Ceremony and Power

Ceremony and Power

Performing Politics in Rome between Republic and Empire

Geoffrey S. Sumi

UNIVERSITY OF MICHIGAN PRESS
Ann Arbor

First Paperback edition 2015

Published in the United States of America by the
University of Michigan Press
Manufactured in the United States of America
⊗ Printed on acid-free paper

2018 2017 2016 2015 5 4 3 2

A CIP catalog record for this book is available from the British Library.

Library of Congress Cataloging-in-Publication Data

Sumi, Geoffrey S., 1963–
Ceremony and power : performing politics in Rome between Republic and Empire / Geoffrey S. Sumi.
p. cm.
Includes bibliographical references and index.
ISBN-13: 978-0-472-11517-4 (cloth : alk. paper)
ISBN-10: 0-472-11517-0 (cloth : alk. paper) 1. Political customs and rites—Rome. 2. Rites and ceremonies—Rome. 3. Rome—Politics and government—265–30 B.C. 4. Rome—Politics and government—30 B.C.–68 A.D. I. Title.
DG254.2.S86 2005
937'.04—dc22 2005012550

ISBN 978-0-472-03666-0 (pbk. : alk. paper)

Parentibus optimis

Shuzo Mark and Sandra I. Sumi

In Memoriam

Michael Akio Omotani

1954–1989

Acknowledgments

This book is a substantial revision of my doctoral dissertation submitted to the University of Michigan. I owe a debt of gratitude to the members of my doctoral committee, in particular my adviser, David Potter, who was instrumental in getting the project started and remained a source of sage counsel and encouragement throughout the long process of transforming it into a book. I have accrued a number of other debts over the years, both institutional and personal. Bruce Arnold, Bettina Bergmann, Cynthia Damon, Paula Debnar, John Ramsey, and Carole Straw all read earlier versions of some or all of the manuscript, saved me from many errors, and provided encouragement at crucial stages. The anonymous readers of the Press also offered helpful comments and suggestions.

Earlier versions of some of the material contained in the book were presented at Mount Holyoke College, Bard College, Williams College, Smith College, and Wesleyan University as well as at meetings of the New England Ancient Historians Colloquium, the Classical Association of New England, and the American Philological Association. The questions and comments from the audiences on those occasions helped redirect my thinking on some crucial points. I had the good fortune to participate in a National Endowment for the Humanities Summer Seminar at the American Academy in Rome led by Bettina Bergmann and Christine Kondoleon, which helped shape many of the ideas contained in the book. Mount Holyoke College provided a faculty grant at an opportune time for another trip to Rome. Completion of the project was greatly facilitated by a Blegen Research Fellowship in Classics at Vassar College. I would also like to thank the editorial staff at the University of Michigan Press, especially those who helped this book see the light—Ellen Bauerle, Collin Ganio, and Christopher Collins. Needless to say, I bear responsibility for all remaining errors.

This book is dedicated to three people: to my parents, who always preached the value of a good education, although I don't think they could have anticipated where their advice would lead me; and to the memory of my cousin, Michael, who (I flatter myself in thinking) would have enjoyed reading this book.

Finally, to my children, Katherine and Christina, for enduring a father whose attention was too often divided, and to my wife, Jennifer, who suffered the most, I can offer only my love and appreciation for their support and understanding.

All translations of Latin and Greek passages quoted in the text and notes are my own unless indicated otherwise.

Contents

Abbreviations

Abbreviations of Latin authors and their works are as indicated on pp. ix–xx of the *Oxford Latin Dictionary* (Oxford 1982) and of Greek authors and their works, on pp. xvi–xxxviii of Liddell, Scott, and Jones' *A Greek-English Lexicon* (Oxford 1968) (with the exception of Cassius Dio, to whom I refer in text and notes simply as Dio).

Full titles of scholarly journals cited by abbreviation in the bibliography can be found in *L'Année Philologique*. The following special abbreviations are also used in the notes:

AE	*L'Année Épigraphique*
BMCRR	*Coins of the Roman Republic in the British Museum*. Ed. H. A. Grueber. 3 vols. London 1910.
CAH	*Cambridge Ancient History*. 12 vols. Cambridge 1923–39. [2nd ed. 1970–.]
CIL	*Corpus Inscriptionarum Latinarum*. Berlin. 1863–.
D-G[2]	*Geschichte Roms*. 2nd ed. Eds. W. Drumann and P. Groebe. 6 vols. Berlin-Leipzig. 1899–1929 (Repr. Hildesheim 1964).
D-S	*Dictionnaire des Antiquités Grecques et Romaines*. Eds. C. Daremberg and E. Saglio. 5 vols. Paris 1877–1919.
FrGH	*Die Fragmente der griechischen Historiker*. Ed. F. Jacoby. Berlin and Leiden 1923–58.
HRR	*Historicorum Romanorum Reliquiae*. Ed. H. W. G. Peter. Leipzig 1914–16.
ILLRP	*Inscriptiones Latinae Liberae Rei Publicae*. Ed. Attilio Degrassi. Florence 1957–72.

ILS	*Inscriptiones Latinae Selectae*. Ed. H. Dessau. 3 vols. Berlin 1892–1916.
Inscr. Ital.	*Inscriptiones Italiae*. vol. 13. Ed. Attilio Degrassi. Rome 1947.
LTUR	*Lexicon Topographicum Urbis Romae*. Ed. E. M. Steinby. 5 vols. Rome 1993–2000.
MRR	*Magistrates of the Roman Republic*. Ed. T. R. S. Broughton. 2 vols. New York 1951. Vol. 3 (Supplement). Atlanta 1986.
OLD	*Oxford Latin Dictionary*. Ed. P. G. W. Glare. Oxford 1968–82.
ORF²	*Oratorum Romanorum Fragmenta Liberae Rei Publicae*. 2nd ed. Ed. E. Malcovati. Milan 1955.
RE	*Pauly's Real-Encyclopädie der classischen Altertumswissenschaft*. Eds. G. Wissowa, E. Kroll, et al. Berlin and Stuttgart 1893–1978.
RIC²	*The Roman Imperial Coinage*. Rev. ed. Eds. C. H. V. Sutherland and R. A. G. Carson. London 1984–.
Röm. StR³	Th. Mommsen. *Römisches Staatsrecht*. 3rd ed. 3 vols. Leipzig 1887–88.

Introduction

Ceremonial Politics

This study is concerned with the relationship between political power and public ceremonial in the Roman Republic, with particular focus on the critical months following Caesar's assassination and later as the Republic gradually transformed into the Principate. The Roman Republic is an especially fruitful time to study such a phenomenon since it was characteristic of politics in this period that the sum of political activity—the demonstration of the ownership and distribution of power—occurred in the open air in full view of gatherings of the Roman people.[1] This study, then, will focus on those public ceremonies at which the elite and governed came into contact, where political power was on display, where the elite attempted to justify its privileged status as political leaders and the people confirmed this status or wrested it away: oratory at public meetings (*contiones*) and the law courts (*quaestiones*), voting assemblies (*comitia*), public entertainment (*ludi* and *munera*) and festivals, funerals, and triumphs. These ceremonies were the stages on which the drama of politics unfolded, came to serve as venues for political discourse, and helped shape the political process. They played a significant role in the political contest following Caesar's assassination and subsequently Octavian's rise to power. Later when Octavian became *princeps* and began calling himself Augustus, he brought these kinds of public performances under his own control and transformed them into the court ceremony of the Principate.

The Fundamental Dynamic of Roman Politics

The importance of public ceremonial in Roman political life of the Republic was due in no small measure to the very nature of Roman society, with its clear distinctions between the political elite and the governed (the actors and spectators in political dramas). On the one hand, the existence of a self-confident and often arrogant elite, who administered the city through political magistracies, sponsored legislation, and conducted foreign policy, required public occasions on which it could display its power and demonstrate its capacity and right to rule. On the other, the ideal of popular sovereignty embedded in the political system through the election of magistrates and enactment of legislation in the popular assemblies required the approbation of the Roman people in virtually all aspects of public life. Thus, the sensibilities and objectives of Roman aristocrats as well as the participation of the Roman people in the political process only heightened the importance of public ceremonial. For this reason, it will be necessary to explore in some detail these two complementary aspects of Roman politics: the Roman aristocratic ethos and the role of the Roman people in politics.

Roman aristocrats lived in the public eye, as Cicero informed his son: "For if anyone from early in his life possesses some claim to fame and distinction, whether he gets this from his father (as I believe you have, my dear Cicero), or through some other fortunate circumstances, all eyes are fixed on him. As a result, people are curious about what he does and how he lives. He spends his time in the spotlight—his every word and deed known to all."[2] Members of the aristocracy had more and greater opportunities for distinction because they lived their lives in the eyes of the people. Yet, their behavior was monitored, questioned, approved, or disapproved;[3] the ultimate arbiters who passed judgment on these activities were the *populus Romanus*. This notion of living life in the public eye was part of the ethos—the code of conduct—that informed the lives and careers of members of the Roman aristocracy.[4] Many aspects of an aristocrat's life were a public document, open and accessible.[5] The dress of senators, a toga with the broad purple stripe, red shoes, and shining ring, boasted their social rank to all those whose gaze fell upon them.[6] Further, they owned homes on the Palatine and the Velia, the Capitolium and Cermalus, all within shouting distance of the Forum, which functioned as a kind of common forecourt for public business and made them even more accessible to the people.[7] The Roman *atrium* house drew the visitor in and directed his line of sight naturally from the entryway (*fauces*) through the open-air common room (*atrium*) to the *tablinum* where the patron and head of the household (*paterfamilias*) stood to await his *clientes* at the morning greeting (*salutatio*).[8] An aristocrat's home was a symbol of his public status (*existimatio*)[9] and a shrine to his family's achievements. The *atrium* housed his ancestors' busts (*imagines*), which were paraded at family funerals and put on display at other public events.[10] Those aristocrats who were so fortunate as to achieve a triumph saw the procession end at their homes, where the spoils of the enemy were often affixed to the walls or displayed outside the door and by the threshold where passersby could stop and gape.[11] Such adornments would remain highly visible and abiding reminders of a family's glory and its role in expanding the empire. It is no surprise, then, that the homes of those adjudged to be enemies of the state were often destroyed as a way of eradicating the living memory of their owners—a kind of *damnatio memoriae*.[12]

A Roman aristocrat's principal objective in his career was to acquire political power and prestige (*dignitas*), wealth and status, and to bequeath as much of this as possible to his descendants. For a Roman aristocrat, the surest path to public distinction was service to the state. The tenure of political office, which brought with it the opportunity for military commands, ennobled individuals and families and came to be the defining characteristic of the Roman Republican aristocracy.[13] Success in political and military affairs, moreover, was celebrated at such important events as the triumph and the aristocratic funeral. Political office also provided opportunities to be in the public eye, in religious processions and at *contiones*, for example. Finally, service to the state also took the form of public largesse—the sponsoring of games and other forms of public entertainment, hosting banquets, and distributing food and cash to the public.[14] In other words, public ceremonies were integral to the lives and careers of Roman aristocrats.

A Roman aristocrat, in order to reach the consulship, the pinnacle of political power and the source of much prestige and renown, had to win the approval of the people in the electoral assemblies (*comitia*) three, and sometimes five, times in fifteen years.[15] The political prestige and power that Roman aristocrats strove to achieve were contingent upon the approval of the people. The exercise of power in the Roman Republic in the hands of a "resplendent elite"[16] had to take place in full view of the Roman people. Thus, the role of the people in the political process in the Roman Republic is essential to our understanding of the relationship between power and ceremonial.

Polybius' famous avowal that the *populus Romanus* conferred honor and distinction on Roman aristocrats through elections and public acclamations (Plb. 6.14.4) affords the Roman people a significant role to play in the political and social life of Rome. This statement and its implications have provoked a lengthy scholarly discussion in recent years on the extent or significance of the "democratic" elements in the Roman Republican constitution.[17] No one can deny the existence of democratic institutions in Rome, such as the legislative and electoral assemblies (*comitia*), but it has long been disputed how many actually participated in these assemblies and whether they could vote freely.[18] The domination of a few select families in the elections for the highest magistracies, especially the consulship, seems to indicate that they could not;[19] in fact, the traditional view has held that these few families controlled every aspect of Roman politics through a complex network of family alliances, political friendship (*amicitia*), and patronage.[20] It has recently been argued, however, that the influence of such social ties has been overestimated.[21]

This argument is based in part on the transformation of Roman society from middle to late Republic. In the third and second centuries BC, primarily as the result of the great expansion of Roman power, the social order in Rome and Italy underwent tremendous upheaval. There was a great movement from countryside to city prompted initially by concerns for the safety of persons and property during the Second Punic War that swelled the urban population of Rome.[22] In the second half of the second century, economic factors were the primary cause of this movement, as members of the lower social orders migrated to the cities and especially to Rome, lured by the varied opportunities that existed there.[23] Perhaps they sought to reap the economic benefits provided by the lavish lifestyle of Roman aristocrats on whose generosity they came to depend long before there were state-supported grain doles.[24] The implementation of these doles only accelerated the process. In any event, the population of Rome increased as a result, perhaps doubling in the century and a half before the Gracchan reforms.[25] The enfranchisement of Italian allies after the Social War and the reforms of Sulla, in particular the increase in the number of praetors and quaestors, led to keen political competition, as members of distinguished families in the municipalities (the *domi nobiles*) came to Rome to embark on political careers but found the consulship largely closed off. The number of praetors increased while the number of consuls remained constant. Some of these same factors—namely, the enfranchisement of the Italian allies following the Social War and the consequent expansion of the citizen body, as well as the implementation of grain doles that had the effect of drawing members of the lower orders of society away from the great aristocratic houses—made the workings of patronage in particular an ineffective way of communicating with the electorate. A more effective means had to be found.

Related to the changes to the institution of patronage was the expanding role of the *plebs* in the legislative process. This fits with the general picture of

Roman politics that Polybius paints for us, but L. R. Taylor, in her discussion of Roman voting assemblies, argues that in the late Republic the primacy of the centuriate assembly was challenged by the more democratic tribal assembly, which passed laws introduced by magistrates. Consequently, consuls "no longer controlled the prizes of empire, [namely] the zones of military commands and the armies assigned to them."[26] Once in office a consul could not push through a legislative package or implement a political program without the approval of the full tribal assembly. The kind of "backroom," secretive, and conspiratorial political maneuvering, the like of which helped forge the alliance of Cn. Pompeius, M. Crassus, and C. Caesar now known as the First Triumvirate, could achieve nothing of lasting importance except through a *lex* passed by the tribal assembly. A vote of the people was also required both for public building projects, an important means of aristocratic display and, most importantly, for extraordinary military commands, such as those of Pompeius and Caesar, which promised the glory of war, the source of so much political power and influence.[27]

Cicero also acknowledges the importance of these assemblies when he claims that they were one of three venues where the people could express their will—public meetings (*contiones*) and public entertainment being the other two.[28] Even though the argument of the speech is somewhat tendentious, inasmuch as Cicero attempted to redefine the terms *populares* and *optimates* as a way of further isolating his political enemies, his statement nonetheless shows that the will of the people, however it might be expressed, was part of the political consciousness of Roman aristocrats. Other evidence confirms that many gatherings of Roman citizens were used to gauge popular opinion, especially ones at the theater. When Caesar entered the theater in July of 59, at a time when he was attempting to control politics in the city along with M. Crassus and Cn. Pompeius, he was greeted with a stony silence. Cicero believed that Caesar would react to this cold reception by sending an angry missive to Pompeius.[29] Caesar's concern at his reception in this public venue shows that Roman aristocrats prided themselves on how the people responded to them, even at events whose primary purpose was not political. Cicero's response, a gleeful (and perhaps erroneous) conclusion that the people stood united in their opposition to the three principals in power at the time, is a further indication that politicians calculated their opponents' popularity based on crowd reactions at such events. Most importantly for our purposes, Cicero, in a letter he wrote less than a month after Caesar's assassination, importunes Atticus to send him political news from Rome or, in lieu of that, public acclamations of the people and the lines spoken by actors.[30] This was one barometer of popular will in an uncertain time.

The traditional role of the people in the political process (as Polybius describes it), the expanding role of the people in the legislative process, the larger electorate in the late Republic, and the consequent increase in political competition, along with the diminished role of patronage, converged to create two important, and closely interrelated, historical changes. First, the traditional political institutions, embodied in the *curia* and the Forum, were no longer adequate venues for political exchange and communication, aristocratic self-advertisement, and performance. These were partially replaced, or supplemented, by funerals, triumphs, and games—by public ceremonies of various kinds.[31]

The second major historical change was the development of a new relationship between ruling elite and *plebs*, in which the *plebs* responded more directly to individual leaders and less to the senate, especially as the senate failed to look out for the interests of the Roman people at large.[32] Political actors in Rome (the *principes urbis*) became increasingly more powerful, as they remained in the public eye for a longer period of time, and as a result there developed a new relationship between these men, on the one hand, and the army and the *plebs urbana*, on the other. This relationship became a cornerstone of the Principate of Augustus, as the *princeps* became the universal patron for all of the Roman Empire. Augustus' predecessors all played a role in helping to develop this relationship and thereby laying the groundwork for his new form of government. C. Marius is credited with, or blamed for, changing the requirements for recruitment of soldiers, thereby enabling his successors to use their armies as a tool to achieve their political objectives.[33] L. Sulla became dictator, reformed the constitution, and remained the abiding power in Roman politics for several years. He was also the first to establish permanent games in honor of his military victories, thus marking the Roman calendar with his own glory (see, chap. 1). Pompeius' extraordinary commands enabled him to achieve unprecedented military victories and helped establish his reputation as world conqueror, which was celebrated at his triumphs and permanently commemorated with the statuary adorning his theater.[34]

Thus, even if we cannot speak of the Roman Republic as a "democracy," it is clear that the Roman people exercised important powers within the constitution, especially their role in the electoral and legislative assemblies, and that, just as importantly, the Roman nobility was eager for their acclaim. At the very least there existed an ideology of popular participation in the political process of the Republic that influenced many of the words and actions of Roman aristocrats.[35] A consequence of this principle is that during this period politics was a drama that took place on several public stages—the Forum and *comitium* or *saepta*, theater and circus, even the homes of the elite, and the streets of Rome. The players in this drama were aristocrats, mostly descended from a small number of distinguished families, and the spectators were the Roman people.

Politics as Performance

This dynamic of the Roman Republic, with elite "actors" staging politics before an audience of the Roman people, encourages the view that in this period in Roman history politics was performed. In fact, there is evidence that the metaphor of politics as performance was deeply embedded in Roman thought. In a famous anecdote, Suetonius describes the emperor Augustus' final assessment of his own life and career in the following way:

> On the last day of his life he asked every now and then whether there was any disturbance without on his account; then calling for a mirror, he had his hair combed and his falling jaws set straight. After that, calling in his friends and asking whether it seemed to them that he had played the comedy (*mimus*) of life fitly, he added the tag: "Since well I've played my part, all clap your hands. And from the stage dismiss me with applause."[36]

Augustus' comparison of his life and career to the performance of a mime, even extending the metaphor with a request for applause as he left the stage, was an explicit acknowledgment that his actions as *princeps* were a performance, a notion that arose perhaps because so much of his career took place in the gaze of the Roman people. This notion of *princeps* as performer was not a result of the advent of monarchy under the Principate but rather owed its development to the nature of politics in the Roman Republic, of which Augustus was himself a product. Cicero, for instance, in a sense anticipating Augustus' last sentiments, suggests that a skilled orator advocating for his client might appear to one watching from a distance to be a famous actor on stage.[37] Cicero clearly viewed oratory as a kind of performance somewhat akin to a theatrical spectacle, with the orator as performer and the people in the audience (the orator's *corona*) as spectators.[38] This analogy presumably could be extended to include the orator speaking at a public meeting (*contio*).[39] Finally, in the "Handbook of Electioneering" (*Commentariolum Petitionis* 52) ascribed to Q. Cicero, the author advises the candidate to "be sure to make your whole candidacy a fine performance (*pompae plena*), brilliant, distinguished, and popular, so that it is a great spectacle with the utmost prestige. . . ."[40]

This metaphor of politics as performance, a necessary first step in the development of a conceptual vocabulary and analytical framework through which we can begin our study of public ceremonial, has emerged from social anthropology. Most useful for our purposes is Victor Turner's notion of human society as a collection of "social dramas,"[41] for this encourages the view of politics not as a function or set of functions, as structural-functional anthropologists would have it, but rather as an arena of activity where communities define who they are through performative action.[42] This approach has the additional merit of studying the changes in political processes that occur over time, which makes it especially congenial to historians. The metaphor of politics as performance in an arena has enormous implications for our understanding of power and public ceremonial by providing a larger canvas on which to situate our analysis of these concepts and their relationship. It also implies that politics is a process or set of actions that takes place before a group of spectators, much like Augustus' characterization of his own career, or Cicero's view of one stage of political activity in the Roman Republic, namely public oratory. Finally, the notion that the performance of politics expresses a community's self-definition suggests that the action of politics is highly symbolic and that it communicates to its audience a sense of self.

Public ceremonies were one type of arena where political activity took place in the Roman Republic, where, in fact, the fundamental dynamic of Roman politics—the interaction of elite and nonelite—played out. The phenomenon of public ceremonial can be approached from several different theoretical perspectives beyond the notion of politics as performance. For instance, public ceremonies have also been described as "imaginative" works built out of social materials that construct a narrative on the social order—or, put more simply, they tell a society a story about itself.[43] They do not merely reflect social reality, but they also directly or obliquely critique and evaluate social life.[44] This is another way of saying that public ceremonies are part of a cognitive system—one that contains crucial information about a society that is open to interpretation; in this sense, they are closely akin to ritual.[45] However we choose to understand these phenomena—whether as a social drama, a story (or text), or a cognitive system—ultimately the end result is the same. Public ceremonies provide information about the society they represent. In words that we used earlier, a community's self-definition is on display at these events.

I would define public ceremonial, then, as symbolic action that is often also ritually prescribed action performed before an audience. The performer is often a person of some political or social standing in the community: in the

Roman Republic, usually a magistrate or ex-magistrate. A ceremony often requires special dress or accoutrements, is performed at a special location (a "stage"), and has some connection with historical time. These elements are also part of a ceremony's ritualistic nature and largely what makes it symbolic.[46] A Roman triumph, for instance, was both ritual and ceremony, which is an indication that the two categories often overlap. Romans attending a triumph knew to expect a certain set of actions (a procession that followed a prescribed route through the city, execution of prisoners of war, sacrifice), the special dress of the *triumphator* (the *toga picta*), and certain accoutrements (*quadriga*, trumpeters, display of spoils of war and placards, prisoners of war). Moreover, it was a ceremony that had a history that dated back to the very foundation of the city and its first king. I choose "ceremony" over "ritual" only because the former term connotes a public and often political action and therefore is more appropriate for the kinds of events discussed in this book, although, as noted earlier, the two terms are not mutually exclusive.

There is also, however, a whole category of public performances that were highly symbolic and important venues for political discourse in the Roman Republic that do not at first glance fall easily into the category of public ceremonial as just defined. Spectacle entertainment, for instance, especially performances in the theater, was performed by actors, persons of low status, not high political or social standing. Nonetheless, their words and actions were often interpreted by members of the audience as politically topical and directed at a major political figure who, at least insofar as he was the focus of the spectators' gaze, became a "performer."[47] Thus, from one point of view, this type of event is not too far removed from public ceremony as we have defined it here. An important point of distinction is that such performances were largely subversive inasmuch as they poked fun at or otherwise undermined the political standing of a person of importance. To a similar end, on more than one occasion slaves disrupted the performance at the theater and occupied the seats reserved for senators and knights.[48] This was not ceremony as much as it was the disruption of routine, the subversion of ceremony and ritual. It was possible for other ceremonies, such as a *contio* or electoral *comitia*, to be disrupted similarly, and these disruptions usually involved collective action or mob violence. Of fundamental importance for our purposes is that such subversive performances still addressed issues of power; but their purpose was to draw power away from the elite and confer it, if only temporarily and often only symbolically, on other individuals or, more frequently, on another social group.

Finally, there were public performances, such as Cicero's return from exile, which involved an individual of high political or social standing (a magistrate or ex-magistrate) and were highly symbolic but cannot be regarded as ceremony, at least insofar as they did not follow a strict ritual pattern. However, the study of such performances, as I will attempt to show in due course, is only enhanced by placing them within the analytical framework of public ceremonial.

Scholars who study the relationship between public ceremonial and power have focused on the question of whether ceremonial is in the service of power or is a type of power in its own right, or whether the relationship is altogether more complex.[49] Two statements from the previous discussion directly impinge upon our understanding of this relationship. The first is that ceremony by definition requires a performer of some political or social standing. In this sense, ceremony was in the service of power as a venue for its display. As we shall see, those in power at Rome often exploited public ceremonial for their own advancement. At the same time, many of the symbolic elements of ceremony—its special dress and accoutrements, its stage, its connection with historical time—all served to elevate the standing of the performer. Public ceremonies, therefore, were the loci where political power was not only on display but also enacted. Thus, public ceremonial was itself a kind of power.[50] In a Roman context, it was precisely in public ceremonial that the two principles of Roman politics—the aristocratic ethos and the ideal of popular sovereignty—intersected. The venues where the Roman people expressed their collective will were also where Roman aristocrats exercised power. This suggests that in the Roman Republic power and ceremonial were closely intertwined, their relationship almost symbiotic in the sense that one could not really exist without the other.

In this study, the discussion of public ceremonies will take place on two levels but not with equal emphasis. On one, such performances can be viewed as social or political institutions that articulate a community's values, as we have already discussed. This fact was recognized by Polybius, who described for his readers a generic aristocratic funeral and the kind of values it inculcated, especially in the young men witnessing it (6.54.3). Polybius was primarily interested in the aristocratic funeral as institution and what this institution could reveal about Roman character and values. The same approach can be taken for a Roman triumph or, for that matter, a *contio* or meeting of the tribal assembly. Any Roman triumph, for instance, expressed the values of Romans and, perhaps more specifically, of the Roman aristocracy, such as valor (*virtus*) or success in war (*gloria*), good fortune (*felicitas*), and the importance of service to the state. A *contio*, when used to inform the city populace of the senate's position on an important political issue, might reflect the ideals of popular sovereignty and *libertas*, as well as political *concordia*, the necessary cooperation between the senate and people of Rome in order for the Republic to flourish. These values were the fundamental principles—the central ideas—of Rome,[51] and they were often expressed at public ceremonies. It is necessary, then, to understand these ceremonies in part as institutions, with their own history and traditions. How they developed, what changes they underwent in the course of Republican history, especially the late Republic, and the values they articulated are all necessary background material for a discussion of a specific funeral, triumph, or *contio*.

This last statement presupposes the second level of discourse about public ceremonial. A specific ceremony, such as Caesar's funeral or Octavian's triumph, has many of these "institutional" features that express certain social values, but at the same time, and more importantly for our purposes, it also has a specific historical and political context that might confirm or undermine some of these same social values, or might even formulate and articulate new ones. In other words, any ceremony has a specific resonance within the political circumstances in which it is performed. There are then symbolic "variables" involved in any ceremony, or, to put it another way, a given ceremony has levels of meaning. At bottom, we have the phenomenon being observed, the action itself—of funeral, triumph, *contio*, or form of public entertainment.[52] The next level is that of signifying action, when the spectators observe the action performed or visual symbol displayed and interpret it to signify something about the actors themselves—their virtues and vices, their political aims and objectives—and in some instances, about the general political situation. Through the symbolism available to him, whether in the location of the ceremony or its connection to past events, a politician could further disclose his political affinities, establish a political ideology, ally himself with others in power, or lend his support for or opposition to a given political issue. For these reasons, it will be necessary to understand the meaning of a given ceremony as a social institution primarily as background for a more detailed analysis of the meaning of ceremonies in their specific historical and political context. In other words, the emphasis of this study will not be on ceremony qua ceremony but on specific ceremonies within a fairly narrow historical context.

Some of the symbolic "variables" (alluded to earlier) in any ceremony are related to time and space:[53] a specific ceremony's implicitly and explicitly drawn connections with both the recent and remote past; and its "topography" or location within the city of Rome. Roman aristocratic funerals are one example of how a ceremony could draw together the past and the present, both in the speech in praise of the deceased (*laudatio*) and the procession of ancestral busts (*pompa*) that celebrated all the important achievements of a particular family throughout Roman history, thus peering back on the political offices held and triumphs won. In this context it is worth repeating T. J. Cornell's assessment that in many ways Rome was the "history of an anachronism,"[54] since Romans preserved in sometimes fossilized form social and political institutions from the Regal Period and early Republic. A penchant in the late Republic and the early Principate for searching for the origins of institutions,[55] sometimes termed "antiquarianism" (which was introduced in part by the need for those in power to link their new and sometimes extraordinary positions to ancient institutions—I am thinking here specifically of Sulla or Caesar), reflected a historical consciousness among Romans of this period that had roots deep in the remote past, even to the point of encouraging the creation of what have been termed "invented traditions."[56] Romans at times invented ceremonies or elements of ceremonies in order to legitimate a new idea by cloaking it in the garb of antiquity. To regard this as antiquarianism obfuscates the true significance of Roman historical consciousness in public ceremonial: references to the past, whether recent or remote, are not mere pedantic indulgences but actually can place the performer at the center of power through his connection with or opposition to past events.

The distant past, then, was very much alive in the late Republic and early Principate, and this past shaped many aspects of public life, none more so than the public ceremonies that we will be discussing. Orators, for instance, often used historical *exempla* as rhetorical hooks on which to hang crucial issues and draw the attention of their audience. T. P. Wiseman has recently suggested that religious festivals were the places where Romans first learned the stories that would become a part of their annalistic history.[57] In a funeral, the ancestral *imagines* adorned the *pompa*, and thus the deceased took his rightful place among the great men of his family and of Rome. In a triumph, the *triumphator* followed the route that past *triumphatores* had followed, made the traditional sacrifice, and held the customary *contio*. In this way, he at least implicitly compared himself to the great *triumphatores* of Roman history. Finally, in the debate over the proposed honors for Ser. Sulpicius, who died on his legation to Antonius in February 43, Cicero proposed that a statue be erected in his honor on the Rostra and that a space ten feet square around the statue be reserved for members of his family during gladiatorial combat and other games (Cic. *Phil.* 9.16). If we assume that others had received this honor—and Cicero does not imply that his proposal in this instance was unique or unprecedented—then we can also assume that at the public spectacles mentioned one could see members of many families crowded around statues of their famous ancestors, outwardly forging the link that connected present and past. In other words, the past, as much as the present, was a part of such ceremonies, which could, in turn, shape the way that Romans understood their past and the relationship of the present to it.

These two dimensions of public ceremonial—time and space—were often interdependent, for the capacity of a particular ceremony to shape the historical consciousness of its audience was at times augmented or at least affected by its location. The topography of the city of Rome was itself a historical document, replete with monuments, temples, or statues, each of which evoked a legend or story from Rome's past. Temples vowed in battle were constructed from the fruits of victory and often adorned with paintings of battle scenes immortalizing that victory; statues honored heroes from the early Republic. These monuments were some of the building blocks of the annalistic tradition,[58] and the enterprising orator at a *contio* or trial could also put them to good use as props in his speech,[59] visual reminders of a heroic past and evidence for the historical *exempla* that he cited. They served a similar function for public ceremonial, bringing the past to life before the gaze of the spectators. This could be done explicitly by the performer, such as the orator mentioned earlier, who loudly vociferated on and gestured dramatically toward monuments that represented a historical tradition; but more often the topography of Rome remained a silent but highly evocative and symbolic stage where public ceremonial took place—a visual landscape of Roman history. It should be noted, too, that in the period under discussion this visual landscape was undergoing substantial changes, which, I believe, would have encouraged further reflections on the past and further shaped Roman historical consciousness. On these images from the past the reality of the present often obtruded. It is at these points of convergence and conflict that this study finds its focus.

Public ceremonies, then, were "centers of power," the loci of political discourse, where the central ideas of Roman culture found expression. This means that the action at public ceremonies was not only highly symbolic, as I have already suggested, but also emotionally charged and highly combustible, which made the eruption of violence a real possibility, as we shall see in our discussion of specific events. These were the arenas of political conflict and resolution, where views on the most disputatious issues of the day were aired and praised or condemned. In many cases, references to past events, whether recent or remote, only served to heighten emotions. For Roman aristocrats, the opportunities for self-aggrandizement were many, as were the perils of public humiliation.

The Present Study

In subsequent chapters, we will examine public ceremonial from Sulla's dictatorship to the end of the reign of Augustus. The focus will be on the events of 44–43 BC, years of political uncertainty and instability, following Caesar's assassination. This period is especially suited for such a study because there was a void in the political power structure left by Caesar's assassination. To fill this void, members of the nobility sought the support of the people and army through the performance of public ceremonial. M. Antonius took advantage of the political uncertainty and used the office of consul to establish his supremacy in the early months after Caesar's assassination. Caesar's name gave Octavian the opportunity to challenge Antonius' supremacy, especially by providing access to public ceremonial, which he used as a means of advertising himself and legitimating his position. The analysis of these events is placed in a narrative framework in order to show more clearly the effect of these ceremonies on the politics of the period and the political rivalries. Attempts at consolidating power and expressions of opposition to those in power occurred at public ceremonial—the loci where the ruling elite staked out their political territory and communicated their political positions to the Roman people. The study of any historical period that experiences a significant transformation inevitably must evince the twin themes of continuity and change. But of particular importance to this study is how these twin themes relate to ceremony. What happens, for instance, to a ceremony's capacity to express a community's sense of self when that community is itself undergoing a transformation, as was the case in the late Republic?

The necessary background for this endeavor is a typology of Roman Republican ceremonial, in which we will examine the generic characteristics and values of each type of ceremony (chap. 1), with some examples from the late Republic, followed by an analysis of public ceremonial during Caesar's dictatorship, since so much of the political activity of the years 44 and 43 BC was a response to Caesar's power (chap. 2). Caesar's place at the center of power informed the trajectory of Roman politics in subsequent years as the rivals for power (Caesarians on one side, conspirators and their supporters on the other) demonstrated in various ways their affection for or antagonism toward the memory of the dead dictator. This process began immediately upon the Ides of March and the ensuing days, when the conspirators delivered a speech at a *contio*, laying out the rationale for their bold deed and when Antonius responded, also at a *contio* (chap. 3). Expressions of outrage over Caesar's murder and the preservation and celebration of his memory largely occurred at the public ceremonies associated with his death and divination, centering on the actions of Antonius at Caesar's funeral and Amatius, the supposititious son of C. Marius, afterward (chap. 4). Antonius' rivalry with Octavian and others who were obstacles to his ascendancy (namely, the conspirators and their supporters) was communicated to the people through public ceremonial (chap. 5). The conspirators' last attempt to shape popular opinion in Rome was Brutus' sponsorship of the *Ludi Apollinares* in July 44, which was almost immediately overshadowed by Octavian's production of games in honor of Caesar's victory and his reconciliation with Antonius (chap. 6). The rivalry between Octavian and Antonius intensified in the autumn of 44, as the former became a more legitimate threat to the latter's power. Once the two principals departed Rome for Mutina, political affairs returned to the senate and there was a noticeable diminution of public ceremonial (chap. 7). After the formation of the Second Triumvirate, the process of consolidating power on the part of the triumvirs was long and tedious and interrupted by pockets of resistance and expressions of opposition voiced at public ceremonial (chap. 8). Later under the Principate, Augustus used Republican ceremonial to create his own imperial court ceremony (chap. 9).

I

Consensus and Conflict

A Typology of Roman Republican Ceremonial

Our discussion of the relationship between power and ceremonial in the late Roman Republic will begin with a framework or typology of ceremonial—an enumeration and general description of the kinds of events that form the focus of this study and their historical development. The purpose of this chapter is not to provide an exhaustive list but rather the principal categories of ceremonics that we will be discussing. These events were usually formal gatherings of the people at which the ownership and distribution of political power were demonstrated. They share characteristics of ceremony, as defined in the introduction, but each is distinctive. *Contiones* and triumphs, for instance, were ceremonies of quite different type—the one quotidian and routine, the other splendid and lavish, full of pageantry and spectacle, the ultimate accomplishment of a Roman aristocrat's career. The disruption of these events frequently became an objective of those intent on undermining the power that was at stake. At many of these ceremonies a tension was palpable between the power and prestige of an individual and the sovereignty of the people, between the celebration of the glory won in the name of Rome and the renown of individual achievements. Consequently, the discussion will focus on the role of ceremonial in creating political consensus and as a stage for social and political conflict. It is not enough to say that public ceremonial reflected the larger political context of which it was part; rather public ceremonial was itself political action.

Oratory before the People

Vergil's striking comparison of Neptune calming the seas to an orator standing before a raucous crowd (*Aen.* 1.142–56), commanding silence through his appearance and soothing an audience with his words, demonstrates the Roman belief in the power of oratory and its importance as a component of statesmanship.[1] At the same time, the fact that the crowd was in need of calming shows that Vergil understood public oratory to be a place of conflict that an orator could resolve through his power, influence, and sometimes his mere presence. An orator's ability to incite or calm a crowd, persuade a jury to acquit his client, or convince an assembly to approve or reject legislation made him a formidable presence on the political scene in Rome.[2] Part of the orator's power and prestige arose from the ceremonial nature of oratory: the formal dress and comportment of the orator, the raised platform from which he spoke, the crowd of spectators looking on, and the sense of oratory as performance. Yet there is evidence that the orator was required to defer to the people, who could pass judgment with shouts—or with silence.[3]

In our discussion of oratory before the Roman people we will focus on two venues, the public meeting (*contio*) and judicial proceeding (*quaestio*). A *contio* was any gathering of the Roman populace or army for the purpose of hearing a speech delivered by a political or military leader.[4] We will focus on two of the three basic types: the *contio* preceding the *comitia tributa*, in which legislation presented, discussed and debated in the *contio* was voted on; and the *contio* convened by a magistrate to inform the citizen body of an issue of public interest, such as the content, course, and outcome of debate in a meeting of the senate.[5] All *contiones* had to be convened by a tribune of the *plebs* or a magistrate or promagistrate with *imperium*, and all speakers were summoned and introduced by the presiding magistrate, although the people could demand a speaker by acclamation. In some cases, a nonmagistrate (*privatus*) could address an assembly but only after being introduced by a tribune of the *plebs*.

The tension mentioned earlier, between the prestige of an individual aristocrat, in this case the presiding official or orator at a *contio*, and the sovereignty of the Roman people was often in evidence at these events, as we shall see. It is worth noting now that this tension was ceremonially acknowledged by the display of the *fasces*,[6] the bundles of rods and axes that were carried by lictors on public occasions as emblems of a magistrate's coercive and punitive powers and were thought to have originated with the kings. The presence of a magistrate with *imperium* at a *contio* required a display of the *fasces*, but since these symbols of regal authority were anathema to the ideal of popular sovereignty under the Republic, they were ceremonially lowered before the people. This custom, ascribed to the great populist politician, P. Valerius Poplicola (Cic. *Rep.* 2.53; cf. 1.62), was a sign of deference to the power of the people, yet it also acknowledged the tension between the sovereignty of the people and the power and authority of a magistrate. This tension erupted most visibly and violently in the late Republic through the breaking of the *fasces*,[7] a dramatic means of undermining the very power and authority that these emblems represented.

In our period, a *quaestio* took place in the Forum Romanum (see fig. 2) on a wooden tribunal constructed for the purpose. The principals involved, both on the side of the prosecution and the defense as well as the presiding magistrate (one of the eight praetors for the year),[8] were often leading politicians whose reputations depended upon the issues at stake and the eventual outcome. Thus, criminal courts were as much a venue for a discussion of political issues of the day as they were a site for judicial proceedings. Since these trials took place in the open air of the Forum and involved some of the most distinguished men of the day, a crowd might gather to hear one of the orators advocating for his client; and since several trials might be ongoing at once, we can envision the crowd moving from one to another, much as it did during a festival as it sought the most striking form of entertainment.[9] A captivating speaker could expect a large crowd (*corona*) to gather in a circle around his tribunal, and orators were known to speak and perform to that audience as much as to the judge and jurors seated on the tribunal with them.[10] The crowd in attendance at a trial, in its turn, could exert some pressure on the participants, creating anxiety on the part of the performers (Cic. *Caec.* 28; cf. *Fin.* 2.74).

One consequence of the metaphor of politics as performance is the expectation that these ceremonies involved a performer performing before a passive audience. As we shall see, this is not necessarily true. A common feature of a *contio* or public trial in this period was the vociferous reaction of the crowd to the speakers on the Rostra to the point where the crowd itself became a part of the whole performance. Whether these responses of the crowd were spontaneous or prearranged by some of the participants is often difficult to prove at such a remove. However, any attempt to orchestrate a crowd's response shows how important the expressed will of the people was to the political elite of Rome.

We can use as an example the public meeting in 67 BC to vote on the proposal of A. Gabinius (*tr. pl.* 67; *cos.* 58). Gabinius proposed to confer a command against the pirates on Cn. Pompeius Magnus.[11] The passage of this law has to be understood as part and parcel of the public meetings (*contiones*) that were held before the people to debate the issues involved prior to the actual assembly in which the people voted. Since our ancient sources do not agree on the precise sequence of events, the following is an attempt to reconcile them.[12]

A debate on this law had already been held in the senate, with A. Gabinius speaking in favor and Q. Hortensius (*cos*. 69) speaking in opposition (Cic. *Man*. 52). This debate continued at a *contio* that was probably held on the day of the voting in the Forum Romanum. First Pompeius and then Gabinius spoke in favor of the bill (*rogatio*). The consul C. Calpurnius Piso lent his prestige to the proceedings when he spoke in opposition, declaring that if Pompeius wanted to be another Romulus (Plut. *Pomp*. 25.9), he might suffer Romulus' fate. The crowd reacted by nearly tearing Piso to pieces—almost subjecting *him* to Romulus' fate instead.[13] Q. Catulus (*cos*. 78), an eminent consular, spoke in opposition to the proposal contrary to Gabinius' expectations (according to Dio 36.30.5), but with greater deference to Pompeius, it seems, than Piso. Catulus opposed the idea of conferring such extraordinary power on one man and attempted to convince the crowd of the folly of the proposal by asking who would replace Pompeius should he be lost. The crowd responded ("You, Catulus") in a manner that appeared to be prearranged. Cicero understood the crowd's response to be an indication of Catulus' distinction, a product of his excellence (*virtus*) and prestige (*dignitas*). But it also had the effect of taking the wind out of his sails by making him appear to be the crowd's favorite, as he apparently had accused Pompeius of being. Catulus retired from the Rostra. It was probably at this point that another tribune, L. Roscius Otho, came forward to speak in opposition to the proposal, but the crowd refused to hear him.[14] Instead of speaking, he held up two fingers to indicate (as Plutarch tells us) that he was opposed to the idea of conferring such power on a single man; the crowd shouted him down. As the people then divided themselves into tribes to vote on the proposal, Trebellius, another tribune, interposed his veto, at which point Gabinius proposed a second law deposing his uncooperative colleague. When seventeen tribes had voted for his removal—one short of the majority necessary—Trebellius withdrew his veto. The law was passed. At this *contio*, the crowd did not wait passively to be told how to vote on this law: it nearly assaulted a consul, encouraged one orator to retire from the Rostra, and refused to hear another. The distribution of power was on display, and the Roman people were full participants.

Audience participation was not limited to *contiones*. We have already noted how orators sometimes "played to the gallery" at judicial trials, demonstrating a keen awareness of audience reaction. The jury could participate in the performance as well. In a raucous scene at the infamous Bona Dea trial of P. Clodius (62 BC), Cicero claims that he came forward to testify amid the shouts of Clodius' supporters and that he was surrounded by the jury who pointed to their bare throats, as if to demonstrate that they would lay down their lives for his.[15] A similar scene played out at the trial of T. Milo in February of 56. When Cn. Pompeius rose to speak, his voice was nearly drowned out by the shouts of Clodius' supporters. When Clodius began to speak, Milo's supporters, among them Cicero, returned the favor. Clodius became flustered (according to Cicero) and began peppering the audience with questions ("Who is starving the people?" "Pompeius!"). Following this, as though on cue, Clodius' supporters began spitting at Milo's supporters. A riot ensued (Cic. *Q.fr.* 2.3.2).

These incidents illustrate how the people could influence the course of a debate at a *contio* or the procedure at a trial, demonstrating further that it is overly simplistic to view such events as merely displays of aristocratic power. Rather it was in oratory before the people that the distribution of political power in the Roman Republic was most visible. Certain elements lent prestige and power to the performer (the appearance of the orator and the location of the speech, for instance), but the presence of the crowd was an abiding reminder that whatever the issues at stake the approbation of the people was necessary for their resolution. The ever-present threat that a *contio* could devolve into rioting showed how delicate was the balance of power between elite and nonelite, and how fragile the harmony that underpinned public order. Attempts to disrupt a *contio* or a *quaestio* and undermine the speaker only brought into sharper relief the question of the ownership and distribution of power. The fact that the crowd's response appeared to be prearranged indicates the level of performance in these ceremonies, even on the part of those in the audience. It also shows that the usual distinction of performer and spectators can become blurred, which has ramifications for our understanding of the relationship between power and ceremonial. If power is conferred partly through performance at such public events, then the crowd on these occasions would have garnered some power at the expense of those eminent statesmen standing on the Rostra or tribunal.

As we can see from the above examples, ceremonies in this period often became high public drama further confirming the metaphor of politics as performance. Another such instance was the prosecution (in 63) of C. Rabirius for the murder of C. Marius' one-time ally, L. Appuleius Saturninus (*tr. pl.* 100), a crime that was alleged to have been committed thirty-seven years previously.[16] Saturninus' popular legislation in 100 eventually provoked the so-called ultimate decree (*senatus consultum ultimum*), compelling the consul

Marius to arm the citizen populace and bring down his former ally.[17] In his defense in 63 BC, Rabirius admitted to taking part in the siege of Saturninus and his supporters on the Capitolium but denied murdering him. The point at issue in the trial was whether the senate had the authority to pass the "ultimate decree" (Dio 37.26.1), in effect calling for martial law, against the sovereignty of the people vested in a tribune of the *plebs* whose person was sacrosanct. The trial, or rather trials, and accompanying events became a dramatic performance, the outward form of which was as politically significant as the very issues at stake.[18]

At a *contio* that preceded the trials themselves, T. Labienus, tribune of the *plebs* and prosecutor, displayed a portrait bust (*imago*) of Saturninus (Cic. *Rab. Perd.* 25). The frequent comparison of public oratory with a theatrical performance and a *contio* with a "stage" (as we discussed earlier) indicates that public speeches in Rome were partly a visual experience. If we imagine a *contio* or *quaestio* in the Forum in which the orator stood on the Rostra or tribunal to address a crowd of citizens in the open air, we have to assume that many in the back of the crowd at a distance from the speaker would have been able to catch only snippets of the speech, a catchphrase or slogan, shouted above the din. This is why the visual aspects of oratory, for instance a prop like Saturninus' *imago* displayed as part of an orator's speech, became communicative components of the performance.[19]

There is no record of how the audience on this occasion reacted to the display of Saturninus' *imago*, but it did elicit comment from Cicero, who, in his speech in Rabirius' defense, wondered aloud where Labienus had found such a portrait, since it had become illegal to display one after Saturninus' death. Since such *imagines* were often displayed at funerals, this prohibition really meant that Saturninus was not to be mourned publicly and thus constituted a form of *damnatio memoriae*, the officially sanctioned eradication of the public memory of a man deemed an enemy of the state. If Cicero's statement is accurate, then it is likely that no one in the audience at Labienus' *contio* would have previously laid eyes on Saturninus' portrait. Further, the display of *imagines* at funerals and in the *atria* of aristocratic households was a right associated with the Roman *nobilitas*.[20] By displaying his *imago* in this way, Labienus was not merely reviving Saturninus' memory but also conferring an honor on Saturninus that was usually reserved for members of more distinguished Roman families. The display of Saturninus' *imago*, then, was a more pointed act at this trial, since it infringed upon the power of the aristocracy and was meant to elevate the sovereignty of the people.

Rabirius might have been found guilty again had it not been for the unusual action taken by the praetor Metellus Celer, who brought down the flag from the Janiculum. Dio explains that in ancient times this action signaled an enemy attack and the consequent adjournment of an assembly, but it continued largely as a matter of form. This gesture towards an antiquarian tradition was consistent with a theme of the first trial, which was conducted in accordance with an archaic legal procedure before two judges (*duoviri perduellionis*) (Cic. *Rab. Perd.* 12). The whole procedure is a further indication of the kind of devotion to archaic and arcane rituals and procedures that permeated political life in the late Republic, for Cicero claims that Labienus, the tribune of the *plebs* who presided at the second trial (a *iudicium populi*), found the ritual of the first in the dusty pages of annalistic history.[21] He was probably right, for the paradigm case for *perduellio* was from the Regal period, the story of Horatius who killed his sister when she mourned the fallen enemy upon her brother's return from war, as retold by Livy.[22] In the trial in 63, Rabirius was found guilty and sentenced to death by the lash and the cross, an antiquarian revival of a long extinct form of punishment. Cicero, however, apparently exercising his consular veto, arrested the proceedings before this grim penalty could be enacted (Cic. *Rab. Perd.* 10–11).

The whole episode shows how politics in this period could be a highly dramatic performance complete with props and a stage. In the end, the guilt or innocence of Rabirius seems to have been of only secondary importance in the grand design of his accusers. Justice in the narrow sense was not what they were after. The fact that the trial took the form of an archaic legal procedure further hindered this narrow enactment of justice. Nonetheless, the very form of a public trial was essential to the process, since it came to be an expression of the sovereignty of the people and thus was the most effective stage for a discourse on the larger issues of the power of the senate and its right to enact the *senatus consultum ultimum*. But to regard the ceremony as a mere stage for political action obscures the reality of politics in this period, for the ceremony was itself political action. This trial exhibits the breadth and depth of ceremony, characteristics that enabled it to resonate symbolically beyond its overt purpose.

Electoral and Legislative Assemblies

Meetings of the electoral and legislative assemblies (*comitia*), as Cicero informs us, were venues where the will of the Roman people could be expressed (*Sest.* 106).[23] In these assemblies, the role of popular sovereignty in the distribution of power was visibly demonstrated through the conferral of a magistracy or (in some cases) a provincial command. The presiding official at the electoral *comitia* was usually a magistrate (the consul at consular elections), at legislative *comitia*, the tribune of the *plebs*. Yet the people, who could influence the proceedings and whose votes ultimately conferred power, were frequently an active and performative audience. Hence, a successful outcome of the *comitia* was the result of a consensus between ruling elite and people as demonstrated by the ceremony itself. *Comitia* are often attested in our sources, but few, if any, of these same sources describe in any detail what a typical one looked like, presumably because these assemblies were routine procedural politics that became noteworthy only when the routine was disrupted by an unusual occurrence or the outcome was especially contentious. In the previous section, we saw how the *contiones*, where legislation was introduced and debated by the people and magistrates, could become quite riotous affairs at which the distribution of power was at stake. Similarly, the disruption of *comitia* was often an effort to manipulate the popular will or undermine magisterial authority, but in either case the distribution of power hung in the balance.

At a typical election, the Roman people gathered in the Campus Martius and crowded, tribe by tribe or century by century, into the *saepta*, or *ovile*, to elect magistrates. The metaphor inherent in *ovile* is apt: the Roman electorate was herded into an enclosure where in early times they elected magistrates by acclamation, later by secret ballot, with all the tribes or centuries casting their votes simultaneously. Meetings of the electoral and legislative *comitia* were formal occasions that apparently required all attendees to don the formal dress of the toga,[24] while candidates at elections were resplendent in white (*toga candida*). There must have been some opportunities for private discussions and debates about the candidates before those gathered in their voting groups actually committed their choices to the wax tablets. At consular elections, one century chosen by lot (called the *praerogativa*) voted first and seems to have exercised a disproportionate influence over the outcome of the election (Cic. *Planc*. 49). In fact, it was so important that attempts were made to control or undermine its influence.[25] Following the vote of the *praerogativa*, the remaining centuries then cast their votes; the votes were counted until one candidate achieved a majority and his victory was announced by heralds to the waiting throng.[26] The tabulation continued until all available offices had been filled.

At the consular elections, the presiding magistrate was the consul who held the *fasces* for July as a result of having been returned first in his own election to the consulship in the previous year,[27] an indication of the prestige attached to the first announced winner and the opportunity for further self-advertisement as a result. Elections were another opportunity for the presiding consul to claim a distinction over his colleague. The presiding consul also announced the winners, thus co-opting his successors and introducing them for the first time to the people.[28] Roman elections, therefore, even after the secret ballot was introduced, retained an atmosphere of voting by acclamation,[29] in the sense that the results were almost instantaneously returned and the victors could enjoy the applause of the voters. Through the declaration of the winner, the presiding magistrate accepted and made public the will of the people.[30]

Pompeius' postponement of an election that promised an uncongenial outcome (see n. 25) was a tactic available only to the magistrate presiding at an election. More extreme measures could be taken by others, most notably the blocking of voters from the voting space or the violent disruption of the proceedings through armed force. For instance, at the consular elections for 55 BC (held in the previous year), the candidacy of the powerful consulars Pompeius and Crassus cowed all potential rivals save one, L. Domitius Ahenobarbus, who enjoyed the not inconsiderable support of the younger Cato.[31] The candidates, along with their supporters, entered the Campus Martius at dawn on the day of the elections. A mêlée ensued, Domitius' torchbearer was killed, and all eventually fled, despite (in Plutarch's account) the heroic attempt of Cato to hold Domitius there. In the end, Pompeius and Crassus were elected consuls.[32]

The tribal assembly, when convened for the purposes of voting on proposed legislation, usually met in the Forum—in our period, in front of the Temple of Castor (see fig. 2)—and voted successively, each tribe taking its turn. The centuriate assembly always met outside the Pomerium in the Campus Martius, whether its purpose was legislative or electoral. Legislative activity took place more sporadically, but in a busy year the tribal assembly could meet frequently.[33] The citizen who was within easy travel distance from Rome and who was politically inclined would have had many opportunities to exercise his right to vote.[34] The first tribe to vote (the legislative equivalent to the *centuria praerogativa* in the electoral assemblies) was determined by lot, but it seems that the presiding magistrate was allowed to choose the first voter from that first tribe (*principium*), whose name was engraved along with that of his tribe on the same bronze tablet that contained the text of the law[35] and was later posted on the Capitolium. As he voted, the first voter was on an elevated platform, visible to all other citizens, as were the voters who followed his example. Thus, even the action of voting itself was a kind of performance, a symbolic enactment of popular sovereignty.[36]

An example of the kind of conflict that could arise during the meeting of a legislative assembly, and the personal danger to which politicians subjected themselves, can be found in Caesar's consulship in 59. Caesar proposed a law distributing lands to the poor and veterans of Pompeius' eastern campaigns.[37] Violence erupted while Caesar was overseeing the voting. As he stood on the Rostra, addressing the people, with Pompeius on one side and M. Crassus on the other (Plut. *Caes.* 14.4), M. Bibulus, his colleague in the consulship, burst in upon him and disrupted the meeting. Some armed men attacked Bibulus and his lictors and broke his *fasces,* the visible symbol of a consul's *imperium.* Bibulus bared his neck and invited them to strike, a gesture that demonstrated his willingness to sacrifice his life for the Republic (App. *BC* 2.11.39; Dio 38.6.2–3). In another account, Bibulus had a basket of dung dumped on his head as a further humiliation (Plut. *Cat. Mi.* 32.3).[38] His friends managed to usher him off to the Temple of Jupiter Stator. M. Cato was then invited to address the crowd, perhaps by one of the tribunes loyal to the senate's cause,[39] but he was carried off by Caesar's supporters and ejected from the Forum. He found his way back to the Rostra by another route, but the crowd refused to hear him. The law was eventually passed.

Dio remarks that there were no objections of substance to this *rogatio.*[40] Again, the issues at stake were larger and more far-reaching than the question of land distribution for Pompeius' veterans. In fact, this assembly had more to do with the amount of power the people were willing to grant to Pompeius and Caesar and, consequently, the authority they were willing to wrest away from the senate. The breaking of the consul's *fasces* was a striking reminder of these larger issues by demonstrating visibly the senate's vulnerability at the hands of the people. In other words, the distribution of political power was brought into sharper focus through the actions taken at this *comitia.*

For Roman aristocrats there was great prestige in election to high office or the passage of legislation, but this prestige was conferred only by a vote of the assembled citizen body of Rome in the *comitia,* an enactment of popular sovereignty. The manipulation of this procedure—whether this consisted of the blocking of the *pontes* or the violent disruption of the voting itself—was an oblique acknowledgment of this important source of political power. Such manipulation, as a disruption of routine, undermined procedure and was an attack on the very form of ceremony.

Public Entertainment: *Ludi* and *Munera*

L. Aemilius Paullus' famous dictum that "a man who knows how to conquer in war was also a man who would know how to arrange a banquet and show" demonstrates the centrality of public entertainment in the Roman aristocratic ethos.[41] An aristocrat demonstrated his wealth and power through his public munificence (*liberalitas*) at state-sponsored games, by putting on a good show and providing a public benefaction.[42] Cicero also includes public entertainment as one of the venues where the Roman people could express their collective will (*Sest.* 106; cf. *Att.* 10.12a.3). These two statements are evidence that in the Roman Republic there was often a significant political component to public entertainment of all kinds—games connected with state-sponsored festivals (*ludi*) and with private funerals (*munera*), banquets (*epulae*), and distributions of food (*visceratione*s).[43] Even though these forms of entertainment cannot be considered routine political procedure in the same way as *contiones* or *comitia*, they nonetheless had long been closely associated with the political process in the Roman Republic, especially for advancing the careers of aristocrats.[44] Yet they also became a way to celebrate military conquest and imperial power and as such became closely associated with the public image and in some cases the public memory of the military dynasts of the late Republic. For these reasons, the focus of our discussion will be on the sponsor of the games as performer—the one who ultimately wields the power on display—and the reactions of the audience, especially as attempts to undermine this power.

Roman aristocrats used public entertainment as a way of converting private munificence (*liberalitas*) into political power, and for this reason public entertainment became highly competitive. Caesar's aedilician games in 65 are a case in point. As curule aediles, Caesar and his colleague M. Bibulus were responsible for the *Ludi Megalenses* in April and the *Ludi Romani* in September, but we are told that Caesar also sponsored games separately from his colleague in order that he alone might enjoy the people's favor.[45] He included the customary *ludi* (games in the circus and theater) and *venationes* (wild beast shows and hunts). But he also decorated the Comitium, Forum, and Capitolium, perhaps with paintings, statues, and other works of art, and constructed temporary porticoes to accommodate the equipment associated with the games. His games thus occupied the important public spaces of the city, and we can imagine these decorated public spaces as an elaborate stage for Caesar's public appearances during the games. Roman aristocrats often went to great expense to make their games distinctive from their rivals. Caesar did this in three ways. First, he supplemented funds provided by the state with his own resources, thus blurring the distinction between public and private. These games, then, were not just a state-sponsored public festival, but Caesar's own creation, and his own success. Second, Caesar also in this year honored the memory of his father (who had died some twenty years earlier) with gladiatorial combat (*munus*), thus bringing himself before the people once again. Finally, Caesar also made known his allegiance to the memory of C. Marius by restoring to the Capitolium the trophies of Marius that had been demolished by Sulla, and by erecting an inscription celebrating one of Marius' most important victories.[46] The witticism attributed to M. Bibulus, Caesar's colleague, that he would play Pollux, the forgotten twin, to Caesar's Castor, is an indication of Caesar's success in distinguishing himself from his colleague.[47]

While in Caesar's aedilician games the competition was principally his colleague in a junior magistracy, L. Sulla Felix used a new set of games to establish a permanent record of his achievements, thus broadening the scope of the competition to include perhaps all of the great men of Roman history. Sulla's *Ludi Victoriae* lasted from 26 October until 1 November, the anniversary of the battle that the games commemorated.[48] It is probable that these were first celebrated in 81, in which case they would have culminated nearly a year of celebrations in honor of Sulla's victories and were to be renewed annually.[49] The second time these games were held (in 80 BC), Sulla summoned athletes and other entertainers from all over the Mediterranean world to Rome, evidence of his great wealth, power, and scope of his influence. Sulla's monopolization of athletes left only the one stade footrace to be run at the ancient Olympic games.[50] Another striking aspect of these games was the display of lions unfettered in the Circus—the first such instance in Roman history (Sen. *Dial.* 13.8). This means that the games were produced on a lavish scale, they contained a notable "first," and they included both Greek-style athletic and perhaps poetry contests as well as more traditional Roman entertainment such as chariot racing.

One question is whether these games bore Sulla's name in the official record (*Ludi Victoriae Sullanae*) and thus commemorated a victory that was in essence Sulla's personal achievement. Although it is unlikely that Sulla so named his games, it is clear that they were as closely associated with Sulla as they were with the victory they celebrated.[51] Since Sulla's good fortune (*felicitas*), for instance, was a prominent part of the advertisement for these games (Vell. 2.27.6), they were an important part of his public image.[52] Games in celebration of victories (*ludi votivi*) were fairly common during the Republic,[53] but they were never made a permanent part of the Roman calendar.[54] Sulla's games were unique and unprecedented. The implicit message was that the victory commemorated by these games did not belong to the Roman people but rather to Sulla himself, demonstrating how Sulla's own achievements became intertwined with those of the state. Sulla communicated this message still further when he opted to have the games renewed annually, placing them on the Roman calendar between the *Ludi Romani* and *Ludi Plebeii*, thus transforming a victory celebration—usually a onetime, ephemeral event—into a regular feature of the Roman calendar. Thus, Sulla became an honoree and benefactor of the Roman people alongside Jupiter Optimus Maximus, and a celebration of Sulla's "personal victory" became routinized as part of the recurring festivals in the Roman calendar.

Thus far, we have focused on the use of public entertainment as a means for a Roman aristocrat to advertise his public image and thereby gain prestige (*dignitas*) and power. But an aristocrat's presence in the theater exposed him to insults spoken by the actors on stage as well as the hisses and catcalls from the rest of the audience.[55] Thus, a Roman aristocrat imperiled his public standing and prestige whenever he entered the theater, for by doing so he placed himself before the people and could be subject to their vociferous disapproval.[56] For instance, in 59 Caesar's entrance into the theater received only a tepid response from the audience, which Cicero surmised would evoke an angry letter from Caesar to Pompeius.[57] Silence could be as loud as boisterous applause. At the *Ludi Apollinares* in the same year, an actor on stage uttered the line "because of our misfortune you are great," which the audience interpreted as a reference to Pompeius and cheered wildly.[58] In 51 Q. Hortensius, the famous orator, was roundly hissed as he entered the theater following his successful defense of a client in a controversial case. The hostile reaction of the crowd almost made him regret his victory, for this was the first time in his distinguished career, we are told, that he had suffered such humiliation (Cic. *Fam*. 8.2.1).

The public humiliation of a distinguished aristocrat in the theater was one way that the Roman people could use public entertainment to express their collective will (Cic. *Sest*. 106). At other times, games became stages for popular protest. In these instances, just as at certain *contiones*, the distinction between performer and spectators became blurred. One set of games that occurred in conjunction with the political ambitions of P. Clodius is a noteworthy example.[59] At the *Ludi Megalenses* (April 56), which Clodius was sponsoring in his capacity as plebeian aedile,[60] the point at issue was the iniquities inherent in the Roman custom of hierarchically arranged seating in the theater. The venue for the protest was a temporary theater adjacent to the Temple of Cybele on the Palatium (*Har*. 24). At a prearranged signal (*signo dato*) a crowd of Clodius' supporters—slaves, according to Cicero—recruited from all the streets of Rome stormed into the theater and onto the stage itself. The consul Lentulus and members of the senate and the equestrian order—all the "good men" (*boni*), as Cicero refers to them—rose in dignified protest, acceding to the crowd, and left the theater, leaving the entertainment to be performed for the mob. The sight of the *boni* giving way to the crowd was a subversion of ceremony and custom. Cicero makes a point of reminding his audience that the *Ludi Megalenses* were the games at which the consul P. Africanus Maior first set aside the front rows of seating for the senatorial aristocracy,[61] thus demonstrating the depth of the crowd's violation of Roman custom when slaves occupied seats reserved for senators. But perhaps it was the crowd itself or its leaders that understood the significance of undermining the particular set of games that evoked the custom of arranged seating, as a show of breaking down (if only temporarily) the barriers that separated the social strata in Rome. In other words, the larger historical context of these games and the custom of arranged seating provided a greater depth and symbolic significance to the crowd's actions.

Public entertainment in the Roman Republic reaffirmed aristocratic preeminence through displays of *liberalitas* and hierarchical seating, and the audience often responded with applause and shouts of approval. Such games were a way of converting public munificence into political power, which made it a venue for competition among aristocrats, or, as in Sulla's case, for establishing a permanent record of his achievements and thus his historical legacy. Just as often, though, the audience in the theater undermined the prestige and authority of aristocrats with catcalls, hissing, and public mockery. The theater, like the Forum or the Campus Martius, was a place Roman aristocrats entered at their peril. Public acclaim might await them—or public humiliation.

The Triumph and *Ovatio*

As a celebration of success on the battlefield (*gloria*), an abiding element of the Roman aristocratic ethos,[62] with a pageantry that bespoke Rome's military might, the skill and courage of its army and the good fortune of the Roman people, the triumph was high national drama and a ceremony of power par excellence.[63] Part of the reason for this was the *triumphator* himself, who in comportment and dress had the appearance of a king or even the king of gods and was the focus of the spectators' gaze. The triumph was often the pinnacle of a statesman's career. The triumph was also a national celebration, involving all segments of Rome's population—senate, magistrates, army, and people. It was a celebration of the achievement of common military objectives and a demonstration of the glorious results that arose from unity and consensus. Yet the power that a triumph conferred on an individual sharpened aristocratic competition and encouraged political gamesmanship. Thus, in the performance of a triumph there existed a tension between the display of the *triumphator*'s power and the celebration of the glory of Rome, between individual achievement and national honor.

The power of Rome was displayed at a triumph through the achievements of the army under the leadership of the *triumphator*. The accoutrements of a triumph were largely the components of a visual imagery of military power and conquest. Carts laden with spoils[64] and gifts sent by subjugated peoples, usually gold crowns, as well as the display of spices and other aromatic substances, were evidence of the material rewards of conquest. Placards depicted important battles, along with the names of the conquered nations, and models of conquered cities could be shown.[65] Images of foreign wars and distant battlefields were thus brought back to Rome. Distinguished royalty or children of royalty ennobled a triumph, the most prominent of whom were executed before the sacrifice.[66] The centerpiece of the *pompa* was the *triumphator*, basking in the glory of his triumphant day. His appearance and dress were that of a king, or even the king of gods. His face was painted red (most likely in imitation of Jupiter[67]), and he wore the purple triumphal dress (*vestis triumphalis*), which consisted of the *tunica palmata*—so named for the palm branches embroidered on it—and of the *toga picta*—the purple toga with gold embroidery—and a gold crown. He carried an ivory scepter and laurel branch, the Roman symbols of victory (App. *Pun*. 66), as he rode in a chariot pulled by four horses. Following him were men he had freed from slavery, who donned for the occasion the *pilleus* of the freedman. The soldiers who followed his chariot sang ribald songs about their commander,[68] and a slave whispered in his ear, "Remember, you are only a man." Perhaps this was to ensure that the *triumphator* would not have designs on the kingship, or that, when he stood in the presence of the king of gods as sacrificer, he should do so with the appropriate humility. The sacrifice to Jupiter on the Capitolium included the dedication of the spoils of war that answered the avowal of spoils and the sacrifice that had marked the beginning of the campaign.

In the middle Republic, when the senate's power and influence over state affairs was virtually complete, especially in military matters, the senate took the prerogative of conferring triumphs. It gradually tightened its grip by effectively limiting triumphs to consuls.[69] Two other victory celebrations, the *ovatio* and the triumph on the Alban Mount, seem to have developed out of the disputes in the senate over the conferral of the triumph proper. The *ovatio* also required the senate's approval, but it was often granted for a victory that was deemed to be of less importance,[70] such as one in a slave war,[71] and thus it accorded the celebrant less prestige than the triumph proper. Even though the *ovatio* was regarded as less prestigious than the triumph proper, its bestowal was still rare. From the first *ovatio* in 503 to 19 BC, when the traditional conferral of triumphs came to an end under Augustus, there were 288 victory celebrations in all, 248 of which were triumphs, only twenty-four *ovationes*, eleven naval triumphs, and five triumphs on the Alban Mount. The comparative infrequency of *ovationes* is not all that surprising when we consider that they really existed only in relation to the triumph: those commanders who were denied a triumph might hope to attain an *ovatio*. Livy's fourth and fifth decades are replete with accounts of debates in the senate in the middle Republic concerning the merits of certain military victories and whether or not they deserved a triumph.[72] The *ovatio* seems to have faded (as did the triumph on the Alban Mount) around the middle of the second century and then to have undergone a transformation, for in the late Republic the only three recorded *ovationes* were all for victories in slave wars, in 132, 99, and 71 BC, which is consistent with what our sources tell us about the conferral of an *ovatio*—that it could be awarded when the enemy was deemed unworthy. Caesar's *ovatio* in January 44 BC, which we will discuss in more detail in the next chapter, was a major departure from the three previous, since it did not celebrate a victory in a slave war; in fact, there was no obvious victory to celebrate. Thus, it is best not to regard the triumph and *ovatio* as static institutions, but rather to observe how they evolved throughout Roman history, including the period on which we will be focusing.

There was also a third ritual, the triumph on the Alban Mount, which existed for the sole purpose of providing a venue for the celebration of a victory that was for some reason not sanctioned by the senate, but it conferred far less prestige.[73] Its location outside the city made the celebrant less conspicuous and the report of the deeds less well known in Rome. By 172 it had become customary, according to Livy (42.21.7), for commanders who were denied a triumph by senatorial decree to celebrate on the Alban Mount.[74] The development of the triumph on the Alban Mount (beginning in 231, when the first was celebrated)[75] coincides roughly with the senate's usurpation of control over the triumph proper.

When we turn to the late Republic, we find that the great conflicts of this period, the civil wars, redirected the evolution of the triumph by challenging some *triumphatores* to find the proper way to celebrate victories over Roman citizens. Sulla's triumph (27 and 28 January 81) is one indication of the difficulties of celebrating victory in civil war. It included two processions (*pompae*) celebrating two victories—one over a foreign enemy (Mithridates) as well as one over a Roman citizen (Marius). The entry in the *Fasti Triumphales* appears to record only the victory over Mithridates[76]—Marius is left unmentioned—indicating perhaps that Sulla desired to downplay his victory in Italy over Roman citizens, at least in the official records. Moreover, it was customary for the victor to put placards on display describing the number of enemy slain or cities captured, or, more visually appealing, models of captured cities and towns could be conveyed in the procession (e.g., Liv. 37.59.3; 38.43.10). Sulla put on display many representations of conquered cities in Greece and Asia, but not a single city in Italy was shown.[77]

Even though it seems that Sulla attempted to downplay his victory in Italy, he still did not shrink from portraying his personal enemies as enemies of the state. For instance, during Sulla's triumphal procession, prominent men and their families who had been exiled during the Cinnan regime marched in a long train wearing garlands and called Sulla their "savior and father."[78] It was not unusual for those rescued from enemy attack to be present in the triumphal procession, as a manifest sign of the good work of the *triumphator* in his role as savior.[79] In this instance, however, the restoration of exiles was an overt reminder of the civil war and the *dominatio* of Cinna and Marius, from which the returning exiles had been rescued. The denigration of his enemies was necessary in order that Sulla could advertise the benefits of his regime. Sulla also made no attempt to distinguish the vanquished in the two processions of his triumph, the one displaying the wealth taken in the war with Mithridates and the other the wealth recovered from Praeneste after the death of the younger Marius. These two processions on successive days could have had the effect of equating the two enemies whose defeat was being celebrated. Thus, the younger Marius, though a Roman citizen, became a *hostis* of the Roman state, like Mithridates. This was a necessary part of the process of legitimation of Sulla's victories, which had come under the auspices of a command his political enemies could claim was not rightfully his, and buttressed his dictatorship, which stood outside the constitution.

Lesser conflicts, the usual rivalries that animated Roman politics, also played out in the granting of a triumph, a process that began when the returning commander addressed the senate, usually at the Temple of Bellona, with a narrative of his accomplishments demonstrating the importance of his victory, followed by a senatorial debate exploring the merits of the request.[80] Some of the most contentious meetings of the senate involved a debate of a general's accomplishments (*res gestae*) and whether they merited the right to triumph.[81] The triumph was such a singular honor and conferred so much prestige and *gloria* that the senate often granted one only after much dispute and contention. Based on the source material, a triumph decreed with unanimous approval was a rare occurrence, although one must admit that the most contentious debates made for the most dramatic retelling. There is also the tradition that personal rivalries had an effect on the outcome of these debates as aristocrats tried to prevent their political enemies from enjoying the benefits of a triumph.[82] In the late Republic, this kind of political gamesmanship surrounding triumphs forced many aristocrats to delay their celebrations for months, even years—and some never achieved this signal honor. L. Lucullus' triumph for his achievements against Mithridates was delayed by the tribune C. Memmius, who tried to convince the people to deny him a triumph. According to Plutarch (*Luc.* 37.1–2), the leading citizens of Rome prevailed upon the people, and Lucullus got his triumph three years after his return from the east.[83] Caesar was hoping for a triumph when he returned from Spain in 60 BC and then to stand for the consulship of 59. He had to receive special dispensation from the senate to stand for election in absentia, since he could not cross the Pomerium and still be eligible for a triumph. His proposal failed in the senate when M. Cato filibustered against it until the senate adjourned (Plut. *Caes.* 13.2). Caesar was forced to choose between a triumph and the consulship. C. Pomptinus, Caesar's predecessor in Gaul, finally achieved a triumph in 54 for his achievements in 62 or 61, following the machinations of his friend Servius Galba, who reportedly enrolled new citizens early in the morning of the assembly that was set to vote on a proposal granting him a triumph.[84] The tribunes of the *plebs* who had been left out of this assembly disrupted Pomptinus' triumph in protest (Dio 39.65.2), which shows how a political dispute that was part of the process of conferring a triumph could mar the ceremony itself. Or, to put it another way, the ceremony of the triumph evinced the conflict that was part of the larger political context. A triumph was emotionally charged precisely because of its role in the ongoing political rivalries, and it often came to symbolize victory not only over a foreign foe but also over one's own political enemies at home.

Disputes over a triumph sometimes arose over the question of who held the right to confer it. In the late Republic, the notion that a triumph was the people's celebration was more strongly felt. The law passed conferring a triumph on Pomptinus in 54 (alluded to earlier), as if to bypass a senatorial decree, confirms that the Roman people could have a hand in conferring a triumph. Laws of this sort were rare, however, with most dating to the early Republic.[85] But since Livy is responsible for these notices, the tradition of the people conferring a triumph by law was known to him in his day, and we should understand it as a tradition of the late rather than the early Republic. Some laws from a more recent period made a triumph possible (by, for instance, extending a command until the day of a triumph or allowing a commander to return for a triumph) but did not confer a triumph per se, as was the case with Pomptinus.[86] Livy describes tribunes of the *plebs*, the guardians of popular sovereignty, as the traditional opponents of triumphs.[87]

They could interpose their veto to prevent a triumph, although it is not clear how often they did so. We have already noted how C. Memmius attempted to block Lucullus' triumph. Ap. Claudius Pulcher (*cos.* 143) celebrated a triumph despite a tribunician veto (Cic. *Cael.* 34; V. Max. 5.4.6; Suet. *Tib.* 2.4), and in protest a hostile tribune of the *plebs* attempted to pull him from his *quadriga*. Cicero was warned against attending senate meetings following his return from Cilicia lest he anger a tribune who would then block his bid for a triumph (Cic. *Att.* 7.4.2). The triumph, the ceremony in which a Roman aristocrat achieved his greatest honor, was also the venue where the reputation (*fama*) of the Roman people and army was at stake.[88] It remained an opportunity for the people to acclaim the general in the city, after the acclamation of the soldiers (*salutatio*) had taken place on the battlefield. Finally, Cicero states that the only true triumph was the acclamation of the whole citizen body for those who had performed a signal service to the state. This is in part Cicero's special pleading, since it so happened that Cicero was honored with precisely this kind of ceremony in April 43, following the battle of Mutina (Cic. *Phil.* 14.13; for a discussion see chap. 7).

Another important historical development of this period was the conferral of triumphal imagery in the form of the triumphator's dress as a special honor to an individual who had enjoyed unprecedented success. The wearing of triumphal dress became an honor bestowed on certain individuals, thus extending the use of this unique garb to other occasions. The right to wear triumphal garb at Roman public festivals was first bestowed on L. Aemilius Paullus following his victory over Perseus (*de vir. ill.* 56), an honor conferred both by a law voted on by the people and a decree passed by the senate. Cn. Pompeius was similarly allowed to wear triumphal dress and a gold crown at the *ludi circenses* and the *toga praetexta* and gold crown in the theater, although Velleius claims that he only exercised this right once (2.40.4; Dio 37.21.4). A similar honor was bestowed on Caesar (Dio 43.43.1). C. Marius arrogated this right to himself when he appeared at the first senate meeting of his consulship in 104 BC having come directly from his triumph still dressed as a *triumphator*.[89] Marius provoked the envy and ill will of his colleagues in the senate. Pompeius only once dressed in this way, probably to dispel such ill will. This honor had the effect of conferring the imagery of the triumph, with its attendant power and prestige, on certain individuals, thus making the triumph and the glory that it offered in a sense a characteristic of these individuals. After this perhaps, Romans could more readily accept the notion of the triumph as being reserved for an individual and members of his family.

In the late Republic, a triumph could only be conferred through the combined efforts of the senate and people of Rome. This was due in part to the political gamesmanship that usually accompanied debates about the worthiness of a general's claims to the right to triumph. But it is also evidence of the place of the triumph as a national celebration, one that resulted from the consensus of the senate and people. Celebrations for victories in civil war were especially difficult for the very reason that they ultimately resulted from a fractious and perilous lack of consensus. Thus, in the late Republic, the usual tension that marked a triumph, between the power and fame of a renowned individual with the success and glory of Rome, was exacerbated by political instability.

Departures and Returns

The pageantry of the triumph informed to a degree two other related ceremonies—the departure and return of a Roman commander. These departures and returns were part and parcel of triumphal celebrations, since the departure (*profectio*) of a military commander often adumbrated victory and triumph, in effect crowning a *triumphator* in anticipation of his victorious return, while the return itself (*reditus* or *adventus*) brought the reality of a triumph even closer. The same tension existed in these celebrations between the glory of Rome and the power of an individual. The departures and returns that we will be considering fall into two broad categories: those of a military type, involving magistrates with *imperium* departing for or returning from military campaign, often with their armies in tow; and those of a nonmilitary type, involving Roman aristocrats who were usually not holding political office (*privati*) but were nonetheless men of high political standing whose departures and returns were often highly symbolic. In both cases, the Roman people played an important role in providing a celebratory sendoff or in welcoming home the returning hero.

Livy captures the drama of a consular *profectio* in his description of P. Licinius Crassus' (*cos.* 171) departure for his campaign against the Macedonian king Perseus. The consul was required to make the appropriate vows (*vota nuncupata*) and don the military cloak (*paludamentum*) before departing from the city escorted by the people.[90] The sight of the commander's change of dress from magistrate to promagistrate (*mutatio vestis*) remained charged with emotion, especially in times of war—a form of high national drama.[91] Livy describes the crowd's sense of anticipation, the anxious thoughts, the acknowledgment of the unpredictable fortunes of war, the fame and prestige of the enemy, the possibility of victory or defeat.[92] The triumph, Livy asserts further, marked the return of the commander to the same gods from which he had departed.[93] Thus, the triumph, ending with a sacrifice to Jupiter Optimus Maximus on the Capitolium and the dedication of the spoils of war just completed, fulfilled the avowal of spoils and the sacrifice that marked the beginning of the campaign. The triumph was only one—albeit the most important one—of a series of ceremonies that included the departure (*profectio*) and return (*reditus*).

Just as the departure of the commander with his army anticipated a triumph, so did his return, even before a triumph had been decreed. Following his victory over Philip V in 196, T. Quinctius Flamininus settled affairs in the Greek east and then led his army back across the Adriatic to Italy. On his return journey, Flamininus seems to have established what would become the traditional route of a commander returning from the east. He landed in Brundisium and marched through Italy in a manner that, Livy tells us, had the appearance of a triumphal procession (*prope triumphantes*), with Flamininus at the head of a column of soldiers, the spoils of war being conveyed behind.[94] While we can only conjecture how this sight might have struck those who witnessed it at the time, we can state with more certainty that Livy viewed this procession as triumphal in form, perhaps because he noticed that it consisted of some of the important features of a triumph proper, including the presence of soldiers and the spoils of war. Moreover, Flamininus' achievements made a triumph seem inevitable.

The return of L. Aemilius Paullus in 167 BC after his victory over Perseus was equally colorful and dramatic. He sailed up the Tiber, standing in a Macedonian royal skiff festooned with weaponry and textiles captured from the king, and was greeted by a huge throng waiting on the banks to welcome their returning hero. Paullus must have looked like the Hellenistic king he had just conquered (Liv. 45.35.3). Comparisons of Paullus and Flamininus were inevitable, since both had defeated Macedonian kings and returned to celebrate great triumphs. We can only guess at what Paullus might have been thinking. Perhaps he bypassed the land route that Flamininus had taken in the hopes of distinguishing his achievements from those of his famous predecessor by staging a return that was even more dramatic. These triumphant returns were the precursors to the imperial *adventus*.[95]

In the late Republic, a general's departure or return was still an event of high drama and emotion[96] that came to reflect the fractious politics of the time. The national drama of the middle Republic often became a ceremony of tension and conflict. One notable return was that of M. Cato from Cyprus in 58 BC. Cato sailed up the Tiber river in a royal skiff, perhaps modeling himself after Paullus, and was greeted by a large crowd, including all the magistrates and priests, the senate, and a large portion of the Roman people.

Plutarch likens his return in appearance and honor to a triumph,[97] mainly because Cato paraded spoils of war through the Forum, thus conforming to prescribed procedure of a triumph proper even though he had not been conferred one. Perhaps he was pessimistic about the probability of gaining a triumph and so used his return as a surrogate.[98] In the end he achieved some success, since the senate decreed that he be allowed to wear triumphal garb at all public festivals. This was a rare honor, as we have seen, and it is indicative of the senate's belief that Cato's accomplishments merited public and formal recognition, although it is not clear why he was not granted a triumph proper.

In 55 BC the two consuls Pompeius and Crassus were accorded commands over Spain and Syria despite the opposition of many in the senate as well as the tribunes. The *profectio* of Crassus, a duly elected consul who was departing the city to fight a formidable enemy, should have been a national drama similar to the departure of P. Licinius Crassus as he set out against Perseus. Instead, it devolved into a spectacle that exposed the political divisions surrounding the conferral of *imperium* that indeed were characteristic of the times: Crassus' departure became an inversion—almost a parody—of a typical *profectio*.[99] When Crassus was offering the customary prayers on the Capitolium, rumors spread of evil omens and portents, in direct contrast to a typical *profectio* that foretold victory on the battlefield, a safe return, and eventually a triumph. Ateius Capito's (*tr. pl.* 55) bold attempt to throw Crassus into prison was thwarted by some of his colleagues. In the face of such persistent opposition, Crassus enlisted the aid of his colleague Pompeius to help ensure the ease of his departure. Undeterred, Ateius set up a brazier near a gate of the city (probably the Porta Capena [see fig. 1]), and, when Crassus approached, he began uttering curses as he threw incense onto the flames. Crassus' ultimate defeat and death at the hands of the Parthians provided our later sources with ex post facto legitimation of these curses. But Cicero also got wind of this spectacle and remarked that Crassus had not fared as well as his "contemporary" (*aequalis*) L. Aemilius Paullus (*cos.* 182, 168), who had once set out against Perseus.[100] Cicero's mention of Paullus in the context of Crassus' departure is further evidence for our claim that Romans often placed more recent events in a larger historical context by associating them with similar events from the remote past and, more importantly for our purposes, that ceremony (or, in this case, the inversion of ceremony) was often the medium through which this interweaving of past and present took place. Cicero's allusion to Paullus' departure shows his contempt for Crassus' ambition to be a great conqueror, intimating that if Crassus could not get his departure right he was unlikely to return triumphant.

Cicero, in a similar way, could use the departures and returns of his political enemies as fodder for his rhetorical diatribes. He, for instance, castigates the *profectio* of L. Piso and A. Gabinius—"two vultures in military dress" (*duo vulturi paludati*)—who set out from Rome accompanied by bad omens and maledictions.[101] He also criticizes the return of Verres, who, after departing in due accord with proper ritual (*vota nuncupata*), had snuck back into Rome at night to visit his mistress (*Verr.* 2.5.34). The view of these events is Cicero's own, and he is obviously exploiting the emotions surrounding such events for rhetorical purposes. Nonetheless, his characterization of these events in this way shows precisely why they should be regarded as symbolic action: through these events a Roman aristocrat constructed his public image by communicating specific political messages. These were the events that people remembered.[102]

As with the triumph proper, the prevalence of civil war in the late Republic altered the development of these ceremonies, making returns of commanders not cause for celebration but a time of fear and trepidation. The best example is Pompeius, who, after his victory over Mithridates in 62, landed in Brundisium, as other commanders returning victorious from the east had done before him, and then made a great show of disbanding his army before proceeding to Rome.[103] He arrived in the city without his army and waited several months for his triumph. Pompeius' actions indicate that he had a model in mind more recent than Flamininus or any other commander from the middle Republic. By disbanding his army, Pompeius wished to demonstrate that he would not follow the example of L. Sulla, who also landed in Brundisium after his victory over Mithridates some twenty years earlier. But Sulla then marched on Rome, captured it from his political enemies, became dictator, and ushered in a reign of terror that included the systematic destruction of his enemies. Sulla's return also anticipated a triumph, but one that celebrated a victory over Roman citizens as well as a foreign enemy.[104]

Thus far, we have focused on departures and returns that involved magistrates with *imperium* departing for or returning from a military campaign. Even this type, though, was subject to some variation in the late Republic, as we have seen, insofar as they related to the ongoing political struggles, especially as these struggles exploded into civil war. Now we can turn to those departures and returns that involved members of the elite who did not have *imperium* nor armies in tow, ones that did not anticipate an actual triumph. Nevertheless, these events involved statesmen who had much at stake and whose reputations were well known to the public; these events were also highly symbolic and were often used to communicate a political message.

The departure of M. Crassus in 62 is an example of how far such an event could diverge from the departure of commanders with *imperium* while still maintaining its symbolic value within the context of the political issues then current. When Pompeius Magnus' return from the east was imminent and when all Rome stood in anticipation of what the world conqueror would do, Crassus, Pompeius' longtime rival, departed the city with his children and valuables,[105] a public performance that was intended to demonstrate that Pompeius' return meant Italy and Rome were no longer safe. (Pompeius understood the symbolic significance of his actions, which is why he disbanded his army immediately upon his return to Italy.) In this instance, Crassus did not intend to emulate a commander departing for his province, but his departure was nonetheless symbolic.

That the triumph was the paradigmatic ceremony for departures and returns is in evidence in Cicero's departure for exile and later his return to the city. In both cases, he described these performances using the metaphorical language of a triumph even though they involved no military campaign. In February 58, Cicero departed Rome following the failure of his most powerful friends (especially Pompeius) to help him fend off the attacks of Clodius.[106] He even donned the garb of mourning, as did many of his friends and relatives, to call attention to his plight and arouse the sympathy and solicit the assistance of the Roman people, as we noted earlier.[107] Before he left the city he ascended the Capitolium and dedicated there a small statue of Minerva,[108] with whom he felt an affinity since he had declared himself Rome's protector and savior, like Minerva, especially during his consulship when he rooted out the Catilinarian conspiracy.[109] Even at this low point in his career, Cicero remained Rome's protector and savior, since his exile from the city was to ensure peace and concord. It is possible that Cicero was emulating Q. Metellus Numidicus, another eminent Roman statesman, who had been forced into exile by the machinations of a tribune and who was even made to say that he went into exile so that no danger would befall the Republic (App. *BC* 1.31.140). But the similarities between the two departures became explicit only after Cicero's return.[110] Precisely what was going through Cicero's mind on the night of his departure is open to speculation, but it is clear that after his return he viewed his exile as essential for the safety of Rome (Cic. *Red. Pop.* 1). At that time, his departure took on symbolic importance, and he linked it closely with his return, which he described with the metaphorical language of a triumph. As Cicero himself told the story of his exile, he saved Rome by departing and would save it again upon his return, fostering his image as Rome's savior.

Cicero's return from exile, modeled in part on that of Q. Metellus

Numidicus, was also greeted with enthusiastic applause. Cicero's speeches and letters provide the most vivid details of his return, which he characterized as being triumphal.[111] Almost immediately after Cicero went into exile, his friends began working for his recall. On 4 August 57 a law passed by the *comitia centuriata* allowed Cicero to return home. Cicero left Dyrrachium on 4 August and on the next day landed in Brundisium to great fanfare. His arrival there coincided with the foundation day of the colony of Brundisium, the significance of which was not lost on the inhabitants, as well as the foundation day of the Temple of Salus (on the Quirinal) in Rome, which Cicero took pains to point out to his friend and correspondent Atticus. It was also the birthday of his daughter Tullia who was there to greet him. The imagery of birth and rebirth became a motif of Cicero's writings of his return.[112] The symbolism of salvation—both Cicero's and Rome's—that had been so important in Cicero's departure persisted in the tradition surrounding his return. Cicero remained in Brundisium until around 11 August[113] when he received a letter detailing the results of the vote and the celebration that attended it. We can only note that he followed the route from Brundisium to Rome that victorious commanders had traversed before him, and on his journey he was greeted by congratulatory delegations dispatched by *municipia*. (There is admittedly no direct evidence that any contemporary made a connection between Cicero's route and the return of a victorious general.) Cicero's arrival in the outskirts of Rome drew even more attention; only his enemies failed to attend. The lower orders (*infima plebs*) welcomed him home with applause at the Porta Capena as they filled the steps of the temples. A similar crowd followed him to the Capitolium and more throngs awaited him in the Forum (see fig. 1).

Cicero would have us believe that the crowds in the city that welcomed his return were there for precisely this purpose; in this he was perhaps moved by the precedent of Metellus Numidicus. We know, however, that Cicero arrived in Rome on 5 September, which happened to be one of the first days of the *Ludi Romani*, the most important festival on the Roman civic calendar. It is likely that the crowds in the city on this occasion had come for the spectacle of the games, not for the spectacle of Cicero's return. Cicero knew the city would be crowded for the *Ludi Romani* and probably planned his return so that it would coincide with the beginning of the festival. He took advantage of the occurrence of one spectacle to stage another.

Furthermore, Cicero later described his entrance into the city in a manner that made it appear like a *pompa triumphalis*. The procession began outside the city at the Porta Capena and wound its way to the Capitolium. He credits P. Lentulus with effecting his return as if he had been conveyed in a golden chariot drawn by decorated horses.[114] As Cicero thought about and then retold in his speeches and letters the circumstances surrounding his return from exile and the actual event itself, it is clear that he used the ceremony of a triumph as a frame of reference—as a model or paradigm, in other words, for understanding and expressing the significance of this event in his life. His return signaled both a victory over his political enemies and a reentry into the life and public activity of a Roman citizen. It remains an open question whether the Roman people or members of the senate who came out to greet him upon his return would have conceived of his performance in these same terms. Was it enough that an aristocrat arrived at the Porta Capena to a waiting throng, passing by the shrines of Honos and Virtus and the tomb of the Scipiones—monuments associated with triumphs past? The topography of Rome was a powerful and evocative set of visual symbols, but could following the partial route of a triumph—through the Forum Romanum and ascending the Capitolium to the Temple of Jupiter Optimus Maximus—evoke in the minds of the spectators the idea of a triumph? These are questions we will attempt to answer when we explore some of the departures and returns and other ceremonies following Caesar's assassination. It has to be admitted that direct evidence is generally lacking. Even if we cannot argue convincingly, however, that these events were "triumphal" in character, we can at least say that they were highly symbolic acts that followed a fairly standard pattern and further that they communicated a specific political message.

Departures and returns should be understood as ceremonies and symbolic action closely related to the triumph. Livy was careful to describe such ceremonies in the middle Republic as high national drama, showing the consensus of the people as they ushered a commander to the gates of the city and hailed his departure for a glorious military campaign. In the late Republic, these same ceremonies were fraught with political conflict, as political rivals used them to advance themselves or undermine the power of their enemies.

The Aristocratic Funeral

A Roman aristocratic funeral (*funus privatum*) celebrated the glory of Rome through the exploits of one of its most famous sons.[115] It also served to convoke Romans of all social strata and, like the triumph, promote important Roman ideals, such as the rewards of service to the state and the fame and glory to be found in martial valor. Polybius could describe a generic aristocratic funeral of his day (ca. 150–125 BC) as a ceremony with a clear social purpose—to inculcate important social values and encourage the younger generation to aspire to great achievements in service to the state (6.53–54). Yet an aristocratic funeral honored the achievements of an individual and his family within the larger context of Roman history. Moreover, like any gathering of Roman citizens, the aristocratic funeral provided the enterprising politician with an opportunity to make a political statement, and indeed funerals became a political forum for the ruling elite. Even as early as the late fourth century funerals began to be used specifically to enhance a political image.[116] By the end of the Republic, the state became involved in honoring the most eminent statesmen, such as Sulla and Caesar, with funerals at public expense (*funera publica*). Thus, the same tension (discussed earlier) between the glory of Rome on the one hand and the power of an individual on the other entangled the aristocratic funeral as well. This tension erupted in mob rioting when the urban *plebs* used these funerals as an opportunity for political protest. A ceremony that had a unifying social force was also fraught with conflict, especially during the last generation of the Republic.

The typical aristocratic funeral followed a standard ritual framework, evoking the fame and accomplishments of the deceased and his family as well as the glory of Rome: display of the body at home; procession of family and friends conveying the body to the Forum (*pompa*); speech in praise of the dead on the Rostra (*laudatio*); cremation or burial. Deviations from this ritual were equally symbolic, at times heightening the sense of drama or undermining aristocratic authority. As often, political considerations prevailed.

The body of the deceased was put on display in the *atrium* of his home for several days before the funeral took place. On the day of the funeral, the place of cremation was prepared and other accoutrements readied. The deceased was customarily carried out of the home by members of his family or his clients,[117] who formed the procession (*pompa*) that conveyed the body to the Forum and laid it on the Rostra (see fig. 2). At the head of the *pompa* were musicians and professional mourners followed by actors who put on the masks (*imagines*) of famous members of the family of the deceased and impersonated the dead.[118] At the end came the family and the corpse. In the case of a funeral at public expense (*funus publicum*),[119] senators and magistrates took the place of the family as pallbearers and conveyed the body to the Forum.[120] The presence of political officials was intended to demonstrate that the deceased's accomplishments directly benefited the *res publica*.

By the same token, at several funerals in our period the Roman people are known to have conveyed the body to the Forum as an indication of their esteem for the deceased. Around 133 BC, a friend of Ti. Gracchus died under suspicious circumstances immediately after Gracchus had passed his controversial agrarian legislation, and the senate was blamed for this death. At his funeral, the crowd—spontaneously, it seems—honored the deceased by carrying his body to the Rostra for the *laudatio*.[121] In 57 L. Licinius Lucullus died; he was the great general who preceded Pompeius in the war against Mithridates. At his funeral, a crowd unexpectedly arrested the procession of young aristocrats carrying his corpse to the Forum and requested that Lucullus be buried in the Campus Martius, where Lucullus himself had buried L. Sulla. This incident is open to one of two interpretations: One is that the crowd was conferring on the deceased the honor of burial within the city limits, a component of the *funus publicum*, but without the senate's consent. The mention of Sulla's name might point in a different direction, however, for Sulla was never popular and Appian implies that his funeral was imposed on the Roman people by members of the senate, rather than emerging spontaneously from their collective will. This would mean that the crowd's request for a public burial was intended to mock the honor bestowed upon Sulla. In the end, the brother of the deceased convinced the crowd that Lucullus should be buried at his estate in Tusculum (Plut. *Luc*. 43.3–4).

One of the most visually striking components of the *pompa* was the display of ancestral masks (*imagines*). This display was highly symbolic and potentially politically significant. It was a right traditionally reserved for the most eminent families, and thus these *imagines* first and foremost bespoke the glory and renown of the aristocracy in general and the family of the deceased in particular. At Sulla's funeral (78 BC), some six thousand busts were on display in a lavish parade that was intended to connect Sulla in the first instance to his ancestral Cornelii.[122] But since his reforms of the constitution had restored the prestige and power of the Roman nobility, his funeral ceremony heralded the dawn of a new age in which this nobility would be supreme. Thus, the parade of *imagines* also demonstrated the supremacy of Sulla's new oligarchy. Clodius' funeral (52 BC) was in a sense the exact inversion of Sulla's funeral, for at Clodius' funeral there were apparently no *imagines* displayed at all (Cic. *Mil*. 33, 86), even though he was descended from a distinguished patrician family. Perhaps the absence of *imagines* was intended to undermine aristocratic authority and present Clodius as a plebeian populist.[123]

The most overtly political use of *imagines* was at the funeral of Caesar's aunt Julia (69 BC), the widow of C. Marius. L. Sulla and C. Marius, whose personal competition and rivalry came to symbolize the complex social and political forces that engulfed Rome in its first civil war, were still, many years after their deaths, at the center of political discussions,[124] one of which Caesar himself provoked when he paraded Marius' busts (*imagines*) in his aunt's funeral procession.[125] Representations of Marius had not been seen publicly, we are told, since the dictator Sulla had them all removed and destroyed in his attempt to eradicate the public memory of his rival. According to Plutarch, the outcry against Caesar for his display of Marius' images was easily drowned out by the shouts of approval from the crowd. Caesar, during the games that he sponsored as aedile in 65, went a step further when he restored the trophies of Marius (demolished by Sulla) on the Capitolium and erected an inscription celebrating Marius' victory over the Cimbri.[126] Caesar's celebration of his aunt's funeral and his aedilician games were opportunities to communicate a political message—a message having reference to figures from the recent past—and Caesar succeeded in establishing himself as a kind of heir to Marius.[127]

The funeral for Caesar's aunt occurred at a crucial time in Caesar's young career, when he was holding his first political magistracy, but it also afforded him the opportunity to continue communicating a political ideology. Following the reforms of L. Sulla, the quaestorship marked a young aristocrat's formal entrée into Roman politics at least in the sense that holders of this office entered the senate upon completion of their tenure (Tac. *Ann.* 11.22.6). It is probable that the increase in the number of junior magistracies caused an increase in the competition for political office as there was a greater number of young aristocrats who had to distinguish themselves from their colleagues if they hoped to advance to the higher offices. Caesar chose to distinguish himself in part by honoring his aunt with a funeral at which he could deliver another speech before the people in the Forum.

Once the *pompa* assembled at the Rostra, a member of the family of the deceased—by tradition his eldest surviving son—delivered a speech in praise of the dead, which functioned as a kind of oratorical commentary on the parade of *imagines* that accompanied the body to the Rostra.[128] In the case of a *funus publicum*, a leading magistrate often delivered the *laudatio*. For our purposes, it is worth pointing out again that the *laudatio*, like all Roman oratory, had an element of the theatrical in it: it was performed on a stage, the Rostra, before an audience, by an orator whose performance was reminiscent of an actor. Cicero describes the rhetoric of the *laudatio* as "a spare and unadorned brevity,"[129] in keeping with the somber occasion. Historical accuracy was not a requirement and in fact was often sacrificed in the interests of an encomium, thus making *laudationes* the bane of historians who attempted to glean historical fact from extravagant adulation.[130] This also shows that the audience came to a funeral expecting to witness the retailing of history, even though this history often had a clear family bias. The *laudatio* told the story of the deceased, his illustrious ancestors, and their place in Roman history, thus providing a larger historical canvas on which to place the accomplishments of the deceased. Funeral orations in honor of especially eminent Romans were delivered at *contiones* in the presence of all Roman citizens. This is another indication that a ceremony celebrating the careers of the members of a specific family could become a highly public event with opportunities for political communication.

In the *laudatio*, the great deeds of the deceased were recounted, and then the speaker turned to the distinguished members of the deceased's family, whose likenesses and clothing were worn by actors. Beginning with the most ancient, he then recounted their glorious deeds (Plb. 6.54.1). In some cases, a *laudatio* contained audacious boasting about a family's history. Caesar, for instance, used the funeral of his aunt Julia to establish the preeminence of his family, dating back to the very foundation of Rome, for in the *laudatio*, Caesar traced her descent back to the legendary kings of Rome, claiming that her mother's family—the Marcii Reges—were the progeny of the ancient Latin king Ancus Marcius.[131] He traced the descent of his own family, the Julian *gens*, even further back, to Aeneas and his mother, the goddess Venus.[132] In this speech, in the Forum before the people, he professed that he was descended from kings and gods; but even when speaking of kings, Caesar's emphasis was clearly on their religious inviolability (*sanctitas regum*). In tracing the Julian *gens* back to Venus, Caesar was not making an original claim—a relative had previously done so[133]—and it was possible for *laudationes* to contain such boasts, especially in the late Republic when this kind of genealogical antiquarianism became a hobby of Roman aristocratic families. Nonetheless, these were bold words coming from the mouth of a man who had just entered the quaestorship and was embarking on his senatorial career.[134]

Despite the ritual framework of the funeral that prescribed a certain set of actions as well as the care and planning that was involved, it was possible in the late Republic for a funeral to erupt into violence through the presence and participation of the crowd.[135] The best attested of the funerals that erupted in rioting and violence are those of P. Clodius in 52 and Caesar in 44.[136] The only other funeral so attested was that of Pompeius Strabo, father of the Great Pompeius, who died of plague in 88 BC. His body was pulled from the bier, presumably during the *pompa*, and dragged through the mud on a hook—a treatment traditionally reserved for tyrants. Senators and tribunes restored order with difficulty and covered his body with their cloaks.[137]

In the late Republic, the aristocratic funeral was an opportunity for elite families to parade their history before the Roman people as a way of demonstrating their privileged status and their capacity to rule, which, in some instances developed into a state-sponsored ceremony honoring an individual's achievements (the *funus publicum*) and in others a forum for popular protest. The funeral at once shows two important developments in this period: first, the increasing power and public profile of the *principes urbis* and the unprecedented honors accorded them, and second, the failure of the traditional political institutions of Rome to acknowledge fully and adequately satisfy the interests of the urban populace.

Conclusion

The typology of Roman Republican ceremony, as outlined in this chapter, is the framework within which our discussion and analysis of ceremony will take place. It is important to bear in mind a few basic themes already discussed in the introduction: ceremony was a means of political communication between elite and nonelite. This political communication was not always "top down," but rather the urban *plebs* could also make its will known, albeit collectively and often through violent action. Public ceremonial was a venue where Roman aristocrats displayed their power and prestige, but these were clearly dependent upon the consent and approbation of the people. Such a display of consensus masked the tension that underlay many of these ceremonies; the tension between the power of an individual and the sovereignty of the people, as well as between the glory of Rome and the renown of individual achievements, often erupted into riotous, even violent, conflict.

2

Dictator Perpetuo

Public Ceremonial during Caesar's Dictatorship

The political career of Julius Caesar,[1] like many of his contemporaries, played out on the stage of public ceremonial, through which he introduced himself to the electorate as well as established, polished, and honed his public image (*existimatio*) and personal prestige (*dignitas*) and displayed his generosity (*liberalitas*) before an audience of the *plebs urbana*.[2] In many ways, Caesar's career was typical of the time in which he lived, especially his appearance in *contiones* and *quaestiones* early in his career and his sponsorship of spectacle entertainment.[3] This is not to deny the importance of his magistracies, especially the consulship in 59 that enabled him to pass important legislation, or the military commands through which he became the conqueror of Gaul and thus equaled the considerable accomplishments of his rival Pompeius Magnus. Rather it is simply a first step in our understanding of the place of public ceremonial in Caesar's career and also, more generally, in the political life of the city of Rome in the late Republic and early Principate. In one sense, Caesar was behaving like a typical Roman aristocrat in acknowledging the sovereignty of the people and allowing himself to appear subject to its approval. Caesar's sole occupation of the center of power during his dictatorship did not ease but only exacerbated the tension underlying many of the ceremonies under discussion as he initiated the process (curtailed by his abrupt and violent end) of transforming them from national dramas to his personal displays of power.

Caesar's Dictatorship: The Background

Following his consulship in 59, when he received an extraordinary command in Gaul as a benefaction of the Roman people, Caesar was absent from Rome for much of the period 58–46, first executing this command and then routing Pompeius. When he finally returned to Rome in late July 46, basking in the glory of his victory in the civil war, he put on in September of that year a series of public ceremonies that in some cases matched, and in others surpassed, the kinds of celebrations that others had held before him. Political advancement was no longer his purpose, for Caesar by this time had ascended to the very pinnacle of power; still he clearly believed it necessary to celebrate his achievements, to share the spoils of his conquests with the Roman people, and to continue to polish and hone his public image. These ceremonies also served to mark the end of civil war, or at least a temporary respite, and provided a needed salve for the still fresh wounds of this conflict. They brought one phase of Roman history to an end and ushered in a new era under Caesar's leadership and helped establish the themes of his rule. Finally, through these ceremonies the dictator began to redefine the ways in which the Roman people related to its leaders.

Before we can discuss in an informed way the ceremonies of Caesar's dictatorship, it is necessary first to assess the nature of his political power and whether we should regard his political ambitions as monarchical; and second to consider his public building projects, especially his transformation of the topography of the Forum Romanum, for both have a bearing on our interpretation of the ceremonies that occurred under Caesar's dictatorship.

It is a gross understatement to say that Caesar remains an enigmatic figure. Even a contemporary such as Cicero could state publicly that "among those still to be born there shall be, as there has been among us, sharp disagreement; some shall extol your achievements to the skies, and others may find something—perhaps the most important thing—missing, if you do not extinguish the flame of civil war and thus preserve your fatherland. . . ." (Cic. *Marc.* 29). Tacitus echoed these same sentiments when he remarked that "the killing of the dictator Caesar had seemed to some the worst, and to others the fairest, of high exploits (Tac. *Ann.* 1.8.6). Livy wondered whether it would have been better for the Republic if Caesar had never been born.[4]

The focus of modern scholarship has tended to be on the scope of Caesar's genius, the nature of his political power, and the loftiness of his political ambitions.[5] Caesar left few hints about his future political plans, which has produced much fodder for scholarly speculation. To some Caesar was the last true Roman,[6] to others the first of the Caesars.[7] The fact is he was both, a transitional figure who transformed Rome of the Republic to Rome of the imperial age. A great deal of scholarly prose has been written in an attempt to understand the nature of Caesar's power, inevitably focusing on the question of whether he intended to found a monarchy. Advocates of monarchy fall roughly into two schools of thought: those who believe that Caesar was especially influenced by Alexander the Great and the concept of Hellenistic kingship and hoped to found a monarchy after the Hellenistic model, complete with divine worship of the king;[8] and those who believe that he was satisfied with a Roman or Italian model of kingship and that he would be a new Romulus.[9] Caesar, for his part, adopted the dress of the Alban kings, but perhaps he did so as an acknowledgment of his family connections to Iulus, the son of Aeneas, and the first of the Alban kings rather than as an adumbration of any aspirations for monarchy of any kind. Most damning to the idea of a Caesarian monarchy is that Caesar never clearly named a successor. Other scholars have been skeptical about attributing specific aims and objectives to Caesar for which there is no direct evidence. Whether Caesar aimed for kingship or not and of what type it was made little difference to his contemporaries. He was after all dictator, a position of unassailable political power that enabled him to pass laws without threat of tribunician veto and to maintain command of the army. He was further named dictator for life (*dictator perpetuo*) around the beginning of February 44 BC, thus securing his position for the foreseeable future. His only other preparations for the future were the appointment of magistrates for the next two years and his plans to lead Roman legions into Parthia. Caesar's position of power at the time of his death, then, his final aims notwithstanding, was incompatible with the ideals of the Roman Republic in the eyes of such contemporaries as Cicero and Brutus. "Caesar was slain for what he was, not for what he might become."[10]

A separate but related issue is the nature of Caesar's divinity and whether he enjoyed divine worship during his lifetime.[11] Caesar's contemporary Cicero enumerates a litany of honors for Caesar: a sacred couch, an image, a gable (probably on the home of the Pontifex Maximus), a priest (Cic. *Phil.* 2.110). This evidence coupled with the large number of extraordinary honors conferred on Caesar after his victory over Pompeius does demonstrate that Caesar was elevated to a plane inhabited by no other Roman. Yet Caesar's principal aim in this regard, I believe, was to achieve immortality through accomplishments extraordinary and unmatched. Cicero remarks that the great men of Roman history are ranked with the immortal gods because, though their bodies are mortal, "the activity of their minds continues for all time." He cites as a model for this view the example of Hercules, who achieved immortality through his accomplishments (*vita*) and courage (*virtus*).[12] Caesar hoped to achieve this kind of immortality—the only true immortality—by defeating the Parthians and ultimately creating an empire whose only boundary was the ocean, thus surpassing the accomplishments of all Romans throughout history and equaling or surpassing the accomplishments of Alexander.[13] I do not think that Caesar wanted to be a monarch in the conventional sense, but he did hope that his accomplishments would overshadow those of his predecessors, and any who might come after him. Thus he could have his own place, a singular perch, in the history of the Roman people.

We can now turn to the modifications made to the Forum Romanum under Caesar's influence (see fig. 3). Following the dedication of Pompeius' theater in 55, Caesar, while still in Gaul, initiated a building project that would culminate in the reconfiguration of the Forum Romanum and construction of a new Forum Julium, with the Temple of Venus Genetrix as its centerpiece. As R. Ulrich has argued (1993), the evidence suggests that Caesar's plans evolved from the time when he first purchased land in 54 BC, with the help of M. Cicero, and his death ten years later. Since Augustus ultimately completed many of these projects, it is also not clear how much we can attribute to Caesar himself or his successor. For our purposes, the main point of the subsequent discussion is that at the time of the events we will be discussing in this and forthcoming chapters, the area in and around the Forum was undergoing a major transformation, not all of it complete.[14] This "incompleteness" symbolized topographically and perhaps evoked some of the political changes taking place at the same time.

First, we shall consider the building activity in the Forum Romanum itself.[15] The Basilica Aemilia was refurbished around 50, marking the northern boundary of the Forum (see figs. 2 and 3). Caesar marked the southern boundary with his own basilica, where shops (*tabernae*) and the Basilica Sempronia once stood. Construction began in 54, and though still incomplete the new building was dedicated as the Basilica Julia in 46, around the time of Caesar's triumph. Early in 44, Caesar began building a new meeting place for the Roman senate to replace the Curia Hostilia, which had burned in 52 in the rioting that occurred during and after P. Clodius' funeral and had been replaced by a new structure dedicated by Faustus Sulla. The new Julian senate house, when finally completed by Augustus and dedicated in 26 BC, was erected roughly on the same site as the old Curia but with a southwesterly, instead of southeasterly, orientation.[16] It is not clear if Caesar himself had planned this new orientation. Furthermore, perhaps necessitated by the reconstruction of the Curia,[17] Dio states that, early in 44 BC, Caesar moved the old Rostra, which had been part of the Curia/Comitium complex, to the spot where the Rostra would stand during the imperial period, in the west end of the Forum, with the Capitolium providing the backdrop, and facing the open area of the Forum proper. At the same time, Caesar restored the equestrian statues of Sulla and Pompeius.[18]

The removal of the Rostra out from under the shadow of the Curia marked a significant break with Republican tradition, for whoever stood on Caesar's new Rostra no longer had the Curia as a backdrop and perhaps would appear less beholden to the senatorial aristocracy (see fig. 3). The Rostra and Curia were as closely linked historically as they were topographically. The focal point of public meetings in the early Republic had always been the senate house (Curia) and the voting enclosure (Comitium). In fact, the original Rostra probably was built onto the Curia and faced the Comitium,[19] thus serving as a platform from which one could address both people and senate; also, it could have been used by senators to inform the people of issues they had debated and decisions they had made in their meetings. At some point after 338, a new Rostra was built, still in the Curia/Comitium corner of the Forum but now between the Comitium and the Forum; in other words, it was moved outward some distance. At some time before the late Republic, orators who spoke from the Rostra began turning away from the Curia/Comitium complex to address the people who gathered in the Forum for *contiones*.[20] The location of the Rostra in close proximity to the Curia, where the senate met, was evocative of the nature of politics in the Republic, for Cicero describes the Curia as a guardian who watches over activity on the Rostra, punishes rashness, and guides a sense of duty and obligation—although (he admits) sometimes to little effect.[21] C. Licinius Crassus (*tr. pl.* 145), during the *comitia*, was the first to lead voters away from the Curia and Comitium and into the Forum proper—and he may have led them to the Temple of Castor. It is likely that this temple was made ready to accommodate *comitia* as early as the mid-second century;[22] in 117 this process was advanced when Metellus Delmaticus increased the size of the tribunal,[23] now called a second *rostra*, thus acknowledging the place of the temple in the new orientation of the Forum, which made the temple a more important site for *contiones* and *comitia*.[24] This combination of factors helped change the orientation of the Forum as the focus moved away from the Curia/Comitium. Thus, Caesar's removal of the Rostra completed a process that had been ongoing since the middle Republic, a process, if you will, of separating the people from the senatorial aristocracy.

Once this reconstruction was complete, and we should remind ourselves that this only happened under Augustus, the Forum became a more defined space, with clearly marked boundaries: on the north, the Basilica Aemilia; on the south, the Basilica Julia; on the west, the new imperial Rostra, which responded topographically to the Regia,[25] standing on the eastern end of the Forum, the headquarters of the Pontifex Maximus—Caesar himself in 44. There was also a new sight line created between the new Rostra and the Regia, the "headquarters" of Caesar. The one who stood on the new Rostra would have the attention of the people gathered before him and the new senate house facing him to his left. The Forum now had a visual center as it never had before. But what was its purpose? Did Caesar imagine that *contiones* would continue to be held here? What about legislative *comitia*? Before we can answer these questions, we have to consider Caesar's other building projects in the city.

Caesar also began construction of his own forum, the Forum Julium, which had as its centerpiece the Temple of Venus Genetrix (see fig. 3).[26] The link between the old and the new forum was provided by the Curia Julia, which faced the new Rostra, but was also attached to the southern corner of the Forum Julium.[27] At one time, Caesar may also have intended that by clearing space in the old Forum he could create a new spatial link with the Campus Martius,[28] where increasingly in the late Republic more and more building had been taking place, but in the end the new Forum Julium blocked access to the Campus Martius. The intended purpose of the Forum Julium—as Ulrich puts it, to "challenge the authority of the old Republican Forum"[29]—can be understood only while taking into consideration Caesar's other important building project in the Campus Martius, a new permanent enclosure for the *comitia tributa*.[30] Meetings of the tribal assembly by the late Republic took place in front of the Temple of Castor, increasingly the locus of much political activity in this period. Cicero and Dio both maintain that the new Saepta was designed for meetings of the tribal assembly only.[31] Dio states further that all elections, except those of the *plebs* (presumably meaning the *comitia tributa*), devolved into Caesar's hands (Dio 42.20.4). If this is true, however, then it is not clear where Caesar and his successors in this project planned for the centuriate assembly to meet. Taylor has argued that the *comitia centuriata* must have met here as well,[32] since it was required to meet outside the Pomerium, comprised, as it was, of Roman citizens in military array. Caesar's decision to build a permanent covered structure for comitial activity gives some indication that the assemblies still had a place in his Rome, although we should bear in mind that under Augustus this structure became a multiuse facility as the site for gladiatorial combat and wild beast hunts (*venationes*) as well as meetings of the popular assemblies.[33] This structure was meant to rival the great Theater of Pompeius that eventually became the southern boundary of Agrippa's complex of buildings in the Campus Martius.[34]

Just as the Saepta Julia was meant to move comitial activity from in front of the Temple of Castor to the Campus Martius, so too the Forum Julium was meant to replace the same temple as a venue for public meetings (*contiones*). The only attested incident at the Temple of Venus, however, recorded to demonstrate Caesar's growing arrogance, was the dictator's failure to rise at the approach of a procession of magistrates, lictors, and senators who were bringing news of extraordinary honors to be bestowed upon him.[35] It is possible to interpret this incident as demonstrating that the temple and forum complex came to be symbolic of Caesar's autocratic power, but it brings us no closer to the purpose of the new temple and forum complex. Ulrich remarks that the similarity between the architectural features of the new Temple of Venus Genetrix and the so-called Metellan phase of the Temple of Castor is so striking as to suggest overt imitation.[36] Most notably, both temples were fronted with a speaker's platform of roughly the same dimensions (100 Roman feet across and a height of 3.50 m), although the Temple of Venus used a different means of access, perhaps intended to provide a greater degree of protection for the speaker. Ulrich concludes from the archaeological evidence that Caesar's new temple and forum complex provided a dramatic yet secure stage from which the dictator could conduct public business, especially *contiones*. The Forum Romanum, by contrast, was "to be treated like a national shrine, lovingly restored at great expense, but no longer the focus of political life."[37]

Caesar had very little opportunity to try out this new topography before he was assassinated. If indeed it was the fate of the Forum Romanum to cease to be the focus of political life, this fate was dramatically altered by Caesar's death, for the Forum remained central to the events after the Ides of March as the site of many of the ceremonies we will be discussing. The Temple of Castor was frequently a site of *contiones*, as was the Rostra in the Forum, including funeral eulogies (*laudationes*), although, as we shall see, it is not clear in every instance from which *rostra* speakers delivered their speeches. Triumphal parades and funerary and other processions continued to move through the Forum Romanum, as they always had. The Forum Romanum was a powerfully evocative symbol of political life in the Republic, and one of the principal questions in forthcoming chapters is how the changing topography affected the ceremonies that occurred there and to what extent the new topography of the Forum evoked the memory of Caesar and his dictatorship or the traditional political procedures of the Republic.

The Popular Assemblies under Caesar

One of Caesar's conditions for appeasement with Pompeius at the beginning of their civil war in 49 BC was that free elections and control of public affairs should return to the senate and Roman people (*Civ.* 1.9.5). This fine-sounding ideal was never realized under the dictatorship of Caesar, whose complete control of these assemblies upset the fundamental balance inherent in the assemblies of Roman citizens that convened to elect magistrates and pass legislation, a balance between the sovereignty of the people and the power of an individual.

Suetonius claims that Caesar shared with the people the appointment of the magistracies other than the consuls: half the magistracies were filled by popular vote, the other half Caesar himself nominated (Suet. *Jul.* 41.2). In Suetonius' scheme, Caesar apparently appointed the consuls as well.[38] Cicero, in an offhand remark, states that Caesar chose the consuls and tribunes, implying that the other magistracies were still left to popular vote (*Att.* 14.6.2). A famous anecdote illustrates the resentment caused by Caesar's control of consular elections. When a consul died on the last day of his office, Caesar appointed C. Caninius Rebilus consul for the remainder of the day.[39] Caesar may have thought he was following custom by ensuring that the consulship remained occupied, but this brief appointment was universally viewed as an egregious transgression of tradition. He also appointed consuls for two years (43 and 42) in anticipation of his Parthian campaign. Our ancient sources suggest that the fate of the lower magistracies was still in the hands of the people in the *comitia tributa*. But at the senate meeting in the Temple of Tellus (on 17 March) following Caesar's assassination, great consternation was aroused by the prospect of invalidating Caesar's *acta*, which meant that those magistrates who were indebted to Caesar for their positions would have to subject themselves to the whims of the electorate (App. *BC* 2.129). This implies a heavy reliance on the dictator's personal influence in the elections for all magistracies.

Caesar exercised his right of recommending candidates for election (*commendatio*), according to Suetonius, by sending a written note to each tribe with the name of the candidate he was recommending. There is no record of whether the people were flattered by such direct personal appeals from the dictator, or resentful that they had been robbed of the power to elect candidates freely. We should remember that Augustus, who was generally more sensitive to form than Caesar, accompanied his candidates in person as they made the rounds of all the tribes (Suet. *Aug.* 56.1). Augustus adopted a more personalized approach to canvassing as a way of distinguishing himself from his predecessor, who at times, it seems, could appear aloof. If this was the case, then Caesar fostered a far different kind of relationship with the electorate in the popular assemblies than he did with his banquets (as we shall see later in this chapter).

Elections under Caesar, from what we can gather, further diminished the exercise of popular sovereignty. No ancient source informs us precisely of the manner of elections under Caesar, but his method of recommending candidates for election does not encourage the view that under his presidency elections proceeded according to custom. Frei-Stolba has suggested that Caesar announced the names of his candidates without actually calling the people to vote.[40] If she is correct, then the performance of voting—the actual enactment of popular sovereignty—only rarely took place. There was no display of consensus between ruling elite and governed, no approbation of the people; elections, then, were no longer ceremonies of popular sovereignty but reaffirmations of Caesar's power. Again, whether the people resented this change is not known.

Caesar's use of the legislative assemblies under his dictatorship follows a similar pattern. The slate of legislation that Caesar passed in this period helped define his public image and administration. Virtually all of his administrative measures, the sum of the achievements of his dictatorship (usually referred to collectively as the *acta Caesaris*), were possible only by making use of the two principal assemblies, the *comitia tributa* and the *comitia centuriata*.[41] L. R. Taylor has pointed out that the fundamental difference between these two assemblies was the manner in which they were held and consequently the nature of those who participated.[42] The *comitia tributa*, especially for legislation that was scheduled at no special time, was generally in the hands of those resident in Rome, although proposed laws were promulgated widely, and, since there was a statutory waiting period between the promulgation of a bill (*rogatio*), its debate in a *contio*, and the subsequent vote in the *comitia*, some residents of the municipalities who had the means could venture to Rome. By contrast, the *comitia centuriata*, which usually met in late July to elect magistrates, beckoned crowds to Rome, and these usually comprised members of the municipal aristocracy, Italian families of local importance, many of whom were members of the equestrian order. This group, Taylor asserts, usually were in agreement with the Roman nobility, and their combined electoral power ensured the election of candidates whom they favored.

She further states in this context that Caesar's decision to use the centuriate assembly as a lawmaking body indicates that he no longer had any reason to fear the power traditionally exercised by the nobility over the municipal aristocracy.[43] On the other hand, the stories of his difficulties with tribunes are well known. Pontius Aquila refused to rise at his triumph in 45 (Suet. *Jul.* 78.2.); Caesetius and Marullus removed a diadem from one of his statues in 44, for which they were deposed.[44] Thus, Caesar used the centuriate assembly because he could control it more easily than the tribal assembly.[45]

In Taylor's mind, Caesar's use of the centuriate assembly as a lawmaking body was based on political exigencies, not constitutional requirements or legal niceties, although we know that the centuriate assembly had long been used as a lawmaking body. The traditional view has it that the tribal assembly largely usurped the legislative functions of the centuriate assembly, especially after 287 BC.[46] In more recent studies on the legislative assemblies, K. Sandberg has suggested that it might be possible to distinguish the legislative activity of each assembly based on its sphere of influence: the centuriate assembly dealt with matters "extra pomerial"—that is, outside the sacred boundary of the city (Pomerium), having to do with "foreign policy" (e.g., declarations of war[47])—while the tribal assembly dealt with matters "intra pomerial."[48] These spheres of influence are clearly indicated by the location of the meetings of these assemblies—the centuriate in the Campus Martius outside the Pomerium, the tribal in the Forum Romanum. Legislation in both assemblies could be introduced only by tribunes of the *plebs*. Sandberg's study, however, traces legislative activity only down to 88 BC, leaving aside the last generation of the Republic, since by that time the Republican constitution was crumbling. In this period, however, the tribal assembly had begun to encroach on the centuriate assembly's sphere of influence, especially in regard to provincial commands (e.g., P. Sulpicius' law on Mithridates in 88, Gabinius' and Manilius' laws on Pompeius' commands in 67 and 66). Sandberg does point out that, after L. Sulla's dictatorship and his reforms of the Roman constitution, curule magistrates were able to introduce legislation to the tribal assembly, which might have developed out of Sulla's weakening of the power of the tribunate. Furthermore, Sulla might have intended the centuriate assembly to take precedence in his new constitution (Sandberg 1993, 81), in a sense "correcting" the primacy of the tribal assembly. Finally, there is some evidence to suggest that, throughout the history of the Republic down to the time of the Gracchi, a dictator passed legislation in the centuriate assembly.[49] This procedure perhaps arose out of the emergency conditions under which a dictator was appointed and the military nature of the office.

What does this mean for our understanding of Caesar's legislative activity during his dictatorship? It might help clarify some of the issues, but it does not answer all our questions. We can state that Caesar used both assemblies for his legislation. Our only evidence for his use of the *comitia centuriata* as a legislative body is a passage in Cicero's *First Philippic*, in which Cicero again raises the issue of the validity of Caesar's *acta*, asserting that his actual laws should be considered his genuine *acta*, while his holographs, memoranda, and papers (*chirographa, commentariola, libelli*) should be ignored (Cic. *Phil.* 1.16–19). Based on section 19 of the *First Philippic*, Yavetz (1983, 108) contends that Caesar's *lex de provinciis*, restricting the duration of provincial commands, was passed by the centuriate assembly, although Cicero does not explicitly say as much. This law fits perfectly with Sandberg's contention that the *comitia centuriata* dealt with matters extra pomerial and perhaps is an indication that Caesar, like Sulla, hoped to restore the traditional spheres of influence to each assembly.

Even though we cannot describe in detail how Caesar modified procedure in the popular assemblies, it is clear that he exercised enormous influence. The outcome of the elections as well as the passage of legislation were confirmation that he controlled two traditionally important avenues to power and prestige in the Roman Republic. The success of his candidates at the *comitia*, announced victorious in a perfunctory reading of names, was also a reminder to Roman aristocrats that they had to go through Caesar to achieve the offices that ennobled them and their families. Presiding over these assemblies was another way that Caesar's growing power was enacted.

Caesar's Victory Celebrations

Caesar oversaw several ceremonies that celebrated his victories in Gaul and in the civil war against Pompeius and his supporters. All of these celebrations displayed Caesar's power and munificence and recognized publicly his great accomplishments on the battlefield. These were national dramas that Caesar exploited for his political benefit, using them to communicate to the Roman people important aspects of his public image. After briefly establishing the chronology of his triumphs and their attendant spectacle entertainment, I will organize my discussion around these five principal themes: how Caesar chose to celebrate his victories in civil war; Caesar's rivalry with his predecessors, especially Pompeius; the global reach of his victories and games; his relationship with the urban *plebs*; and his relationship with the nobility.

Caesar celebrated his first four triumphs in September 46 BC over Gaul,

Alexandria, Pontus, and Africa; his fifth triumph, for his victory in Munda (Spain), took place in the fall (perhaps October) 45.[50] In the triumphs of 46, it is probable that Caesar was present to celebrate the *Ludi Romani*, which traditionally ran from 4 to 18 September. After a day's respite, he commenced his triumphs on 20 September, allowing one day for each and (in all probability) one day's respite in between. Hence, there was a triumphal procession on 20, 22, 24, and 26 September.[51] The last triumph coincided with the dedication of the Temple of Venus Genetrix in Caesar's new forum, which was celebrated by a lavish banquet, a portion of which took place in the forum itself.

We only have a few indications in our sources about the reception of these games among the urban populace and soldiers present in the city. Entertainment on this scale and of this variety, marking the end of civil war, attracted a huge number of visitors to Rome. So many, in fact, that tents were set up to house them. Another anecdote demonstrates the depth of ill will that these games could provoke. Caesar reportedly used fine silk to shade the spectators from the sun (Dio 43.24.2), which roused the ire of the soldiers, who resented such expense on the citizens' behalf and not their own. Caesar was forced to deal harshly with the rioters, and reportedly executed one of the ringleaders and ordered the *pontifices* and Priest of Mars to execute two others in the Campus Martius and put their heads on the Regia.[52]

Another anecdote in our tradition provides further evidence for the growing discomfort about Caesar's unrivaled power. On the first day of his triumph, celebrating his victories in Gaul, while Caesar was being conveyed across the Velabrum, the axle of his *quadriga* broke. Caesar, therefore, completed the procession in spectacular fashion, ascending the Capitolium on his knees,[53] abject before the king of the gods. If this story is true, it might also have been a way for Caesar to deflect the criticism that resulted from one of the extraordinary honors decreed by the senate—that of a bronze statue of him standing on a likeness of the world with an inscription declaring him a demigod.[54] Other honors were equally lavish. The senate decreed a *supplicatio* lasting forty days. Further, Caesar was granted the right to have four white horses draw his *quadriga*, perhaps in imitation of Camillus, and to be accompanied by as many lictors as he currently had with him, along with those from his first and second dictatorships.[55] In his triumph, Caesar expressed clearly that, despite all these extraordinary honors, Jupiter was the only king of Rome.

Stories like these persist in our tradition because Caesar's contemporaries scrutinized his ceremonies for clues to Caesar's intentions in order to find reasons for praising or blaming him. The reasons are clear. On one level,

Caesar's victory celebrations were traditional ceremonies that dated back to the earliest period in Roman history and thus had a historical depth, as we discussed in the introduction. At the same time, these same ceremonies could not avoid allusions to the recent past, since they partly commemorated victories in civil war and were meant to demonstrate that Caesar's accomplishments surpassed those of his predecessors, especially Pompeius Magnus. Thus, the civil war remained a subtext of Caesar's victory celebrations. We discussed in the previous chapter some of the challenges facing Sulla when he celebrated his triumph in 81. Some elements of Caesar's (triumphal) displays evoked the sadness rather than the elation of the spectators: for instance, the arms and armor taken from Roman citizens who had fallen in the war in Africa (Dio 43.19.2; cf. App. *BC* 2.101). As if in anticipation of the ill will that might be directed toward him and his triumphs, Caesar was careful not to inscribe the names of any Roman citizens on lists of peoples conquered or to display depictions of the battles of Pharsalus or later in his fifth triumph, Munda.[56] Such displays would have reopened the wounds of civil war, which his famous *clementia* was supposed to heal.[57] His moderation in this regard was not without its limits, however, for he did show the deaths of some prominent Roman citizens such as Q. Scipio and Cato the Younger. The latter's unbending opposition to Caesar's tyranny transformed him into the symbol of republican freedom (cf. App. *BC* 2.101.420). Pompeius himself was noticeably absent (App. *BC* 2.101.419).

Pompeius' memory was present, however, in less direct ways. Caesar's quadruple triumph trumped Pompeius' magnificent triple triumph in 61.[58] Moreover, Caesar's first four triumphs commemorated victories on three continents, as Pompeius' had sixteen years earlier, and adumbrated world conquest. There were two visual symbols that made the comparison even clearer. The first, in the procession of the Gallic triumph, was a depiction in gold of the Rhine, Rhone, and Oceanus, showing visually the territory that he had brought under Roman sway (Flor. *Epit.* 2.13.88), thus challenging Pompeius' status as world conqueror.[59] The second we alluded to briefly in the introduction. On display at his Pontic triumph was a placard with the slogan *veni, vidi, vici* (Suet. *Jul.* 37.2; cf. Plut. *Caes.* 50.3), an alliterative expression of how quickly Caesar had prosecuted the war against Pharnaces, the aspiring monarch of Pontus, as an example of the swiftness for which Caesar had become famous and, at the same time, contrasting his speedy victory with Pompeius' years of struggle against the great Mithridates, father of Pharnaces.[60] As Suetonius tells it, within five days of arriving on the scene and within four hours of sighting the enemy, Caesar routed him in a single pitched battle, at Zela on 2 August 47 BC.[61] Caesar then made a statement to the effect that Pompeius' reputation for success in military campaigns (*felicitas*) had been manufactured from victories over such feeble enemies as Pharnaces (*inbelle genus hostium*). It is not known when Caesar belittled Pompeius' accomplishments in this way, but his words provide a gloss on the otherwise laconic slogan that appeared in this triumph. Thus, Caesar used this triumph to situate himself and his accomplishments within the larger history of Rome's military campaigns against the kingdom of Pontus.[62]

Such allusions to Pompeius and Caesar's other enemies in the civil wars must have been unpleasant reminders to many of the spectators at Caesar's triumphs. In order to deflect the spectators' attention from the harsh reality of the civil wars, Caesar created and displayed battles involving only foreign enemies. In an area of the city known as the Codeta,[63] probably located across the Tiber near Caesar's *horti*,[64] an artificial lake was excavated for a mock naval battle (*naumachia*) between "Tyrian" and "Egyptian" ships of all sizes (biremes, triremes, and quadriremes). This form of entertainment, in which condemned prisoners were made to reenact a famous naval battle from history, became common in the imperial period. There is no attested instance of a naval battle between Egyptians and Tyrians. Perhaps Caesar was creating historical fiction rather than history, but this mock battle nonetheless showed his ability to produce a spectacle on a large scale and in so doing recreate the past.[65] Caesar also produced a mock infantry battle in the Circus Maximus (see fig. 1), each consisting of five hundred infantry, thirty cavalry, and twenty elephants. We do not know if this was a reenactment of a historical battle, since the opposing forces are not named. In any event, these mock battles reminded those present that wars could be waged that did not involve Roman fighting Roman.

If the creation of mock battles was intended to deflect attention from the harsh reality of the civil wars, it did so by directing the spectators' gaze to distant lands and a more remote past. Caesar similarly directed attention to the remote past when he attempted to distinguish from those of his predecessors the games that marked the dedication of the Temple of Venus Genetrix, which commenced on the last day of his triumphs (26 September). He did so by establishing a *collegium* responsible for the cult of Venus Genetrix, whose responsibilities presumably included preparing and producing these games;[66] he thereby refused to follow Sulla's precedent of having a magistrate preside over his games.[67] We can understand Caesar's reasons for doing so if we remember that two of the most ancient Roman festivals, the *Consualia* and the *Equirria*—both of which were traditionally dated to the reign of Romulus—were managed by priestly colleges.[68] Thus Caesar could make his games appear more ancient and perhaps even connect them to the founding of

Rome. In this scenario, he might have wanted his own *Ludi Veneris Genetricis* to celebrate a second founding of the city.[69]

A more direct reference to the founding of Rome can be found in Caesar's revival of the *Lusus Troiae*. This ceremony, last witnessed during the dictatorship of Sulla (Plut. *Cat. Mi.* 3.1) but, according to legend, contemporary with the city's founders, spoke to both the remote and recent past. It consisted of an equestrian exercise involving young men of noble rank who performed complicated maneuvers on horseback and was thought to have been brought to Italy by Aeneas and revived by his son Iulus when the latter was king of Alba Longa.[70] It thus had a history that evoked the role of the Trojans in the founding of Rome. Early in his career, as we discussed (see chap. 1), Caesar publicly laid claim to his family's descent from the goddess Venus as well as the legendary kings of Rome. The construction of the Temple of Venus Genetrix, the centerpiece of his new forum that these games were celebrating, was only the most grandiose demonstration of this royal and divine genealogy that remained a part of Caesar's public image. Caesar's revival of the *Troia* must be seen as part of this process of interweaving his own family's legends into the fabric of Roman mythology.[71] This form of entertainment, moreover, with its connection to the distant past and founding of Rome, has all the signs of being an invented tradition—invented perhaps by Sulla who "revived" it in order to advertise his special devotion ultimately to Venus. In a similar way, Caesar may have been reclaiming the *lusus Troiae*, recently taken over by Sulla, for the Julian *gens*. From this point forward, the *lusus Troiae* became a regular feature of games and other celebrations under the direction of Augustus.

Caesar's power that was on display at these ceremonies emerged in part from the way in which he situated himself and his accomplishments in the larger sphere of Roman history through his connection with the remote past and the mock battles that demonstrated his ability to recreate the past. His power was also worldwide, stretching from one end of the empire to the other. We have already seen how his triumphs celebrated victories on three continents and that representations of the Rhine and Oceanus were on display. This "global" reach appeared in his entertainment as well. Wild beast hunts customarily showed the sponsor's ability to procure rare and exotic animals. At Caesar's games, the hunts went on for five days, at which a giraffe was put on display for the first time (Dio 43.23.1–2). He also sponsored Greek athletic contests, which took place in a temporary stadium in the Campus Martius. If these were like Sulla's games in 80 BC (see chap. 1), Caesar would have recruited athletes from all over the Mediterranean world. Even some of the dramatic festivals performed in the city underscored the breadth of the empire of which Caesar was now taking control. In different areas of the city (*regionatim*) and in all languages (Suet. *Jul.* 39.1) plays were performed, to illustrate the cosmopolitan character of the city at the center of a worldwide empire. Caesar was not just first man in Rome; he was first man of the world.[72]

All public entertainment was a display of munificence on the part of the sponsor. Caesar's large-scale mock battles as well as the procurement of animals for the hunts or athletes for Greek-style contests all demonstrated his great power and wealth, which he was willing to share with the Roman people. Games associated with victory and conquest offered the celebrant the additional opportunity of distributing the spoils of war. It was customary, dating back at least to the middle Republic, for Roman *triumphatores* to reward their soldiers with cash payments, their share of the spoils of victory, often offered in conjunction with the triumph itself.[73] Caesar's cash payment to his soldiers after his triumph thus adhered to tradition (App. *BC* 2.102.422), but his distribution of grain and olive oil to the people that exceeded the usual dole, as well as a cash award, was unprecedented,[74] but it reflected a relationship with the *plebs* that had a long evolution. It developed out of the political ideology and rhetoric of the late Republic that Ti. and C. Gracchus had initiated, for they declared that the Roman people should share in the spoils of empire.[75] Caesar made this rhetoric a reality through his generous donatives. He further established a precedent that Roman emperors were compelled to follow in their dealings with the urban *plebs*.

Caesar's relationship with the *plebs* was reified in a lavish public banquet. Such banquets were a customary conclusion to funerals and games, and occasionally triumphs, but this banquet celebrated in particular the dedication of Caesar's new forum and temple. If Ulrich's interpretation of the function of this space is correct—that Caesar intended to use it as the space for *contiones*—then this banquet, in which the Roman people played such an important role, functioned as a kind of rite of inauguration, introducing the people to a space that would in a sense be their own. Caesar sponsored feasting on this occasion that was unprecedented on two levels (Suet. *Jul.* 26.2): first, the scope and scale went beyond anything that had been done before; second, and more importantly, Caesar changed the principle of the usual aristocratic wooing of popular support by creating a more personal relationship with the Roman *plebs* through these banquets. This is shown most clearly in his ceremonial entrance following the dinner itself. He entered his forum wearing slippers and garlanded with flowers, appearing as the host of a private dinner party with the Roman *plebs* as his invited guests. He then processed home, presumably across the Forum Romanum to the Domus Publica, accompanied by a large crowd and a retinue of elephants carrying torches. A longer and more lavish procession would have taken him to his estate and *horti* across the Tiber, where the entertainment could have continued.[76] Plutarch tells us that Caesar feasted the people (with a banquet and distribution of meat) while they reclined on twenty-two thousand *triclinia* (Plut. *Caes.* 55.4). Each *triclinium* (three *klinai*) seated nine persons, meaning that Caesar on this occasion entertained and fed 198,000 people—a number that tests the bounds of our credulity. The logistics of entertaining such a large crowd are mind-boggling; it is likely that Caesar established a new magistracy devoted primarily to the production of banquets on this scale (Plin. *Nat.* 14.66). Where such a banquet could have been held is also unclear. Other banquets are known to have taken place in the Forum Romanum (Liv. 39.46.2–3). At least part of the banquet took place in Caesar's recently dedicated Forum Julium (Dio 43.22.1), but since it could not have accommodated all of the participants in a feast of such magnitude—in fact, there was no single venue in the city that could have—it is probable that Caesar followed the procedure he used for his theatrical performances and entertained the people throughout all the regions of the city (i.e., *regionatim*) (Suet. *Jul.* 39.1).

One unusual aspect of Caesar's games was the frequent participation of members of upper orders of Roman society. Among the many dramatic productions, for instance, was a play written and performed by Decimus Laberius, a knight who was lavishly rewarded for his efforts and then allowed in striking fashion to make his way from the stage to the fourteen rows reserved for members of his order. Thus, in one symbolic gesture he was transformed from a déclassé stage performer to a member of the equestrian order. At a gladiatorial combat (*munus*) in the Forum, a man from a praetorian family was pitted against a former senator.[77] Such combats between members of the nobility were rare and usually frowned upon, but they occurred with greater frequency in the imperial period.[78]

Caesar's final triumph occurred in the fall of 45, after he had returned from Spain, having completed the final phase of the civil war in his campaign against the elder son of Pompeius. This his fifth and final triumph was the only one that overtly and unapologetically (it seems) extolled a victory over Roman citizens.[79] As a result, the tribune Pontius Aquila refused to stand as Caesar entered the city in his *quadriga*, some evidence for the growing animosity toward him (Suet. *Jul.* 78.2). Caesar's use of an ancient festival, the *Parilia*, was perhaps an attempt to forestall any animosity over his victory celebration. The *Parilia*, in origin a shepherd's festival, fell on 21 April, the anniversary of Rome's foundation,[80] but, after news of Caesar's victory at the battle of Munda arrived (or was made to arrive) on the eve of this festival in 45, it was expanded to include chariot racing (*ludi circenses*).[81] Since the *Parilia* marked the foundation of the city, it was also associated with, among other things, Romulus' murder of Remus[82]—the fratricide that Romans believed prefigured the civil wars of the late Republic.[83] Therefore, the civil war between Pompeius and Caesar, which ended with the battle of Munda, was only part of a larger cycle of internecine strife among Romans. By arranging for the news of Munda to reach Rome on the eve of the *Parilia*, Caesar demonstrated that he had brought this cycle to a close on the anniversary of the very day it had begun. A new age had dawned.[84] Caesar could advertise himself as a second founder of Rome, replete with all the imagery of birth and rebirth, and use yet another existing ceremony to celebrate his victory.[85]

Caesar's return to Rome from Spain was planned well in advance, as Cicero's letters of August 45 attest. I argued in the previous chapter that returns of this type were ceremonial and high national drama. L. Aelius Lamia (*aed. pleb.* 45)[86] visited Cicero at his estate in Tusculum, bringing a letter from Caesar that stated clearly that he planned to be in Rome before the *Ludi Romani* (4–18 September) and urged Lamia to put every effort into the preparations for these games so that he would not have to hurry himself for nothing.[87] Cicero considered meeting Caesar in Alsium (along the Via Aurelia) before he reached Rome (Cic. *Att.* 13.50.4) but apparently changed his mind. As Caesar's entourage moved closer to Rome, a throng of senators came out to greet him. The city would have been especially crowded, as Caesar no doubt had hoped, in anticipation not only of his arrival but also of the games that were imminent. In his entourage, Caesar gave privileged positions to three men who would appear prominently in different versions of his will: M. Antonius, D. Brutus Albinus the conspirator, and C. Octavius the future Augustus.[88] Antonius rode with Caesar himself while the two younger men came immediately behind. It perhaps would be taking this evidence too far to say that Caesar intended to indicate possible successors in this public display,[89] but it is striking that Augustus used his court ceremonies for precisely this purpose, to present his heirs to the public and perhaps even rank them in order of succession (see chap. 9).

It is likely that Caesar's triumph itself occurred in close conjunction with the second celebration of the *Ludi Veneris Genetricis*, but the precise date is unknown.[90] We do know that one of Caesar's lieutenants was allowed to celebrate his own triumph on 13 October and that this triumph came after Caesar's by a few days (Quint. *Inst.* 6.3.61). If the games in honor of Venus were on the same days in 45 as they had been in 46, they would have commenced on 27 September and run into early October. Therefore, Caesar's triumph would have occurred during or immediately after the games. There is some evidence for preparations for games in the summer of 45,[91] but we hear nothing about the games themselves. It is likely that Suetonius' account of spectacle entertainment associated with Caesar's triumphs (described earlier in this chapter) includes the kind of entertainment at the games in 45 as well.

As we turn to the year 44, when Caesar's victory was complete and his power largely unchallenged, his predominance in public ceremonies only increased. In January of this year, two months before his assassination, Caesar celebrated the *Feriae Latinae*, a festival consisting of a procession to the Alban Mount followed by a sacrifice and banquet at the Temple of Jupiter Latiaris. Based on what we know about this festival, Caesar, as consul, was acting perfectly in accord with tradition in celebrating it on this occasion. The celebration of the *Feriae Latinae* further linked Caesar to the early kings of Latium—a connection he advertised by wearing the red boots of the Alban kings on this occasion (Dio 43.43.2). The senate granted Caesar the unprecedented honor of entering the city on horseback following this festival, which is recorded as an *ovatio* in the *Fasti*,[92] the victory celebration known as the "lesser triumph." It is curious that Caesar would have wanted to celebrate an *ovatio*, a comparatively minor ceremony according to tradition, especially in view of his celebration of four triumphs in 46, complete with a banquet and games in honor of Venus, and a fifth triumph a few months before this *ovatio*. The *ovatio* at first glance hardly seems a necessary addition to Caesar's long list of extraordinary achievements and many unprecedented honors. Moreover, since he had celebrated all his previous victories with the triumphs cited, there was no obvious victory for this *ovatio* to celebrate.[93] Finally, it is also curious that he chose to join his *ovatio* with a celebration of the *Feriae Latinae*. The key to understanding the significance of this victory celebration lies in the combination of the two ceremonies. The *ovatio*, as a kind of triumphal celebration, was associated with military victory, but a military victory of a certain type—one that came quickly and without bloodshed (Gel. 5.6.20; Plut. *Marc.* 22.5). Along these same lines, the *Feriae Latinae* was a festival celebrating peace and concord.[94] These ideals were of direct significance to Caesar at this time, since he had recently endured some criticism for his triumph for Munda, a victory in a civil conflict. His performance of these two ancient ceremonies, I will argue, allowed him to reassess the victory and underscore the concord and peace that he hoped his new regime would bring. Thus, it was crucial to his public image at this time and therefore merits a detailed discussion.

It is characteristic of the history of the Republic that we tend to know more, or at least are told more, about the origins of an ancient festival (such as the *Feriae Latinae*) than about what meaning such a festival might have had for those witnessing it at the end of the Republic. The *Feriae Latinae* was one of the *conceptivae*, meaning that it occurred annually but had no fixed date on the civic calendar. The consuls were the presiding officials of this festival, or in their absence a dictator could be named; when the consuls entered office in January, they set a date for its observance—usually the end of April. The consuls were required to conduct this festival before they set out on military campaign, and it became a part of the consuls' routine to set the date of the *Feriae Latinae* and request a decree from the senate to confirm it.[95] This festival was clearly one of great antiquity, which is presumably why Romans took such pains to preserve it. By tradition all members of the "Latin League," the loose organization of city-states located in Latium, observed this festival,[96] which symbolized peace, community, as well as the shared culture and religion of the Latin peoples. This festival could serve as the basis for Caesar's reassessment of his victory.

One of the important questions about this festival for our purposes is who the Latin representatives were and how they were selected. Livy, in describing the celebration of the *Feriae Latinae* in 176 BC, calls the representative from Lanuvium a *magistratus*.[97] Otherwise, these representatives are unnamed in our sources. Since, in the case of Rome, the consuls and other magistrates participated in this festival, it is reasonable to assume that the other towns sent their elected magistrates as well who were members of prominent local families. There are indications that, as Roman power expanded through the middle and late Republic, the number of towns participating in this festival decreased. In a famous passage, Pliny mentions the original 30 *populi Albenses* that participated in this festival (Plin. *Nat.* 3.69). Scholars have pointed out that this list reflects a pre-urban Latium and probably are names of clans (*gentes*) who were the original participants in this festival before the advent of the city-states.[98] Members of these clans must have continued to serve as representatives as long as their clans survived. One of Pliny's purposes, however, was to demonstrate how many of these communities had died out by his day. Cicero also informs us that some of these communities—he mentions in particular Gabii, Bovillae, and Labici—found it impossible to select delegates for this festival (Cic. *Planc.* 23). It is not clear why this was so; perhaps it was due to a general depopulation, or perhaps the families whose members traditionally had served this function had begun to die out. In any case, it seems that there was a shortage of eligible representatives to assist the Roman magistrates in performing the sacrifice on the Alban Mount that could have imperiled the continued performance of this sacred rite.

It should also be noted, in a similar vein, that Latin cities were home to some of the most prominent aristocratic families in Rome. In fact, many patrician families originated in these cities and made their way to Rome (the Julii and Servilii from Alba Longa[99] can serve as two notable examples). It is probable, then, that many of the representatives present at the festival were members of prominent Roman aristocratic families who maintained some ties to their hometowns. T. Annius Milo (*pr.* 57) (although a plebeian) was from the town of Lanuvium and was journeying there to nominate a *flamen* for Juno Sospes (*ad flaminem prodendum*) in his capacity as dictator when he had his infelicitous encounter with P. Clodius on the Appian Way (January 52) (Cic. *Mil.* 27; Asc. 31C). If Milo served in this capacity, then other aristocrats presumably could have served as representatives of their hometowns at the celebration of the *Feriae Latinae*.

The purpose of this rather long, and at times circuitous, line of reasoning is to demonstrate that the *Feriae Latinae* was likely a festival that involved above all members of the Roman aristocracy, and perhaps especially members of old patrician families. This festival then was an opportunity for Caesar to demonstrate *concordia* and harmony among the aristocracy, a *concordia* created and fostered by himself as a result of his victory.[100] This was desirable since his victory had come in part as a result of his reliance on Italian elements against Rome.[101] The *Feriae Latinae*, with its emphasis on Latin unity, was perhaps a demonstration of Caesar's commitment to the old patrician families over some of the newcomers on the scene. It should also be noted in this context that the consuls under Caesar's dictatorship from 48–44 BC exhibit a favoritism toward patricians.[102] I have also shown, however, that there may have been a shortage of representatives for the *Feriae Latinae* in the late Republic. If this was the case, it is further likely that this festival could not have remained unaffected by one of the privileges granted to Caesar during his dictatorship, namely promoting families to patrician status,[103] some of whom could have sent representatives to participate in this festival. In this case, the *Feriae Latinae* in this year could have celebrated Caesar's new aristocracy, including provincials whom he had rewarded with senatorial rank and even one with the consulship, the Spaniard Cornelius Balbus.

The second element in Caesar's celebration in January 44 was his return to the city on horseback in an *ovatio*, dressed in triumphal garb. The date of this event, 26 January, was duly recorded in the *Fasti*.[104] The *ovatio*, like the triumph, was associated with military victory and dated back to the very beginnings of the Republic, but its occurrence, as I indicated in chapter 1, was comparatively rare. In the late Republic, again, as I argued in chapter 1, the *ovatio* underwent a transformation and became associated in particular with slave wars, which means that for Caesar's audience in January 44 the *ovatio* was a ceremony that many had never witnessed in their lifetimes and those who had seen it would have had as a point of comparison only the *ovatio* of M. Licinius Crassus in 71 for his victory over the slave army of Spartacus. Caesar's *ovatio* was unusual, as I stated earlier, because there was no obvious victory to celebrate. What also set Caesar's *ovatio* apart was the entry in the *Fasti*, which contains no mention of an enemy, stating merely Caesar's name, title, the date, and *ovans ex monte Albano*. By not naming an enemy Caesar removed his victory from a specific historical context: he was not celebrating a particular victory, I believe, but rather the concept or even ideal of victory. Victory over a foreign enemy had always benefited Roman society, bringing a cessation of hostilities, wealth, prosperity, and peace. Victory in civil war was another matter. Sulla's victory, for instance, brought wealth and prosperity for some but only suffering for others. Caesar had no desire to reawaken the animosity that arose following his celebration of his victory in Spain, but he did want to acknowledge the potential benefits of all his victories—the most important of which was a long-awaited peace. It is worth noting that in the fall of 40 BC Antonius and Octavian used the *ovatio* for precisely this purpose: each was decreed an *ovatio*, even though there was no war and no victory to celebrate; rather it ceremonially confirmed their recently concluded peace agreement, known as the Pact of Brundisium.[105]

The tradition that the *ovatio* was associated with victory in a slave war seems to have been a development of the late Republic. A second and perhaps older tradition, which might have been what Caesar had in mind, suggests that the *ovatio* celebrated a military victory of a certain kind, namely one that came quickly, without dust (*inpulverea*) and without bloodshed (*incruenta*).[106] The swiftness of his Pontic victory Caesar had already advertised in an earlier triumph, and this swiftness, as I noted earlier, became characteristic of Caesar's actions. The tradition that the *ovatio* celebrated a "dustless" or "bloodless" victory is further elaborated upon by Plutarch, who tells us that the celebrant processed on foot wearing shoes, not by chariot, accompanied by flute music, so as to appear "unwarlike" (ἀπόλεμος) and "friendly" (ἡδύς). Plutarch expresses his conviction that it was the manner in which a general won a victory that determined whether he was awarded a triumph or an *ovatio*. One who resorted to armed conflict was awarded the more fearsome triumph. By contrast, one who employed diplomacy, persuasion, and negotiation celebrated the peaceable *ovatio*. Plutarch bases this on the different crowns worn by the celebrants. A *triumphator* and his soldiers wore the laurel crown associated with Mars, but in an *ovatio* the celebrant wore the myrtle crown of Venus, the matriarch of the Julian *gens*. Further, the accompanying flute music was also symbolic of peace (*Marc.* 22; cf. Gel. 5.6.22).

Whether Caesar had all this in mind when he chose to celebrate an *ovatio* on this occasion we cannot determine with certainty. However, the *ovatio* and the *Feriae Latinae* did share certain themes in our tradition, most notably an association with peace. For Caesar himself the two ceremonies also allowed him to advertise again his family heritage, which he first articulated in his funeral oration for his aunt (see chap. 1), namely his descent from the Latin kings on his maternal side and ultimately from Venus on his paternal side. If Plutarch is correct that the general in an *ovatio* entered the city on foot wearing shoes or slippers (βλαῦται [Marc. 22.2]), then Caesar's entrance on horseback wearing the red boots of the Alban kings would have been a marked departure from tradition, drawing closer attention to his royal lineage.

There was an antiquarianism associated with the *ovatio* and the *Feriae Latinae*, which takes on the appearance of fossilized remnants of the early Republic; yet we should not think of festivals of this kind as simply antiquarian indulgences with little relevance to the Rome of Caesar's day, since Romans so often used the remote past to frame current political debates, as Caesar was doing here. The *Feriae Latinae* certainly hearkened back to the distant past, but it also had undergone a transformation since its inception, for it is likely that many of the representatives of the Latin city-states were now members of the Roman nobility. Caesar was using this festival, associated with peace and concord, with truces and cessation of hostilities, as a way of celebrating reconciliation and reunification, not of the old Latin city-states but of the Roman aristocracy and hence of the Roman world itself. The addition of the *ovatio* underscored this theme of reconciliation.

The postscript to Caesar's reassessment of his victory had potentially damaging consequences for his renewal and advertisement of *concordia*, for the people who greeted Caesar upon his return from the Alban Mount hailed him king, to which he gave his famous reply that he was Caesar and not a king.[107] This public denial of kingship had little effect. When a diadem later appeared on one of his statues, two tribunes, Caesetius and Marullus, removed it, presuming that Caesar would want it so. Caesar responded by convening the senate in the Temple of Concordia and procuring a decree that deposed the tribunes from office and sent them into exile (Suet. *Jul.* 79.1; App. *BC* 2.108.149). The location of this senate meeting, however, was perhaps to demonstrate that, despite the pleas of the people for Caesar to take the title of king, Caesar was committed to the ideal of *concordia* recently expressed by his participation in the *Feriae Latinae* and subsequent *ovatio*. Perhaps Caesar objected because the people had made the offer of kingship to Caesar, and therefore only Caesar could refuse it. Caesar also desired his refusal to be unequivocal, and this could be accomplished only if he did so himself.

Caesar at the *Lupercalia*

As we turn to Caesar's second public denial of kingship, we must bear in mind not only the changes in the topography of the Forum Romanum but also Caesar's purpose behind these changes and, finally, their effect on political life, especially as the setting for public ceremonial. Caesar's second denial of kingship occurred at the festival of the *Lupercalia,* which fell on 15 February.[108] This followed closely the *Feriae Latinae* and *ovatio,* but it was all the more necessary after Caesar was named dictator for life earlier in February. Caesar desired to distinguish his new magistracy from a more traditional monarchy. Caesar's use of this festival as a stage for clearly communicating to the Roman people his own views on his power demonstrates again how important such events could be even for someone in his position. Caesar sat atop the Rostra on a golden chair, dressed in a *toga purpurea,* the dress of the Roman kings, with a garland on his head (*coronatus*).[109] In Cicero's account, M. Antonius is held up for especial blame. Antonius approached, suitably attired for the occasion, and offered Caesar the diadem. M. Aemilius Lepidus, who had just been named Caesar's master of horse, turned away when Antonius offered Caesar the diadem and made his feelings known with a groan (*gemitus*) and gloomy look (*maestitia*).[110] The crowd also groaned. Caesar brushed the diadem away and the crowd cheered. The imperfect verbs in this passage indicate several repeated attempts on the part of Antonius to crown Caesar, as our later sources make more explicit. Antonius then knelt down to make one final offer, which Caesar also declined. The respective roles of Antonius and Lepidus in Cicero's version of the *Lupercalia* can be attributed in part to their place in the politics of late 44 and early 43 BC, when the *Second Philippic* was published and the *Fifth Philippic* delivered. Cicero used their performances on 15 February—or rather his interpretation of their performances—in order to make his political case first for the perils of Antonius' supremacy and later for the possibility of Lepidus' acting as an agent for peace.

It is highly unlikely that Antonius was so bold as to act on his own initiative when he offered Caesar a diadem. Likewise, as modern scholars now generally agree, it is just as unlikely that Lepidus would have made such a public declaration of his feelings in full view of the Roman people unless Caesar knew that he would do so. The whole ceremony, involving the dictator, his colleague in the consulship, and his master of horse, was carefully prearranged, I believe. Caesar's purpose was to refuse publicly the kingship that the people had offered.

Nicolaus' account differs from Cicero's on a few points of detail and adds to the cast of characters involved in the ceremony. A certain Licinius, perhaps one of the *Luperci*,[111] was the first to offer Caesar a diadem, placing it at his feet. The crowd shouted for M. Lepidus to place the diadem on Caesar's head, but Lepidus refused. Lepidus' behavior is a striking point of comparison between the two accounts. In Nicolaus' version, Lepidus is depicted as simply refusing to intercede in Caesar's coronation, despite the pleas of the crowd, which turned to him in his capacity as Caesar's *magister equitum*. In Cicero's account, a much more dramatic rendering of the episode, Lepidus' refusal is punctuated by a gesture (turning away) and a facial expression that clearly signaled his disapproval of the action taking place on the Rostra. Nicolaus goes on: C. Cassius, one of the conspirators, feigning complicity in this whole endeavor as a way of diverting suspicion away from the conspiracy, picked up the diadem and placed it on Caesar's knees; P. Casca, another conspirator, was also present and had a hand in this (or so Nicolaus' account implies). It is not surprising that mention of the two conspirators, whatever their motivation might have been to be present at, and possibly participate in, Caesar's coronation, dropped out of Cicero's version of this event, for their presence would have served only to embarrass the conspirators. It is not clear why they were present on the Rostra for the performance of this ceremony in the first place. Neither man was a *Lupercus*, as far as we know; Cassius did hold a magistracy in this year—*praetor peregrinus*—but that office has no obvious relevance to the festival at hand. P. Casca was not a magistrate in this year, holding the tribunate only in 43. It is possible that Caesar included them in this ceremony to bear witness to his grand refusal of kingship and as evidence of his *concordia*.

Amid the noise of the crowd, which kept shouting for Caesar to accept the diadem, and Caesar's persistent refusal, Antonius rushed up and placed the diadem on Caesar's head; Caesar removed it and cast it into the crowd. Antonius apparently retrieved it and offered it a second time, while the crowd shouted, "Hail, King!" Caesar again refused and had the diadem delivered to the Capitolium to be placed in the Temple of Jupiter Optimus Maximus, the true king of Rome, which action he duly recorded in the *Fasti*. According to Plutarch, Caesar also knelt down, as a final gesture of vulnerability, pulled back his toga, thus exposing his neck, and invited anyone to cut his throat.[112] Since Romans had no ritual that existed for the sole purpose of denying kingly power, Caesar had to modify an established one. As we shall see in a later chapter, this is a procedure that Augustus wholeheartedly adopted.

Nicolaus also describes the audience on this occasion as divided in its sympathies toward the performance and the performers. Those in the back of the crowd applauded when Caesar refused the diadem, while those near the Rostra shouted for him to accept it and not reject the will of the people. Nicolaus' description of a crowd divided in its sympathies might very well reflect the reality of the situation. Caesar was a controversial figure, and it is unlikely that all in Rome would have approved of his position. Moreover, if this whole performance was carefully planned in advance in order to provide Caesar with the opportunity to refuse the kingship publicly, as I believe it was, it is possible that the Caesarians planted in the audience a group near the Rostra who were instructed to cheer the presentation of the diadem, since the other participants in the drama, most notably Antonius, still had political careers to think of, and they ran the risk of incurring the wrath of the crowd if the crowd believed that they were acting on their own and not at the behest of the people. The whole performance was politically risky, but Caesar must have thought it necessary in order to lay to rest the notion that he coveted kingship.

According to Nicolaus, this ceremony had a stirring effect on the conspirators, providing clear evidence of what they previously had only suspected.[113] What Nicolaus means by this is open to interpretation. He implies that, after the performance of the *Lupercalia,* the conspirators believed even more deeply that Caesar had to die. If he is correct, then Caesar's grand refusal of kingship failed to hit its mark. What went wrong? One possibility is that the location of the ceremony and the surrounding topography only undermined the message that Caesar was trying to communicate. I suggested earlier that Caesar, by moving the Rostra to the center of the Forum and taking it out from under the watchful gaze of the senate, topographically dismantled an important Republican ideal. When Caesar renounced the kingship from this new Rostra during the *Lupercalia,* the topography served to undermine the solemn and symbolic performance of his rejection of the diadem offered by Antonius. Caesar brushed the diadem aside, but to his left were only the remains of the Comitium and the old Rostra, evocative symbols of the Republic that had to be dismantled to make room for the new Curia. He claimed that he was no king, but the new Rostra on which he sat and the new Curia rising to his left declared otherwise. One month later Caesar lay murdered at the foot of the statue of Pompeius Magnus, and the conspirators cried out that a tyrant had been justly slain.

Conclusion

One of Caesar's most formidable challenges was to describe to the Roman people the nature of his power and to characterize his victory, one that was won at the expense of many Roman citizens and ultimately of the Republic itself. Caesar never adequately reconciled his defeat of Roman citizens on the one hand with his *clementia* on the other, although he did attempt, I believe, through the *Feriae Latinae* and *ovatio* in January 44 to deflect some of the criticism leveled at him by reassessing his victory on that occasion and then later by publicly refusing the kingship at the *Lupercalia*. Caesar further tested the bounds of the traditional ceremonies of the Roman Republic by becoming the principal performer at a variety of public events. These ceremonies enabled him to remain at the very center of Roman politics. But what distinguished him from his predecessors was the way that he exploited public festivals (*Parilia, Feriae Latinae, Lupercalia*) in addition to the assemblies, triumphs, *ludi*, and so on. For Caesar the attraction of these festivals was that they were a recurrent feature of Roman public life, celebrated in annual rhythm as part of the calendar of festivals. The memory of some of his achievements, most notably his victory at Munda announced at the *Parilia*, was made more permanent through its connection to an existing festival. Thus, Caesar's memory pervaded the Roman calendar of festivals, later beguiling the conspirators' attempts to proclaim him a tyrant as his memory became the focal point of the political struggles following his assassination.

3

Standing in Caesar's Shadow

The Ides of March and the Performance of Public Oratory

As Caesar lay dead in the theater of his former son-in-law and rival, his imprint was everywhere visible not only on the events of the time but also on the calendar of festivals and the physical landscape of the city of Rome itself. Virtually every festival, triumph, law, or speech contained an overt or oblique reference to Caesar's memory. The next five chapters of this study discuss and analyze the public ceremonies following Caesar's assassination. The typology of Republican ceremonial, as outlined in the first chapter, will still determine the kinds of events we discuss, but it will be necessary now to do so within a chronological framework in order to understand how such ceremonies informed and were informed by the events of this period. The themes of consensus and conflict will still dominate our discussion, but invariably efforts at building consensus, and the inevitable conflict that arose when these efforts failed, played out across the great divide that separated those endeavoring to preserve Caesar's memory from those intent on restoring his assassins.

To his contemporaries Julius Caesar was a controversial figure. Following his assassination the controversy only deepened. If we glance ahead a bit, to January 42, we find the members of the Second Triumvirate granting Caesar a series of posthumous honors, overtly declaring him divine. This elevation of Caesar to the ranks of the gods set in motion the final confrontation between his supporters and the conspirators that culminated in the battle of Philippi

(Dio 47.18–19.3). M. Brutus, a few months later, minted a coin that celebrated the assassination of the tyrant, depicting a freedman's cap (*pilleus*) between two downward pointing daggers, with the subscript referring to the Ides of March ("EID[ibus] MART[is]").[1] These two radically different treatments of the late dictator demonstrate in stark terms the vast chasm that separated the triumvirs and conspirators. Each side, in an effort to win over popular opinion, presented their mutually incompatible assessments of Caesar and his dictatorship that came to be a component of the public ceremonies occurring in the months following his assassination.

The expression of these assessments of Caesar and his dictatorship was part of the discourse of political power in this period, a discourse that began formally on the day that Caesar was murdered and continued in the months following, usually at ceremonies before the people. A great deal of this chapter will be devoted to the *contiones* (public meetings) of the conspirators on one side and Antonius and his supporters on the other, as they wrestled over control of the urban *plebs* and Caesar's veterans. Both sides realized that the Roman people and the soldiers provided access to power. We shall see that Brutus and Cassius claimed to have murdered a tyrant while surrounded on all sides by the visible reminders of the "tyrant's" extraordinary honors and benefactions, including the new topography of the Forum and the reconstruction of the Curia. Antonius, on the other hand, began to use the memory of Caesar and the consequent popular unrest to his political advantage, as he allowed the people to exert pressure on the senate to uphold Caesar's *acta* even as they decreed an amnesty for his murderers.

First let us look at a brief outline of the historical context.[2] Immediately after Caesar's murder, Brutus had hoped to address the senate gathered in the *curia* of Pompeius' theater (see fig. 1), explain his actions, and declare the Republic restored; instead he was left standing in an empty hall after the senators not directly involved in the conspiracy fled the senate house. Panic and terror devolved into chaos and confusion. The panic spread to the theater proper, where a gladiatorial *munus* was being held. It quickly emptied. There was looting in the marketplaces.

The conspirators rushed out of the *curia* of Pompeius and sought refuge on the Capitolium (see fig. 1). In some accounts, they were accompanied by gladiators who had been hired by D. Brutus to act as an armed guard. It is possible, however, that gladiators rushed from the theater to the senate house, and their fortuitous presence caused greater panic for Caesar's supporters in the senate who thought that they were there to spill more blood. Once on the Capitolium, the conspirators were joined by senators, many of whom had had no hand in the assassination but wanted to demonstrate their support after the fact in an attempt to bask in some reflected glory.[3] The conspirators fled the senate house following Caesar's assassination, one of them carrying a freedman's cap (*pilleus*) symbolizing the freedom that they hoped would result from their actions. When they reached the Capitolium, they raised their daggers and waved them at the crowd, shouting that they had slain a tyrant and restored liberty. Thus, *pilleus* and daggers, the two symbols that appeared prominently on coins minted in 42 BC (see n. 1), featured in the later historical tradition of Caesar's assassination and its aftermath. The conspirators, chief among them M. Brutus, presumably believed that the removal of the tyrant would lead to the immediate restoration of the Republic, although it is unclear what form they expected this to take.[4] The senate's failure to give immediate sanction to the conspirators' actions forced Brutus and his allies to turn to the people, but they never did so with complete aplomb. Perhaps they did not wish to appear too reliant on popular politics and hoped instead that the senate would initiate all political activity. The evidence suggests that they wanted the support of the people but were never able to obtain a fair hearing. Within several hours of the assassination, it appears that the streets were no longer safe for the conspirators, and this clearly hampered their ability to win over the will of the people. Once a measure of calm prevailed, the conspirators emerged from the Temple of Jupiter and descended into the Forum to deliver a speech from the Rostra before a crowd of the urban *plebs*. Two days later, outside the Temple of Tellus where the senate was meeting to debate whether to punish the conspirators or invalidate Caesar's dictatorship, M. Antonius (*cos*. 44) addressed an assembly of citizens who had gathered there. Probably on the same afternoon (that is, on the afternoon of 17 March), Brutus again addressed the Roman people, this time on the Capitolium, with the intention of responding in part to Antonius' speech. Around this time, Antonius and Lepidus sent their sons to the Capitolium as hostages, while Brutus and Cassius came down to dine with them. This act of private hospitality was the first evidence that an amnesty had taken hold. Then finally the consuls for the year, M. Antonius and P. Dolabella, who had taken the place of the dictator Caesar, appeared at a *contio* to praise the amnesty that had been agreed upon at the senate meeting at the Temple of Tellus and celebrate the cessation of hostilities and the renewal of *concordia*.

The *Contiones* of the Conspirators (15 March)

It is not always easy to disentangle the events immediately after Caesar's assassination from our sources, some of which provide conflicting accounts.

The evidence for the *contiones* at this time is similarly murky. Cicero, for instance, refers to a *contio Capitolina*, presumably a speech delivered by Brutus on the Capitolium, a copy of which Brutus sent him later in 44, around 18 May, with a request for his editorial advice before its publication.[5] The evidence of Cicero makes it clear that there was a *contio* on the Capitolium, but he does not inform us when it occurred. Plutarch, who generally preserves a tradition favorable to the conspirators, describes a *contio* held by Brutus on the Capitolium on the Ides of March that received a favorable hearing from those in attendance.[6] Appian also preserves a speech that Brutus delivered on the Capitolium, but he dates it after the senate meeting at the Temple of Tellus, probably on the afternoon of 17 March (App. *BC* 2.137–142.592). Neither Nicolaus nor Dio records a *contio* on the Capitolium, but both describe one in the Forum (Nic. Dam. 26a.99–100 [*FrGH* 90, F130]; Dio 44.21.1). The second *contio* that Appian records might have dropped out of the other sources. The fact that Brutus ultimately published only one written version suggests that only one *contio* had been convened. Another possibility is that Appian found this speech—a speech of Brutus on the Capitolium—in one of his sources and, since it seems to respond to the charges made by Antonius outside the Temple of Tellus, thought that it must have postdated Antonius' speech. In this scenario, the second *contio* that Appian mentions was probably based on the published version of the *contio* Brutus held on the Capitolium immediately after the murder. If it seems to answer charges made later, this is only because, in editing it for publication, Brutus had the opportunity to make revisions that would naturally include a refutation of these later accusations.

The historical tradition, then, consistently describes a *contio* in the Forum shortly after Caesar's assassination (either on the same day or the next) and a *contio* on the Capitolium, which suggests that the conspirators convened two *contiones*. The two most probable dates for the *contio* on the Capitolium are either the Ides of March, immediately before the *contio* in the Forum (so Plutarch), or 17 March (or thereabouts), after the senate meeting at the Temple of Tellus (so Appian). The evidence allows for no easy solution. Plutarch's account, as noted above, has Brutus deliver only a brief speech on the Capitolium to a few supporters before being encouraged to address a larger crowd in the Forum. It is doubtful whether such a speech on the Capitolium would have constituted a *contio*, inasmuch as only a small portion of the Roman citizen body (it seems) was present. Moreover, we should bear in mind that Brutus chose to publish the *contio* on the Capitolium, an indication that he deemed it of greater importance than the *contio* in the Forum. Brutus' remarks on the Capitolium on the Ides either would have been hastily prepared or a version of the speech that he had hoped to deliver to the senate immediately after the assassination.[7] On the other hand, if the conspirators had held a second *contio* on the Capitolium after the Ides, they would have had more time to prepare their remarks, and the finished product would already have merited publication even before Cicero lent it his editorial hand. Thus, it is possible to reconcile the accounts both of Plutarch and Appian by positing a *contio* in the Forum on the Ides of March followed a few days later (but before the reading of Caesar's will and his funeral) by a second *contio* on the Capitolium, where the conspirators were sequestered.

In chapter 1 we discussed at some length the performance of public oratory at a *contio,* which lent prestige and dignity to the orator who was expected to command his audience with the magnificence of his appearance and the power of his words and gestures. The *contio* was equally a ceremony of popular sovereignty, symbolized by the downward tilt of the magistrate's *fasces,* in which the Roman people were asked to approve or reject proposed legislation or were kept apprised of issues of public importance. The conspirators' *contio* on the Ides of March still contained many of these ceremonial aspects, but in all probability they were overshadowed by the confusion and terror caused by Caesar's assassination. Before the conspirators appeared, the audience would have known very little about what had happened in the *curia* of Pompeius' theater, and, by the same token, no one knew for certain what would happen next. All of this must be borne in mind as we analyze this *contio*.

We shall begin with a discussion and analysis of the location of the speeches that occurred on the Ides of March. This discussion will also have a bearing on events that we consider in later chapters. Most of our sources identify the location of this first appearance of the conspirators as the Rostra in the Forum, after the conspirators had come down from the Capitolium, but it is not clear which Rostra is meant. The possibilities are the old Rostra, which was part of the Curia/Comitium complex in the northwest corner of the Forum, the *rostra* on the Temple of Castor, or the new Rostra Caesaris, recently moved by Caesar in the early part of 44 (see fig. 3). The old Rostra had long been associated with the senatorial aristocracy and elite politics, while the Temple of Castor came to be the platform of choice for politicians like P. Clodius, who, as tribune of the *plebs* in 58, enacted from its *rostra* a number of pieces of legislation designed to win the favor of the urban *plebs*. Therefore, the old Rostra would have been the location most evocative of the Republic and senatorial politics and, for this reason, the most suitable for Brutus' speech, especially if Brutus desired to eradicate the memory of the dead dictator by reviving the Republic. As we discussed in the previous chapter, however, Dio tells us that Caesar had begun to transform the Forum early in 44, which included moving the Rostra to its more familiar location in the west end of the Forum, where it would remain for the rest of the imperial period. It is likely that two statues of Caesar already stood here, one showing him as the savior of the citizens, wearing the *Corona Civica,* and the other as the deliverer of the city from siege, wearing the *Corona Obsidionalis*.[8]

The evidence of Cicero provides some corroboration, for Cicero also held *contiones* in the Forum after January 44, and, from a statement that he makes in the *Sixth Philippic,* it is clear that when Cicero was delivering this speech before a *contio* on 1 January 43 he was speaking not from the old Rostra but from the new one built by Caesar. This *contio* followed the long-awaited meeting of the senate held at the Temple of Jupiter on the Capitolium that marked the beginning of the year of the new consuls, C. Vibius Pansa and A. Hirtius.[9] In the middle of this speech, Cicero gestured toward an equestrian statue erected in honor of L. Antonius, brother of the future triumvir, with a dedicatory inscription calling him patron of the thirty-five tribes.[10] He describes the statue as being "on the left" (*a sinistra*) without giving any indication from whose perspective he means, his or his audience's. He later states, however, that this statue stood in front of the Temple of Castor (*ante Castoris*) (section 13). If this is true, the statue could not have been on the speaker's left whether he was standing on the old or new Rostra, but it could have been on the audience's left if Cicero was speaking from the new Rostra. It follows, therefore, that Cicero must have meant the audience's left when he used the phrase *a sinistra* and further that he elected to speak from the new Rostra Caesaris. It also seems reasonable to conclude that Cicero would have opted for the new Rostra only if the old Rostra were unavailable.[11]

The evidence of the *Sixth Philippic* does not provide definitive proof for the location of the conspirators' speeches in the Forum on the Ides of March, but it is highly suggestive. If we are correct in our reasoning, then we must conclude that the conspirators' speeches were also delivered from the new Rostra, a location that would have produced a striking and provocative scene. I argued in the previous chapter that Caesar's building program reoriented the Forum by making the new Rostra its visual center. The conspirators delivered their speeches denouncing the tyrant and proclaiming freedom for the Roman people from the structure that the tyrant had built, where Caesar himself had renounced the kingship in February; the recently dedicated but still incomplete Basilica Julia was to the speaker's right, and statues of Caesar the savior and deliverer stood before him. On the conspirators' left was the new Curia Julia, still under construction. If the conspirators had hoped that the assassination of Caesar would revive the Republic, then the topography of Caesar's Forum, in particular the leveling of the Comitium and the turning of the Curia toward the new Rostra, would have proclaimed loudly to the conspirators' audience that the glorious days of the Republic were long past. If the Republic were to survive somehow, it would do so only in a drastically altered state.

Thus, the stage for the *contiones;* what of the rest of the performance? Our later sources are not in accord when they describe the *contiones* in the Forum on the Ides of March. Plutarch's accounts in his various *Lives* tend to focus on the figure of Brutus, who, it seems, became spokesman for the conspirators immediately after Caesar's murder (Plut. *Caes.* 67), although Plutarch acknowledges that Brutus was accompanied by his coconspirators as well as other senators. Nicolaus also preserved a speech of Brutus in the Forum in a lost work (Nic. Dam. 26a.100). Appian, on the other hand, has both Brutus and Cassius appear on the Rostra together, along with the other conspirators and their supporters, to deliver a speech to the people. Dio similarly refers to the conspirators as a group and does not single out Brutus for special mention at this time (44.21.1). It is probable that the conspirators and their supporters were present in the Forum as a group and that Brutus was not the only speaker. In fact, Appian's account of a "joint" speech of both Brutus and Cassius perhaps reflects the public face of the conspirators as they tried to demonstrate the broad support for their endeavor as well as their collective guilt, in a manner similar to the murder of Caesar itself, in which all the conspirators had participated. In my view, Appian's account is more likely correct. The success of the conspiracy depended on action in concert. No single person was responsible for the act; it was a collective effort to show the widespread distrust of and hatred for Caesar's power. Since the conspirators together assassinated Caesar, they addressed the crowd together.[12] The presence of other senators (as Plutarch contends) was a welcome sign of approbation for the conspirators.

How carefully did the conspirators plan and organize this *contio*? Amid the fear and uncertainty that prevailed after the senate meeting, it is unlikely that they could have planned it at all. We are told that Brutus hoped to address the senate after Caesar's assassination but was unable to quell the panic, to which the conspirators were not immune, as their flight to the Capitolium shows. No more than a few hours could have elapsed before the conspirators addressed the crowd. We have to imagine a hasty consultation to determine the next course of action, involving the conspirators and those senators who joined the cause only after the fact. The decision was made to hold a *contio*, whose purpose presumably was to gauge popular opinion, calm the crowd, and win the approval of the Roman people for the assassination of Caesar. Several speakers addressed the crowd, including L. Cornelius Cinna (*pr.* 44), Caesar's former brother-in-law, and P. Dolabella (*cos. suff.* 44). How carefully the conspirators thought through the remarks Cinna and Dolabella would make on this occasion is not known. But certainly, if they hoped for a return to constitutional government, it was necessary to solicit the opinions of the magistrates in office. In fact, since it was customary for magistrates to weigh in on important issues at a *contio* (e.g., the Gabinian law, discussed in chapter 1), the speeches of Cinna and Dolabella conformed to procedure. The conspirators might also have hoped that, since Cinna and Dolabella were not privy to the conspiracy beforehand, they might provide greater legitimacy to the conspirators' deed afterwards.[13] In most ancient accounts, the actions and words of these two, both of whom spoke in favor of the conspirators, encouraged the conspirators to address the crowd in the Forum.

The praetor Cinna came forward first (it seems), laid aside the insignia of his magistracy, and castigated Caesar in a speech on the Rostra (V. Max. 9.9.1). Cinna's dramatic gesture of removing his insignia before the people impugned Caesar's control of the electoral assemblies during his dictatorship, an overt rejection of Caesar's *acta,* the first step in declaring him a tyrant. But this demonstration also placed Cinna in the awkward position of relinquishing a magistracy, with the loss of its attendant power and prestige, and reverting to the status of a *privatus*. Cinna's action could also be interpreted as a rejection of a personal benefaction and caused some in the crowd to become restive.[14]

Appian claims that Dolabella also spoke, having taken up the *fasces* and insignia of the office of consul at this time, since he had been selected *consul suffectus* by Caesar for the remainder of the year. Dio states rather that Dolabella delivered a speech first and then ascended to the Capitolium and became consul.[15] This is an issue worth considering since it has a bearing on Dolabella's appearance and consequently our understanding of this *contio*. The installation of a consul required ceremony, including a procession to the Capitolium and sacrifice,[16] but it is unlikely that Dolabella would have had the opportunity to participate in such a ceremony before this *contio*. If so, then Dolabella either delivered his speech dressed as a *privatus,* for he held no other magistracy, or he hastily donned the insignia of consul and found some lictors to carry his *fasces* while he addressed the people in the Forum. The latter is improbable since it would have been an egregious violation of Roman custom for Dolabella to don the insignia of the office of consul without due ceremony. But if we assume for a moment that this did happen, what would it have meant? The *fasces* had become a symbol of Caesar's dictatorship, especially after he was allowed to be attended at his triumph in 46 BC by the number of lictors that were then with him as he returned to Italy from Africa in addition to those lictors from his first and second dictatorships—a minimum of 36 in all.[17] It is not known whether Caesar as dictator in 44 had possession of the *fasces* continually throughout the year or the traditional exchange of *fasces* between the consuls was being observed. My guess is that the former was the case since Caesar had been accorded the special honor of having his *fasces* decorated with laurel (*fasces laureati*), as a permanent reminder of his victory.[18] But even if Caesar had shared the *fasces* with Antonius somehow, he probably would have acted as the ranking consul in 44, which means that he would have carried the *fasces* in the odd-numbered months, including March. In any event, Dolabella's acquisition of the *fasces*, however he managed it, would have been as redolent of Caesar's memory as it was of the Republic restored.

If, as is more likely the case, Dolabella had not yet donned the insignia of his new magistracy, then his appearance at this *contio* would have been a striking complement to Cinna's demonstration: here were two magistrates, both selected by Caesar, one rejecting his office, the other eager to enter his, but both ultimately dressed as nonmagistrates. Their prestige and authority rested on the legitimacy of Caesar's dictatorship, and yet both spoke against him. These speeches would have done nothing to allay the fears and dispel the confusion the Roman people must have been feeling.

Our sources tell us little about the physical appearance of the conspirators at the *contio* in the Forum immediately after Caesar's murder, but it is possible to surmise how they might have looked to their audience. Brutus and Cassius, for instance, would have been formally attired, wearing the *latus clavus* and *toga praetexta* as well as the insignia of the office of praetor. This magistracy also entitled them to be attended by two lictors carrying *fasces*, but we are not told explicitly that lictors were present. Several eminent senators escorted the conspirators to the Forum, thus demonstrating their support for, and approbation of, the tyrant's murder and—perhaps this was the conspirators' hope—lending the bold deed some political legitimacy (Plut. *Brut.* 18.12). The people were understandably awestruck at the sight of these senators, perhaps because the senate had only recently lavished extraordinary honors on Caesar, and its members were now treating his murderers as heroes. What's more, many of those who were privy to the conspiracy were themselves friends of the slain dictator and direct beneficiaries of his clemency.

The most striking aspect of Brutus' appearance, and that of the other conspirators, was the result of their participation in Caesar's murder. Brutus, along with the rest of the conspirators, had rushed from the *curia* of Pompeius' theater with their togas wrapped around their left arms for protection and their hands smeared with blood and holding their daggers aloft (Plut. *Brut.* 18.7). We are not told whether Brutus was still holding his dagger when he addressed the crowd on the Capitolium or later in the Forum, although it would have been a bold visual symbol of the end of tyranny. Appian does maintain, however, that Brutus' hand was still visibly bloody (*BC* 2.122.512), and it is likely that, in the mêlée, blood had spattered on Brutus' toga. The sight of a Roman magistrate with blood on his hands and clothes, surrounded by others similarly attired, must have run counter to the crowd's usual expectations for the appearance of an orator. In fact, the dress of the orator—the toga—was symbolic, of the Roman people, civil discourse, the Forum, and, ultimately, peace.[19]

The actual words that Brutus spoke on this occasion are lost. Even the published version of the *contio Capitolina* probably did not contain a verbatim account of the speech Brutus delivered either at the *contio* in the Forum or on the Capitolium. In fact, the apparent existence of only one published speech suggests that it was a compilation of the two *contiones*, perhaps leavened with some statements that the conspirators in hindsight wished they had made. The versions of Brutus' speech(es) that are available to us in our later sources exist at a still further remove from Brutus' published *contio*.[20] Dio claims that the conspirators spoke against Caesar and in favor of democracy, while urging all to take courage (44.21.1). Appian's version is more elaborate (*BC* 2.122.514). Brutus and Cassius, evincing no humility, praised each other for a deed well done, offered congratulations to the city, and thanked Decimus Brutus for supplying gladiators for their protection. They further urged the Roman people to imitate their ancestors, who expelled from Rome the last kings. And these kings had not ruled by force as Caesar had done but were elected in accordance with the laws. They called for the restoration both of Sextus Pompeius, the son of Caesar's rival in the civil war, who was still fighting Caesar's generals in Spain, and of Caesetius and Marullus, the two tribunes who had been deposed from office after removing a diadem from Caesar's statue.

A speech that consisted of an attack on Caesar as a tyrant and praise for the Republic was perfectly suited for the occasion. The other details of Appian's version are plausible under the circumstances. The conspirators' exhortation to the Roman people to emulate their ancestors was an allusion to the story of M. Brutus' putative ancestor, L. Brutus, who expelled Tarquinius Superbus and served as one of the first consuls of the new Roman

Republic. This legend became a recurring theme in the rhetoric of the conspirators and their supporters. Cicero, for instance, states that "there is still one hope, that the Roman people will at some point emulate their ancestors."[21] Cicero also refers to the legendary Brutus in the *First Philippic* (13) and claims that his deed served as a model for the conspirators' actions. M. Brutus, for his part, hoped to put on a production of Accius' *Brutus* at the *Ludi Apollinares* in July 44 (see chap. 6). The story of L. Brutus was not merely a product of the circumstances surrounding Caesar's assassination, for it was already part of M. Brutus' family history, along with the story of Servilius Ahala, the assassin of the would-be tyrant Sp. Maelius in the fifth century BC. The two stories taken together were part of M. Brutus' claim to be a tyrannicide. He had almost a decade before Caesar's assassination advertised both connections on coinage, when there hung in the air rumors of Pompeius' ambitions for extraordinary powers.[22] The tradition of L. Brutus, and M. Brutus' relationship to him, clearly became part of the public discourse in the aftermath of Caesar's assassination, and it is possible that it was introduced at the conspirators' speech on the Ides of March as Appian has it.[23]

The conspirators' call for the restoration of Sextus Pompeius had a twofold purpose. First, it was a tribute to his father, Caesar's rival, who had enjoyed great popularity throughout his career and who, after his defeat at the hands of Caesar and subsequent death, became an important political symbol to the conspirators because he came to represent the political freedom that perished under Caesar's tyranny. The murder of Caesar took place in the *curia* of Pompeius, and Caesar's body fell at the foot of Pompeius' statue. To some this was providential. In fact, we are told that Cassius nodded in the direction of Pompeius' statue just before the murder as if to invoke his memory (Plut. *Brut.* 17.2). At some point later in the year (but before 2 September, when the *First Philippic* was delivered), Pompeius' statue was put on display and, according to Cicero, wildly cheered. We do not know what the occasion was; the *Ludi Apollinares* sponsored by Brutus in July 44 are a possibility (Cic. *Phil.* 1.36). The name of Pompeius Magnus still resonated with the veterans in the city, many of whom had served under him but later became Caesar's soldiers; some of these men were probably present at the conspirators' *contio*. Furthermore, Caesar himself had restored a statue of Pompeius to the Rostra, providing a visual point of reference for the conspirators at this *contio*.

Second, the mention of Sextus Pompeius was an acknowledgment that the conspirators lacked the military force to rival Caesar's supporters. Brutus advocated Sextus Pompeius' recall, in the hope that the son would take the place of the father,[24] and, in the weeks following the murder, the conspirators and Cicero kept close track of the movements of Sextus. In late June Cicero was wondering if Pompeius' son would be the leader in the next civil war (Cic. *Att.* 15.21.3; 15.22).

The conspirators' call for the restoration of Caesetius and Marullus was meant to cast Caesar's dictatorship as an affront to the ideal of popular sovereignty—specifically, the role of tribunes of the *plebs* as representatives of the lower orders of society. The story of Caesar's harsh treatment of these tribunes is presented in virtually all our sources as evidence that the dictator was becoming a tyrant, and their clash over the diadem was viewed as one of the primary causes of the conspiracy.[25] The very statue of Caesar that received the crown and was at the center of the dispute stood on the Rostra where the conspirators spoke. Perhaps it was the presence of the statue that encouraged them to include a statement about the deposed tribunes in their speech in the hopes that it would attract the support of the Roman people. At the consular elections immediately following the tribunes' banishment, the names of Caesetius and Marullus appeared on many of the ballots. Who was responsible is not known, but it was probably intended to show the electorate's displeasure at their fate (Suet. *Jul.* 80.3). Certain fundamental ideals of popular sovereignty and equal protection under the law were embodied in the power of the office of tribune (*tribunicia potestas*).[26] These ideals were established during the Struggle of the Orders,[27] but they remained contentious issues even in the late Republic. Caesar's confrontations with tribunes have been well documented, as I noted earlier (see chap. 2). The conspirators apparently believed that their call for the restoration of the deposed tribunes would be sufficient to remind the Roman people of Caesar's challenges to tribunician power and would offer further proof that they had indeed slain a tyrant.

This lengthy discussion only proves that Appian's version of the conspirators' speech in the Forum is a plausible reconstruction, assembled as it was from the kind of conventional rhetoric the conspirators and their supporters were known to have used to justify Caesar's assassination. We cannot go so far as to claim that this represents what Brutus and Cassius actually said. But even if Appian is wrong in some of the details, it is likely that he has got right the general tone of the speech. The conspirators attacked the nature of Caesar's power as a tyranny whose very existence was a violation of the freedom on which the Republic had been founded and called for a restoration of constitutional government. But this speech was at least in part undermined by its location, with its many visible reminders of Caesar's dictatorship.

How did the audience react? The conspirators apparently hoped to be hailed as tyrannicides by the Roman people, their actions acclaimed, their words lauded. Instead, the audience in the Forum greeted the conspirators with a stony silence or, in response to Cinna's actions, angry words. The presence of Caesar's veterans, always a cause of concern for the conspirators, and the popularity of Caesar are two factors to explain such a reaction. Did the conspirators' claim to have restored freedom appeal to the people?

M. Brutus had long claimed a connection to the great tyrannicides of Roman history, as we noted above. The tradition that graffiti appeared on his praetor's tribunal and elsewhere in Rome chiding him for not measuring up to his distinguished ancestor is an indication that this connection was widely acknowledged (see n. 23). Brutus' very appearance on the Rostra might have evoked this connection without his ever uttering a word. But Cassius reportedly remarked to Brutus that these graffiti were inscribed not by shopkeepers and the like, but by members of the aristocracy (Plut. *Brut.* 10.6), who had the most to gain from the removal of Caesar from power. If this is an accurate assessment of the political context for these graffiti, then one wonders how effective any allusion (whether implicit or overt) to the *exemplum* of L. Brutus would have been to an audience that partly comprised shopkeepers. Was this an *exemplum* that concerned the history and freedom of the elite and spoke mainly to their interests and ideals?

A slogan attendant upon all of the conspirators' words and actions was *libertas*, the restoration of political freedom following the removal of the tyrant. We have already mentioned the *pilleus* and daggers as visual symbols of *libertas* and tyrannicide. By invoking *libertas* in this way, the conspirators were using rhetoric frequently voiced by politicians of the Republic who regularly appealed to the sovereignty of the people. The question is whether the audience on this occasion—a gathering of the urban *plebs* and perhaps some of Caesar's soldiers, a heterogeneous group comprised of freedmen, resident aliens, poor freemen, and others—embraced the "freedom" that the conspirators proclaimed, for this freedom seems to have been tantamount to political power for the senatorial aristocracy, with no guarantees of peace and prosperity for the Roman people.[28] It is important to note that *libertas* as a political symbol or ideal had a different resonance for the various members of Roman society, depending on their social rank.[29] For aristocrats, like the conspirators, it meant that the game of politics would be played on a level field. In this sense, it was closely allied with personal prestige (*dignitas*), so much so that the diminution of one caused the diminution of the other. In other words, a careful balance had to be struck between *libertas* and *dignitas*, since an individual's self-interested pursuit of *dignitas* would have the inevitable effect of infringing on another's *libertas*. This is in part what led Brutus and the others to assassinate Caesar. For the Roman *plebs*, *libertas* provided many important safeguards and rights: protection from wanton abuse by a magistrate (although this may have decreased in importance during the late Republic), the right to vote in an election (including the important secret ballot),[30] freedom of association,[31] economic freedom, and political independence. The question is whether Caesar's dictatorship, in the eyes of the Roman *plebs*, constituted an infringement on these fundamental rights. It is likely that they did not feel oppressed by Caesar's "tyranny" any more than they had by the previous regime.[32] At the time of the conspirators' *contio*, I believe, *libertas*, as a symbol or even a slogan, did not have the same stirring force or emotional appeal that it once did, mainly because of the ambivalence that many felt toward Caesar as he rose to power and held the dictatorship.

There is one example that can illustrate what I mean, although it dates to the early months of the civil war between Pompeius and Caesar. In early March 49, after Caesar's successful siege of Corfinium, and while he was journeying to Brundisium in pursuit of Pompeius, Cicero wrote to Atticus of conversations that he had been having with townspeople (*municipales*) and country folk (*rusticani*), presumably living in the vicinity of Formiae, where Cicero was then resident. After describing how these people had come to admire Caesar and loathe Pompeius, Cicero remarks, "They care for nothing other than their fields, small estates (*villulas*) and petty investments (*nummulos*)."[33] There is a disdainful tone in Cicero's words because, as he sees it, these people failed to understand the larger constitutional issues at stake in Caesar's march into Italy and the consequent flight of the consuls and Pompeius. The very Republic was in peril. For these *municipales* and *rusticani*, however, the larger constitutional issues were far less important than peace and economic prosperity that would guarantee stability; as a source of this stability they looked not to Pompeius, and the senatorial aristocracy that he represented, but to Caesar.

The symbol of *libertas*, therefore, may have had less effect in stirring the people to action in March 44, since Brutus' ideology and vision of the future was contingent upon the restoration of the Republic—a condition that would do nothing to improve the livelihoods of many of those in his audience.[34] The debate over the fair distribution of wealth from military conquest and economic exploitation of the provinces dated back to the great expansion of the second century when the influx of wealth greatly widened the gap between rich and poor. Ti. Gracchus first eloquently demonstrated the inequities of this distribution when he stated that the Roman people were called the conquerors of the world, yet they could not afford a single clod of earth to till.[35] C. Gracchus took this rhetoric a step further when he styled himself the defender of the public treasury (*aerarium*) against the depredations of the aristocracy (from the viewpoint of his enemies, Gracchus' spending programs were a threat to the *aerarium*).[36] When Caesar tried to gain access to the *aerarium* in 49 to obtain funds for his campaign against Pompeius, a tribune blocked his way.[37] The message of Gracchus and other *populares* was clear: the people had a right to share in the revenues of the empire.[38] For this reason, Gaius pointed with pride to his moderate administration as proquaestor in Sardinia, claiming that he did not pillage the province, as was customary for most Roman officials.[39] Cicero, speaking in support of the *lex Manilia,* which conferred the command against Mithridates on Pompeius, perhaps his most *popularis* speech, also declared the people's right to the revenues from the provinces, reminding his audience that Mithridates stood on the threshold of Asia (one of the richest provinces in the empire), and, if he succeeded in invading it, the economic repercussions would be felt in Italy.[40]

On the Ides of March, Brutus' strongest appeal was to *libertas*, but this was losing its allurement in a time of domestic conflict and civil war. The best evidence for Brutus' failure to appeal to the interests of his audience was the profound silence that greeted his words. It was perhaps a speech that would have received a better hearing in the Curia than in the Forum.

On one level, the very existence of the conspirators' *contio* demonstrated their willingness to exhort the urban populace, thus acknowledging the interests of the urban *plebs* and Caesar's veterans. But by doing so, Brutus also subjected himself to the will of the people, for he had to demonstrate his ability to win over the people, hear their acclaim, or suffer a loss of personal prestige—or, in the dire circumstances in which he spoke, personal injury or even loss of life. Appearing before the Roman people was always a perilous undertaking in the late Republic, but Brutus had no choice. In fact, Cicero criticized him for not attempting to do more (Cic. *Att.* 14.10.1; cf. *Att.* 14.14.2; 15.11.2).

On another level, M. Brutus' allusion to his putative ancestor, L. Brutus, advertised a great accomplishment of a member of his family—not at all unusual in the politics of the late Republic—but this relationship entitled him to claim to be a tyrannicide, which in turn lent him a prestige and authority appropriate for the occasion. Moreover, bound up with this *exemplum* was the central idea of freedom as embodied in the transition from the Regal period to the Republic (Liv. 2.1.1–2). I argued that Brutus might have miscalculated the emotive value of this particular idea to his audience on this occasion, but his efforts nevertheless show how an ancient story could be made to serve a practical political purpose. He persisted in his belief that this story and the ideals it expressed were the best way to communicate with the Roman people. In the Roman Republic, the messy game of politics was often elevated by such *exempla* from Rome's remote past.

The conspirators' retreat to the Capitolium following their *contio* is evidence both of their failure to win the acclaim of the people as well as the continued uncertainty over the loyalty of Caesar's veterans and consequently their own personal safety on the streets of Rome. The *contio* was a ceremony that could confer great power or snatch it away, as we have seen, but this was a power largely built on consensus, the political harmony between elite and nonelite. At the conspirators' *contio* on the Ides of March, they tried to build consensus on the foundation of *libertas* and the death of the tyrant, but this failed to move their audience. While Cinna's performance was intended to demonstrate his willingness to forego the dictator's benefaction, it only underscored the ultimate source of his authority—Caesar himself. This might have had the consequent effect of drawing attention to the ultimate source of Brutus' and Cassius' authority as well. This *contio* in the end was just short of an embarrassment for the conspirators, all eminent men, many of them magistrates, who collectively could not summon the *auctoritas* necessary to win the crowd. Caesar cast a long shadow, obscuring much of what the conspirators hoped to accomplish.

The *Contiones* of Caesar's Supporters

The evening after Caesar's murder was taken up with negotiations between Antonius and Lepidus over their next course of action. Antonius required Lepidus' support since the latter had troops under his command. We can imagine similar discussions undertaken by the conspirators as they remained sequestered on the Capitolium. The conspirators sent envoys to Antonius to discuss the future of the state. He postponed his reply until the next day. In the meantime, Lepidus appeared in the Forum and convened a public meeting. Antonius decided to call a meeting of the senate for the next day (17 March) at the Temple of Tellus, during which the fate of the conspirators and the memory of Caesar's dictatorship would be at issue.[41] During the meeting, Antonius and Lepidus convened two *contiones* to present their views of Caesar and his fate.

The *contiones* of Caesar's supporters on 16 and 17 March were in part a response to the conspirators' speeches, for they presented a quite different view of the dead dictator. More importantly, these *contiones* were a political power play, an opportunity for Lepidus and Antonius to demonstrate that they could win over an increasingly restive crowd. Their goal was to create a measure of consensus centered on the figure of Caesar and the preservation of his memory.

Amid the confusion following Caesar's assassination, M. Lepidus was more visible than M. Antonius. As Caesar's master of horse, he had troops under his command, which he led first to the island in the Tiber and then to the Campus Martius. He communicated with Antonius on the evening of 15 March, presumably to discuss their course of action. That night or the next day, he entered the Forum and commanded his troops to take control, so that they could exclude the conspirators from Rome's political center while allowing himself and Antonius ready access. At dawn on 16 March, Antonius appeared in arms, and Lepidus, as if to demonstrate his control of the Forum and perhaps to test the will of the people, stood on the Rostra and delivered a speech castigating the conspirators and calling for vengeance for Caesar's murder (Nic. Dam. 27.103). It is probable that Lepidus was communicating the wishes of his troops, who would have been ardent in their desire to see the conspirators punished. For this *contio* he would have been dressed in military garb (the *paludamentum*), not the toga, an unusual appearance for an orator at an assembly of Roman citizens.

The words and actions of Antonius and Lepidus contrasted sharply with the speeches by the conspirators and their supporters the day before, as was their appearance in military garb accompanied by Lepidus' troops. The *contio* was both a civilian and military ceremony, but in this instance both soldiers and civilians were present as well as Caesar's veterans. Lepidus' dress and the presence of his troops, who had spent part of the time after Caesar's murder occupying the Forum (the very location of this *contio*—the political center of Rome), would have been a vivid reminder of the threat of civil war and the consequent violation of civic harmony and tranquility. The conspirators had called for calm and a peaceful restoration of constitutional government; Caesarians were crying out for vengeance and bloodshed.

The supporters of Caesar took counsel later that day. Lepidus continued to express his desire for vengeance against the more moderate counsel of C. Vibius Pansa and A. Hirtius, Caesar's appointed consuls designate for 43. Antonius decided to preserve the conspirators and work through the senate. He called a meeting of the senate for the next morning at the Temple of Tellus. Appian tells us that Antonius chose this location for the meeting of the senate because it was near his home (formerly Pompeius') in the Carinae district, and he did not dare risk a meeting in the Forum because D. Brutus' gladiators were close at hand, perhaps on the Capitolium protecting the conspirators.[42] What we know of the temple's location bears out this assessment of Antonius' motives. It was on the Carinae, just northeast of the Forum, where Pompeius' Domus Rostrata (Antonius' residence at the time) was located.[43] The location was clearly important to Antonius, and from what we know this was the only senate meeting ever held here.[44]

During this meeting, Antonius held a *contio* before a crowd of people who had assembled outside the Temple of Tellus (App. *BC* 2.130.542). Such a *contio* was the customary way for a consul to communicate to the Roman people the actions taken in a meeting of the senate. Antonius' *contio* on this occasion went beyond what was customary, since it was his first opportunity to address the people after Caesar's assassination. He used this speech to praise the dead dictator and appeal to the interests of the people. In a letter dated 20 June, Cicero writes of a *contio* at which he was present and heard Caesar referred to as "a most distinguished man."[45] Cicero's language in an earlier letter, dated 21 April, suggests that he had seen a written version of the same *contio*.[46] Since Cicero had left Rome by 6 April, the *contio* in question must have occurred before this time, and in all probability it was the *contio* that Antonius delivered outside the Temple of Tellus on 17 March.[47] His praise of Caesar in this speech clearly indicates that he intended to preserve the memory of the dead dictator, even against the interests of the conspirators and a majority of the senate. Thus, in his first public statements after Caesar's murder, Antonius showed that he was playing both sides: in the senate, he helped forge an amnesty for the conspirators, but in a *contio* before the people and Caesar's veterans, he took pains to preserve Caesar's memory.[48]

The appearance of Antonius at this *contio* merits comment. Antonius presumably would have been attired as consul, with *toga praetexta* and *latus clavus*, and accompanied by lictors bearing the *fasces*, symbols of the power of his office, although, as we have just noted, the meaning of the *fasces* became somewhat more ambiguous after Caesar's dictatorship. Under his toga, however, Antonius wore chain mail, which he displayed to the people assembled before him. He was so armed, he claimed, as a safeguard against possible violence. This threat may have been real, since in later letters Cicero often derides the conspirators for their failure to assassinate Antonius as well on the Ides of March. With this visible demonstration of personal peril, Antonius intended to show the dangers that a consul and friend of Caesar faced in the aftermath of Caesar's murder.[49] The toga, of course, was the dress appropriate to the Forum and associated with peacetime activities, but in combination with the chain mail Antonius sent a clear signal that civil war was at hand.

Appian adds that the crowd responded with an ambivalent reply: some continued to cry out for peace, a condition that would have had to include some accommodations for the conspirators, while others demanded vengeance for Caesar's murder, which would have resulted in the conspirators being branded as criminals and subjected to prosecution (App. *BC* 2.130.544). Those demanding vengeance were largely veterans of Caesar's campaigns, whom he had settled in cities throughout Italy (Nic. Dam. 17.49 [*FrGH* 90, F130]). This is the first instance after Caesar's murder of a crowd divided in their demands, with one side favorable to the conspirators, and the other supportive of Caesar. This split became even more noticeable in the following weeks, especially as more of Caesar's veterans flocked to the city, which only worsened an already cloudy and uncertain political scene, since the political figures who took part in these ceremonies had to take into account the composition of the crowd that came to hear them speak (see chap. 4).

For the content of Antonius' speech, we must rely again on Appian's account. Antonius demonstrated his allegiance to Caesar's memory in two other ways. The crowd cried out for peace; in response, Antonius made reference to the oath sworn by the senate to preserve Caesar's life, thus introducing another political symbol that put the conspirators on the defensive. He averred that peace, though a desirable end, was difficult when oaths meant nothing.[50] Peace, Antonius went on, was rooted in fundamental goodwill, a trait that the conspirators obviously did not possess.

Antonius made reference to this oath again when he explained his reasons for not actively exacting vengeance for Caesar's murder. His first duty as consul, he asserted, was to protect the common good, which, he claimed, was Caesar's also when he spared those who eventually were responsible for his murder. He referred, of course, to Caesar's famous *clementia*, and, by portraying Caesar as a victim of treachery, he intended to make the conspirators' deed all the more heinous.[51] *Clementia* differed from *libertas* in that originally it was not an evocative catchword but simply a personal virtue. Caesar turned this virtue into his own personal slogan, and it became one of the defining characteristics of his regime. After his death, Antonius used this slogan of Caesar's effectively as a catchword against the conspirators, both in his *contio* outside the Temple of Tellus and in his funeral speech (*laudatio*) for Caesar (Dio 44.45). While the concept of mercy as a virtue had a long history in Rome and was considered traditionally and fundamentally Roman,[52] the use of the word *clementia* to describe this virtue was relatively recent.[53] In fact, *clementia* rarely appeared before the civil war of 49, and then it virtually burst on the scene, especially as a part of Caesar's own rhetoric. His actions at Corfinium, when he spared all those who were taken in the siege, became a famous exemplum of his *clementia*.[54] It is possible that Antonius was responsible for minting coins bearing the slogan "Clementia Caesaris."[55] A temple was to be built in honor of Caesar's *clementia*, although no trace of it or any dedications exist.[56] Antonius skillfully applied this slogan to his own circumstances by showing that he was trying to avoid Caesar's fate in his efforts to effect a peaceful solution to the crisis.

According to Appian (*BC* 2.131), M. Lepidus, who was present alongside Antonius at this *contio*, also delivered a speech to the people. He began to speak from the Temple of Tellus, but then the crowd summoned him to the Forum so that all could hear. Lepidus ascended the Rostra, moaned, and wept as he recalled a recent occasion when he and Caesar had appeared on the Rostra together.[57] His appearance in military garb again, like Antonius' chain mail under his toga, would have foreshadowed the coming civil conflict.

Antonius and Lepidus strove to demonstrate their affection for Caesar's memory at their *contiones* after his death, but the manner of their dress and the presence of soldiers at Lepidus' speech would have shown that their power depended on military might, in striking contrast to the conspirators' *contio*, whose only supporters were members of the senate. The *contiones* of Lepidus and Antonius were a power play designed to demonstrate their control of the city and to intimidate their rivals.

Brutus' *Contio* on the Capitolium

After the *contiones* of Antonius and Lepidus were held and the amnesty decided at the senate meeting, the conspirators summoned the people to the Capitolium, where Brutus addressed them in a speech that Appian records and Cicero mentions only briefly. Cicero's description of the *contio Capitolina* in his subsequent letters often focuses more on what should have been said than what was said. Without describing the contents of Brutus' speech in any detail, Cicero also praises its eloquence highly, except to say that considering the theme (ὑπόθεσις) and the character of the speaker (*persona dicentis*), he would have spoken with greater fervor (*ardentius*) (Cic. *Att.* 15.1a.2). We can infer from Cicero's remarks that in his view Brutus failed to play the proper role in his speech, without stating explicitly what he thought that role was. In a letter to Atticus, however, Cicero declares that he had cried out that the senate should be summoned by the praetors (i.e., Brutus and Cassius) and that through the efforts of the good men (*boni*) much could have been accomplished, although he fails to specify precisely what this was (Cic. *Att.* 14.10.1; cf. *Att.* 14.14.2). In a later letter, he adds that the conspirators should have incited the people to action and taken on the leadership of the whole state (Cic. *Att.* 15.11.2).

The location of this *contio* is also of interest. The Capitolium, as we suggested earlier, was not the usual venue for *contiones*, except those that preceded a gathering of the tribal assembly (*comitia tributa*), which sometimes met on the Capitolium for the purposes of voting on legislation.[58] In fact, in Appian's version of the *contio* under discussion, Brutus felt compelled to defend his choice of the location, stating that the conspirators' occupation of the Capitolium should not be interpreted as an admission of guilt, thus acknowledging the importance of the location of a *contio*. Why not descend to the Forum and deliver another speech from the Rostra? The city streets had become dangerous, and Lepidus' troops accompanied by a crowd had occupied the Forum itself almost continually since Caesar's murder. The Capitolium thus remained the safest place for the conspirators, as they attempted to find a political solution to the crisis.

The first question we should address is: Why was Brutus chosen to speak on the Capitolium? I argued earlier that, on the Ides of March, both Brutus and Cassius delivered speeches. Much later, when a speech was necessary to rally the troops in preparation for the battle of Philippi (summer of 42), Cassius was selected to speak first on the grounds that he was the elder (App. *BC* 4.89.376). Why was the same criterion not used on 17 March? The presence of a statue of L. Brutus on the Capitolium, where the conspirators had fled, along with statues of the seven kings of Rome provided a striking juxtaposition of the tyrant and the tyrannicide. The more recent addition of a statue of Caesar erected next in line after L. Brutus (Dio 43.45.4; cf. Suet. *Jul.* 76.1) perhaps encouraged the selection of M. Brutus to speak on behalf of the conspirators,[59] for this created a second pairing of tyrant and tyrannicide and gave the conspirators the moral high ground in the contest over Caesar's memory.

The one point that Brutus made in this speech that is worthy of note demonstrates the importance of Caesar's veterans to both conspirators and Caesarians. I have already shown that Brutus' demand for the recall of Sextus Pompeius may have been largely for the benefit of ex-Pompeians among Caesar's troops in the city. According to Brutus, the conspirators' enemies also slandered them "about the colonies" (App. *BC* 2.139.580). This charge must have been that the conspirators, if allowed to attain power, would ignore the needs of Caesar's veterans and not provide them with the land to which they felt entitled. Brutus, as one might expect, assured the soldiers in his audience that they would be allowed to keep any land that had been granted them, but he made this statement only after a long harangue against the practice of Caesar and Sulla in this regard, imputing that they had intentionally set the soldiers at odds with their fellow countrymen. Caesar and Sulla managed this, Brutus argued, by settling veterans on the land left by displaced Italians, contrary to the usual practice of finding unoccupied land elsewhere.[60] Not only that, but Caesar and Sulla settled their veterans under their standards and in military organization so that they could never really enjoy peace—and they were continually threatened by the people whom they had displaced.[61] The accuracy of Brutus' charges is questionable, but the rhetoric could have still been effective with two important segments of the urban populace: Caesar's veterans and those displaced by the colonies. In both cases, Brutus promised to rule with a fairer hand and, by addressing the economic conditions of his audience, was correcting an oversight he made in his earlier speech. This indicates that, upon reflection, Brutus realized that initially he had made a serious miscalculation: appeals to *libertas* were not sufficient; eventually he had to address the interests (*commoda*) of the Roman people.

The fact that the conspirators felt it necessary to hold another *contio* even after the senate had declared an amnesty can only mean that they understood this amnesty to have limited effect in ensuring their well-being. The ratification of Caesar's *acta* meant that Caesar's memory was still alive and that they had to compete with Antonius and Lepidus for the support of Caesar's veterans and the urban *plebs*. This was the last time that the conspirators addressed the Roman people directly in a *contio*.

The Consuls' *Contio*

The next day (18 March), Antonius and Lepidus sent their sons as hostages to the Capitolium to persuade Brutus and Cassius to come down to the Forum. The consuls convened another *contio*,[62] probably on the same afternoon, in which the decrees of the senate were read aloud and the amnesty made public. In Appian's account, which is the most detailed, the people loudly applauded when Brutus and Cassius appeared and demanded that the consuls and conspirators reconcile before they allowed the consuls to speak. It is not clear how heartfelt this reconciliation was for the participants, but it did summon up at least a breath of peace in a city that was perilously close to another civil war. It is also worth noting that the leaders responded to the crowd who demanded that the two parties reconcile. The reconciliation was further cemented through the exchange of dinner invitations, with Lepidus entertaining Cassius, and Antonius Brutus.

This *contio* symbolized reconciliation, inasmuch as it gathered members of the opposing parties in one place, but it also declared a victory for those who supported an amnesty for the conspirators, in particular Cicero, who was one of the speakers on this occasion. Our source tradition is silent about Caesar's veterans, who must have resented the accommodation of the conspirators first effected in the senate meeting at the Temple of Tellus and later publicly proclaimed at this *contio*, who had persisted in their demands for vengeance at recent *contiones*. For now, those who had cried out for peace at those same *contiones* emerged victorious. The issue of Caesar's status and the position of the conspirators in the political structure of Rome were hardly settled, for the senate at its next meeting decreed that Caesar would be honored with a public funeral and that his body was to rest in the Campus Martius, thus ending any hope that this period of tranquility might endure. The first stage in this political contest, the public meetings, largely ended in a draw, but the next, Caesar's funeral, turned the tide of popular opinion against the conspirators and prepared the way for a new champion of the people.

Conclusion

Our discussion of these public meetings is severely hampered by the confused and lacunose accounts in our sources, especially the later tradition, which requires perhaps an overreliance on the versions of the speeches of Brutus and Antonius that appear in Appian. Yet it should also be clear from our discussion that in the aftermath of Caesar's assassination political discourse took place between each of the leaders and the people at public ceremonies, the loci of political power in the late Republic. The content of this discourse tended to focus on how each side dealt with the memory of Caesar. The conspirators claimed to have killed a tyrant and in so doing restored freedom and civil order. Antonius and Lepidus, on the other hand, mourned the death of Caesar and demonstrated through their appearance in military dress that civil order had been thoroughly disrupted by the actions of the conspirators. Even if we cannot be certain of the contents of the speeches described, the ability of Antonius (on one side) and Brutus (on the other) to control and persuade the people was a demonstration of their ability to influence politics at the time. Power and prestige could emerge from the ceremony of the *contio*, as could public humiliation. In the *contiones* after Caesar's murder, all of this depended on how one treated Caesar's memory.

4

Caesar ex machina

Ceremony and Caesar's Memory

The *contiones* immediately after the Ides of March demonstrated that Caesar's memory and how it should be preserved shaped the words and influenced the actions of the political leaders at the time. In other words, political power was directly linked to the posthumous honors awarded Caesar and consequently to the ceremonies in which his memory was publicly celebrated. The political prestige of Caesar's supporters, as well as the fate of the conspirators, depended upon the status of Caesar himself. If he had been judged a tyrant, then his body would have been impaled on a hook, dragged through the streets of Rome, and thrown into the Tiber River; his *acta* would have been annulled, his will invalidated, his fortune confiscated, his memory condemned.[1] Therefore, a burning question of the time was whether Caesar should be buried, and what the nature of his funeral should be; equally important was the reading of his will. Every time a privilege was granted to the memory of Caesar, his supporters rallied and the conspirators shuddered. In this chapter, we will focus on the ceremonies surrounding Caesar's death, which only increased the city crowd's hostility toward the conspirators. At the same time, the arrival of Amatius, a slave who claimed to be descended from the great Marius, the erection of an altar in Caesar's honor on the site of his impromptu cremation in the Forum, and the activities of the urban *plebs* and Caesar's veterans in the vicinity of this altar hastened the departure of the conspirators from Rome, directly affecting the course of politics in the months to come.[2] As news of Caesar's death spread throughout Italy, however, more of his veterans flocked to the city in anticipation of his funeral and burial (Nic. Dam. 17.49 [*FrGH* 90, F130]). Thus the crowd in the city grew increasingly more Caesarian than the seemingly divided one that had listened in silence at the conspirators' *contio* in the Forum or had simultaneously demanded peace and vengeance at Antonius' speech at the Temple of Tellus. For the conspirators the streets of Rome were still dangerous, but they became even more so after Caesar's funeral. We will see once again how public ceremonial was a demonstration of political power by the elite and by the people. The ceremonies discussed in this chapter, especially Caesar's funeral and ensuing demonstrations under the leadership of Amatius, also demonstrate the crowd's ability to manage a ceremony separately from the political elite—and at times with consequences that the elite did not anticipate or desire.

The Reading of Caesar's Will

When one considers the importance of the posthumous honors for Caesar, it is not surprising that Caesar's will provoked a tumult when it was read in Rome,[3] helped turn the tide of popular opinion against the conspirators forever, and put Antonius in a precarious political position. It also brought Octavian, Caesar's principal heir, back into the public consciousness and later in the year allowed him entrée into political life, especially through the medium of public ceremonial. On the evening of the murder, when Antonius took possession of Caesar's papers from Caesar's wife, Calpurnia, he presumably also received Caesar's will, which Caesar had deposited at the Temple of Vesta after completing it on 13 September 45. Caesar's father-in-law, L. Calpurnius Piso, demanded that the will be read, and this took place in Antonius' home (Suet. *Jul.* 83.1). At some point, the terms of the will became known to the people, perhaps through a public reading at a *contio*. Plutarch (*Brut.* 20.1) says that Antonius' supporters demanded that the will be read publicly, while Appian (*BC* 2.143.596) asserts it was the people who made this demand. If Appian is correct, then his account shows how the people were participating in the ceremonies involving Caesar's memory from the outset. We should also note that the "people" increasingly included Caesar's veterans, who perhaps could have exerted greater pressure on the political leaders.

By the terms of the will, the bulk of Caesar's property went to his grandnephew, C. Octavius, and the remainder to two other grandnephews, L. Pinarius and Q. Pedius. Caesar's practice of including the *plebs* in his donatives, which began in the celebration of his victories in September 46, continued after his death, for he bequeathed a small sum to each Roman citizen living in the city, and to the people as a whole he also left his suburban estate (*horti*) across the Tiber for use as a public park. Thus Caesar treated the *plebs* almost as if they were members of his family, in a sense placing his personal relationship with the Roman people, one that he had fostered throughout his career, in a formal, legal framework. This bequest obligated them to honor his memory and encouraged them to view the conspirators not as liberators and tyrannicides but as traitors and murderers.

At the end of the will (*in ima cera*), Caesar provided for Octavius to take his name and thus, in a sense, join the Julian family; but he still allowed the possibility that a son might be born to him after his death, and he named as guardians for this as yet unborn heir some of the assassins, while D. Brutus was honored as secondary heir. Dio states that the assassins, along with Antonius and D. Brutus, were named guardians for Octavius (Dio 44.35.2), but he seems to be confusing Octavius with the son yet to be born, since Octavius would have been legally independent (*sui iuris*) at this time and in need of no guardian. Suetonius' account is clear on this point. Dio also asserts, as does Florus, that M. Antonius was named secondary heir along with D. Brutus, but his account of the terms of the will is so confused that it is hardly trustworthy. It is possible that Antonius was left out of the will entirely,[4] although no direct evidence for this exists. In any case, the terms of the will must have stunned Antonius, for he was a longtime ally of Caesar who had been granted a privileged place in the return from Spain six months earlier (Plut. *Ant.* 11.1; see chap. 1)—a place ahead of Octavius and D. Brutus—who now found himself either demoted or utterly ignored in Caesar's last words. As a result, his position as leader of Caesar's supporters was now less secure, and he was compelled to engage the support of those among the urban *plebs* who especially longed for Caesar, in particular Caesar's veterans.

Octavius was probably equally surprised to discover the terms of the will, since there is no evidence to suggest that he was privy to it beforehand.[5] We can be certain that by the time he arrived in Naples on 18 April, he was determined to accept the inheritance,[6] including not only Caesar's colossal fortune but also his name. Adoption of this kind, known as testamentary adoption, was mainly for the purpose of carrying on the name of the deceased (*condicio nominis ferendi*) and of perpetuating his memory, not for extending the family line.[7] The heir so designated could take on the name of the deceased, but it was not required, and the new heir did not enter the testator's family.[8] Octavius' adoption in this manner raised two important issues that affected his plans and behavior over the course of the next several months. First, if the primary purpose of testamentary adoption (under the *condicio nominis ferendi*) was commemoration of the dead, then he was under a more pressing obligation to nurture Caesar's memory. Second, if adoption in this manner did not make him legally Caesar's son in the same way as if Caesar had adopted him while still alive (*inter vivos*), then Octavian could be vulnerable to charges that he was not Caesar's true heir. This is probably why he persevered in getting a law passed by the curiate assembly to sanction the adoption, and why Antonius relentlessly opposed it (Dio 45.5.3–4; see chap. 7).

Thus, the public reading of Caesar's will had a threefold effect: First, the people now had a vested interested in seeing Caesar's murder avenged, and they further showed that their interests were fully integrated into the politics of the time; second, Antonius was in a more defensive position politically, especially as regards Caesar's veterans. He could believe that he would no longer be viewed as Caesar's heir. Finally, Octavian was brought back into public consciousness, and he would have to be reckoned with shortly.

Caesar's Funeral

The reading of Caesar's will was closely followed by his funeral[9] (ca. 20 March),[10] a ceremony that had a profound effect on the politics of this period. On one level, a Roman aristocratic funeral demonstrated the rewards of service to the state and the fame and glory to be found especially in martial valor. It celebrated the achievements of an elite family by honoring its most recently deceased member. On another level, especially in the late Republic, this ceremony became increasingly entangled in the political issues of the day. We have already seen, for instance, how Caesar demonstrated his allegiance to Marius by celebrating the death of his aunt (chap. 1). Thus a funeral became a political platform for the enterprising politician. A funeral could also become a venue for political protest, as the funeral for P. Clodius in 52 attests. Caesar's funeral loudly proclaimed the urban *plebs'* affection for Caesar's memory and the threat under which the conspirators lived. It also secured Caesar's memory through the actions of Antonius and the rioting of the crowd.

The rioting that erupted at Caesar's funeral was a reflection of the many competing interests at stake in the confused political situation after his assassination and of the opposing views of his position in the state. The amnesty achieved at the senate meeting at the Temple of Tellus was a tottering house of cards. By ratifying Caesar's *acta,* the senate failed to condemn Caesar as a tyrant while declining to punish his murderers. A separate debate then ensued, in which it was decided that Caesar should be honored with a public funeral, even though Cicero's friend Atticus, for one, expressed the dangers to the conspirators if the man they murdered for being a tyrant was honored in this way (Cic. *Att.* 14.10.1). Caesar's funeral both reflected and exacerbated the uncertain political situation.

We are not told who was responsible for suggesting that Caesar be honored with a public funeral (*funus publicum*), which technically the state, not the family, organized and paid for.[11] There is a long list of those who may have been involved in the planning and execution of Caesar's funeral, including Caesar himself, who left instructions for his funeral in the hands of Atia, his niece and the mother of Octavius.[12] The mention of Atia in this context raises the question of whether her husband, L. Marcius Philippus (*cos.* 56), a consular who seems to have supported the conspirators' cause, could have exercised a mitigating influence over those who may have been inclined to use the funeral as a way of exalting Caesar and consequently denigrating the actions of the conspirators.[13] L. Piso, Caesar's father-in-law, took part in the reading of Caesar's will—not surprisingly since, for a time at least, Caesar's papers were in the hands of Piso's daughter and Caesar's widow, Calpurnia. According to one account, he also conducted Caesar's body into the Forum for his funeral (App. *BC* 2.143.598). There was also the consul Antonius, who delivered the *laudatio* and, according to Appian, presided over the entire celebration like the leader of a chorus (*choregos*) (more on this later in the chapter). Finally, there was the crowd that took control of the funeral at the end and performed an impromptu cremation of the body in the Forum and attacked the homes of the conspirators. It is impossible to know whether this rioting was somehow arranged in advance, or even whether it was the expectation of those involved in planning the funeral. Cicero and many later sources clearly put the blame on Antonius, as if he orchestrated the crowd's response through his own actions at the funeral. But, as I will try to show, there are reasons to believe that the violence erupted spontaneously following the *laudatio* and display of the corpse on the Rostra.

We discussed earlier how Roman funerals tended to play out in a ritual framework, consisting of a display of the corpse at home (lying in state), procession of relatives and the masks of the ancestors (*imagines*) to the Forum, display of the corpse on the Rostra, speech in praise of the deceased (*laudatio*), singing of the dirge (*nenia*), and removal of the body for burial or cremation. Caesar's funeral adhered to this basic framework, but some of the elements were modified and other new ones apparently added that made this event more theatrical and spectacular.

The funeral celebration customarily began with the preparation of the body, which was washed, anointed, and then dressed in the insignia of the highest office the deceased had achieved in life. The body was then displayed for seven days in the *atrium* of the home where the deceased had lived.[14] At the time of his death, Caesar was residing in the Domus Publica as Pontifex Maximus, but he also owned a villa across the Tiber where Cleopatra was then staying (Cic. *Att.* 15.15.2). Since only five days appear to have elapsed between his death and funeral, Caesar's body could not have been put on display in customary fashion. The unrest in the city and the condition of his body would have made such a display difficult. Some may have witnessed the conveyance of Caesar's body to his home from Pompeius' theater on the Ides of March,[15] but to others it would have remained out of view from the time it was carried home until it was dramatically unveiled on the Rostra during the funeral celebration.[16] Keeping the body out of public view in this way heightened the effect of other devices that called attention to the condition of the body on display during the funeral.

The absence of the customary period of lying in state makes it appear as though the funeral was put on hastily. The condition of the body might have precluded its display, thus shortening the period between death and funeral, but I am inclined to think that the uncertain political situation was the principal cause of this omission. The amnesty agreed upon at the Temple of Tellus failed to quell the fierce debate over the whole question of the legitimacy of Caesar's dictatorship and the validity of his *acta*. There was always the possibility that this amnesty could be revoked and Caesar still declared a tyrant. In the political contest then underway, it was not clear who would ultimately prevail. If Caesar's enemies managed to attain a position of preeminence, then the dead dictator might still be declared a tyrant and his body given the hook and thrown into the Tiber, leaving his allies in a precarious political position. A quick funeral and burial would have preserved the posthumous honors accorded Caesar and consequently placed Antonius and other Caesarians on firmer footing.

Before the procession (*pompa*) itself could begin, it was necessary to set up a bier at the place of cremation—in Caesar's case the Campus Martius next to the tomb of Julia—and to ready the Rostra (see fig. 3) for the display of the body and for the *laudatio*. A gilded shrine modeled after the Temple of Venus Genetrix was placed on the Rostra as a reminder of Caesar's divine heritage. Inside this model was a couch of ivory with coverlets of purple and gold, and at its head stood a trophy (*tropaeum* [Suet. *Jul.* 84.1]), probably a spear (cf. App. *BC* 2.146.610), holding aloft the robe Caesar was wearing when he was killed. It was customary, as Picard points out (1957, 30), to erect a trophy to mark the grave of a man who died a violent death, especially on the field of battle. But Picard argues that Caesar's divinity was the overriding factor: the ivory couch was equivalent to a *pulvinar* and the funeral a *lectisternium*.[17] Further, the model shrine prefigured the Temple of Divus Julius, which would be vowed in January 42 and dedicated in August 29 by Octavian, and the trophy was a stand-in for a statue of Caesar. That the gilded shrine was modeled on the Temple of Venus Genetrix simply shows the connection between the cult of Divus Julius and the matriarch of the Roman *gens*.

While this is a plausible interpretation, I would argue that the trophy would have had a greater impact on the audience as a military or political rather than religious symbol. The reason for this is that the idea of a model shrine and trophy was probably already part of Caesar's instructions for his funeral, but the trophy was modified after his murder to include the clothing he was wearing when he was killed. By honoring Caesar at his funeral in the manner of a soldier killed in battle, his death became the death of a warrior and his murderers the enemy. If Caesar was wearing the dress of a *triumphator* or that of a commander (*paludamentum*) when he was slain—symbols of the height of his glory—the crime of the conspirators would have been all the more heinous. Caesar's robe became a central feature of Antonius' performance later in the funeral ceremony.

Following the period of lying in state and once the bier and Rostra had been readied, the funeral proper began with the *pompa funebris*, in which it was customary for members of the deceased's household, including slaves and freedmen, as well as his relatives, friends, and *clientes* to escort the corpse to the Forum where the *laudatio* was delivered. The *pompa* was where the prestige of the deceased was most prominently on display, for the size of the procession attested to his generosity and influence as well as to the affection felt by those who were in his debt. For Caesar's funeral, a herald announced that those bringing gifts (*munera*) should travel through all the streets, without any order of precedence, so that the offering of gifts could be completed in a day (Suet. *Jul.* 84.1). This implies that the crowd on hand for Caesar's funeral was of unprecedented size. It also shows, however, that the customary "hierarchy" of precedence in the marching order of the *pompa* was at least partly abandoned, which might have encouraged the rioting that later erupted.

Suetonius adds that the body was carried into the Forum by magistrates (Suet. *Jul.* 84.3), as was generally the case in a public funeral. It is unlikely, for obvious reasons, that Brutus and Cassius and the other conspirators who held magistracies in this year participated in this procession, and, despite the amnesty decreed by the senate a few days previously and the *concordia* that was celebrated at a recent *contio*, their absence would have served as a further reminder of their role in the unsettled political situation. In a society that placed such importance on seeing its political leaders perform in public, the conspirators' invisibility could only have diminished their personal prestige and perhaps undermined the amnesty.

The funeral *pompa* followed, conducted by L. Piso, Caesar's father-in-law, along with magistrates and ex-magistrates carrying Caesar's bier. Caesar's body in all probability had been kept at Caesar's villa across the Tiber.[18] Included in the procession were musicians (*tibicini*) and actors (*scaenici artifices*), the latter hired to dress up in Caesar's triumphal garb and impersonate him. Our sources for Caesar's funeral do not mention the customary parade of funerary busts (*imagines*) that celebrated the family of the deceased. These images became much more than private icons requiring the family's homage; they were often displayed publicly at festivals, especially at the funerals of eminent men and, in the late Republic, women as well. They became symbols of achievements and triumphs of a bygone age and allowed Romans to relive their city's storied past.[19] The collection of these images at a funeral turned the event into a public celebration, not only of the men and their families who were represented but also of Rome itself, for it was in the faces of these famous men—the Scipiones, Caecilii Metelli, Aurelii Cottae, Aemilii Lepidi—that the glory of Rome's past came alive; it was their stern countenances that challenged the young men of Rome to rival the achievements of their ancestors and sustain Rome's *dignitas* (Plb. 6.53–54; cf. Sal. *Jug.* 4.5). The absence of such a parade at Caesar's funeral is especially odd considering his antiquarian interests and his own display of such *imagines* at the funeral for his aunt. This would have been an appropriate place to celebrate yet again the family lineage of which he frequently boasted. The presence of the model of the new Temple of Venus perhaps was intended as a substitute for the busts of his mortal ancestors, serving as it did as a reminder of Caesar's divine heritage. Furthermore, the actors who marched in the procession dressed as Caesar enacted the achievements of the deceased alone. In this case, the absence of *imagines* could have underscored Caesar's divinity.[20]

Once Caesar's body had been placed on the Rostra (presumably next to the model shrine of the Temple of Venus Genetrix), the stage was set for the *laudatio*. Our sources present strikingly contrasting views of the *laudatio* given by Antonius in honor of Caesar, and this has led to a continual disagreement among modern scholars. Cicero refers to this *laudatio* only twice in his writings. In a letter to Atticus dated 19 April, in which he generally mourns the unfortunate outcome of the Ides of March, he remarks: "Do you remember that you shouted that our cause was lost if he [Caesar] was given a funeral? But he was also burned in the Forum and praised with a pitiful speech, and slaves and brigands were made to attack our homes with torches."[21] In the *Second Philippic*, he claims that Antonius, in effect, lit the firebrands of the mob himself with his inflammatory *laudatio*: "That eulogy of yours was a fine piece of work, as was your excessive emotion, your incitement to anger. You, yes, you, lit those firebrands and the torches with which Caesar was cremated."[22] The second statement should be read as an attack on Antonius, who was a more dangerous enemy in October than he had been in April. The first statement is less accusatory, although it still shows that Cicero regarded the *laudatio* as an important component of Caesar's funeral and linked it closely with the mob violence that erupted, even if there was no clear cause and effect. Our later sources are no more helpful. Both Appian and Dio put speeches into the mouth of Antonius—Dio's version is especially lengthy (App. *BC* 2.144–45; Dio 44.36–49)—but, as we have noted, the later versions of these speeches may or may not accurately reflect what was actually said. Dio states that Antonius' speech was ornate and brilliant but somehow inappropriate for the occasion (Dio 44.35.4).

Suetonius' account is notable in that Antonius gave no *laudatio* at all but rather provided a commentary to a herald's recitation of the decrees passed in Caesar's honor.[23] Suetonius' version perhaps bears the marks of his own sources. Since we know that Suetonius had access to the imperial archives, especially for his earlier biographies, it is possible that his account represents the official version of events. The rivalry between Octavian and Antonius in the months immediately following Caesar's assassination centered on who would become his legitimate heir. Octavian had the advantage of being named heir in Caesar's will, while Antonius was mentioned only secondarily, if at all. But Antonius still acted as Caesar's heir on occasion in order to ingratiate himself to the veteran soldiers, whose presence in the city after Caesar's assassination contributed to the political instability (see chaps. 5 and 6). It is my contention, therefore, that Augustus may have wanted to downplay Antonius' role at Caesar's funeral, the one occasion on which he himself had been unable to perform his duties as heir. This version made its way into his memoirs and ultimately into Suetonius' text.

In Appian's account, the rather mundane theatrical elements in the *laudatio* for Caesar were heightened by Antonius' virtuoso performance. As Antonius delivered the *laudatio*, Caesar's body remained hidden. Following the *laudatio*, Appian states that Antonius stood on the Rostra as though he were on stage; he girded up his toga to allow greater freedom of movement, a direct violation of the orator's dress code, which required that the left hand hold the excess of the toga, leaving the right hand free for gesturing. Antonius, on this occasion, needed both hands free. He stood close to the bier, bent over the body, then straightened up, holding up his hands in witness to Caesar's divine birth and praising him as a deity (App. *BC* 2.146.607). And then, changing the cadence of his speech, he recited the battles fought and the victories won by Caesar and all the nations he brought within the Roman empire, lauding in particular Caesar's conquest of Gallic tribes, who three hundred years previously had sacked and burned Rome.[24] He altered his voice from clear and high to low and dirgelike. As the crowd's furor rose to a fever pitch, Antonius dramatically flung back the coverlet that clothed the body of Caesar and lifted on the end of a spear Caesar's robe,[25] torn and bloody, to show the assembled crowd, who, like a chorus, moaned in lamentation. After this the crowd chanted other lamentations, accompanied by funeral music, and Caesar's deeds and manner of death were again recited.

Appian's account differs from but is not incompatible with Suetonius'. Both mention the robe, but Suetonius has it in the gilded shrine on a trophy (as we discussed earlier), while Appian apparently has it covering Caesar's body on the bier. But whence, then, the spear? He could have gotten it from one of the soldiers in the audience, but it is more likely that the spear was part of the trophy and that Antonius simply held the trophy aloft and waved it so that all could see, since inside the shrine it would have been invisible to most in the audience.[26]

One question is whether any of this, as Appian describes it, is credible. I believe it is for two reasons. First, since Appian's account tends to be less favorable toward Cicero, we should not think that he is attempting to blacken Antonius' memory by holding him solely responsible for the violence that erupted at Caesar's funeral. Second, we have discussed the strong connection between acting and oratory, one that apparently was acknowledged by the leading practitioners of both occupations in the late Republic, although the two were regarded as clearly distinct. Cicero benefited from watching the performances of actors as a young orator in training and turned to actors for advice especially on that aspect of oratory known as *actio* or delivery (Plut. *Cic.* 5.4). Gesture, and for that matter any kind of visual aid or prop, was especially important because in practical terms it was difficult to communicate to a large crowd in the Forum with only the spoken word. A gesture such as Antonius made on this occasion or his display of Caesar's robe to the crowd communicated to them much more effectively than any words he could have uttered. The so-called Asianic style of oratory, known for excessively flowery language and metaphors, of which Antonius was known as a skilled practitioner, may have exercised especial influence in the sphere of *actio*. Antonius' performance perhaps demonstrates his "Asianist" leanings.[27]

The theatrical and spectacular nature of Caesar's funeral was heightened further by an appearance of the deceased himself. This "Caesar" stood presumably on the stage of the Rostra and began naming his enemies to whom he had granted clemency, and then uttered a refrain from a play of Pacuvius, "Oh that I should have spared these men to slay me."[28] This was presumably an actor, a mime, portraying Caesar, whose presence is our best evidence for the professionalization of the Roman aristocratic funeral. Polybius states that the *imagines* of deceased members of an aristocratic family were an important part of the funeral celebration. Those who resembled these deceased members in size and stature donned the masks and the insignia of the highest office that they had achieved and, thus attired, processed to the Forum, where they seated themselves on the Rostra and became a topic of the *laudatio*. It is not clear from Polybius' account whether the wearers of these masks were living members of the family or professional actors hired for the purpose (Plb. 6.53.6). He also makes no mention of anyone wearing a mask that represented the man whose funeral was being celebrated. We do have other evidence that, around Polybius' time in Rome, at L. Aemilius Paullus' funeral (160 BC) for instance, a professional actor could be hired to portray the deceased (Diod. 31.25.2)—a tradition that seems to have continued into the imperial period.[29] The presence of someone, whether a professional actor or member of the family, dressed as the deceased and imitating him in word and gesture was a customary part of the Roman funeral.

Suetonius' account of Caesar's funeral provides some corroboration of Appian's: he tells us that at Caesar's funeral, as I mentioned earlier, there were flute players and actors in the *pompa*. Suetonius tells us that these actors dressed as Caesar the *triumphator*, wearing the garb that Caesar had worn in his four triumphs. Apparently his fifth triumph, the one that celebrated his victory in Munda over Pompeius' sons, was not represented, perhaps an indication that the controversy over it, as a victory in a civil war, was still percolating (see chap. 2). In any event, we can imagine four Caesars marching in the funeral procession and then occupying curule chairs near the Rostra for the *laudatio*, where Antonius could punctuate certain references to Caesar's triumphs during his speech with a gesture toward the appropriate "Caesar" seated in front of him. One of these Caesars in all probability arose to name Caesar's enemies and speak the line from the tragedies of Pacuvius and Acilius. When Appian claims that "Caesar himself appeared to speak" at his funeral, we have to imagine a professional actor impersonating Caesar, transforming the funeral into a theatrical celebration. Moreover, the funerary mime's performance on the Rostra was the most overt attack against the conspirators, whose names must have been among those mentioned, and, along with the sight of Caesar's bloodied robe, stirred the crowd to a frenzy.

A final theatrical device that was used to depict Caesar at his funeral further enraged the crowd. The source again is Appian: While the crowd at the funeral was venting its sorrow, someone raised above the bier a wax image of Caesar showing all twenty-three wounds over his body and face (App. *BC* 2.147.612). The image was rotated to give all mourners an opportunity to view the representations of the wounds.[30] In Roman funerals the body was frequently on display, not only in the days before the funeral but during the procession itself. But Romans tended to show the deceased as he had looked in life, apparently preferring to remember him in that way, from the initial display of the body in clothing that showed the highest office he had achieved, to the use of actors to portray the dead man and imitate his gestures and mannerisms. From Appian's description this wax image appears to be a theatrical device of some kind, of the sort that introduced divinities into the theater (Plat. *Crat.* 425d; *Clit.* 407a). I have already noted other theatrical elements of this ceremony, but they seem to be in keeping with the spectacular nature of the evolving Roman funeral. This kind of *deus ex machina* device, however, was apparently unprecedented and perhaps hinted at Caesar's divinity. The presentation of the body in its wounded and bloodied state runs counter to this interpretation, since we might expect Caesar to be shown in a pristine state as befitted a god. But most likely this consideration was outweighed by the anger on the part of Caesar's supporters, who desired to show the enormity of the crime committed by the conspirators. They could do so with an image that showed Caesar in the state in which he had died, without the necessity of exposing the corpse itself.

This anecdote raises again the question of the credibility of Appian's account. The image of Caesar that was put on display in this unique and unprecedented fashion was made of wax and showed realistically all twenty-three wounds. This was a full-body image, not just a mask but an effigy. Such effigies are attested at Roman funerals, especially at the type known as the *funus imaginarium*, that is, a funeral with an image, although this type of funeral is not attested until much later. According to the *Historia Augusta*, Septimius Severus honored Pertinax, one of his predecessors, with a *funus imaginarium et censorinum* (*Script. Hist. Aug. Vit. Pert.* 15.1). He did so because Pertinax's body had already been buried by Didius Julianus, although it had not been accorded the customary honors for an emperor; this is presumably why Septimius honored him anew. From this account we can infer that a *funus imaginarium* took place when the body of the deceased was not available for burial—and perhaps only if it had already received the rites of burial. We do not know how common such funerals were, but we can imagine that as the empire expanded and as Romans spent more time in the provinces and perhaps died there that they could have become quite common.

In any event, whether through the tradition of the *funus imaginarium* or for some other reason, effigies of the deceased increasingly became a part of Roman funerals, especially, it seems, in the late Republic; this is something, we should remind ourselves, that Polybius does not mention. At Sulla's funeral, the women of Rome contributed such a large quantity of spices that they filled 210 litters, and there was still enough left over to construct out of frankincense and cinnamon an image of Sulla and another of a lictor (Plut. *Sull.* 38.3). If we look ahead slightly to Augustus' funeral in AD 14 we hear that the city of Rome was virtually populated with images of the deceased *princeps:* during his funeral *pompa* his body was hidden, but a wax replica in triumphal garb was visible, which was carried from the palace by the magistrates elected for the following year; a second Augustus of gold came from the Curia Julia, and a third appeared in a triumphal chariot. All three images were conveyed in his *pompa* followed by images of his ancestors. The imperial funerals of the second and third centuries may have consisted of a double ceremony in which the body of the emperor was cremated, while his wax image remained intact for a few days before it was also cremated; in the second ceremony, an eagle, a symbol of the emperor's apotheosis, was made to fly aloft while the image was consumed.[31]

If we continue to assume that Appian is correct in his description, then the question becomes, who was responsible for this device and what purpose did it serve? The "who" must be whoever made the arrangements for the funeral, but as I indicated earlier it is possible to construct a list of possible participants without knowing if it was a collective effort or if one person, say Antonius, took over preparations. Certainly from Appian's account one might expect Antonius to have been responsible since he otherwise took center stage, especially in his performance of the *laudatio*. Because many aristocrats had access to actors, sometimes in their own households, any of those involved could have been responsible.[32] The funerary mime as well as this contraption were shown immediately after the *laudatio* and in Appian's account can be read as part of the same performance. First, a mime uttered provocative lines from tragedy and named Caesar's murderers; then the victim himself appeared, graphically portraying the wounds he suffered at the hands of his enemies, and was raised aloft by a theatrical device. Appian's account, even if it is high drama, has the merit of being internally consistent.

Following the *laudatio* and display of the body, it was customary in a public funeral for the magistrates or senators to convey the body to its place of burial. In the case of Caesar's funeral, however, following Antonius' dramatic unveiling of the deceased, the crowd took control of the ritual.[33] A pyre had already been prepared in the Campus Martius, but there arose a dispute over where Caesar should be buried (Suet. *Jul.* 84.3). The *plebs* took up the body on their shoulders, a rare but not unprecedented honor,[34] and carried it to the Capitolium to cremate it there among the gods.[35] When the priests prevented this, the crowd returned to the Forum. While the people stood divided as to where Caesar should be cremated, two figures appeared and directed the crowd to place the body immediately in front of the Regia (Suet. *Jul.* 84.3) (see fig. 3). Burial within city limits was an honor reserved for only a few whose services to the state had been exemplary. In remote antiquity, P. Valerius Poplicola left such a meager estate when he died, so legend has it, that his family could not afford a funeral in keeping with his esteemed position in the state.[36] The senate decreed the expenditure of funds from the public treasury to defray the costs of the funeral and allowed him to be cremated and buried at the foot of the Velia.[37] Soon after Caesar's funeral, the people erected an altar on the spot of his cremation, which became a rallying point for his supporters and the center of cult activity for Caesar that arose under the leadership of the false grandson of Marius, Amatius. The fact that this cult arose so soon after Caesar's death is eloquent testimony to his divine status in the hearts and minds of his veterans and, it seems, a large segment of the city population.

It is worth pausing for a moment to consider one unusual aspect of the story of Caesar's impromptu cremation, namely the appearance of two figures who directed the crowd to place Caesar's body near the Regia. This anecdote appears only in Suetonius' account of Caesar's funeral.

> Lectum pro rostris in forum magistratus et honoribus functi detulerunt. quem cum pars in Capitolini Iovis cella cremare pars in curia Pompei destinaret, repente duo quidam gladiis succincti ac bina iacula gestantes ardentibus cereis succenderunt confestimque circumstantium turba virgulta arida et cum subselliis tribunalia, quicquid praeterea ad donum aderat, congessit. (Suet. *Jul.* 84.3)
>
> *[A group of magistrates and ex-magistrates carried [Caesar's] bier down into the forum, in front of the Rostra. Some in the crowd wanted to cremate his body in the Temple of Capitoline Jove, others in the Theater of Pompey. Suddenly two figures appeared, each one girded with a sword and carrying two spears; they set fire to the bier with blazing torches, and immediately the crowd of bystanders piled up dry branches, benches and seats, and whatever else was to hand as an offering.]*

This passage from Suetonius is our only authority for the sudden and timely appearance of two figures, armed with swords and carrying spears, who directed the divided crowd at Caesar's funeral to the appropriate place for the cremation of his body. Although Suetonius does not identify them as such, these figures were probably understood to be the twin sons of Zeus, Castor and Pollux, whose temple stood just to the south of where the body lay. Precisely when this story was first told and how it found its way into Suetonius' narrative is difficult to determine, but it likely developed immediately after Caesar's funeral. There was no other occasion between that event and Suetonius' time that would have encouraged the development of such a story. Only in the aftermath of Caesar's funeral, when the altar was erected on the spot of his cremation, would there be a need for such a story to explain the location of the cremation and make a claim for divine sanction.

We can pinpoint three factors that might have encouraged the development of this story. First, it must have been told in part because of the proximity of Caesar's cremation to the Temple of Castor. Second, the traditional mythology of Castor and Pollux—involving frequent epiphanies on the battlefield to aid a flagging army and their later physical presence at their own temple to announce the victory that they helped procure to those awaiting news at home[38]—might have also encouraged the development of this story. Finally, since there also exists a story of the Dioscuri appearing to announce Caesar's victory at Pharsalus (Dio 41.61.4), there was already a connection between the traditional mythology of the Dioscuri and Caesar's military victories. The story of the Dioscuri's appearance at Caesar's funeral, however it was invented and developed, shows that old myths could be recast and adapted to fit a "contemporary" context.

Further rioting ensued. A crowd of angry mourners first burned the meeting room where Caesar had been killed and then laid siege to the homes of some of the conspirators and attempted to burn them, exacting vengeance for the humiliation and murder of Caesar,[39] but domestic servants warded them off. In the mêlée that followed, the unfortunate tribune Helvius Cinna perished. Mistaken for his namesake, the praetor Cinna who had delivered a speech on the Ides of March condemning Caesar, the tribune was torn to pieces by the angry crowd (App. *BC* 2.147.613; V. Max. 9.9.1) and his head paraded on the end of a spear around Caesar's bier.

A reconsideration of the political circumstances in which Antonius found himself might shed some further light on his role in arranging Caesar's funeral and in particular in the rioting that ensued. Antonius had been left out of Caesar's will, or at least placed in a secondary position to the young Octavius; he had no troops at his disposal, while Lepidus did. At this time, he still needed the support of the senate, and in fact he adhered fairly consistently to a policy of accommodation with the conspirators during the first few weeks following Caesar's murder, supporting the amnesty and celebrating *concordia*. Even Brutus voiced his approval (Cic. *Att.* 14.8.1). Under these circumstances, it is hard to understand why he would intentionally rouse the crowd to attack the homes of the conspirators at Caesar's funeral. At the same time, the contents of Caesar's will imperiled his position as leader of the Caesarians, thus increasing the necessity of the support of the urban *plebs* and Caesar's veterans. Antonius was caught between competing interests, and perhaps he thought his best hope for political supremacy lay (in the short term at least) in attempting to accommodate both the conspirators and the urban *plebs*. His performance at Caesar's funeral was intended first and foremost to honor the memory of Caesar, and thus he acted in the manner of his heir, even though legally he had no such standing. It is possible he never intended to inflame the people against the conspirators, for he was still actively supporting the amnesty at this time, but rather he hoped only to honor Caesar's memory in a way that would please the *plebs*, veterans, and Caesar's supporters without causing undue strain on the fragile amnesty. Besides, the crowd needed no rhetoric, and perhaps no theatrics, from Antonius to rouse them, for the sight of Caesar's body and the recital of the senatorial decrees in his honor were sufficient provocation.[40] It is possible that the crowd's angry outburst went beyond what Antonius or anyone else had anticipated.

The Arrival of Amatius and the Monument in Caesar's Memory

Caesar's funeral profoundly influenced the political climate of Rome in the following months. The conspirators never again enjoyed a position of influence with the urban populace, bearing the brunt of the people's anger, which left them politically impotent and personally at risk, despite the amnesty adopted at the Temple of Tellus and Antonius' continued policy of reconciliation, a policy that was forced upon him by political circumstances. Even though the reading of Caesar's will and his funeral had succeeded in turning popular opinion against the conspirators, Antonius had failed to win over either Caesar's veterans, many of whom were still in the city, or the senate, which still favored the conspirators. It was incumbent upon him, therefore, to support the amnesty and come to terms with Caesar's murderers, for if the amnesty failed the issue would be decided by legions that Antonius did not yet have under his control.[41] His efforts to win over the senate, however, might have cost him the support of the urban *plebs*. The actions of the *plebs* demonstrated that it was no longer willing to respect deals struck within the closed walls of a senate meeting. It also perhaps confirmed that, after generations of political unrest and several years of bloody civil war, the old propaganda of fighting for the *libertas* of the senate and people was no longer enough to mobilize the majority. The *plebs* went looking for a new champion—but one that also kept alive the memory of the old. They found him first in Amatius, who established a cult in honor of Caesar, and then, after he was removed by Antonius, in Octavian, who inherited Caesar's name and sought to take his place.

By early April,[42] a Greek named Herophilus, who had taken the Latinized name of Amatius, was present in Rome.[43] He claimed to be the grandson of C. Marius, through his son and Licinia, daughter of the eminent orator L. Crassus. This made him a relative of Caesar through Marius' wife Julia.[44] Amatius had approached Cicero in May 45, claiming a special relationship to the great orator as well because of Cicero's connection to Marius, who hailed from the same hometown of Arpinum, and requesting Cicero's aid in his defense on a charge that is not stated. Cicero politely declined and encouraged him to seek out C. Caesar instead (Cic. *Att.* 12.49.2). This Amatius was apparently a man of some wealth, for after Caesar's return to Rome, following his victory over Cn. Pompeius the younger, Amatius opened his gardens to the people and entertained them there (V. Max. 9.15.1), perhaps in imitation of Caesar. Attended by a large retinue, including some women related to Caesar who were apparently convinced of his legitimacy, Amatius approached C. Octavius, Caesar's grandnephew, in the fall of 45 before Caesar's return from Spain, requesting that he be recognized as a member of Caesar's family (Nic. Dam. 14.31–32 [*FrGH* 90, F128]). Octavius put him off by suggesting that only Caesar could make such a decision. We hear later that Caesar banished him from Italy for reasons that are not known (V. Max. 9.15.1; Cic. *Att.* 14.6.1). Perhaps Caesar worried about this false Marius' apparent skill at cultivating the people's affections.

This was the man who returned to Rome upon hearing of the death of Caesar, saw to the erection of a monument in Caesar's memory, and threatened the safety of the conspirators (App. *BC* 3.2.3). Cicero claims that he was a runaway slave (Cic. *Phil.* 1.5), but Cicero often lambasted his political enemies, or those of whom he disapproved, in like terms. How did Amatius acquire such popularity? What were the mechanisms by which he gained access to the Roman people even when Roman magistrates with *imperium*, such as Brutus and Cassius, were completely blocked off? Valerius Maximus informs us that through Amatius' claim to be descended from Marius he was able to become *patronus* to many colonies of veteran soldiers, towns (*municipia*), and guilds (*collegia*) (V. Max. 9.15.1). If this is true, then the citizens of these towns and colonies, many of whom were firm allies of Caesar, could have provided Amatius with a ready-made crowd for his demonstrations, even before he arrived in Rome. Once in the city, his influence with the *collegia* would have enabled him to mobilize even more of a following.[45] If the *collegia* were the primary mechanism through which he gained access to the people, then we have to regard Amatius as another Clodius, or, perhaps better, another Sextus Cloelius (Clodius' henchman). Amatius' apparent wealth (how else could he be a *patronus*?), political skill, and influence, as well as the following that he was able to garner, indicate a man of considerable talent, but his ultimate fate—execution on the instructions of the consul Antonius—is evidence for noncitizen status.

Much of Amatius' activity centered on the makeshift monument erected in Caesar's memory on the site of his impromptu cremation. According to Suetonius, the monument, a solid column (*columna*) of Numidian marble, was nearly twenty feet high and inscribed with the words, *Parenti Patriae* ("Father of the Fatherland"). Further, the *plebs* began to regard this as a place to settle disputes and swear oaths in Caesar's name.[46] These demonstrations and the ensuing harassment of the conspirators by the *plebs* confined Brutus and Cassius to their homes (Cic. *Att.* 14.5.2). The crowd then occupied the portion of the Forum where the monument was located, between the Temple of Castor and the Regia,[47] thus taking control of Rome's political center. Also at this time, Antonius failed to thwart a conspiracy of Caesar's freedmen, and perhaps Amatius was involved.[48] News of Amatius' actions reached Cicero in Fundi before 12 April (*Expecto quid de Mario*). What he heard did not please him (Cic. *Att.* 14.7.1). About this time the conspirators fled Rome.

Amatius' growing popularity could no longer be ignored, not only because he threatened the safety of the conspirators, but also because he was beginning to encroach on Antonius' position as successor to Caesar.[49] On 13 April the consul had Amatius arrested on the orders of the senate and summarily executed, his body impaled on a hook, and presumably dragged through the streets of Rome to the steps of Gemonia and eventually hurled into the Tiber River.[50] This execution was itself ceremonial, which Antonius could use to demonstrate the fate of those who endeavored to exploit the urban crowd. In his desire to win the senate's approval, Antonius either grossly underestimated or casually dismissed the anger of the *plebs*, who seized the Forum in protest; Antonius responded by dispatching troops to clear the Forum but to little effect.[51]

The popularity of Amatius showed that there was room for others on the political scene in Rome who were loyal to Caesar's memory. Amatius' execution summoned up praise from the conspirators, but for Antonius it also removed a rival for the affection of Caesar's veterans. Not coincidentally around this time Antonius published the *contio* that he had delivered at the Temple of Tellus on 17 March, in which he praised Caesar as a most eminent man.[52] By disseminating these remarks more widely, Antonius was hoping to demonstrate his own efforts to preserve Caesar's memory. Antonius continued to play both sides of the political divide at this time as he worked to consolidate his power.

Public Demonstrations for the Conspirators

All but lost in the events honoring Caesar's memory and especially the activities of Amatius were the conspirators and their supporters, who in most cases seemed to stand idly by as Caesarians took center stage. There was, however, one demonstration apparently in support of the conspirators that took place in the theater—a further indication that the conspirators and their supporters had been all but precluded from the Forum, the more traditional venue for communicating with the people. Cicero mentions this demonstration only briefly in one of his first letters to Atticus, dated 8 April, following his departure from Rome: "I received two letters from you yesterday. From the first I learned of the theater and Publilius, good indications of popular accord. The applause for L. Cassius seemed rather funny to me" (Cic. *Att.* 14.2.1). The allusion is to the mime performance of Publilius Syrus, most likely performed at the *Ludi Megalenses*, in honor of Cybele, which traditionally ran from 4 to 10 April,[53] although it is not clear if the customary festivals were still being observed on their usual days in the calendar. Cicero provides no details about the demonstration—who or what was involved or how it came about. We do know from other instances how such demonstrations tended to play out, such as at the performance at the *Ludi Apollinares* in 59 (Cic. *Att.* 2.19.2; see also chap. 1). In that instance, the performer on stage uttered lines that were deemed relevant to the current political situation, in particular to the attempts by Caesar, Crassus, and Pompeius to control politics in Rome, and were loudly applauded. The mime of Publilius might also have included a line (or lines) that was thought to refer to the current political situation, and the audience reacted in a way (perhaps with applause or with requests to repeat the line) that Cicero (and others) interpreted as being favorable to the conspirators. The applause for L. Cassius, the brother of the conspirator, was perhaps also taken as a good sign, even though he had been supportive of Caesar, which is probably why Cicero found humor in it.

We must remember also that this festival and demonstration occurred when Amatius was most active in celebrating the memory of Caesar. If the demonstration on behalf of the conspirators was an accurate reflection of popular will, then how are we to understand the actions of Amatius in honor of Caesar? The *plebs urbana,* almost always inaccurately described in our sources as a homogenous crowd, was in fact a complex and variegated group whose composition must have varied depending on the motivation for its gathering, the political issues involved, and other such variables as time of year.[54] But at this time, early April 44, there seems to have been concurrent demonstrations occurring in the public spaces in Rome that celebrated both Caesar's memory and his assassination. The explanation for this dichotomy lies, I think, in an increasingly widening split in the *plebs urbana,* with those on one side hoping for a return to peace and stability, an admittedly ill-defined group, and those on the other bent on vengeance for Caesar's murder, comprising mostly Caesar's veterans and other ardent Caesarians, such as his freedmen. This split mirrors the political complexities of the time, as Romans attempted to weigh the dictatorship of Caesar against the actions of the conspirators.[55] In the end, this demonstration in support of the conspirators seems to have had little practical effect, for the conspirators were forced to leave the city just a few days after it occurred.

The Conspirators' Departures from Rome

I include a section on the conspirators' departures from Rome with some hesitation since so little information about them survives, particularly the departures of those who set out to govern provinces in the spring of 44. A brief discussion is warranted, however, if only because we then can establish what we do *not* know about these ceremonies. Without detailed discussions in our sources, it will be necessary to rely heavily on our discussion of departures in the first chapter.

The departure of many of the conspirators should have followed the procedures for magistrates with *imperium,* and in some cases (e.g., D. Brutus) *imperatores*, departing for their provinces. The political climate in the city, however, did not allow these procedures to be followed, which would have undermined the authority and *dignitas* of the "heroes." Once Caesar had been murdered and the crowd at his funeral had carried firebrands to the conspirators' homes, the conspirators had no choice but to leave the city quickly while maintaining as much *dignitas* as possible. A letter from D. Brutus to M. Brutus and Cassius, dated just days after Caesar's funeral, shows the conspirators in a quandary as they pondered their future.[56] The fact that the conspirators were compelled to communicate by letter shows how dangerous the streets of Rome had become. In this letter, D. Brutus described a meeting with A. Hirtius, who was acting as Antonius' representative, in which he asks for a free commission (*legatio libera*), "so that they could find an honorable pretext for departing the city." Failing that, they hoped for a province, which would also require the assistance of the consul Antonius, and this was by no means assured.

M. Brutus was under the special constraint of being *praetor urbanus*, and as such could not be absent from the city for more than ten days without a *senatus consultum* or a *lex* passed by the *comitia tributa* granting him a special dispensation (Cic. *Phil.* 2.31). Negotiations began soon after Caesar's murder (Cic. *Fam.* 11.1; *Phil.* 1.2) and continued until the conspirators finally left Rome.[57] From the evidence of Cicero's letters we can surmise some of the details of their departure and come close to pinpointing the date. The conspirators were still in Rome as late as 11 April, first mentioned as being confined to their homes and then later attested as having a meeting with Antonius.[58] Brutus surfaced in Lanuvium around 13 April.[59] From a senatorial decree on the Jews mentioned by Josephus that was confirmed on 11 April, we know that the senate met on that date (Jos. *AJ* 14.10.10). We can assume, then, that on or about that date (ca. 10 or 12 April) a *senatus consultum* was passed that allowed Brutus to depart from Rome; from Cicero's testimony we know that the proposal came from Antonius (Cic. *Phil.* 2.31). As I mentioned earlier, an honorable means for Brutus' departure was likely in the works for some time. As soon as one was found, Brutus wasted little time in leaving the city (no more than a day or two). Cicero's surprise at Brutus' sudden appearance in Lanuvium shows that Brutus had left so quickly and unexpectedly that he had no time to inform Cicero of his plans. The city was still a dangerous place for the conspirators, and Brutus would not have wanted his *profectio* to attract any undue attention.[60] D. Brutus' departure was even more significant in some ways since he was a proconsul leaving for his province. If Decimus just vanished from the city, as I expect he did, he would have hardly looked the part of the military commander departing on campaign.

It is worth noting that Brutus and Cassius later attempted to represent their willingness to relinquish their magistracies much in the same way that Cicero tried to portray his departure into exile. That is, they stated in a letter to Antonius dated 4 August that they would depart Italy for Greece "in the interests of civic harmony (*concordia*) and freedom (*libertas*)" (Cic. *Fam.* 11.3.3). We have no evidence for how they represented their departure from Rome in April, but it is possible that they made similar claims in order to cast it in the best possible light. In any event, the conspirators' departures, apparently unseen by the Roman people, were consistent with their ever diminishing public profile in the weeks after Caesar's murder. Their refusal to confront the people in the customary ceremonies that shaped political life in Rome only diminished their prestige and reduced the likelihood that other opportunities would arise.

The Demonstration at the *Parilia* and Dolabella's Response

Soon after the conspirators' departures from Rome the demonstrations on Caesar's behalf seem to have reached a peak (around the middle of April), from what we can glean from Cicero's often laconic remarks in his letters to Atticus. About this same time, several days in the Roman calendar were usually set aside for the *Ludi Ceriales* (12–19 April). This festival would have been an especially appropriate venue for demonstrations in Caesar's memory, since Caesar had recently created a new magistracy (*aediles ceriales*) to oversee it.[61] It is probable, however, that because of Amatius' demonstrations this festival was postponed for a month.[62]

The execution of Amatius and postponement of the *Ludi Ceriales* did little to quell the demonstrations in Caesar's honor. Since news of Caesar's victory at Munda arrived in Rome on the eve of the *Parilia* (21 April), the anniversary of Rome's foundation, he had increased the importance of this festival by adding games in the circus, as we mentioned earlier. Dio states that the circus games of the *Parilia* in this year were held in slight regard, meaning perhaps that no public funds were provided for their celebration; in other words, that aspect of the festival that the dictator Caesar had added for the sole purpose of celebrating his victory at Munda was not observed. A demonstration did take place at this festival in 44, stage-managed by Caesar's supporters, which found its way into Cicero's correspondence primarily because Q. Cicero *filius*—nephew both to Cicero and Atticus—shamed the family name by donning a garland in Caesar's honor.[63] Others, of course, were involved as well, but Cicero mentions only a Lamia by name, probably L. Aelius Lamia (*aed. pl.* 45).[64] Cicero singled him out because he considered Lamia a friend and ally who had supported his recall from exile (cf. Cic. *Fam.* 11.16.2; 12.29.1). Lamia's experience as aedile in the previous year made him especially suited to organize this tribute to Caesar at the *Parilia*, and perhaps Cicero regarded him as ringleader.

We can infer from a later letter of Cicero's, as well as what we know generally about this festival, how the celebration in April 44 might have played out. Cicero was not at all pleased that young Quintus had taken part in this ceremony and apparently asked his brother to find out why he had participated. He relayed to Atticus Quintus' response: "As for those who were wearing garlands, when the son of your sister was called to account by his father, he wrote back that he had worn a crown to honor Caesar, he had taken it off to mourn him; finally he says that he gladly bears censure for loving Caesar even after his death."[65] It is likely that those involved performed the ceremony, as established by Caesar in 45, with the exception of the races in the circus. If so, then they would have formed a procession from the Capitolium to the Circus, as is customary before such *ludi*, but on this occasion they donned garlands in honor of Caesar's victory and accompanied a statue of Caesar. When they arrived at the Circus, they removed the garlands and mourned the death of Caesar.[66] This event is the first indication that Caesar's memory would be preserved through the many festivals that became connected to his rise to power. We discussed earlier how Caesar made use of existing festivals for his own political gain and how scrupulously he recorded some of his actions in the *Fasti*. The celebration of the *Parilia* in April 44 demonstrates how Caesar's memory remained attached to such festivals, which complicated the conspirators' efforts to expunge it. The original purpose of this festival—to celebrate Rome's founding—seems secondary if not utterly lost amid the preservation of Caesar's memory.

The unrest in the city finally came to a head in late April, after Antonius had departed for Caesar's veteran colonies in the south, leaving in charge his colleague Dolabella, Cicero's erstwhile son-in-law. Dolabella dealt harshly with the demonstrators, making full use of the cross and the Tarpeian rock.[67] He also had Caesar's monument (*columna*) removed and let out a contract to have the space repaved. In so doing, Dolabella reclaimed the public space of the Forum, which Caesar's supporters had occupied almost continuously since his funeral. The act of clearing the area where the monument had stood was an attempt to eradicate any last traces both of the spontaneous cremation of his body and of the monument itself, which marked the spot where the cremation had taken place. Dolabella's actions, in particular his use of the Tarpeian rock, were a display of consular authority and power in the face of a recalcitrant crowd. This rock, or cliff, most likely located on the southwest corner of the Capitolium,[68] had long been symbolic of the power of the tribunes in protecting the welfare of the *plebs* against arbitrary acts of magisterial authority.[69] In the late Republic, its use became politicized as tribunes used or threatened to use it against their political enemies, but in these cases the targets still seem to be magistrates in office.[70] Dolabella, by contrast, used the Tarpeian rock as a form of punishment for the followers of Amatius and supporters of Caesar, who seem not to have posed the same kind of threat to the welfare of the people as a magistrate abusing his authority. Cicero's remark (Cic. *Att.* 14.16.2) that the lower orders of society were clearly showing their approval of Dolabella's actions might indicate the continued presence of a split in the *plebs urbana*, as one side remained more vocally Caesarian and the other more hopeful of a peaceful resolution to the crisis. In any event, Cicero was elated, called Dolabella the leader of the *optimates*, and dared to hope—in vain, as it turned out—that this would give the conspirators a chance to return to the city (Cic. *Att.* 14.16.2).

Conclusion

The ceremonies that we discussed in this chapter, from the reading of Caesar's will to Amatius' demonstrations in April, revived and celebrated Caesar's memory amidst the mourning for his loss. The power gained by the performer at the ceremonies was partly reflected from Caesar himself, whose memory was revived and celebrated and his death mourned. The theatrical nature of Caesar's funeral, partly under the direction of the consul Antonius, it seems, heightened the sense of drama and provoked the fury of the crowd that was then vented on the conspirators. Caesar's funeral is only the most noteworthy illustration of how the urban *plebs* and Caesar's veterans could play a part in directing the action at such events, forcing the political elite to become spectators. In the case of the ceremonies for Caesar's memory, the collective action of the crowd ultimately had enormous consequences for those who stood on both sides of the political contest. The conspirators were compelled to remain out of the public eye, thus missing opportunities to communicate with the people and generally engage in politics; finally they departed the city with no fanfare. Antonius, to preserve public order and the fragile amnesty, had to take drastic action against Amatius. In the end, the events discussed in this chapter turn a page in Roman history, as Amatius' death and the conspirators' departure left the stage clear for Antonius to take greater control over public affairs and for the arrival of Octavian.

5

The Arrival of Octavian and the Ascendancy of Antonius

The events surrounding Caesar's funeral and Amatius' execution did nothing to resolve the questions over Caesar's memory, beyond forcing the conspirators to abandon the city. Without Brutus and Cassius to accommodate, Antonius could focus his efforts on the consolidation of his own power through the recruitment of Caesar's veterans and laws passed in the tribal assembly. Our discussion of public ceremonial in this chapter will focus on Antonius' legislative activity as well as the highly symbolic returns of Antonius and Octavian to Rome.[1]

Antonius began to show his hand already in April, when he made public the contents of Caesar's memoranda (Cic. *Att.* 14.12.1) and then appropriated the money that Caesar had deposited at the Temple of Ops (Cic. *Att.* 14.14.5). By the end of April, Antonius began using both for his own ends. Antonius himself departed for Caesar's veteran colonies in search of military support, partly in response to D. Brutus' departure for Gaul. While Antonius was absent, Octavian arrived in the city to accept Caesar's inheritance and name, which he did with two public appearances in the Forum in Rome. As background for his arrival in the city and return to public life after Caesar's death, we will briefly describe the ceremonies in which he participated earlier in his life before his departure for Apollonia in December 45. Octavian, as we shall see, had acquired a measure of experience in the public eye mostly at Caesar's side, an experience that would help him clear his way through the thicket of Roman politics after he returned. His public declaration in a *contio* of his intentions to accept Caesar's inheritance made him the primary preserver of Caesar's memory—a defining role in the early months after his return. Finally, Antonius returned to Rome in late May, emboldened by the support of veterans, some of whom now served as his bodyguard, and initiated a series of laws in the *comitia tributa* at the beginning of June that were intended to placate these same veterans and win the support of the people, thus strengthening his political position. A further law allowed Brutus and Cassius to leave Italy. Despite the presence of Octavian in Rome, the ground was prepared for Antonius' supremacy.

Octavian's Early Career

Before we can appreciate fully the significance of Octavian's arrival in Rome following Caesar's assassination, we must consider the ceremonies early in his career so that we can gauge his public profile before his return to Rome. As we shall see, after Caesar's assassination, Octavian did not emerge chrysalis-like on the political scene in Rome. Rather he had enjoyed a public profile during Caesar's dictatorship and must have been a familiar face to the people as well as Caesar's veterans.

Octavian (born C. Octavius) was a member of an equestrian family from Velitrae, although he spent most of his early youth in the city of Rome with his mother, Atia, the niece of Julius Caesar, and stepfather, L. Marcius Philippus (*cos.* 56). His own father, C. Octavius of senatorial rank, died in 59 when Octavian was only four years old. Octavian's connection to Caesar's family was in evidence at an early age, for he made his first public appearance in his twelfth year (i.e., age eleven) (51 BC) when he delivered the *laudatio* at his grandmother's funeral, Caesar's sister, presumably standing on the Rostra in the Forum Romanum (*pro contione*) (see fig. 2).[2] He assumed the toga of manhood (*toga virilis*) four years later, when he was age fifteen (on 18 October 48 BC), taking part in the customary ceremony in the Forum.[3]

Soon after this, Octavian was elected in the gaze of the Roman people[4] to the pontifical college in place of L. Domitius Ahenobarbus, one of Caesar's staunchest enemies. Nicolaus narrates the two events (Octavian's donning of the *toga virilis* and election to the pontificate) in close order as if they happened on the same day, with Octavian moving seamlessly from one ceremony to the next. If Nicolaus' chronology is correct,[5] then Octavian's election occurred just two months after Domitius was killed at the battle of Pharsalus in August 48 (Caes. *Civ.* 3.99.5). If this chronology appears too narrow in that it might not allow sufficient time for news of Pharsalus to reach Rome and Caesar's instructions for the election to be received and carried out, we can only offer as evidence Caesar's legendary swiftness (he himself, however, did not return to Rome until September 47) and his desire not to allow vacancies in official positions to remain unfilled. He notoriously filled the consulship with a replacement (*suffectus*) on the last day of 45, so that that office would not be vacant (see chap. 2). Octavian's ceremony (or ceremonies), whether this was precisely Caesar's intention or not, would have expressed a striking change that emerged after Caesar's victory, as the young man, grandnephew of Caesar, entered manhood and took the priesthood of a member of one of Rome's oldest and most distinguished aristocratic families. We can only guess at the reaction of Domitius' friends and supporters when they witnessed the scion of a great aristocratic house replaced by a boy from Velitrae. The Roman people seem only to have been in awe.

The procedure of Octavian's election to the priesthood deserves brief mention. The priestly colleges historically controlled their membership through a procedure now known as cooptation. When a priest died, the surviving members of the college selected his replacement (on what principle, we do not know) and enrolled him in the college. Since 104 BC, ironically after the proposal of another Domitius Ahenobarbus (*cos.* 96), cooptation was abolished. The members of the college retained the right to nominate candidates, but the final choice was in the hands of a special session of the tribal assembly (with seventeen of the thirty-five tribes casting their votes).[6] Thus, Octavian, through his nomination to the pontificate, acquired the experience of standing for election in the tribal assembly.

The pontificate, moreover, conferred enormous prestige on aristocrats who achieved it, as did membership in the other three priestly colleges. The *pontifices* had the important responsibility of advising the senate concerning the proper performance of religious rituals and the propitiation of the gods following prodigies. They were also the guardians of the *libri pontificii*, archival records containing, among other things, lists of consuls and other magistrates (*fasti*) and year-by-year accounts of events in Rome (*annales*), and they saw to the regulation of the calendar. Although the Pontifex Maximus, the dictator Caesar in 48 BC, was the head of the college, he traditionally did not nominate members for election.[7] It is difficult to believe, however, that Caesar was not at least partly responsible for Octavian's nomination in 48.

Octavian's next public duty was a ceremonial office that summoned him to the center of the city, as prefect of the city during the celebration of the Latin Festival (*praefectus urbi Feriarum Latinarum*), perhaps in 47. In this capacity, Octavian ceremonially fulfilled the duties of the consuls while they were conducting the festival on the Alban mount.[8] This was not at all an unusual appointment, according to Dio (49.42.1), but he may be thinking of the imperial period. This was only a ceremonial office, without lictors or *fasces*, it seems, or other emblems of power, such as the curule chair,[9] but it afforded Octavian a visible public presence sitting atop a tribunal in the middle of the Forum (perhaps at the Temple of Castor). According to Nicolaus, some people approached Octavian for advice on legal matters (5.13), but this seems to be outside the scope of this ceremonial office. Others approached just to see the young man.

Octavian also participated in Caesar's African triumph in 46, following Caesar's triumphal chariot, presumably on horseback (Nic. Dam. 8.17), resplendent in military decorations even though he had not participated in the campaign. He also accompanied Caesar on the rounds of the temples for the customary sacrifices and to the theaters and at banquets. Finally, Caesar turned over to Octavian the management of one set of spectacles in the Greek theater, and Octavian was so assiduous in fulfilling this duty that he remained in public view even on the hottest day and consequently succumbed to illness (Nic. Dam. 9.19).

We hear little about Octavian's public life after Caesar's triumph in 46 and before his departure for Apollonia in December 45. He belatedly joined Caesar in Spain during the latter's campaign against the younger son of Pompeius Magnus and returned to Rome in advance of Caesar. He then rode out to greet Caesar upon his return from Spain and accompany him back to Rome, riding in a privileged position next to D. Brutus but behind M. Antonius, as we discussed earlier (see chap. 2). We hear no more about him, although Caesar held another triumph and games in celebration of his final victory in the fall of 45. By December, Octavian had departed for Apollonia.

Much of the above account depends to a large degree on the narrative of Nicolaus of Damascus, who was a close contemporary of the emperor Augustus and probably a witness to many of the events that he himself describes, which makes him a valuable source, although he frequently expresses his admiration for Augustus. There is some evidence of what sounds like special pleading, when Nicolaus, for instance, claims that Caesar had already made Octavian his son during his dictatorship and boasts that their relationship was close.[10] Nicolaus was at pains, it seems, to establish that Octavian was Caesar's legitimate heir and that Caesar made this clear while he was still alive. But Nicolaus himself admits, and other sources corroborate, that Octavian had to be informed that he had been named principal heir in Caesar's will (Nic. Dam. 17.48 [*FrGH* 90, F130]). Nevertheless, there is no reason to doubt the public performances in which Octavian participated, although some, like his term as *praefectus urbi Feriarum Latinarum*, might have been subject to some embellishment. Octavian apparently had some experience in the ceremonies that informed so much of political life in the late Republic and had a public profile by the time that he departed for Apollonia. The fact that Amatius approached him in the fall of 45 in Caesar's stead is some indication of how well known Octavian was. Caesar's assassination, then, did not thrust him into public life as much as it required him to return to it prematurely and under unforeseen circumstances.

Octavian's Return

In our earlier discussion of public ceremonial in the late Republic, we attempted to show that the departures and returns of military commanders in the middle and late Republic were ceremonies like triumphs, often replete with the same kind of imagery of victory and conquest. The metaphorical language of a triumph was also transferred to Cicero's return from exile, which demonstrates that the returns of famous Roman aristocrats, whether strictly speaking of a military character or not, were highly symbolic performances that often communicated political messages. We should bear this in mind as we consider the returns of Octavian and Antonius in May 44.

Octavian's return to Rome after Caesar's murder was indicative of the uncertainty of the political situation.[11] Octavian was studying in Apollonia, waiting to join Caesar on his Parthian campaign, when the first of two letters from his mother, Atia, arrived, bearing news of Caesar's assassination. This letter (likely dispatched on 15 March, or soon thereafter) beckoned Octavian to Rome with vaguely worded advice: "be a man; consider what is necessary and act; follow fortune and opportunity."[12] After taking counsel with his friends, Octavian decided to postpone a final decision about returning to Rome until he learned more of what was happening there, in particular how the people and Caesar's veterans were disposed.[13] Octavian's decision to disembark near Lupiae, south of Brundisium, is an indication of his uncertainty, caution, and even fear over how the troops in Brundisium would receive him.[14] When he arrived in Lupiae, he heard news of what was happening in Rome, the fate of the conspirators, the actions of Lepidus and Antonius, the contents of Caesar's will, including his inheritance and adoption into Caesar's family, as well as the disturbances that roiled Caesar's funeral. He received a second letter from his mother, confirming all that he had heard and importuning him again to return to Rome. A letter from his stepfather, Philippus, also arrived, urging him to forego the inheritance, refuse the name of Caesar, and lead a quiet life free of politics. This advice, which Octavian refused to heed, was consistent with Philippus' political sensibilities. Instead, according to Nicolaus, Octavian determined to succeed Caesar in both name and power and avenge his murder.[15] Our sources describe Octavian's character at this time in a variety of ways.[16] He is at once bold and cautious, decisive and wavering, reflective and opportunistic; he pushes ahead and holds back. His initial caution was dispelled by the news from Rome and then by the reception of the troops in Brundisium who received him as Caesar's son (App. *BC* 3.11.36).

Since Nicolaus' narrative breaks off at this point, we have to turn to Appian's account of Octavian's journey through Italy to Rome. He departed Brundisium with an entourage made up of Caesar's soldiers, veterans, and presumably some of Caesar's friends. It is possible that some of these friends of Caesar came from Rome to greet the young heir, act as counselors, or use him as an instrument for their own advancement. We have little evidence for the identities of those in this group before Octavian reached Rome.[17] For now, we have to assume that most who joined Octavian were those military men (officers and staff) whom Caesar had sent in advance to make preparations for the Parthian campaign and whom Octavian had already been entertaining while in Apollonia (Nic. Dam. 17.46 [*FrGH* 90, F130]). As Octavian passed through Italy on his way to Rome, Caesar's veterans rushed together to meet him in large numbers, while the citizens of many towns remained aloof (App. *BC*. 3.12.41). Appian's account might reflect the different stages of Octavian's journey, for the veteran colonies that likely would have welcomed the young Caesar were located principally in the *ager Campanus* (our sources mention Casilinum, Calatia, Volaterrae, and Capua[18]), while the first stage of his journey, presumably following the Via Appia, would have taken him past many *municipia* (e.g., Silvium, Venusia, Aquilonia, and Beneventum) that would have had less reason to receive him enthusiastically. These differing responses to Octavian's appearance along the route from Brundisium to Rome might be a further indication of the uncertainty many felt toward the political turmoil in Rome. Many of the *municipia* might have been afraid to demonstrate allegiance to any political figure without knowing the final outcome of the tumult in Rome. If civil war erupted again, backing the loser promised only suffering. Neutrality might have seemed the safest course of action.

Octavian's dismissal of many of Caesar's veterans who came to greet him on his journey to Rome (App. *BC* 3.12.41) reveals that Octavian was aware that his return was a performance that could communicate a political message; he was careful to send a message of peace rather than war. Octavian's journey on this occasion did follow the traditional route of the triumphant commander who was returning from an eastern campaign, and it was attended in much the same manner with soldiers and veterans accompanying him and some townspeople hailing him as he passed. While it is true that Octavian was a *privatus* at this time, not wearing the *paludamentum* of an *imperator* and otherwise lacking many of the accoutrements of a returning *imperator*, he was at the head of a column of veterans and soldiers winding its way from Brundisium to Rome and therefore could look the part of the *imperator*, perhaps even *triumphator*. Yet if Octavian's journey to Rome was at all reminiscent of the return of a military commander, he might have appeared more like a Sulla in 84 or Pompeius in 62 in the sense that his return occurred in an atmosphere of political confusion and trepidation, with the threat of civil war imminent, rather than the return (say) of the triumphant T. Flamininus in 194. This is why he was determined to dismiss his soldiers as he advanced.

Even if Octavian's return does not fit neatly into any of the categories of ceremony we have established—calling it a "triumphant return" is perhaps an overstatement—nonetheless, Octavian himself was apparently aware that it was a highly symbolic event, and he was careful of the kind of message that it communicated. Further, the responses of the townspeople to Octavian's passage, whether enthusiastic or aloof, were themselves a performance that communicated their allegiance in the current political struggle in Rome and had ramifications for its outcome.

Octavian's return to Rome proceeded at a measured pace, an indication of his caution as he continued to assess the support he might receive from all quarters, including Caesar's veterans, the Roman people, and the senate. We know from Cicero's letters that Octavian was in Naples on 18 April, visiting his stepfather (and presumably his mother) and paying his respects to Cicero in Puteoli on 22 April (Cic. *Att.* 14.10.3; 14.11.2; 14.12.2), at which time Cicero heard from L. Cornelius Balbus, a close ally of Caesar's, that Octavian planned to accept the inheritance (Cic. *Att.* 14.10.3), the first step in becoming heir to Caesar's name and fortune. Despite his caution in approaching an elder statesmen like Cicero, our sources present a compelling picture of an unwavering Octavian determined to accept Caesar's inheritance.

Octavian likely entered Rome around the beginning of May, at a crucial time in the ever-shifting political circumstances.[19] The mere fact of his presence in the city where the conspirators dared not go caused Cicero to shudder (*Att.* 14.12.2). Moreover, Antonius had recently put Amatius to death and then departed for Caesar's colonies to solicit the support of his veterans. Dolabella had also recently (late April) taken action to thwart demonstrations in Caesar's honor by toppling the monument in front of the Regia in the Forum and ruthlessly crushing the ensuing protests (see chap. 4). The death of Amatius and Antonius' absence from the city meant that Octavian had fewer obstacles blocking his access to the Roman people and Caesar's veterans, who, as a consequence of Dolabella's actions, had failed to preserve Caesar's memory. Octavian arrived to accept the name and inheritance of Caesar and to carry out the terms of his will, thus keeping alive his memory when it was being threatened anew. Whether Octavian planned his arrival to coincide with these events is unknown. But as we argued above, he understood his journey through Italy to be a performance with political moment, and he was likely also aware of how it affected and was affected by the larger political scene in Rome. He therefore might have timed his arrival in Rome to be of the greatest political advantage to himself.

The later tradition has Octavian arriving in Rome adorned with a celestial crown in a show of divine sanction for his undertaking. Precisely how Octavian's arrival was viewed by contemporaries is more difficult to ascertain, but the later tradition, incredible as it may sound, is not wholly without merit. When Octavian appeared at the city gate (probably the Porta Capena [see fig. 1]), an arc appeared in a cloudless sky around the sun, or the orb of the sun itself was curved in the shape of an arc, shimmering with the colors of a rainbow, as if heaven itself were crowning him.[20] On the surface, this story might appear to have been an invention of Augustus' *Memoirs*, along the lines of the tradition describing his conception by the god Apollo.[21] But there is evidence to suggest that this celestial phenomenon happened in much the same way as our tradition presents it. One scholar has argued that the phenomenon that our sources describe is, in modern terms, a halo.[22] He assumes that Octavian arrived in Rome in late April around 9 a.m.,[23] proceeding along the Via Appia from the southeast, the sun directly behind and above him (at 35°). The crowds waiting to greet him faced the sun, making it appear as though Octavian was being crowned by this halo as Velleius describes. Another suggestion is that the attested eruption of Mt. Aetna in the spring of 44 produced a veil over the sun, obscuring its light and creating this kind of celestial phenomenon.[24] In any event, we have good reason to accept the account in our sources at least in general terms, and, even if the significance of this celestial event gained retrospective importance after Augustus rose to power, it still would have provided a spectacular backdrop for Octavian's entrance into the city.

Soon after his arrival, Octavian made two appearances in the Forum. First, he approached C. Antonius (*pr.* 44), the brother of the consul, and at the praetor's tribunal publicly accepted Caesar's name and inheritance

(App. *BC* 3.14.49). Later, perhaps on the same day, Octavian delivered a speech at a *contio*, convened by L. Antonius (*tr. pl.* 44 and the other brother of the consul), where he could formally announce to the people his plans to accept Caesar's inheritance (Cic. *Att.* 14.20.5; 14.21.4; 15.2.3). As a *privatus* Octavian could address a *contio* only after being introduced by a tribune of the *plebs*, which raises the question of why L. Antonius allowed Octavian to address the people. Syme (1939, 115) avers that Octavian "persuaded" the tribune to convene the *contio*, without discussing what form this persuasion might have taken. To my knowledge only U. Gotter has proposed a politically plausible reason: perhaps L. Antonius hoped that, in the absence of the consul M. Antonius, Octavian would act as a counterpoise to Dolabella, who at the time was favoring the cause of the conspirators.[25] Lucius, however, could not have predicted how the people might react to Octavian's speech and by introducing Octavian in this way he ran the risk of affording him a public standing that he otherwise could not have obtained. If, on the other hand, we assume that Octavian's two public appearances in the Forum occurred in succession on the same day, then it is possible that the crowd, which had likely gathered to witness Octavian's appearance on the praetor's tribunal, demanded that he be allowed to address them, as we have seen crowds do on other occasions. L. Antonius could refuse the demand only at his own peril. Lucius also might have convinced himself that in accommodating Octavian he was honoring the memory of Caesar, an action that was especially prudent in the aftermath of Dolabella's ruthless suppression of the protests surrounding the death of Amatius.

We can only guess at the content of Octavian's speech. It likely contained a restatement of his intention, which he had already made public in Brundisium (according to Nicolaus), namely that he would take the name of Caesar and fulfill the obligations of Caesar's will by distributing his bequests to the people.[26] Octavian did not actually distribute this money until after his adoption was sanctioned by a law passed in the curiate assembly, scrupulously adhering to Roman custom.

In any case, Octavian gained access to the people of Rome, from whom Brutus had been barred because of his absence from the city, much to Cicero's regret. It is noteworthy, too, that Cicero received a copy of Brutus' *contio Capitolina* around the same time that he received a copy of Octavian's *contio* (*Att.* 15.1a.2). The arrival of Octavian and his speech to the people might have prompted Brutus to publish his own speech that would counterbalance that of Octavian. This is another indication of the conspirators' failure to maintain a public profile in Rome even as Caesar's heir was making appearances in the city and in the Forum.

Octavian's presence near the place of Caesar's cremation, especially following Dolabella's destruction of the monument in the dictator's memory, must have had a stirring effect on Caesar's supporters. Octavian addressed the people from an elevated position, either from the *rostra* in front of the Temple of Castor or from the Rostra built by Caesar (see fig. 3). Thus, Octavian made his first public appearance following his return to Rome, standing amid the new topography of the Forum, as initiated by the very man whose inheritance and name he was accepting. Depending on the precise location of his speech, he was either adjacent to or facing the Domus Publica where Caesar had lived and near where the people had erected a monument in his memory. Accompanied by Caesar's veterans, Octavian could have appeared as though he were restoring them to the place of Caesar's cremation, from which Dolabella had banned them in late April.[27] Near to hand stood the Basilica Julia, the remains of the Curia Hostilia, Comitium, and old Rostra, with the new Forum Julium and Temple of Venus further back. The Forum was the location of Caesar's famous renunciation of kingship at the *Lupercalia* in February and where his funeral had taken place. In fact, Caesar had been eulogized by Antonius on the Rostra itself. At the same time, Caesar's *columna* had been removed, along with many of the statues erected in his honor. The new topography of the Forum evoked the memory of Caesar, his dictatorship, and his conquests, as well as the recent efforts to eradicate that very memory. We have discussed previously how common it was for such ceremonies to draw together the remote and recent past to create a larger historical context for understanding current political issues. At this *contio*, the images of the recent past were far more prominent, owing mainly to the restructuring of the topography of the Forum. In other words, there was a "newness" to this *contio* that could only have been reaffirmed by the youthfulness of the man delivering the speech. It is impossible to state with certainty the effect this setting had on Octavian and his audience without more direct evidence, but the sight of Octavian addressing the people in the Forum would have evoked the kinds of images and ideas that Caesar's veterans cherished and the conspirators and their supporters loathed.

We discussed earlier the fortuitous timing of Octavian's arrival. Another factor that might have lured Octavian to Rome at this time was the celebration of a festival of great importance to Caesar that had been postponed from the previous month. To have one's arrival coincide with an important festival, something that Cicero did when he returned from exile, and Caesar when he returned from Spain in the fall of 45, was not at all unusual.[28] Appian tells us that, when Octavian attempted to honor Caesar by bringing his *sella* into the theater at a festival that he fails to name, he was prevented from doing so by the aedile Critonius and appealed futilely to Antonius for help.[29] Furthermore, Nicolaus adds that Octavian's attempt to display the *sella* in the theater at the *Ludi Victoriae Caesaris* (20–ca. 28 July, see chap. 6) was the second such occurrence, but he fails to mention when the first one was (Nic. Dam. 28.108 [*FrGH* 90, F130]). The only games that fit the chronology are the *Ludi Ceriales*.[30] Ceres,[31] a member of the Aventine triad, along with Liber and Libera, was also a goddess of great significance to the Roman *plebs*, and the *Ludi Ceriales* were a celebration reserved especially for them. Caesar recognized the political capital to be gained from elevating this cult to a new status by designating a special magistracy for the production of its games. Since the evidence of Cicero's letters suggests that Octavian arrived in Rome around the beginning of May, the *Ludi Ceriales* must have been postponed for about one month from their customary place in the calendar (12–19 April) until mid-May. The cause of the postponement in all probability was Amatius' demonstrations and the general unrest in the city,[32] since the celebration of this festival at its customary time would have provided Amatius another venue for further demonstrations. This solution is not without difficulties, since it requires the postponement of a festival of great importance—an unusual action, perhaps even unprecedented[33]—but so were the circumstances. First, by making his arrival coincide with this festival and second, by introducing Caesar's sella into the theater during a performance, Octavian was beginning the long process of preserving Caesar's memory, which was now irrevocably connected to many festivals on the Roman calendar, including the *Ludi Ceriales*.

Octavian's return to Rome was a flurry of events with several public appearances. Octavian's attempts to preserve Caesar's memory through his *contio* and more visibly at the *Ludi Ceriales* must have brought him more forcefully to the attention of Caesar's veterans in the city, yet he seems to have withdrawn from the public eye in the month of June. He might have been so thoroughly engaged in his preparations for the games in honor of Caesar to be held in July that he preferred to remain silent and invisible. More likely, Antonius' control of the city at this time with an armed guard gave Octavian little reassurance that he could be safe.

Antonius' Return

When Antonius returned to Rome after visiting Caesar's veteran colonies, he arrived with a column of soldiers at his command.[34] Our only source for this return is the later reflections of Cicero, who describes Antonius' return with highly charged and colorful language that all but declares the consul an enemy of the state (*hostis*).

> Then there was your return to Rome—what a disruption of the entire city! I remember Cinna, who was too powerful, then Sulla, who was a tyrant, and most recently I have seen Caesar the King. Perhaps there were weapons, but they were few and hidden. But how barbaric was this display of yours. They follow with swords drawn in a marching column. We see litters of shields being carried. These things we have gotten used to, Conscript Fathers; we are hardened by habit.[35]

Cicero, who described the departures in 58 of Gabinius and Piso in a similar fashion (see chap. 1), knew how to use such ceremonies to his rhetorical advantage. Cicero groups Antonius with Cinna, Sulla, and Caesar—despots all who marched on Rome with an armed force like an enemy of the state. But Antonius was consul, the defender of the city, and champion of *libertas*. If the image of shields conveyed on litters was not a figment of Cicero's imagination, such a display could only underscore Antonius' newly found military backing. But this also ran counter to the kind of displays customarily seen at returns of this sort. There were no spoils of war, no signs of a war concluding, but rather only of one about to begin.

Antonius himself no doubt would have advertised his return differently. He easily could have called himself Rome's savior and enumerated all the reasons to justify such an appellation. We know that he did so on two other occasions. As we discussed earlier, after the senate meeting in the Temple of Tellus, Antonius appeared before a *contio*, wearing an armored breastplate beneath his tunic, which he showed to the crowd as an indication of the peril he faced in behalf of the Republic (App. *BC* 2.130.543; see chap. 3). At a later *contio*, he called himself the guardian of the city (*custos urbis*) and described his efforts to protect Rome.[36] He could have explained his recruitment of soldiers and subsequent march on Rome in the same way: he was returning to defend the Roman people, not enslave them. D. Brutus was in Gaul mustering his forces; C. Trebonius was on his way to Asia where he soon would have access to enormous resources and manpower; M. Brutus and Cassius had fled from Rome but were still in Italy—and who could say whether they would attempt to regain their *dignitas* through force of arms? It appeared that everyone had an army except the consul who was obligated to defend the state. Cicero has cast a long shadow, and his portrayal of Antonius makes it difficult to recover Antonius' version of events.[37] But even

Cicero's distorted account demonstrates again the importance of such ceremonies, which became representations of the politicians themselves, of their character, and of their ambitions, whether this was communicated through oratory or by some other means.

Antonius' Supremacy

Politics in Rome between Octavian's arrival in May and the games in July were dominated by Antonius, as he attempted to strengthen his political position partly through the legislation passed by the popular assemblies. Since the *comitia* had come fully under the control of the dictator Caesar in recent years, we have to imagine that they still bore the stamp of his influence. The *comitia* were routine political procedure that spoke of the sovereignty of the Roman people, but they were subject to disruption in the late Republic. Antonius turned to the *comitia* after the senate became less accommodating. Moreover, the ability to convince the people to pass legislation generally brought great power and prestige, but for Antonius in particular at this time it also allowed him to emerge from under the shadow of Caesar. The laws that Antonius proposed to the people in June evince quite different political objectives than his earlier laws, which provoked the opposition of the conspirators and their supporters. First, we will review Antonius' earlier legislation before we begin our discussion of his legislation in June.

Laws passed in 44 after the Ides of March were mostly proposals of the consul, M. Antonius, and we can surmise that his brother Lucius as tribune of the *plebs* was responsible for actually bringing them before the people. In the first weeks after Caesar's assassination, Antonius was willing to work through the senate in an effort to maintain the spirit of compromise that had prevailed at the senate meeting in the Temple of Tellus on 17 March. At that meeting, not only were Caesar's *acta* confirmed, but as a consequence his assassins were granted important positions of power (e.g., D. Brutus as governor of Cisalpine Gaul). In a later meeting or series of meetings of the senate around 11 April, which must be inferred from a note in Josephus and letters of Cicero,[38] Antonius continued his policy of compromise and effected several important decrees. Brutus was granted special dispensation to be absent from Rome for more than ten days, necessitated by his position as urban praetor (Cic. *Phil.* 2.31). An agreement was reached with Sextus Pompeius, rescinding his proscription and confiscation of his property (App. *BC* 3.4.11; Dio 45.9.4). This was clearly a nod toward the conspirators and their supporters since they advocated accommodations with Sextus Pompeius (App. *BC* 2.122.514), and the conspirators (and the *boni*) continued to look (in vain as it turned out) to Sextus for leadership in the weeks after the murder.[39] The final decree that can be dated to this period allowed Antonius to acquire for himself and his consular colleague, P. Dolabella, the provinces of Macedonia (important because of the large number of troops sent there in preparation for Caesar's campaign against the Parthians and the Getae) and Syria respectively.[40]

Three other Antonian laws, Cicero argued in the following year, were passed without due regard for the auspices and had to be passed anew (Cic. *Phil.* 5.7–8, 12). All dealt with the memory of the dictator: a law abolishing the dictatorship, another allowing Antonius to found colonies for Caesar's veterans, and a third ratifying Caesar's *acta*. The law abolishing the dictatorship, marked out for especial praise by Cicero, seems nothing more than Antonius' deference to the will of the senate and the conspirators, and as such it is probably to be dated to April, when Antonius was still adhering to his policy of compromise and reconciliation. It cost Antonius nothing—he had no designs on the office—and it was welcomed by those who despised Caesar's power. It also, ostensibly at least, placed an obstacle in the path of anyone else who aspired to Caesar's position.

The law on founding colonies for Caesar's veterans, many of whom had been an obtrusive and often disruptive presence in the city since shortly after Caesar's murder, was of significance for three reasons: first, it provided these veterans with long sought after compensation for their terms of service; second, it was a lure for them to leave the city; and third, it provided Antonius with a pretext for departing Rome and journeying to southern Italy on a recruiting mission to acquire military support on the grounds that he was settling veterans in these new colonies. It must, therefore, have been included with Antonius' other laws that were passed in April. It might at first glance seem odd that the senate would approve a law that provided Antonius with such an opportunity, but in Appian's version of the *contio Capitolina,* Brutus had expressed support for such a law (*BC* 140–41.589). Furthermore, if it was passed amid the demonstrations around Caesar's altar organized by Amatius and performed by Caesar's veterans, then the senate may have felt that they had no choice but to appease the veterans in an effort to preserve order in the city.

The law ratifying Caesar's *acta* was undoubtedly the least popular in the eyes of the conspirators and their supporters, for the obvious reason that it confirmed the constitutional legality of Caesar's position and denied the notion that he was a tyrant. The amnesty struck at the Temple of Tellus, however, rested in part on the legality of Caesar's *acta,* and it is likely that Antonius would have wanted to confirm this by a *lex* as soon as possible.

Thus, this law must have been passed in April as well. Cicero also states that this law was passed not only against the auspices but also without the customary three-market-day promulgation (*trinum nundinum*) (*Phil.* 5.8).

In some of the legislation that we have discussed, in particular the laws that resulted from the meeting of the senate mentioned by Josephus (on 11 April), Antonius followed the traditional procedure for passing bills into law by sending them through the senate for its stamp of approval before introducing them to the people in the tribal assembly. It is clear from Cicero's later testimony, however, that Antonius also passed laws under inappropriate conditions, for example against the auspices or contrary to the *Lex Caecilia Didia,* which required that three market days pass between the promulgation of a law and its vote in the assembly. This period was crucial to the legislative process, during which much of the debate concerning the proposed legislation took place in *contiones*. Violations involving the taking of the auspices depended upon one's political loyalty, as M. Bibulus' attempt to thwart Caesar's legislation of 59 demonstrated.[41]

Thus far Antonius' legislation was largely accommodating to the conspirators and their supporters, but upon his return to Rome with close to six thousand soldiers in his entourage after his trip to southern Italy to visit and add to Caesar's veteran colonies, his policy abruptly changed. A meeting of the senate had been called for the Kalends of June when, rumor had it (Cic. *Att.* 14.14.4), Antonius would take Cisalpine Gaul in place of Macedonia, thus depriving the conspirator D. Brutus of his army. When many members of the senate boycotted the meeting in protest,[42] Antonius proposed his legislation directly to the tribal assembly, foregoing the customary waiting period between promulgation of a law and its vote. It is not clear, then, who would have been in Rome to participate in the vote on his legislation. Many *nobiles* fled the city soon after Caesar's assassination, including the likes of Cicero, Brutus, and Cassius, as well as L. Philippus, Octavian's stepfather, leaving mainly the urban *plebs*, Caesar's veterans, and supporters of Caesar and Antonius to cast their ballots.

Appian describes this meeting of the *comitia* in early June in a puzzling passage. First, he claims that Octavian afforded Antonius his full support, although this is unlikely. Octavian and Antonius had had their first face-to-face meeting in May, in which Antonius apparently made it clear that he did not approve of Octavian's plans to accept Caesar's inheritance (App. *BC* 3.14.49–20; cf. Vell. 2.60.3; Plut. *Ant.* 16.2–3). Further, Antonius now had the support of a contingent of Caesar's veterans after his trip to southern Italy and would have required no backing from Octavian. Perhaps Appian is confusing the reconciliation of Antonius and Octavian that took place after the latter's sponsorship of the *Ludi Victoriae Caesaris* in July (see chap. 6) and this earlier meeting of the *comitia* in June. Appian's description of this assembly only gets more confused:

> When the day for the voting arrived, the senate expected that the assembly would be called together by centuries (τὴν λοχῖτιν), but while it was dark their opponents roped off the forum and summoned the tribal assembly (τὴν φυλέτιν), which had gathered by prior arrangement. The common people, although they were irritated with Antonius, still voted in his interest because Octavian stood by the ropes and asked them to do so.[43]

This translation includes the emendation that virtually all editors accept, the transposition of τὴν φυλέτιν and τὴν λοχῖτιν. H. White in his Loeb edition defends this emendation by stating that Antonius' law could not have passed had he used the centuriate assembly, but this assertion raises the question of whether the centuriate assembly was more or less subject to manipulation than the tribal assembly. More to the point is the restriction that the centuriate assembly, because of its military origins, had to meet outside the Pomerium, usually in the Campus Martius. According to Appian, no one in Rome at the time knew which assembly would vote on Antonius' legislation. In the emended version of Appian's text, the senate "expected" the people to be summoned by centuries, but they were instead summoned by tribes. Perhaps the reason for the senate's expectation is that Antonius' legislation included proposals that dealt with matters both extra pomerial (exchange of provinces, grain commission for Brutus and Cassius), which had been in the classical Roman Republic customarily in the sphere of influence of the centuriate assembly. In the late Republic, however, the tribal assembly had begun to encroach on the centuriate assembly's sphere of influence and had begun to pass laws on the provinces, as we discussed earlier (see chap. 2). So it seems probable that the senate could have expected the centuriate assembly to be convened by Antonius in June 44 only if Caesar had established a practice that raised this expectation, and in fact, Cicero informs us, as we discussed earlier, that Caesar's law regulating the assignment of the provinces was passed in the centuriate assembly.[44] Perhaps a law that contravened it, as Antonius' law did, would also have to be passed by the same assembly. The passage in Appian is by no means conclusive—it cannot be in its confused state—but it does provide some further evidence that Caesar attempted to restore to the assemblies their traditional functions.

When the senate meeting on the Kalends of June failed, Antonius introduced legislation before the people beginning the next day.[45] We can use Cicero's comments in his letters and the *Philippics* to reconstruct the package of legislation that Antonius pushed through the public assembly (although not without some gaps).[46] Antonius succeeded in effecting an exchange of provinces, taking for himself the important province of Gaul from D. Brutus (in exchange for Macedonia) and granting to himself and P. Dolabella, who was to govern Syria, a term of five years, in contravention of the recently enacted *Lex Julia de provinciis*.[47] There had been a rumor as early as 27 or 28 April that Antonius planned such a move (Cic. *Att.* 14.14.4; cf. *Att.* 15.4.1 [dated 24 May]), and we find confirmation in a letter of Cicero's that Dolabella was appointed governor of Syria and that Cicero's legation under him would last five years (Cic. *Att.* 15.11.4 [dated 8 June]).

Also passed at this time was a *Lex Antonia agraria* that made all available public land eligible for distribution among Caesar's veterans and needy citizens, and it formed a commission, headed by L. Antonius with both M. Antonius and Dolabella as members, to see that the law was put into effect.[48] Primarily because of his trip to southern Italy in April and May and the large number of troops and veterans that were gathering in Rome in the days before the senate meeting on the Kalends of June, there had been rumors that Antonius planned some legislation in the interests of Caesar's veterans. Cicero mentions that he received a letter from L. Antonius reassuring him that he need not fear losing his estates (presumably as a result of this legislation) (Cic. *Att.* 15.12.2 [dated 10 June]). In a later letter, Cicero asks whether C. Antonius will also be a member of the commission (*Att.* 15.19.2 [dated 16 June]). Thus, we can conclude that sometime between 2 and 9 June this *lex agraria* was passed.

In a letter discussing the Buthrotian affair,[49] Cicero also mentions a law that was passed about this time concerning Caesar's *acta* (Cic. *Att.* 16.16C.2 [dated ca. 11 July]). It apparently gave the consuls, along with a commission (*cum consilio*), power to make investigations (*cognitionem dedit*) and decide on Caesar's *acta*. Nothing else is known about this law, but it is possible that it was passed in order to settle disputes concerning Caesar's *acta*, which had become a source of much controversy after the Ides of March.

In the *Philippics*, Cicero provides a modicum of information beyond what we can learn from his letters. In his effort to portray Antonius as a lawless usurper bent on absolute power, Cicero focuses on the procedure rather than the specifics of the legislation itself, demonstrating again that in Roman politics form often took precedence over content. In the *First Philippic*, Cicero remarks that Antonius ignored the senate and moved his legislation through a gathering of the *comitia tributa*, with the people themselves absent or unwilling, implying that this vote was not a true expression of popular will.[50] In other words, Antonius' legislation was not the product of consensus, but rather it was a reflection of the ongoing conflict over Caesar's memory and the status of the conspirators. Cicero makes this point in more vivid terms when he describes how he expects the assembly will appear when Antonius' legislation is put to the vote: "The Forum will be closed off; all approaches will be blocked; armed guards will be deployed in many places."[51]

In the *Second Philippic*, Cicero further attacks Antonius' legislation: "The one who would have defended Caesar's handwritten notes for his own gain overturned even those distinguished laws so that he could destroy the state. He extended the length of provincial commands; the same man, when he should have been defending Caesar's *acta*, both in public and in private, destroyed Caesar's *acta*."[52] Cicero attacked the procedure that Antonius followed because it was procedure that legitimated the consul's power and authority more so, it seems, than the substance of the legislation that he enacted. In other words, it was the public display of power that counted, and this is what Cicero was determined to subvert.

At this time, it was also imperative for Antonius to settle the question of the conspirators' future once and for all, but in a way that would not allow them an opportunity to gain any political power—or worse, gather an army. Cicero received a letter from Balbus on 2 June that told him of another meeting of the senate planned for 5 June, in which the senate would offer Brutus and Cassius a commission of the grain supply (in Asia and Sicily respectively). Cicero viewed this as an insult to the *dignitas* of the "heroes" (*Att.* 15.9.1; cf. 15.10). In a famous letter, Cicero describes a meeting with the conspirators around mid-June in Antium to decide on their course of action. Cicero advised Brutus to accept the Asiatic commission only because it would keep him safely away from Rome (*Att.* 15.11.1–2). While Cicero was offering this counsel, Cassius came in to proclaim that he would refuse the grain commission and go to Achaea instead. In the midst of Cicero's pontificating about lost opportunities on the Ides of March, Servilia, Brutus' mother, who was also present at this meeting, promised to have the commission removed from the senatorial decree. We hear no more about this and must assume that she was not successful.

If Antonius' legislative program did not adequately clarify his change in policy and his growing ambitions, then the words that he spoke at the passage of this legislation certainly did. The evidence for these words is only circumstantial, but it is weighty nonetheless. In the *Third Philippic* Cicero states:

> [Antonius] had indeed declared in a public meeting that he would guard the city, and that he would keep an army near the city until the Kalends of May. Just like the proverbial wolf guarding the sheep! Would Antonius really guard the city, or would he pillage and harass it? He further stated that he would enter the city and leave it whenever he wished. What about the fact that he stated in the presence of the Roman people, while sitting on the *rostra* of the Temple of Castor, that only the victor would survive?[53]

In this passage, Cicero appears to be recording several statements that Antonius made at one or more assemblies of Roman citizens (either *contiones* or *comitia*), one of which was held at the Temple of Castor, but the date of this event (or events) is open to question. Cicero quotes these statements again in the *Fifth Philippic:*

> Who is there who can consider M. Antonius a citizen rather than a very harsh and cruel enemy, one who sat in front of the Temple of Castor while the Roman people were listening and declared that only the victor would survive? Do you really think, senators, that he spoke more menacingly than he would have acted? What about what he dared to say in a public meeting, namely that he, after he left office, would remain near the city with an army and enter as often as he wished?[54]

The statements of Antonius that Cicero quotes in these two speeches taken together create the following composite:

1. Sitting in front of the Temple of Castor he said that only the victors would survive (3.27; 5.21).
2. He would be the guardian of Rome (3.27) and, after leaving office (5.21), would keep an army near Rome until the Kalends of May (3.27) and would come and go as he pleased.

Because the statements are bold, provocative, and seem to adumbrate civil war, Frisch assumed that there was only one *contio* and that it took place after the middle of November, when Antonius and Octavian both returned to the city with troops as their rivalry came to a head.[55] Cicero, after all, delivered the *Third Philippic* in December 44, and an argument can be made that he would have referred to a recent *contio* rather than one that had taken place several months previous. The added detail that Antonius claimed he would enter the city "after he left office" (*cum magistratu abisset*) also seems to point to a date in November, when his consular year was almost over.[56] But the fact that Antonius made some of these statements while sitting at the Temple of Castor precludes a *contio:* at a *contio* an orator must stand. It is my contention, therefore, that these statements were made on separate occasions—one of which clearly was a *contio,* as Cicero attests, but the other must not have been.

It is possible to date Antonius' first statement that "only the victor would survive" somewhat securely. In a letter dated 22 or 23 June, in the context of discussing the probability of civil war, Cicero quotes a statement of Antonius: "But our friend Cytherius [sc. Antonius] [states that] only the victor will survive."[57] If we put these sources together, the letter and the speeches, the only conclusion is that Antonius made this statement while sitting on the *rostra* of the Temple of Castor (see fig. 3) at some occasion before Cicero penned the letter to Atticus in late June.

When was this earlier statement made? An appropriate occasion would have been after Antonius' return to Rome, when the troops now at his disposal emboldened both his words and deeds. The crucial piece of evidence for dating this speech is its location and Cicero's description of Antonius, for he says that Antonius was "sitting in front of the Temple of Castor" when he uttered these words. Magistrates could be seen sitting in front of the Temple of Castor when they were presiding over the *comitia tributa* that often met in front of this temple to elect minor magistrates and vote on legislation.[58] Antonius would have had to do precisely this when he sponsored a number of laws in the first week of June.

Also at this time, Cicero was predicting civil war with Sextus Pompeius (Cic. *Att.* 14.22.), providing Antonius with an obvious target for his bellicose words. It should be noted that it was in the context of discussing the possibility of civil war with Pompeius that Cicero quoted the statement of Antonius in the letter dated 22 or 23 June. If Pompeius was not enough of a threat, there was also D. Brutus, who had by this time assumed command of his troops in Gaul and was preparing for the possibility of war (Cic. *Att.* 14.13.2 [dated 26 April]; cf. 15.4.1; 15.5.3). As part of Antonius' legislative package in June, he deprived Decimus of his province and had it conferred on himself. With his rhetoric, Antonius could have been laying the groundwork for this, even as the people were assembling to vote on this very legislation. In essence, he was declaring civil war.

Antonius' legislative program after 1 June signaled a change in his policy and his relationship with the senate and conspirators. The words that he uttered while overseeing the *comitia* that passed this legislation only reaffirmed what the legislation itself indicated. These laws settled some important political questions that arose after Caesar's murder having to do with Caesar's *acta*, Caesar's veterans, and the fate of the conspirators. Finally, the passage of this legislation demonstrated that, if Antonius controlled the assemblies, he could achieve his political objectives without recourse to the senate. This influence was so important in the larger scheme of Roman politics that Cicero attempted to undermine it by claiming that the Roman people were not in fact present when Antonius proposed his legislation, or participated only unwillingly. A tendentious argument perhaps, but one that demonstrates how the will of the people expressed at the legislative assemblies conferred power.

Conclusion

It is difficult to assess the effect of Octavian's return to Rome, spectacular though it may have been, and his initial public appearances in the Forum on the consciousness of the urban *plebs* and Caesar's veterans. (Certainly Cicero and Antonius seem dismissive.) Perhaps at this time, Caesar's murder was still too fresh and the political situation still too uncertain. Furthermore, Antonius' execution of Amatius and Dolabella's clearing of the Forum might have cowed Caesar's supporters for a time. It is best to consider Octavian's initial foray into politics at this time as the first step in a long process of introducing (or reintroducing) himself to the urban populace and of declaring his intentions to honor the terms of Caesar's will and preserve Caesar's memory. Certainly later, as we shall see in the next two chapters, Caesar's veterans lauded him for this and threw their support behind him as Caesar's rightful heir. In May and June 44, however, Antonius was the only one who could dispense practical benefits through legislation in the tribal assembly. His remarks at the Temple of Castor further clarified his ambitions, if we extract Cicero's later pejorative comments about it. With Antonius exercising his full consular authority, Octavian and the conspirators were left with few opportunities to entice the support of the people. The doors of the Curia were closed to them and the *comitia* in the hands of Antonius and Caesar's veterans. Brutus and Octavian, in the hope of drawing the gaze of the people, turned to an important ceremony of popular politics, the sponsorship of public entertainment, in order to win the acclaim of the people.

6

Politics and Public Entertainment (July 44 BC)

Following Antonius' passage of legislation at the beginning of June, the conspirators' future was more clouded than ever.[1] Returning to Rome was out of the question, but the grain commission, a feeble gesture on Antonius' part, offered no brighter prospects. The conspirators' access to the people through public ceremonial had largely been closed off, but Brutus as praetor urbanus was responsible for sponsoring the *Ludi Apollinares* in July 44. Cicero's letters and our later source tradition attest to the importance of these games to the conspirators. Brutus' failure to sponsor them would have subjected him to further humiliation,[2] but, with the presence of Caesar's veterans in Rome, the streets remained perilous. Brutus eventually acceded to Cicero's advice and decided to put on the games in his absence but still in his name (*suo nomine*) (*Att.* 15.11.2); he began preparations soon after their meeting in mid-June.[3] Later in the same month, Octavian took it upon himself to produce games in honor of Caesar's victory (*Ludi Victoriae Caesaris*), which also served as funeral games.

The focus of this chapter will be the public entertainment that was sponsored in the month of July 44 BC, and other ceremonies closely associated with it. Public entertainment in the late Republic was often a form of political communication, whether as a means for an aristocrat to demonstrate his *liberalitas* or to publicize a candidate campaigning for office. The games of July 44 had no such connection to the electoral assemblies, but political communication was all important. Brutus hoped to reconnect with the Roman people after his long absence from the city, remind them of some of the ideals that compelled the conspirators to act, and thus, in some form or fashion, reenter public life in Rome. Octavian, on the other hand, hoped to continue the process of honoring the memory of Caesar through the games that he sponsored and thereby remain in the public eye. The two sets of games with utterly incompatible messages showed that the memory of Caesar remained at the heart of the politics of this period.

Brutus' Sponsorship of the *Ludi Apollinares*

There are two points of background to Brutus' games in July 44 that are necessary to establish before we can consider Brutus' games themselves. First, the *Ludi Apollinares* became noteworthy as a venue for political demonstrations in the late Republic, although there is nothing in their origin or early history that would explain such politicization.[4] One example is the famous line of the actor Diphilus at the *Ludi Apollinares* in 59, when the First Triumvirate was attempting to take control of the politics in the city. "Because of our misfortune you are great," he uttered with reference to Pompeius.[5] The crowd cheered wildly and demanded several encores. When Caesar entered the theater on this occasion he heard only silence, while Curio the younger enjoyed great applause, especially from the fourteen rows of *equites*. This apparently induced the triumvirate to consider repealing the *Lex Roscia*, which had granted the knights the privilege of sitting in the rows immediately behind the senatorial aristocracy.[6] This law had caused controversy previously, during Cicero's consulship, when its author, L. Roscius Otho, was greeted at the theater with applause from the knights and hissing from the people; the hissing and applause became insults cast back and forth, and a riot would have ensued had the consul Cicero not quelled the tumult with a speech from the Temple of Bellona.[7]

Two years after Diphilus' celebrated line, the *Ludi Apollinares* were once again a venue for a political demonstration. In July 57, two months before Cicero's return from exile, a crowd of the urban *plebs* (*infima coacta multitudo*) disrupted the *Ludi Apollinares* at a time of severe scarcity of grain by driving from the theater the spectators who were there to enjoy the entertainment.[8] Asconius comments on these games because they were sponsored by L. Caecilius Rufus (*pr.* 57), whose home, Cicero tells us (Cic. *Mil.* 38), was once besieged by Clodius. It is not clear whether the two events were connected. It was customarily the aediles, not the praetors, who were responsible for the grain supply to the city,[9] but the crowd might have targeted Caecilius Rufus because the praetor urbanus was responsible for the general welfare of the city. Cicero tells us of several plays performed on this occasion whose lines were understood to refer to Clodius or himself, including Accius' *Brutus*, a play about the famous L. Brutus and the founding of the Republic, in which lines about king Servius Tullius were interpreted as pointing to another Tullius, namely M. Cicero.[10] This performance took place, and these lines were spoken, at the *Ludi Apollinares* in July of 57 BC, after a senatorial decree on Cicero's recall from exile was announced in the theater.

The *Ludi Apollinares* might have become politicized in this way in part from their place on the calendar—in July just before the consular elections were to be held. In fact, one likely purpose of these games, particularly by the late Republic, was to provide entertainment for Roman citizens from the municipalities who had made the journey to Rome to exercise their right to vote. Therefore, the atmosphere in the city during the *Ludi Apollinares* was highly politicized, providing, as they did, an opportunity for both current candidates and those who would not stand for another year to vie for votes.[11] Did the spectators taking their seats in the theater expect to hear actors utter lines that were politically topical? Did this make the spectators more receptive to political messages? Could such receptiveness be exploited by those sponsoring the games? These are difficult questions to answer, but Brutus' preparations for his games suggest that he hoped the audience would be.

The second point of background to the *Ludi Apollinares* concerns the memory of Caesar. Once Caesar came to power, the *Ludi Apollinares*, like many other festivals and games on the Roman calendar, became associated with Caesar's person and his victories. This festival was especially important because it was celebrated in the month of Caesar's birth. In a letter to Atticus, Cicero describes a *pompa* that included statues of Caesar and Victory in close proximity. This *pompa* was probably part of the *Ludi Apollinares* of 45 rather than the *Ludi Victoriae Caesaris* of that year, as has long been thought.[12] The presence of the statue of Victory hardly proves that these games were the *Ludi Victoriae*, since all *pompae* before circus games likely included this deity because of her importance to athletic contests.[13] There is all the more reason for the presence of Victory at the games of Apollo since they were established, according to tradition, in order to ensure victory (*victoriae ergo*) (Liv. 25.12.15; Macr. 1.17.27). In any case, the production of the *Ludi Apollinares* previous to Brutus' games was partly devoted to Caesar and his military victories.

Finally, the most recent games and festivals before Brutus' *Ludi Apollinares* were all rife with memories of Caesar: the games that celebrated his return from Spain and triumph in the fall 45; the *Feriae Latinae* in January 44; the *Lupercalia* in February; the demonstration at the *Parilia* in April; and Octavian's attempted display of Caesar's *sella* in May, probably at the postponed celebration of the *Ludi Ceriales*. When Brutus decided to sponsor the *Ludi Apollinares*, he was confronted with the challenge of being overwhelmed by Caesar's memory, both in the recently celebrated festivals and in the *Ludi Apollinares* themselves, which included Caesar's birthday within its span of days. In a sense, if Brutus hoped to achieve his political objective of being recalled to Rome, he had somehow to reclaim these games for the Republic by removing Caesar's memory.

Brutus' involvement in the preparation for these games was extensive. He traveled to Naples to confer with actors and, through the agency of friends, attempted to recruit Canutius, an actor of great fame, to participate in the stage productions that were part of the entertainment. Brutus undertook the customary expense and preparations for these games, as had become a common feature of public entertainment in the late Republic, including the procurement of large numbers of wild animals for a show. Brutus left explicit instructions that all the animals were to be used in the games and none sold or left out.[14] There is no mention in our sources about circus games, but these traditionally were included in the *Ludi Apollinares*.[15]

The best example that illustrates how Brutus attempted to reclaim the games for the Republic was his desire to produce Accius' *Brutus*—a *fabula praetexta* about the famous Brutus who drove the kings from Rome and founded the Republic and *libertas*.[16] This was a play of both personal and political importance for Brutus, for he had advertised his connection to two of the most famous tyrannicides in Roman history, L. Brutus and Servilius Ahala in 54,[17] and probably at his *contio* on the Ides of March, as we discussed earlier (App. *BC* 2.122.514; see chap. 3). Moreover, in the events leading up to the assassination of Caesar, Brutus' heritage became both a subject of graffiti and a rallying cry for opponents of Caesar's regime (App. *BC* 2.112.469; Plut. *Brut.* 9.6–7). We do not know when Accius' play was first performed, but it was restaged at the *Ludi Apollinares* in 57 (as mentioned earlier) before M. Brutus' attempted revival in the games of 44. It was a play, therefore, that already had a history of being part of the political discourse of the late Republic, and its lines topically applied to ongoing political debates—in 57, for instance, to Cicero's return from exile. Brutus may have hoped to begin a debate about the nature of Caesar's power and the political status of the men who attempted to destroy it. This was a potentially powerful tool for the conspirators, who were searching for a way to convey their political messages to the people—a difficult task without access to the public spaces of the city where political communication took place. It is not clear how effective a tragedy would have been as a vehicle for disseminating propaganda or encouraging the Roman people to reconsider the plight of the conspirators or reflect more generally upon the political situation in Rome. What is clear is that Brutus would not have gone to such lengths if he thought it futile. The famous legends from Roman history were useful points of departure or frames for even the most controversial political debates of the late Republic. They remained, it seemed, completely relevant. Most importantly for our purposes, these political discussions, whether framed by a legend from the remote Roman past or not, occurred most frequently at public ceremonies before the people.

Brutus could also reclaim the *Ludi Apollinares* for the Republic by repeating the rhetoric that the conspirators and their supporters continued to employ in defiance of Caesar's memory. We discussed earlier the display of Pompeius' statue, which occurred some time before 2 September, when Cicero delivered the First *Philippic*. We have no indication from Cicero when this took place, but a public festival seems the most likely occasion, and, considering that the memory of Pompeius was evocative of the opposition to Caesar, the *Ludi Apollinares* would have been the appropriate festival. What's more, the Theater of Pompeius was a possible venue for the *ludi scaenici* portion of this festival, and it was a place replete with statues of Pompeius. There was no better way to deny Caesar's influence and reclaim these games for the Republic than to display the statue of Caesar's great enemy, who in the rhetoric of the conspirators was developing into a symbol of Republican freedom.

Since, however, Brutus was not present himself to supervise the production of these games, he missed the many opportunities for public appearances that they provided; for instance, the *pompa circensis*, where the presiding magistrate was most visible, presumably had at its head C. Antonius, who had assumed the management of the *Ludi Apollinares* in Brutus' absence (App. *BC* 3.23.87), instead of Brutus himself. C. Antonius might also have been responsible for a change in the program: instead of the *Brutus*, Accius' *Tereus* was performed (Cic. *Att.* 16.5.1). It is not clear what, if any, symbolic value the *Tereus* would have offered for Brutus and the conspirators. If, however, Brutus was disappointed, we do not hear of it in our sources. In fact, Cicero claims he was pleased with the performance of the *Tereus*, because it was well received by its audience (Cic. *Att.* 16.2.3). Any applause was important, for it could be interpreted as a signal that the Roman people longed for Brutus' return (*Att.* 16.2.3; *Phil.* 1.36).

Appian informs us of a demonstration that took place in the theater during Brutus' games that complicates our understanding of the popular reaction to these games and hence to the cause of the conspirators. A crowd approached the theater shouting for the recall of Brutus and Cassius. When the rest of the spectators in the theater were moved to pity, another crowd rushed into the theater and stopped the show until the demands for the conspirators' recall ceased (App. *BC* 3.24.90). As an expression of popular will, this demonstration as well as the counterdemonstration are consistent with the general pattern of crowd behavior we have seen thus far in the months following Caesar's assassination. A portion of the city populace remained sympathetic to the conspirators' cause and even actively supported it, while another portion was more loyal to Caesar's memory. Appian's language makes it appear as though part of this demonstration was orchestrated from the top down, for he claims that the crowd shouting for the conspirators' recall had been paid to do so and that the spectators in the theater were manipulated to feel pity, perhaps through some kind of display or performance. When the second crowd rushed in to stop the show, the first crowd presumably was still making its demands. Appian's account implies that the stopping of the show pressured Brutus' supporters to relent. This passage is slightly puzzling, but if Appian is correct, then his account shows a ceremony being manipulated to communicate a specific message—in this case, to evoke pity for the conspirators' plight and prompt their recall. It also shows, however, that the Roman people did not always buckle under to such manipulation.

A more debilitating blow to Brutus' efforts was the advertisement of these games as beginning not on the Nones of Quinctilis but on the "Nones of July" (Cic. *Att.* 16.1.1). This reaffirmed the extraordinary honor of naming the month of Caesar's birth after him, an honor that continued to be a source of dispute between Caesarians and supporters of the conspirators. Octavian persevered in attempting to uphold these honors, especially the ones regarding Caesar's *sella* and crown, in the face of opposition from several quarters, including the consul Antonius. The oblique reference to Caesar through the announcement of the commencement of the games, on this occasion, was an obvious affront to the conspirators and frustrated Brutus' efforts to obscure Caesar's memory. Cicero was outraged, and Brutus was so upset that he sent explicit instructions for the hunt following the games to be advertised as beginning on the fourteenth of Quinctilis (Cic. *Att.* 16.4.1).

It is difficult to assess the impact of Brutus' games from such a distance. There can be no doubt that he lavished money on them. Cicero makes the claim that the Roman people expressed their true sentiments at these games, demonstrating with their applause their longing for Brutus.[18] But no matter how much acclaim was showered on Brutus—either directly or indirectly because of these games—the conspirators failed to achieve their ultimate goal of being recalled to Rome. Based on this outcome, we have to assume that the conspirators failed to communicate their message effectively. The performance of Accius' *Tereus* instead of the *Brutus*, the use of "Nones of July" to advertise the games, as well as the demonstration in the theater combined to cast a shadow over Brutus and keep Caesar's memory alive.

Antonius' *Contio*

There is a brief notice in Cicero's *First Philippic* (8) that Antonius delivered a speech at a *contio*, but its precise date and content are uncertain. It likely took place between the two sets of games (ca. 15–19 July)[19] and addressed Octavian's reported stand for a vacancy in the college of tribunes (or his support of a candidate for that office) or his request that he be allowed to display Caesar's diadem and chair at the games he was preparing to sponsor in Caesar's memory. If this is correct, this *contio* showed that a deep rift still remained between the two who professed to be heirs to Caesar, and it is no surprise that Cicero was pleased with what he read.

Cicero's remarks about this *contio* are brief. In the *First Philippic*, in the context of discussing the reasons for his return to Rome in August 44, following an aborted attempt to sail to Greece, he mentions that he received from some residents of Rhegium, a town on the toe of Italy, a copy of Antonius' speech, the contents of which pleased him so much that he considered returning to Rome (*Phil.* 1.8). He later received a copy of Brutus' and Cassius' *edictum* (manifesto) and letters from them as well asking that all ex-praetors and ex-consuls be present at a full meeting of the senate (*frequens senatus*) on 1 August. The people who conveyed these documents from Rome also reported that a settlement between Antonius and the conspirators was imminent, and the conspirators would be allowed to return to Rome.[20]

Cicero's statements have led scholars to believe that Antonius considered a rapprochement with the conspirators around this time and attributed his change of heart to popular demonstrations at Octavian's games, some of which may have included criticism of Antonius. Because Cicero mentions a *contio* in the context of this rumored settlement, it has been assumed that Antonius made some overtures to the conspirators at this *contio* or otherwise indicated a willingness to yield to their interests. In a recent article, J. Ramsey (2001) has convincingly argued that Antonius' political position was as strong as ever during the summer months, since he had acquired an armed force, and his two brothers holding magistracies were staunch allies. He had no need to turn to the senate for support. If no such settlement was imminent, whence the rumors to that effect? They were probably the result of the popular demonstrations at Brutus' games and the hopes that the conspirators and their supporters invested in the senate meeting on 1 August.

If we remove a possible settlement between Antonius and the conspirators from the political scene, then Antonius' *contio*, while pleasing to Cicero, must have addressed other issues then current. Antonius' *contio* was an intrusion on the public entertainment sponsored by Brutus and Octavian. It afforded the consul, who may have felt himself fading into the background, an opportunity to address the people and challenge an appearance of Octavian in the Forum. There are four incidents generally datable to the summer months of 44 that show Antonius' efforts to thwart the plans and diminish the standing of his young rival. First is the report that Octavian hoped to stand for the office of the tribune of the *plebs*, which had become vacant when Helvius Cinna had been killed by a mob at Caesar's funeral, but there is disagreement as to the date.[21] Antonius refused to allow it. Second, Antonius maintained his longstanding opposition to a curiate law sanctioning Octavian's adoption. Third, Antonius denied Octavian's request that he be allowed to display Caesar's chair and crown in the theater. Finally, Antonius refused to allow Octavian to speak in a judicial proceeding from an elevated position (Dio 45.7.3). The aim of Antonius' opposition to a curiate law was to prevent any kind of procedural legitimation of Octavian's adoption by a traditional political institution. The final two incidents can be interpreted similarly. Octavian claimed that he sponsored the games for Caesar due to a family obligation, as if to show that he was a full-fledged member of the Julian *gens*. On the face of it, Antonius' refusal to allow the display of Caesar's chair and crown was an attempt to diminish the prestige of these games—a sign of his contempt for his young rival. His refusal, however, might have been politically more subtle. The senatorial decree that accorded Caesar this extraordinary honor did so only for the traditional games on the Roman calendar. By refusing to allow the display of Caesar's emblems of power, Antonius asserted that Octavian's games, which had been moved to July in just this year, were not legitimate, thus in essence denying Octavian's claim of a family obligation and further separating Octavian from Caesar's family.

The last incident cited above—Antonius' refusal to allow Octavian to speak from an elevated place—also impinges upon Octavian's status as Caesar's legitimate heir. Dio tells us that when Octavian wished to speak from an elevated place at a judicial proceeding on some matter, as he had become accustomed under Caesar, Antonius would not allow it, and he further had his lictors forcibly remove Octavian from the Forum (Dio 45.7.3). In response, Octavian avoided the Forum, a dramatic display of the personal insults and indignities that he had suffered at the consul's hands. The precise circumstances surrounding this incident are unknown as is its date; perhaps we should understand as the context the lawsuits against Caesar's estate, which, according to Appian, occurred about this time (*BC* 3.22.80–82). Dio narrates this incident closely with the one involving Caesar's *sella,* but his account of the summer months of 44 is admittedly confused. Since it is unlikely that Octavian could have avoided the Forum during the games that he was sponsoring in honor of Caesar's victory (20–ca. 28 July), his salient absence must have occurred before the games began or after they were over. In any event, Antonius' removal of Octavian underscored the differences in their political status and power—the one a magistrate with *imperium,* the other a *privatus*—as well as their difference in age. Yet by denying Octavian a privilege once accorded by Caesar, Antonius was also asserting Octavian's feeble claim on membership in Caesar's family.

Any or all of these issues could have formed the content of Antonius' *contio,* but the issue that would have touched Cicero most deeply was Antonius' refusal to allow Octavian to display Caesar's chair and diadem. In an earlier incident, Cicero congratulated the tribunes for a job well done concerning Caesar's chair (*Att.* 15.3.2), although admittedly the details of this incident are unknown. In any case, Antonius' *contio* would have put Octavian on the defensive on the eve of his games, which was probably Antonius' objective. The evidence of a rift between Antonius and Octavian was perhaps enough to please Cicero.

Octavian's Sponsorship of the *Ludi Victoriae Caesaris*

While Brutus and Cassius formed the focus of Cicero's thoughts during the summer months of 44, Octavian was still on his mind, although we know little of his actions during this time. He was presumably making preparations for his own games since we know that he first conceived of the idea in May and had already chosen his assistants.[22] His decision to put on games in honor of Caesar perhaps came as a result of his own failed attempt to display the *sella* and diadem at the *Ludi Ceriales* in May. In one letter, Cicero expresses his belief that Octavian seemed to be well disposed to the conspirators but still could not be trusted (Cic. *Att.* 15.12.2). We remarked earlier that Octavian seems to have dropped out of sight after his arrival in Rome in May and his first public appearances in the Forum. The rift between Antonius and Octavian as well as Octavian's forcible removal or absence from the Forum in the days leading up to his games kept him out of the public eye and perhaps diminished his standing. These games thrust him back into public view in dramatic fashion.

Octavian's games took place from 20–ca. 28 July[23] and were associated with a festival honoring Caesar's patron deity and the divine matriarch of the Julian *gens*, Venus Genetrix. Many of the details of Octavian's production of these games, such as the types of contests held, have been lost in our sources, which tend to focus primarily on the appearance of a comet that was later interpreted to be a sign of Caesar's apotheosis. We will consider first the origin of these games, since this has a bearing on the presentation and reception of Octavian's games, before we discuss other features for which we have some evidence.

These games had been established by Caesar and celebrated for the first time on the last day of his triumph (26 September 46); at that time, they combined a *munus* in honor of his daughter Julia with *ludi* that celebrated his conquest of Gaul and other military achievements—all within the context of the dedication of a temple to Venus. It was clearly a performance devoted to the celebration of his family, which may have encouraged Octavian to use these games in order to call attention to his adoption. It has long been held that these games were moved to late July in the year 45 so that they would occur in the month of Caesar's birth, and at that time they were renamed the *Ludi Victoriae Caesaris*.[24] The evidence for the change of date, from September to July in 45, is the letter of Cicero (discussed earlier) in which he makes an oblique reference to Caesar and Victory, stating that during a festival (which Cicero fails to name) the people withheld their applause even from a statue of Victory because of her undesirable neighbor (*malum vicinum*) (Cic. *Att.* 13.44.1). If Ramsey and Licht are correct in their conclusion that Cicero was referring in this letter to the *Ludi Apollinares* in July 45 and not the *Ludi Victoriae Caesaris*, this can only mean that the games in honor of Venus were not moved to July until 44 and, most importantly, that Octavian himself must have been responsible for this change. The reasons for it are not hard to find. Quinctilis was the month of Caesar's birth, the name of which had recently been changed to July as one of his extraordinary honors (App. *BC* 2.106.443; Dio 44.5.2). Octavian also may have discovered Brutus' plans to reclaim the *Ludi Apollinares* by putting on a production of Accius' *Brutus* and otherwise degrade Caesar's memory. By September, when the festival of Venus Genetrix was scheduled to be held, Octavian would have lost the opportunity to "trump" Brutus' games and fashion his public image as Caesar's rightful heir.

With his sponsorship of these games Octavian publicly declared his desire to preserve Caesar's memory. Both Suetonius and Dio state that Octavian sponsored the games in honor of Venus Genetrix when no one else dared—not even those who had been empowered to do so.[25] In the face of Antonius' repeated assaults against him in the days leading up to these games, Octavian's willingness to sponsor them is an indication of his obdurate boldness. Dio also stated that the circus games at the *Parilia* were neglected, although, as we have seen, a demonstration in Caesar's honor did take place. If we add to this Brutus' recently completed games through which he at least attempted to reclaim a place in the political power structure at Rome, and that Antonius was occupied in establishing his own image apart from Caesar, then it is possible to state that Caesar's memory was being neglected. Octavian's second reason for sponsoring these games was to place his adoption on firmer ground by demonstrating that he was a member of Caesar's family. In fact, Octavian stated publicly that a family obligation required him to organize the *Ludi Victoriae Caesaris* (Dio 45.6.4), as if to show that he intended to act as Caesar's legitimate heir, even though he only enjoyed the sanction of Caesar's will, a still somewhat tenuous link to Caesar's family. Antonius had continued to thwart Octavian's efforts to have his adoption legally sanctioned (as we mentioned earlier), leaving Octavian's legal status as Caesar's heir in question (Dio 45.5.3–4).

Octavian previously had preserved Caesar's memory by acknowledging the extraordinary honors that the senate decreed to Caesar, especially the display of Caesar's chair and crown at all festival games. Octavian's first attempt to bring these emblems of Caesar's power into the theater in May was opposed by the aedile Critonius, as we discussed earlier (see chap. 5). Octavian, perhaps at a *contio*, asked Antonius for permission to do the same at his games in July but again was denied.[26] Antonius may have miscalculated the strong feelings his refusal would arouse, whatever those reasons might have been, for when Octavian entered the theater after failing in his efforts, he was roundly applauded by the spectators, both the people and Caesar's veterans, who were angry that he was not allowed to honor Caesar's memory in this way (Nic. Dam. 28.108 [*FrGH* 90, F13])). Their continued applause for Octavian throughout the performance is the best evidence for his popularity as a result of the sponsorship of these games.

These games were made more memorable by the appearance of a comet during daylight hours in the northern sky for seven days. Comets were traditionally believed to be the harbingers of misfortune and evil.[27] This comet's short life span (the shortest of any comet on record, according to Pliny [*Nat.* 2.90]) might have encouraged the belief that this was an unusual occurrence with special significance. Later when Octavian erected a statue of Caesar in the Temple of Venus with a star above its head, the comet was taken to be a sign of his apotheosis.[28] The erection of this statue is significant for two reasons. First, it initiated a process whereby Caesar's statues, many of which had fallen soon after his assassination, were replaced. Second, it was a bold statement confirming Caesar's divinity. The metamorphosis of the comet that had appeared in the sky into a star that appeared above the head of Caesar is also significant. There was a long tradition of belief in the divinity of stars, and this image was used in Hellenistic art to signify the divinity and immortality of a king.[29] The star had already appeared on Roman coins before Caesar's comet flew across the sky, although the honoree was usually a god, not a mortal.[30] An issue of P. Sepullius Macer offered an innovation, for it shows a star behind Caesar's head on the obverse and Venus and Victoria on the reverse.[31] The *communis opinio* holds that this was a posthumous issue that served Octavian's propaganda.[32] Weinstock argues rather that this star saw its origin either in the star of Venus—which soon became Caesar's star—or, more likely, that it owed its origin to Hellenistic times and was symbolic of the divine ruler.[33] Under this interpretation, the comet was a fortuitous occurrence that Octavian exploited in order to bring the symbol of the star—already current—into greater prominence. The meaning of the star before the appearance of the comet is debatable; afterwards there can be little doubt.[34] Thus Octavian made clear his position on the subject of Caesar's divinity.

But all of this came later. The effect of Octavian's games—the comet notwithstanding—on the politics of these crucial months is no easier to assess than that of Brutus' games, mainly because we are so poorly informed about the details. Aside from the brief mention of the applause for Octavian in the theater, the appearance of the comet dominates the historical tradition. But Octavian's reception in the theater shows that Caesar's veterans favored those who preserved Caesar's memory, and therefore the games themselves would also have appealed to this segment of the Roman populace. From this vantage point, Octavian's games were completely integrated within the larger political context that included appeals to Caesar's veterans, from Brutus' and Antonius' *contiones* after the Ides of March to Antonius' legislation in June, which ensured that many of these same veterans would not lose their land allotments as a result of Caesar's death. As we discussed earlier, Octavian's great disadvantage politically was that he was precluded from the assemblies and the senate. Public ceremonial, such as his *contio* and these games, was the only means through which he could communicate with the Roman people and Caesar's veterans and also acquire a measure of political prestige—but he remained secondary to Antonius.

The Reconciliation of Octavian and Antonius on the Capitolium

Antonius was dismissive of Octavian when they first met in Pompeius' gardens in May. Octavian remained silent and invisible for the month of June, perhaps in fear for his life as Antonius exercised greater authority over politics in the city. If anything, earlier in July, the rift between Octavian and Antonius only widened: Antonius refused to allow Octavian to speak from an elevated place and drove him from the Forum. Octavian responded by remaining out of public view. We do not know how long his absence from public life persisted, but it ended in public fashion first with the games he sponsored in late July and then through a reconciliation with Antonius at the end of July or the beginning of August. Why did Antonius agree to reconcile with Octavian so publicly after treating him so dismissively? Did Antonius fear his young rival's growing popularity and power? Was he responding to the applause of Caesar's veterans for Octavian in the theater? The most probable scenario is that Antonius had little choice in the matter, for Caesar's veterans demanded this reconciliation and he could refuse only at his peril.

Several events took place around the time of Octavian's games, some of which are impossible to date with certainty. In mid- to late July, Brutus and Cassius published an edict and dispatched letters to consulars and ex-praetors requesting that they attend a senate meeting on the Kalends of August, when Antonius, rumor had it, would yield, a compromise would be reached, and the conspirators finally allowed to return to the city.[35] In their edict, they outlined their plans to abdicate their offices and retire into voluntary exile "in the interests of concord and freedom" (Cic. *Fam.* 11.3.3 [*concordiae ac libertatis causa*]; Vell. 2.62.3). The contents of this *edictum*, directed mainly at Antonius (Cic. *Fam.* 11.3.1), was read out to the people, probably at a *contio* in the Forum,[36] and thus served as a way for the conspirators to communicate with the Roman people, replacing the *contio* proper. At the meeting of the senate on 1 August, L. Calpurnius Piso, Caesar's father-in-law and moderate Caesarian, criticized Antonius. The precise nature of Piso's criticism is unknown, but it evoked Brutus' profuse praise (Cic. *Att.* 16.7.5, 7).

At some point after Octavian's games, Caesar's disenchanted veterans, troubled by the continued hostility between Antonius and Octavian, demanded that the two reconcile, and they arranged a meeting on the Capitolium.[37] Nicolaus describes the resentment of the soldiers at Antonius' treatment of Octavian, especially after the *Ludi Victoriae Caesaris*. The soldiers first approached Antonius and requested that he meet with Caesar's heir. When Antonius agreed, they asked that he lead them to the Temple of Jupiter on the Capitolium. The soldiers then proceeded to Octavian's house and offered to escort him to the Capitolium for the meeting.[38] Octavian's initial trepidation was soon dispelled by the soldiers' good wishes, and he quickly agreed. The soldiers escorted him through the Forum to the Capitolium where he met with Antonius and was reconciled—a reconciliation that was perhaps confirmed by a sacrifice in the temple.

Antonius had something to gain from this performance, too, namely the favor of the soldiers, and, although these soldiers declared their support for both Octavian and Antonius, it was only Octavian whom they regarded as Caesar's true heir. When Caesar's soldiers gathered at Octavian's house and were trying to convince him of their good intentions, one of them shouted out that Octavian should take courage and realize that they, the soldiers, were all his κληρονομία—his "inheritance." Now, whether or not this actually took place as Nicolaus describes it, we cannot be sure. We can be fairly certain that this is how Augustus himself wanted this event to be remembered, which means that he viewed the reconciliation as a significant event in his career, when Caesar's military power began to pass into his hands. But if this incident did happen as Nicolaus describes it, then it shows that Caesar's veterans in the city were willing to regard Octavian as Caesar's legitimate heir without the official sanction of the curiate assembly.

This reconciliation followed the pattern of other reconciliations of important political figures, of a kind that had occurred earlier in Roman history, although in this instance, the unequal political standing of the two principals—one a consul, the other a *privatus*—was unusual. The sight of soldiers, however, accompanying first Antonius and then Octavian through the Forum to the Capitolium was striking. In order to understand the importance of this ceremony, we must consider first other such reconciliations.

The Roman Republic owed its vitality in part to political competition and rivalry, essential aspects of the Roman aristocratic ethos. Such competition could also be dangerous and destructive, if taken to extremes. For this reason, it was necessary at critical times in Roman history for rivals to lay aside their differences in the interests of a higher good, the stability and harmony of the state.[39] Such reconciliations are frequently attested in our sources. In the midst of the Second Punic War, M. Livius Salinator and C. Claudius Nero (*coss.* 207), who had remained political enemies since the testimony of the latter had been instrumental in sending the former into exile in 219, initially put off reconciliation even though they were about to engage the Carthaginians in battle. The senate insisted that they reconcile in the interests of civic harmony (Liv. 27.35.5–9; V. Max. 7.2.6a). The political situation was less critical in 179 when the two censors for that year, M. Aemilius Lepidus and M. Fulvius Nobilior, longstanding political enemies, were compelled to undertake a public reconciliation. After taking their curule chairs on the Campus Martius at the beginning of their censorship, Q. Caecilius Metellus, accompanied by a large crowd, approached and asked that they put their differences aside. The two men aired their grievances against each other, shook hands, and the crowd escorted them to the Capitolium.[40] This was a reconciliation through public acclamation, which shows that powerful leaders could accede to the demands of the people. Perhaps the most famous of such reconciliations occurred in 70 when the consuls for that year, Cn. Pompeius and M. Crassus, who had clashed throughout their term of office, finally came to terms (Plut. *Crass.* 12.4–5; cf. *Pomp.* 23.1–3). While speaking before a *contio* in the Forum, the two consuls were interrupted by C. Onatius Aurelius, a member of the equestrian order, who leaped onto the platform and related a dream in which Jupiter appeared to urge the two rivals to reconcile. Crassus made the first move by clasping Pompeius' hand and addressing him personally. He then turned to the people with words of praise for Pompeius. With the civil war of Sulla and Marius still a vivid memory, this reconciliation took on greater significance. Similar memories of the more recent civil war between Caesar and Pompeius, and the fear that a fragmentation of the Caesarians might lead to a loss of their benefits, might have prompted the soldiers to urge the reconciliation of Antonius and Octavian.

There are two fundamental differences between the processions described here and the one enjoyed by Antonius and Octavian. The first was the relative status of the two participants. In general, other reconciliations involved aristocrats of roughly equal standing, in terms of political power, prestige, and age. It is possible that the reconciliation of Octavian and Antonius had an equalizing effect (if only temporarily) whereby Octavian matched or came close to matching the status of Antonius.

The second major difference was the presence of the soldiers. In our tradition, the soldiers orchestrated this ceremony, demanding the presence first of Antonius and then of Octavian and compelling them to reconcile. The mere presence of soldiers within the Pomerium was unusual; the leadership that these soldiers displayed on this occasion, their efforts to effect a reconciliation, also would have raised the issue of the distribution of political power. Where was the senate in all of this? The location and movement of this ceremony is also potentially significant. The soldiers accompanied both men to the Capitolium in separate processions that went through the Forum

Romanum. Octavian and Antonius marched through the Forum at the head of an army going to the Capitolium to perform a sacrifice. To those watching, did this reconciliation look like a triumph? We lack the direct evidence to answer this question with authority. Without the other visual symbols of a triumph, such as the dress and *quadriga*, it seems unlikely. We discussed earlier, however, how Cicero viewed his return from exile as triumphal in character, even though his procession to the Capitolium also lacked the customary accoutrements of a triumph (see chap. 1). Cicero also enjoyed a similar kind of procession led by a crowd of the urban *plebs* after news of the battle of Mutina reached Rome in April 43. Again, he describes this procession as a kind of triumph.[41] What we can say is that such events were highly symbolic, and this particular performance gave the participants a chance to demonstrate that they had acquired the favor of Caesar's veterans. As I suggested earlier, the ability to control the crowd, whether in its civilian or military capacity, was a sign of authority and prestige. This reconciliation, whether precisely triumphal or not, was an enactment of such authority; for Octavian this was critical.

It is impossible to overstate the importance of the participation of the soldiers in this ceremony. Indeed, that the soldiers initiated the procession, not unlike the mob at Clodius' or Caesar's funerals, shows how a public performance, once the sole province of the aristocracy, was subsumed under the leadership of an element of the Roman populace, providing them with the means and opportunity to influence politics. Octavian, of course, had a hand in preparing the way for this to happen by boldly claiming his inheritance in a *contio*. In other words, Octavian used his progress through Italy and return to the city in April and May 44 and the games in July to present himself in a way that appealed to the soldiers, and the soldiers took it from there. Even if we conclude, as other scholars have done,[42] that it was in fact Antonius or Octavian (or perhaps both) who actually arranged this ceremony, and the army was only a willing participant, this event still demonstrates the importance of popular participation in the politics of this period. Antonius and Octavian were willing to put aside their differences (only temporarily, as it turned out) as the result of collective action: they had to demonstrate that they were acceding to the will of the army.

Octavian's public image was still incompletely formed, but the two ceremonies in which he participated during the summer of 44—first the games in honor of Caesar's victory and then his procession and reconciliation with Antonius—brought him into public view in dramatic fashion and helped cement his ties to Caesar and Caesar's veterans. Antonius' willingness to meet Octavian on equal terms on that occasion shows that he was now compelled to take his young rival more seriously than he had at their first meeting in May. This heightened Octavian's public standing, which in turn enabled him to visit Caesar's veteran colonies in the autumn and collect a following that for a time put Antonius on the defensive and garnered the praise of Cicero. The veterans' affection for Octavian also forced Antonius to step up his efforts to present himself as Caesar's true heir. Before their departure for Gaul in November, the rivalry between Antonius and Octavian intensified.

Conclusion

The games in July 44 are evidence that such ceremonies still had a place in the politics of Rome in our period, but Caesar cast a long shadow, and it was impossible in the end, it seems, for Brutus to eradicate Caesar's memory from his production of the *Ludi Apollinares*. His absence from Rome was equally debilitating to his cause, for he was unable to be a visible presence during the games, nor could he ensure the presentation of Accius' *Brutus* or the proper advertisement of the games as beginning on the Nones of Quinctilis. Octavian's task in a sense was simpler, since he endeavored to preserve and honor Caesar's memory. The success or failure of these games cannot be assessed from the meager evidence in our sources, but only in the larger historical context. What happened next—the conspirators' departure from Italy, the reconciliation of Antonius and Octavian—indicate that these games were at least a part of a process that was beginning to become more clearly defined. With all political avenues blocked, the conspirators' only hope now was restoration through military force. Octavian, on the other hand, in the ceremony of reconciliation was treated as Antonius' equal. The soldiers' claim to be Octavian's inheritance, and in fact the entire procession to the Capitolium, anticipated in one ceremony what Octavian hoped to achieve through the curiate assembly: the official sanction of his adoption in Caesar's will. In one important respect, through the efforts of Caesar's veterans, Octavian had become Caesar's true heir.

7

Rivalry and Reconciliation

Ceremony and Politics from Autumn 44 to the Formation of the Second Triumvirate

This chapter covers a much longer period than the four previous, about sixteen months from the failure of the reconciliation of Antonius and Octavian at the end of July to the formation of the Second Triumvirate, the coalition of M. Aemilius Lepidus, Antonius, and Octavian that would dominate Roman politics until the battle of Actium. This period was marked first by the rivalry between Antonius and Octavian, which played out in *contiones* before the people, the supremacy of the senate in the early part of 43 BC in the absence of the two rivals following their departure to Gaul, and the return of a victorious Octavian in the summer of 43 after the battle of Mutina, his election to the consulship, and the trial and conviction of the conspirators in absentia. We will be a witness to the development of Octavian's political image as he successfully recruited legions to thwart Antonius' plans. Many in the senate threw their support behind him and, in the first senate meeting of 43, following the investiture of the new consuls, Hirtius and Pansa, acting on Cicero's proposal, decreed him an official command with praetorian status and followed this with the rare honor of an equestrian statue. Octavian's role in aiding the consular armies and rescuing D. Brutus at Mutina strengthened his position and enabled him to return to Rome to stand for the consulship.

Antonius' *Contio* at the Temple of Castor

The autumn of 44 was marked by the growing rivalry between Octavian and Antonius following the failure of their reconciliation and the return of Cicero to active political life with the delivery of the *First Philippic* at the senate meeting on 19 September and the publication of the *Second Philippic* in late October.[1] Cicero's rhetorical sallies against Antonius in the September meeting, which followed L. Piso's attack on Antonius in the August meeting, were more focused and demonstrated a stronger and more eloquent opposition in the senate than Antonius had heretofore faced. But Antonius still had his supporters in the senate, and others favored peace and accommodation over another bloody civil war. Part of Antonius' strategy was to turn to Caesar's veterans and the city populace. He did so in two ways, first, by representing himself as Caesar's heir, which also had the consequence of challenging Octavian's claims to this title; and second, by assailing the conspirators anew. Thus, he endeavored to preserve Caesar's memory, which was the most important lesson he learned from the outcome of events in the summer months.

As we have discussed in previous chapters, Octavian, since his arrival in Rome in early May, continued to keep Caesar's memory alive, which increased his popularity among Caesar's veterans through his support for the decrees passed by the senate that had conferred extraordinary honors on Caesar (as discussed in chaps. 5 and 6). Antonius began to follow suit in September.[2] First, we hear that through legislation passed by the *comitia tributa* he added a fifth day in Caesar's honor to the *Ludi Romani*—probably to the portion of the festival devoted to games in the circus—extending the festival as a whole until 19 September.[3] Through this legislation, the precise date of which is uncertain, Antonius responded in part to Octavian's games in July. In other ways, too, Antonius emulated the young Caesar. Soon after the *Ludi Victoriae Caesaris,* Octavian had erected a statue of Caesar in the Forum Julium, in the Temple of Venus Genetrix, with a star above its head, as we discussed earlier (see chap. 6). Two months later, Antonius erected his own statue to Caesar on the Rostra with the inscription, "To our father, for his great services" (*Parenti optime merito*),[4] thus following the precedents established by Caesar's veterans and his young heir and at the same time invoking one of the extraordinary honors that the senate had granted to Caesar—the title of *Parens Patriae*.[5] The public and political importance of this monument and inscription are clear, but they were also meaningful on a personal level, for Antonius was again participating in the process that he himself had initiated at Caesar's funeral, that Amatius and the veterans had continued in April, and that Octavian also continued after his arrival, of preserving and celebrating Caesar's memory. It was the obligation above all of an heir to carry out this process, as Octavian well knew, and it is likely that Antonius erected this statue also as a way of showing his personal relationship to Caesar.[6]

On October 2, soon after the erection of this statue, the tribune Ti. Cannutius introduced the consul Antonius at a *contio* at the Temple of Castor. We can infer from Antonius' criticism of Cannutius that he should be included among Antonius' political enemies.[7] Does this fact have a bearing on how we understand Cannutius' role in this *contio*? That the consul's political enemy convened this *contio*, and not a political ally or even Antonius himself, probably indicates that this *contio* was not of Antonius' own choosing and might mean that he was responding to a specific request or facing a hostile crowd. Moreover, Cicero's *First Philippic* might have put Antonius on the defensive. We discussed earlier (see chap. 5) some remarks that Antonius made from this location probably in June when he was presiding over the *comitia* that passed his legislation. At that time, the Temple of Castor was the backdrop for his statements that spoke of war. At the *contio* in October, he railed against the conspirators—a manifest sign, if one was needed, that the amnesty had been rescinded. Antonius declared the conspirators traitors to the state and impugned Cicero at the same time, claiming that he had masterminded the plot against Caesar (Cic. *Fam.* 12.3.1). These were stronger and harsher words than Antonius had been accustomed to uttering. We can attribute them to a growing and more vocal hostility in the senate, articulated by Cicero in particular, and a greater willingness on Antonius' part to call for vengeance for Caesar's murder, which he had calculatedly avoided in earlier months.

Octavian's Return to Rome and *Contio* in November

A little over a month later, Octavian returned to Rome at the head of two legions of soldiers and from the same location delivered a speech in which he declared his hopes of realizing the honors that Caesar had attained in his lifetime.[8] This is a ceremony that defies simple categorization. It was a return of a commander with his troops that culminated with a *contio* before an assembly of soldiers and urban *plebs*. This moment, when Octavian had acquired an army without benefit of a magistracy, was of such importance that its recollection became the starting point of the *Res Gestae*, demonstrating that at a later point in his life Octavian now Augustus, viewed this event as the commencement of his public career (Aug. *Anc.* 1.1).

Octavian arrived in Rome around 10 November in the middle of the festival known as the *Ludi Plebeii*, the games in honor of the Roman *plebs*. It is likely that he planned this in much the same way that Cicero's return from exile in 57 was made to happen on the first day of the *Ludi Romani*. Caesar also had hoped to return following his victory in Spain during the *Ludi Romani*. Soon after Octavian arrived in the city in May, he tried to display Caesar's *sella* and crown at the *Ludi Ceriales*, a festival that had taken on a new significance under Caesar's rule and one that was especially important for the Roman *plebs* (see chap. 4).

Before we consider the contents of Octavian's speech, it is necessary to examine the route of his return. Octavian was returning to Rome from the south and followed the Via Appia to the Temple of Mars just outside the city.[9] The area around this temple was known as the mustering point for troops before battle (Liv. 7.23.3) as well as the starting point of the annual parade of knights (*transvectio* or *recognitio equitum*), which took place on 15 July (*Vir. Ill.* 32.3). Octavian entered the city at the Porta Capena (see fig. 2); from there he would have made his way to the Circus Maximus. At this juncture, he had to make a choice: he could proceed through the Circus Maximus to the Forum Boarium, then up the Vicus Tuscus (through the Velabrum) and approach the Temple of Castor, the site of his *contio*, from the rear; or, and this seems to me more likely, he could skirt the Palatium and enter the Forum along the Sacra Via, thus following the second half of the route of a triumph (see fig. 1). This second route afforded him two advantages: first, he could proceed to the Temple of Castor past Caesar's altar, which stood in front of the Regia. Later in his *contio*, he acknowledged the presence of this altar with a significant oath and gesture. Second, this was a route rich in symbolism that allowed Octavian to look the part of a *triumphator* returning with his troops.

Once Octavian arrived in the Forum, he held a *contio* at the Temple of Castor (see fig. 3), surrounded by soldiers carrying concealed daggers, and delivered a speech to a crowd of Caesar's veterans and the Roman people. Standing on the tribunal of this temple, he spoke from an elevated place, which Antonius previously had tried to prevent (Dio 45.7.3). The mere presence of Octavian on the *rostra* of the Temple of Castor would have been something of a personal vindication and a rebuke of Antonius' political manhandling of him in July. Many of the spectators would have been standing immediately in front of the temple's tribunal or on the Gradus Aurelii. To the left of the temple, from the audience's perspective, was the Lacus Juturnae, where, legend had it, Castor and Pollux watered their horses after the battle of Lake Regillus and announced the victory to the Roman people.

To the right was the Basilica Julia, dedicated by Caesar in 46 but still unfinished even in 44. Caesar's altar, set up again by the army after Dolabella had destroyed it, stood just behind and to the left of where most of the people would have been standing (not far from the Gradus Aurelii) and possibly now had at its summit a statue of Caesar.[10] There were statues in front of the temple, in particular one of Q. Marcius Tremulus (*cos.* 306),[11] who after successfully suppressing a rebellion of the Hernici was awarded a triumph and decreed an equestrian statue in the Forum.[12]

Our evidence for the contents of Octavian's speech at this *contio* consists of brief statements in our later sources and a laconic remark in Cicero, thus rendering a complete reconstruction impossible. We still can use this evidence to determine some of Octavian's statements. Cicero's remarks are worth quoting in full:

> As to public affairs: many prudent things you've said on politics, but nothing more prudent than your last letter. For although at the present time that boy is nicely beating Antonius back, nonetheless we should await the outcome. But what a speech! I received a copy. He swears that "he be permitted to achieve his father's honors" and stretches his hand to the statue. I wouldn't want to be saved by such a one![13]

"What a speech!" Cicero quips, yet he quotes directly only the oath that Octavian swore and describes the gesture Octavian made towards a statue of Caesar, adding, for good measure, a line of Greek. It is not clear if we should read Cicero's exclamation as a sign of his indignation and exasperation at the audacity and excess of a young man reaching for things beyond his grasp, or as an oblique compliment and grudging admiration for a striking *contio* that, if nothing else, put Antonius on the defensive. In order to answer this question, we must consider the oath and gesture in more detail.[14]

The language of Octavian's oath was somewhat unusual: "swears 'that he be permitted to achieve his father's honors.'" *Honores* was an ambiguous term in the context of Caesar's career, especially his dictatorship. On the one hand, it was the word used most often to describe the political offices that Roman aristocrats so coveted,[15] and it was used to describe an aristocratic career (*cursus honorum*). Thus, Octavian by this oath could express his hopes of becoming quaestor, aedile, praetor, and consul, as Caesar had before him—perhaps not an overly ambitious statement. On the other hand, *honor* was also the word used to describe a special honor, such as a triumph,[16] and further in Caesar's case it could refer to all the extraordinary honors decreed by the senate following his victory over Pompeius, some of which adumbrated his divinity. Dio informs us that Octavian used part of his speech to praise the accomplishments of Caesar, which would indicate a full detailing of all of Caesar's *honores*, from the more typical (*cursus honorum*) to the most extraordinary (45.12.4).[17]

There is, however, a note of caution in Octavian's oath. In swearing an oath, most Romans declared their intentions to take some action.[18] A magistrate entering office, for instance, swore that he would act in accordance with, and not violate, the law now generally known as the *Lex Bantina.*[19] Octavian, by contrast, swore (*iurat*) that "he be permitted to achieve his father's honors," instead of swearing that he actually *would* achieve these honors. Hence the translation, "swears 'that he be permitted. . . .'" In other words, there was some caution in how Octavian phrased this oath. This caution perhaps arose from his status as *privatus* and the refusal of Cicero to meet with him in Capua and later to come to Rome. Octavian still required the support of the senate (the *boni*) and he had no desire to alienate them. Octavian expressed this desire in Appian's version of his speech when he claimed to be the "obedient servant of his fatherland" and that he was prepared to oppose Antonius (App. *BC* 3.41.169). The former claim in particular might sound like an empty platitude, but in the political rhetoric following Caesar's assassination it takes on greater significance, for in letters that he wrote after the battle of Mutina Cicero attempted to prevent the "defection" of L. Munatius Plancus and Q. Cornificius by admonishing them to remain loyal to the Republic.[20] With his statement Octavian perhaps was demonstrating a further departure from Antonius and a willingness to side with the "Republicans."

However, I am more inclined to think that Octavian's expressed caution was a gesture toward the soldiers and urban *plebs*. The cautious language of his oath might have been intended to demonstrate that he was acting at the behest of the army—they would "permit" him to achieve his father's honors—in much the same way that he allowed himself to be reconciled with Antonius in late July following the request of Caesar's veterans. His success depended on the loyalty and good will of his troops, which he was quick to acknowledge. In fact, Octavian praised the soldiers who had shown him allegiance and even claimed that they had "elected" him to preside over the state, which sounds like an acknowledgment of popular sovereignty.[21] Later the army brought him the *fasces* and demanded that he declare himself praetor (App. *BC* 3.48.194). The location of this *contio*, the Temple of Castor, lent itself to such acknowledgments, since it was a site for often contentious *contiones* in the late Republic, partly due to its function as a place for voting on legislation. Furthermore, the *Lex Bantina* includes a provision that magistrates are to stand in front of the Temple of Castor, facing the Forum, and swear an oath to abide by the statute.[22] If the Temple of Castor had indeed become associated with magistrates entering office, then Octavian's *contio* and the oath that he swore on Caesar's statue would have given an official quality to his act. With his statement that the soldiers had elected him to lead, Octavian was both making plain the source of his authority and appealing directly to the people. After Caesar became dictator, elections to most magistracies ceased to be held in the traditional manner, since he provided a portion of the slate of candidates for election (see chap. 2). Under these circumstances, the temple as a symbol of popular sovereignty would only have been heightened. Octavian had long recognized the importance of elected office and rumor had it that he had hoped to stand for a vacant place in the college of tribunes (App. *BC* 3.31.120), as we discussed earlier. If our later sources accurately reflect Octavian's actual words on this occasion, then it is possible that Octavian presented this *contio* as an election of sorts, providing symbolic legitimation to his otherwise unconstitutional position.

Next we should consider the significance of Octavian's gesture. The first question is, toward which statue did Octavian gesture? If Octavian wanted to honor Caesar, in all probability he would have sworn his oath on a statue of Caesar himself. There were several possibilities. Statues of Caesar stood on the new Rostra in the posture of savior, wearing the *Corona Civica* and *Obsidionalis*. In making the gesture of raising his right hand toward one of these statues, Octavian would have turned his body slightly to the left, raised his right hand and pointed in that direction. The crowd naturally would have turned and gazed in the same direction, catching sight of the new Rostra with statues of Caesar, which was to be the centerpiece of Caesar's reconstruction of the Forum. There was also the statue of Caesar that Antonius had erected earlier in the fall with the inscription *Parenti optime merito*. If Octavian had sworn an oath by this statue, it could only have elicited a cry of admiration from Cicero. We know that the rivalry between Octavian and Antonius had become more fierce in these months, as I indicated earlier, and the rivalry culminated in the two rivals making trips to Caesar's colonies in an effort to win over his veterans. Octavian kept Cicero well informed of his progress (Cic. *Att.* 16.11.6; cf. 16.14.1), and this likely is what Cicero was referring to when he said that Octavian was "nicely beating Antonius back" (Cic. *Att.* 16.15.3; see n. 13). In this contest to be Caesar's legitimate heir, the veterans decided the issue; when Octavian declared in his speech that the veterans had elected him to preside over the state, he was audaciously proclaiming his victory over Antonius. It would have been a stirring tour de force for Octavian to culminate his victory in this rivalry with an oath sworn on the very statue that Antonius had erected declaring his own devotion to Caesar.

Another possibility is that Octavian swore this oath by a statue that was closer to hand, and therefore we must assume that a statue of Caesar now stood atop the altar, which his veterans had reerected in his memory, perhaps as early as the end of May.[23] Octavian, like members of the urban *plebs* and Caesar's veterans, was swearing an oath at a monument to Caesar's memory, which must have raised the issue of Caesar's divinity once again.[24] The question of Caesar's divinity first came to the fore when the senate conferred on him a series of extraordinary honors after his victories in the civil wars, many of which had been voted in the first months of 44. Octavian's interpretation of the comet that appeared at the *Ludi Victoriae Caesaris* as a sign of Caesar's apotheosis made it impossible to put this issue aside. The language of Octavian's speech, which specifically mentioned Caesar's honors (*parentis honores*), would have raised the issue once again. Among many divine honors—such as a temple and a priesthood in Caesar's honor—the senate also decreed that men swear by his *genius*.[25] This admittedly did have a precedent in private cult, as family members could swear by the *genius* of their *paterfamilias*,[26] but the urban *plebs* were preserving this honor in their own way by using Caesar's altar as a place for settling disputes and swearing oaths—not by his *genius*, but by Caesar himself (*per Caesarem*).[27] In other words, they took a traditionally private honor and raised it to a public one, making Caesar the object of public cult. Octavian had done his best since his arrival in Rome to ensure that these divine honors were carried out, as evidenced by his attempts to introduce Caesar's *sella* into the theater at the games in May and July. His oath on this occasion brought Caesar's cult to the forefront once again.[28]

Furthermore, Octavian was implicitly acknowledging the efforts of Caesar's veterans and the urban *plebs* to preserve Caesar's memory, even against the wishes of members of the senate and the consul Dolabella, who had destroyed the monument in April (see chap. 4). With this gesture and oath, then, Octavian showed his allegiance to Caesar's most ardent supporters, especially those who had remained tenaciously faithful to Caesar's memory, which at the same time constituted a departure from the cause of the conspirators, the *boni*, and of course Cicero himself. Under such circumstances one can only read Cicero's laconic *At quae contio!* as a sign of his indignation at Octavian's temerity.[29]

We can now turn to the line of Greek with which Cicero concludes his remarks on Octavian's *contio*. These words again express misgivings about

Octavian, perhaps directing ironic attention to his capacity as savior. We cannot know how literal Cicero was being, but it is possible that he purposefully was mimicking—or mocking—the rhetoric in Octavian's own speech, in which the young Caesar presented himself as Rome's savior. The notion that Octavian might have presented himself in this way is not so far-fetched, for he knew that by bringing troops to Rome he was thwarting Antonius.[30] Such a claim was another way of drawing a connection to Caesar, whose image as Rome's savior was commemorated by two statues on the Rostra.[31] Further, the image of Octavian as savior informed the rhetoric of Cicero in the *Philippics* and in his later letters. In the *Fourth Philippic,* for instance, delivered in December 44, when Octavian's return and *contio* were still fresh, Cicero called Octavian the bulwark of the state's salvation and freedom (4.4). In his speeches to the senate, Cicero echoes many of these sentiments, stating for instance that Octavian, in raising this army, "spent his inheritance lavishly." He then quickly corrects himself and says that Octavian did not "spend it lavishly; he invested it in the preservation of the Republic."[32] Later in the same speech, Cicero claims that Octavian freed the Republic through "private initiative," a sentiment later echoed by Augustus himself in his *Res Gestae*.[33] In a later speech, Cicero proposes to confer extraordinary honors on the young man, comparing him with other young commanders in Roman history—Scipio Africanus, T. Flamininus, and of course Pompeius Magnus (Cic. *Phil.* 5.42–51). The evidence is admittedly only oblique, but it is possible that Octavian tried to cast himself in the role of savior and thus present as a heroic deed his unconstitutional act of leading an army to Rome while still only a *privatus*.

Octavian's status as *privatus* raises the question of his appearance on this occasion. There are only two possibilities. The first is that he was outfitted for war, wearing the cloak of a military commander (the *paludamentum*), which would have been consistent with his appearance as a general returning with his troops, since that garment was a mark of military command. In the same way that the toga was symbolic of peace, the *paludamentum* was emblematic of war, and thus his wearing of it would have been a declaration of war against Antonius. Our sources, however, make it clear that the *paludamentum* was in essence a military badge or honor, and as such it was reserved for *imperatores*.[34] Octavian was still only a *privatus*, lacking *imperium* and any official sanction from the senate or the people to muster an army. For him to arrogate to himself the privilege of wearing a *paludamentum* would have been an egregious violation of Republican custom. It is not clear whether he would have been so bold. The second possibility, that he was dressed in the toga of a *privatus*, raises other thorny issues. Thus attired Octavian would hardly have looked the part of an *imperator* at the head of his troops. Rather his dress would have loudly declared his status as a nonmagistrate, underscoring that his authority, such as it was, was based entirely on the strength of his army, which in turn would have taken on the appearance of a personal bodyguard.[35]

The reaction of the crowd in Appian's account perhaps is evidence for Octavian's overreaching on this occasion, for Appian tells us that many of Octavian's soldiers, after they had heard his address—which apparently to them constituted a declaration of war against Antonius—expressed their unwillingness to march against their former commander, forcing Octavian to allow them to leave. He distributed a donative, watched them depart, and returned home himself (App. *BC* 3.42.172). He was able to bring them back into the fold later. Dio, on the other hand, maintains that Octavian received praise both from his own following and from the rest of the crowd that had gathered (Dio 45.12.6). If we can accept that both accounts reflect differing versions of what actually happened, then this is once again evidence for a divided crowd in the city, with some inclined toward war and others clamoring for peace.

Octavian's *contio* drew together the accomplishments of Caesar and also the activity of popular politicians in the late Republic at the Temple of Castor. As Octavian stood on the tribunal of the Temple of Castor and spoke of his father's accomplishments, the crowd listened, some of them standing next to the altar of Caesar that had been erected on the site of his cremation, where the twin deities had made their appearance. The location of Octavian's *contio*, along with the content of his speech and his striking oath and gesture, came together to inscribe a complex text that had at its heart claims for Caesar's divinity.

Antonius' Return and *Contio*

Antonius returned to Rome with armed followers soon after Octavian departed. In a speech to his troops and the Roman people, he made it clear that he was unbowed by Octavian's successes. The returns of the two rivals and their *contiones* in rapid succession demonstrated the importance of addressing the people in the Forum before undertaking any action. These ceremonies also showed how the political landscape had changed as the two political rivals became antagonists and prepared the Roman people for the imminent military confrontation.

The chronology of events during Antonius' few days in Rome in November 44 is uncertain.[36] He likely arrived around 20 November and called a senate meeting for the 24th when he hoped to declare Octavian a public enemy (*hostis*) (Cic. *Phil.* 5.23; cf. 3.20; 13.19). He prepared the way for this decree by publishing edicts denigrating Octavian's family[37] and then convening a *contio* in the Forum (Cic. *Phil.* 3.27; 5.21). A report that the Martian Legion—one of the three Macedonian legions en route to Ariminum—had diverted to Alba Fucens in order to defect to Octavian forced a change of plans. Antonius hastily departed Rome before the senate meeting could be held and proceeded to Alba Fucens in the hopes of winning the soldiers back. He was greeted with a volley of arrows and returned to Rome. News of the Fourth Legion's defection to Octavian disrupted but did not postpone the meeting of the senate on 28 November. Antonius moved for a vote of thanks for M. Lepidus for his success in coming to terms with Sextus Pompeius in Spain (*Phil.* 3.23), and there was a distribution of the praetorian provinces.[38] Antonius then departed for Tibur where he harangued his troops and was joined by members of the senate and equestrian order before departing for Ariminum and Gaul (App. *BC* 3.46.188–89).

Since Antonius was returning to Rome from the south, he would have followed the same route as Octavian with the same potential symbolism of a victorious commander returning with his troops. Antonius' disposition, however, was more desperate, having recently seen two legions defect to Octavian, and his posture more defensive, in a manner perhaps similar to his *contio* on 2 October. Our only contemporary source, Cicero, castigates Antonius' return as being destructive to the state. He marched into Rome in an armed column, marking down houses for confiscation and distribution to his supporters, while the Roman people looked on and groaned.[39] Cicero later claims that Antonius departed the city for Tibur, dressed in his commander's cloak but avoiding the people, the Forum, and the main streets of Rome under the cover of night (*Phil.* 3.24; cf. App. *BC* 3.45.187). At the very least, Antonius' departure was hasty, for many senators and distinguished members of the equestrian order later went to meet Antonius in Tibur and gave him a brilliant sendoff to Ariminum and the province of Gaul, as if in compensation for his unattended departure from Rome (App. *BC* 3.46.188–89). Antonius' departure from Tibur partially corroborates Cicero's claims, but it also shows that the consul still had many supporters among Rome's political elite.

In Antonius' *contio*, before he departed, he claimed that he would be the guardian of Rome and, after leaving office, would keep an army near the city until the Kalends of May and would come and go as he pleased (Cic. *Phil.* 3.27; 5.21). The first part of his statement, that he would be the "guardian of the city," presupposes the military threat posed by Octavian and his newly recruited troops. It is also a counterclaim to Cicero's later rhetoric that

Antonius' return was destructive to the state. Antonius would maintain that he recruited the troops under his command for the protection of Rome against his young rival. This *contio* should also be viewed as part and parcel of Antonius' published edicts impugning Octavian's family. Despite his later rhetoric in support of Octavian, even Cicero remained ambivalent about him and his motives (*Att.* 16.8.1; 16.9; 16.14.1). We can imagine that other senators would have been equally grave about the prospects of Octavian's rise to power and therefore receptive to some of Antonius' claims. Antonius then went on to state that, after his term as consul expired (on 31 December 44 BC), he expected to station an army near the city until the Kalends of May and "come and go as he pleased." The "Kalends of May" to which he refers (*Phil.* 3.27) must, then, belong to the year 43, but it is unclear what the significance of this date was. Did Antonius intend to delay his departure to Gaul for four months after the expiration of his consulship? This is unlikely given the circumstances created by Octavian's successes. His assertion that he would come and go as he pleased fits the circumstances of his rapid entry into the city and his equally rapid departure.

Whatever Antonius actually said at this *contio* has been forever reconstituted through the machinery of Cicero's rhetoric, but it is improbable that the consul's message would have been reassuring to many in the crowd. The consular *fasces* were presumably lowered as custom required, but this must have seemed an empty gesture to the people in attendance whose sovereignty was now powerless to arrest the tide of civil war. This "ceremony of popular sovereignty," then, demonstrated clearly where the reality of power now lay, as long as troops were allowed to enter Rome or remain on its outskirts—in the hands of the consul and his army. Hope of peace now fluttered away, and those in Rome had to await the outcome of the war.

Cicero and the Supremacy of the Senate

Following the departures of Octavian and Antonius, the gaze of the city turned toward the investiture of the moderate Caesarians A. Hirtius and C. Vibius Pansa as consuls. We can only speculate about how the ceremony of investiture might have looked to those witnessing it. The years 49–44 marked the dictatorship of Caesar, during which time he also held the consulship in 48 and 46–44. This was the first investiture of new consuls in a half dozen years that did not include Caesar in some direct capacity, although his influence might still have been felt, since he had appointed Hirtius and Pansa as well. Antonius' enemies in the senate could have used this ceremony of investiture, which, if typical, included procession, sacrifice, and oath to demonstrate a restoration of normalcy and order to the politics of the time. That it was immediately followed by the customary meeting of the senate in contrast to the previous months was an outward sign that the consuls would work with the senate. The Curia again became an institution of importance in the political arena.

Our sources for these months, from December 44 to April 43, focus on the senatorial debates over how to deal with the two rivals for Caesar's power, Antonius and Octavian. Reports of these debates and the actions taken by the senate were communicated to the people through *contiones*.[40] In a speech delivered to the people of Rome on 20 December 44 (the *Fourth Philippic*), following a meeting of the senate summoned by the new tribunes, and on 1 January 43 (the *Sixth Philippic*), following the first meeting of the senate in the consulship of Hirtius and Pansa, Cicero praised and glorified both Octavian and D. Brutus, calling the former a savior and hero and the latter a protector and liberator, while he denigrated Antonius as an enemy of the state. Cicero was introduced to the first *contio* by M. Servilius (*tr. pl.*) and to the second by P. Appuleius (*tr. pl.*). In a later speech, Cicero claims that the people summoned him to both *contiones* (Cic. *Phil.* 7.22), but if this means something other than that the tribunes, as representatives of the people, invited him, it cannot be confirmed. Cicero, although a nonmagistrate (*privatus*), was still an understandable choice to speak at the first *contio* (in December), especially in the absence of the consuls for 44, Antonius and Dolabella, both of whom had departed the city. He was one of the most senior consulars and the leading orator of the day. At the second *contio*, one might expect that Hirtius or Pansa would have stood before the people, since they had just presided over the inaugural senate meeting of their year, but again it was apparently Cicero's oratorical abilities that brought him to the fore (Cic. *Phil.* 6.1).

In all likelihood Cicero delivered these speeches from Caesar's new Rostra, in the shadow of Caesar's statues, a fitting location for a speech that in part praised the young Caesar. Cicero was dressed in a toga, although, as he himself acknowledges,[41] military dress would have been more appropriate to the occasion since an important topic in both speeches, but especially the *Sixth Philippic*, was the question of whether Antonius should be declared an enemy of the state (*hostis*). In this way, Cicero drew attention to his appearance as a symbol of the confused and even contradictory state of affairs, in which the senate in Rome was earnestly trying to maintain an air of peace, while in the provinces troops were being levied and trained for imminent war.

In these speeches delivered to the people, Cicero employed familiar rhetoric of the late Republic, frequently invoking the freedom of the Roman people.[42] He also treated the recent return of first Octavian and then Antonius to Rome in the late autumn of the previous year. Octavian's recruitment of soldiers and march to Rome without the benefit of either *imperium* or *auspicia*—a blatantly unconstitutional act—becomes in Cicero's rhetoric a deed worthy of official senatorial commendation, by which Octavian both liberated and saved the Republic (Cic. *Phil.* 4.4; cf. *Phil.* 3.3); thus Cicero praises him with words often reserved for a *triumphator*. On the other hand, Antonius' return, which to some might have appeared remarkably similar, was, in Cicero's words, potentially deadly and destructive (Cic. *Phil.* 3.3; 4.3; cf. *Fam.* 12.25.4). In a manner that has now become familiar, the ceremonies of these two men through Cicero's rhetoric were treated as the focal events by which their images were constructed.

The *Sixth Philippic* also demonstrates the importance of topography in oratory. During his speech, as a way of punctuating important points, Cicero gestured to three statues erected in honor of L. Antonius (*tr. pl.* 44), brother of the consul. The first stood in front of the Temple of Castor, with the inscription "The thirty-five tribes to their patron" (Cic. *Phil.* 6.12). The second statue's exact location is not known, but it also bore an inscription that read, "The Roman knights with public horse to their patron" (Cic. *Phil.* 6.13). Finally, the third statue's inscription read, "To L. Antonius, patron, from Janus Medius" (Cic. *Phil.* 6.15). The Janus Medius was an arch—a gateway—where bankers and money changers conducted their business. Its location is unknown, but it probably stood in the middle of the Forum, perhaps near the Rostra.[43] Cicero's comparison of the first statue of L. Antonius to others that stood in the same location, in particular that of M. Tremulus, the conqueror of the Hernici, shows how the topography of the Forum was evocative of the past and further how an orator could use this topography—and the past that it evoked—to frame a current political debate. Cicero implies that L. Antonius did not merit a statue standing next to a great hero of the past. Cicero's mockery of these statues notwithstanding, L. Antonius' self-representation as patron of these groups, and further the existence of these statues commemorating these relationships, show that he embraced the concept of universal patronage as part of his public image, which later the emperor Augustus also adopted.[44]

These two speeches also provide some evidence for the dynamism of oratory, especially at *contiones*, when the Roman people could respond to questions posed by the speaker or interrupt him with shouts and acclamations.[45] On several occasions in these two speeches, Cicero acknowledges the shouts of the crowd, first in assenting that Antonius was a *hostis* (4.2 and 4.8), then in cheering Cicero's mention of the young Caesar (4.3) and D. Brutus' edict

(4.7); in the later speech, the crowd jeered the statues of L. Antonius (6.12). Even in this time of senatorial supremacy, Cicero found it necessary to record the reactions of the urban crowd at these *contiones* in order to provide evidence that his political strategy enjoyed the full support of the Roman people.

Cicero remained in the public eye in the weeks leading up to the battle of Mutina (App. *BC* 3.66.269), as those in Rome waited expectantly for the return of the embassy that the senate had dispatched to Antonius at the beginning of January. The ambassadors, L. Piso and L. Philippus, returned about one month later—the third member, Ser. Sulpicius, having died en route—with demands, not concessions, from Antonius as he lay siege to Mutina where D. Brutus was trapped. The senate passed the ultimate decree. As the siege dragged on, rumors flew about that Antonius was becoming amenable to negotiations for peace. The senate decreed a second embassy in early March, but it never departed Rome. Instead, the consul C. Pansa conducted his troops to Gaul to raise the siege and rescue the beleaguered D. Brutus. News of the fighting in the vicinity of Mutina reached Rome on 20 April. A crowd of the urban *plebs* escorted Cicero to the Capitolium in an impromptu triumphal procession. A *supplicatio* (thanksgiving) lasting an unprecedented fifty days was decreed, but the initial rejoicing became somewhat muted when it was learned a week later that both consuls had perished and that Antonius had managed to elude his captors. Later in the spring, the senate debated appropriate accolades for the generals, D. Brutus and Octavian, who had remained loyal to the Republic. But the senate's failure to appease Octavian, who now had the additional forces of Hirtius and Pansa at his disposal and the ambition to achieve the highest political office, its act of declaring Antonius a public enemy, who had escaped Mutina with his army largely intact, and Lepidus' unwillingness to oppose Antonius or Octavian, led to the seemingly inevitable coalition of these three men over the course of the summer. The events in Gaul caused a dramatic shift in the political landscape in Rome as power coalesced in the hands of these three men.[46]

Festivals and Public Entertainment in 43 BC

Dio tells us that only a few minor festivals were celebrated in Rome in 43 because of a lack of funds (Dio 46.31.4). Cicero mentions the *Liberalia* (17 March), the *Quinquatria* (19–23 March), and the *Parilia* (21 April), all of which were celebrated at some level, but perhaps not in traditional fashion. We are told that the consuls departed Rome before the *Feriae Latinae*, but only because Dio records this in a long list of omens that foretold the coming disaster at Mutina (Dio 46.33.4). The major *ludi*—*Ceriales*, *Florales*, *Apollinares*, *Romani*, and *Plebeii*, not to mention *Victoriae Caesaris*, recently moved to July by Octavian—are not recorded in any of our sources. A possible reason for this is that the magistrates usually responsible for public entertainment were lacking. Broughton has a long list of magistrates for this year (*MRR* 2.334–57) but only one aedile, a certain Volusius, is attested, and we hear of him only because he was one of the proscribed.[47] However Caesar might have modified electoral procedure in his dictatorship, most magistrates seem to have been filled in this the first full year after his death. The dearth of named aediles is, therefore, striking. Although arguments from silence are always perilous, it is possible that the year 43 was the beginning of a trend that we see more fully attested in the Triumviral period, when candidates for the aedileship were often lacking because of the expenses involved in producing the requisite public entertainment.[48]

Cicero's Triumphal Procession (April 43 BC)

A rumor spread in Rome around 18 or 19 April alleging that Antonius had been victorious at Mutina, Pansa had been killed, and Cicero planned to take up the *fasces* and become consul on the *Parilia* (21 April). This rumor proved sufficiently credible that the tribune P. Appuleius convened a *contio* on 20 April to dispel it. The crowd exonerated Cicero on this occasion with a uniform acclamation of its belief that his intentions toward the Republic were only the most noble (*optime cogitatum*) (Cic. *Phil.* 14.16). This rumor might have gained credibility in part because it alleged that Cicero's power play would take place on the *Parilia*, the traditional date of the founding of Rome, and an appropriate festival at which to celebrate the beginning of a new era. But it had become even more appropriate due to more recent celebrations. Caesar himself had used the *Parilia* as an occasion for celebrating his victory at Munda by arranging for news of this battle to reach Rome on the eve of this festival in 45, and later expanding it to include circus games. In 44, following Caesar's assassination, his supporters arranged a demonstration on the *Parilia*, acknowledging the importance of this festival for Caesar's victory by wearing garlands in his honor (see chap. 3). Cicero, by taking up the *fasces* on this day, could have been reclaiming the festival for the Republic by celebrating its own victory, one that brought an end to the period of tyranny begun by Caesar's dictatorship and continued by Antonius' supremacy.

A few hours after this *contio*, new dispatches arrived with stories of the heroism of the consuls Hirtius and Pansa, the fortitude of D. Brutus, and the courage and daring of the young Caesar. A crowd of the urban *plebs* went to Cicero's home and escorted him to the Capitolium, as if in triumph. Cicero describes this procession in the *Fourteenth Philippic*, in the middle of a debate over whether the victorious commanders at Mutina should be saluted as *imperatores* along with the decree of a public Thanksgiving:

> If anyone had killed a thousand or two thousand Spaniards, Gauls, or Thracians, the senate would name him *imperator* by what has become common custom. When so many legions and such a great multitude of the enemy have been killed—I say "enemy," although those enemies within the walls do not wish this—will we not confer the honor of a Thanksgiving on our most distinguished leaders, and add the title *imperator*? Those liberators of this city should enter this temple with the same esteem, joy, and congratulations, that I enjoyed yesterday when, because of my accomplishments, the Roman people conveyed me in an *ovatio* and almost a triumph to the Capitolium, and then escorted me back home! For this in my judgment is the only true and genuine triumph, when the whole citizen body in unison congratulates those who have served the state well.[49]

We discussed earlier how *profectiones* (departures) and *reditus* (returns), traditionally part of a cycle of rituals associated with triumphs (chap. 1), could spawn variations such as Octavian's return to the city in November. It was also possible for triumphlike celebrations to take place in an impromptu fashion, such as the one Octavian enjoyed through the efforts of Caesar's veterans in the summer of 44 (see chap. 6).

Cicero claims that this impromptu procession was an *ovatio* and almost a triumph. He perhaps felt justified in making such a claim because this procession partially traced the formal route of a triumph, thus adhering to a clearly defined ritual framework. The starting point was Cicero's home, which was located at the foot of the Palatium,[50] near the Forum itself; the crowd then entered the Forum and proceeded down the Sacra Via to the Rostra and then up the Clivus Capitolinus to the Capitolium, the destination of all *triumphatores*, and finally he was escorted back home again. The topography of Rome was highly evocative in and of itself, but it became even more so when linked together by the formal *pompae* that were such an important part of public life in this period. In other ways, Cicero's claim to an *ovatio* or triumph seems forced. Since Cicero was proceeding on foot, and not riding into the city in a chariot, it was more appropriate to call this procession an *ovatio*, but it wanted for more than just the chariot: Cicero was not outfitted as a *triumphator* (being without the customary scepter and crown), and there was no army, no prisoners, no spoils of war. There was a victory to celebrate, but one in which Cicero himself had participated only from afar. In fact, he states that he was escorted in this fashion because of the accomplishments (*res gestae*) of those commanders on the battlefield, clearly acknowledging his role as surrogate for the absent consuls and proconsuls. Under these circumstances, it is not surprising that Cicero felt it necessary to explain what he meant: a genuine triumph, he asserts, occurs when one who has served the Republic well receives the tributes of the whole citizen body. He implies that the *senatus consultum*, the chariot, the triumphal garb, perhaps even the spoils of war were not as important for a triumph as was the acclamation of the people. This is what constituted a true triumph.

Cicero's argumentation in this case is somewhat tendentious, inasmuch as he was exalting the procession in his own honor and in honor of those absent commanders as much as triumphs duly decreed by the senate—as he himself acknowledges (Cic. *Phil.* 14.13)—but it still shows how important such events were as expressions of popular sentiments and how Cicero could use such expressions to his rhetorical advantage. It is also worth noting that in a typical triumph the people were usually passive spectators, on hand to cheer the *imperator* and army, to jeer the prisoners of war, and to share in the wealth and glory that military conquest provided. In this instance, however, they were not just spectators but participants: they took control of a ritual that they usually just observed, in a manner similar to the crowd at Caesar's funeral (see chap. 3) or Caesar's veterans orchestrating the reconciliation of Antonius and Octavian (see chap. 6). I believe that this is part of a larger trend in the late Republic of the people exchanging the role of spectator for that of participant. Cicero's explanation of what constituted a true triumph is an ideological construct that acknowledged this exchange of roles.

As Cicero describes it, this procession was an unabashed celebration of victory, but, as happened so often in the late Republic, such celebrations were for victories in civil war, in which the enemies were also citizens of Rome. Sulla and Caesar were compelled by tradition to use the customary ritual of the triumph even when their victories involved Roman citizens. Both attempted to deflect criticism by emphasizing their victories over foreign enemies and downplaying those involving Roman citizens, but there remained an incongruity in the use of these ceremonies, which had long glorified the expansion of empire, for the celebrations of victories in civil war and the slaughter of Roman citizens. I argued that Caesar was acknowledging this incongruity when he used the combined celebration of the *Feriae*

Latinae and an *ovatio* in January 44 to reassess his victory in Spain, and perhaps all his victories in the civil war (see chap. 2). This incongruity also finds expression in Cicero's discussion of the *supplicatio* that should be decreed, he argued, along with a formal salutation of the victorious commanders as *imperatores*.[51] Cicero further states that there was no precedent for the two honors, *supplicatio* and *salutatio*, to be separated—that is, one granted without the other. Cicero's concern to resolve this issue can only mean that the separation of the two honors was raised as a kind of compromise measure to appease those in the senate who still supported Antonius. The question was whether it was appropriate to salute as *imperatores* those generals who were victorious in a battle over Roman citizens. In the end, Cicero proposed a *supplicatio*, in support of P. Appuleius' proposal, a monument in honor of those who perished in the fighting and funds for their survivors (Cic. *Phil.* 14.36–38).

The other question is what these kinds of ceremonies meant for those participating in and observing them. If it is true, as I have suggested, that a ceremony can comment on the social order, then such a ceremony should take on even greater importance when the social order is undergoing a transformation, as was the case at the end of the Republic. In the case of Cicero's "triumphal" procession, the urban *plebs* took a military ceremony and made it a civilian one and in so doing reminded its audience that the triumph was, after all, a ceremony for the people, too, who could celebrate military achievements and in turn reap the fruits of victory. I suggested earlier in the context of Antonius' *contio* in November that the people might have felt helpless to stop the imminent war. This procession, as an expression of popular will in a military context, when troops and discharged veterans frequented the city and had become a powerful political force, demonstrated an elation at the end of war and the advent of peace. For Cicero this triumph was a validation of his career as orator, statesman, and advocate of peace (*auctor pacis*), for it afforded him in return for accomplishments in a civilian or domestic sphere some of the renown usually reserved for military commanders. Not all glory was won for accomplishments away from Rome.

The Senate after Mutina

Cicero's letters attest to the efforts of the senate, following the victory of the Republic in the battle of Mutina, to restore its traditional prestige and authority in a rapidly changing political climate. Cicero was in constant communication not only with the conspirators, the Bruti and Cassius, but also with other provincial commanders whose loyalty to the state was a pressing concern. He corresponded frequently with C. Asinius Pollio (*procos.* Hispania Ulterior), L. Munatius Plancus (*procos.* Gallia Transalpina), and Q. Cornificius (*procos.* Africa), and less so with M. Aemilius Lepidus (*procos.* Gallia Narbonensis and Hispania Citerior), who had already shown an allegiance to Antonius.[52] In an official dispatch, Plancus enjoined upon the senate to arrange for land for his soldiers upon discharge so as to ensure their loyalty to the state, and later Cicero promised to take up the cause himself (Cic. *Fam.* 10.8.3; 10.22.2). The senate attempted to win over Octavian's troops in more direct fashion by sending envoys who were instructed to offer cash awards directly to the soldiers when Octavian was not present (Dio 46.41.1). More than any other senatorial action in this year, this demonstrates how the senate was attempting to reassert its control of the military that it had first begun to lose when C. Marius reformed the army and Sulla marched on Rome.[53] The senate's envoys were given a cool reception. Octavian decided to acquire the consulship through force; he led his troops to Rome.

The senate also attempted to retake control of the dispensation of honors. We have already seen how the senate decreed the honor of an equestrian statue to Octavian, but this was only after Caesar's veterans accompanied him to Rome. After Mutina, it was proposed that D. Brutus be awarded a triumph for his part in the victory. The fallen consuls and soldiers were also granted public funerals and their surviving relatives special honors that would keep their memories alive (Cic. *Phil.* 14.36–38). Cicero also proposed that Octavian be awarded an *ovatio* (Cic. *ad Brut.* 1.15.9), a fine distinction but clearly subordinate to D. Brutus' triumph.[54] Cicero's letters also suggest that there was an attempt to restore a sense of normalcy to the elections, in the sense that they would be contested, where possible, in the traditional fashion. Their timing was very much open to question. Elections were normally held in July, but there was some effort to postpone them until August or even January, perhaps to ensure that all qualified candidates would have the opportunity to return to the city to stand for them (Cic. *Fam.* 10.26.1 and 3). The consulship for 42 was already settled; D. Brutus and L. Munatius Plancus had been appointed by Caesar, and there seems to have been no attempt to dislodge them—such an attempt would have directly contravened Caesar's now officially sanctioned *acta*. The praetorship was another matter. Elections for praetor in particular, whenever they might be held, promised to be hotly contested. Cicero's letters of commendation for L. Aelius Lamia (*Fam.* 11.16 and 17), for instance, could have been written at any time in the late Republic, for they bear no traces of the political uncertainty and threats of civil war that hung over Rome.[55]

Octavian's Return to Rome (July/August 43 BC)

Octavian's return to Rome in August 43 provided him another opportunity for self-advertisement and display. He had two specific objectives: first, to achieve the consulship;[56] and second, to obtain official sanction for his adoption by Caesar. To achieve these objectives he relied on the assemblies of the Roman people. To these specific objectives we can add a third more general one: to continue exploiting the memory of Caesar to his own political advantage.

The circumstances and topography of Octavian's return to Rome evoked the memory of Caesar, for he too came from Gaul, as Caesar had done a half dozen years earlier, even leading his troops across the Rubicon.[57] The sight of a commander returning to Rome from Gaul amidst the uncertainty and fear of civil war might have conjured up memories of Caesar's rapid advance to Ariminum in the winter of 49. Octavian advanced on Rome so quickly that his enemies were unable to muster an adequate defensive force for the city.[58] The arrival of legions from Africa as well as rumors of the Martian and Fourth Legions' defection from Octavian lifted the spirits of those in the city who opposed the young Caesar, but this soon proved to be a false hope. Octavian seized an area north of the Quirinal hill (see fig. 1), stationed his army there, and then proceeded to the Forum with a small bodyguard, most likely marching down the Flaminian Way to the Campus Martius, being greeted along the way by well-wishers. He entered the city the following day from the Campus Martius and turned toward the Forum and in particular the Temple of Vesta, where he met his mother and sister.

In Appian's account of Octavian's return the Quirinal hill figures prominently as the place near which Octavian stationed his troops while he made his way to the Forum. Since Octavian was arriving from the north, perhaps entering the city through the Porta Collina, the Quirinal was one of the first places that he reached and was at least in part a strategic location, a promontory from which he and his men could oversee activity in the city.[59] Octavian's precise point of entry into the city was also important. If, for instance, he entered the city on the north side of the Forum, his route would have taken him past the Forum Julium and Temple of Venus, perhaps evoking even more comparisons with Caesar. If, on the other hand, Octavian entered the Forum from the area of the Circus Flaminius and passed through the Porta Triumphalis, his route at least in part would have followed the procession of a triumph with all its attendant symbolism. After the battle of Mutina, the senate had voted against Cicero's proposal that Octavian enter the city in an *ovatio* (Cic. *ad Brut.* 1.15.9). This return would have given him the opportunity to celebrate a triumphal procession, or at least a portion of one, without the official sanction of the senate, in a manner similar to his reconciliation with Antonius in the summer of 44 and Cicero's procession following news of the victory at Mutina. Such a procession offered the political advantage of conferring a modicum of a *triumphator*'s glory without having to acknowledge the unpleasant side of this victory, namely that it was won over Roman citizens, despite Cicero's claims to the contrary. After his election to the consulship, Octavian had the city in his hands. He easily could have demanded a triumph or *ovatio* at that time, which the senate was too enfeebled to deny. He chose not to make such a demand, I believe, because he did not wish to celebrate a triumph for a victory in a civil war; not only that, such a triumph would have placed him in a politically untenable position, for he was also probably at this time already considering reconciling with Antonius and Lepidus. Such a reconciliation would have been impossible had Octavian celebrated a triumph for the victory at Mutina.

Octavian had reason to be genuinely concerned for the welfare of his family, since members of the senate had designs on using them as hostages. It is not clear, however, how much to read into his reunion with his mother and sister at the Temple of Vesta. Vesta's temple housed the public hearth of Rome,[60] whose fire symbolized Roman power and might, *imperium*, and security.[61] We do know that Augustus later established a new relationship with Vesta, including her, along with Apollo, in his imperial residence on the Palatine, explicitly connecting his welfare with that of the people of Rome.[62] Did Augustus simply invent this connection? Ovid called Julius Caesar a "priest of Vesta" (Ov. *Fast.* 3.699; 5.573; *Met.* 15.778), referring to the office of Pontifex Maximus. Ovid's reference is perhaps only retrospective, having in mind Vesta's new role in the Principate, but it is equally possible that these changes were initiated by the dictator Caesar, and Augustus was only following his lead. Ovid states that Vesta was received into the home of her relative (*cognatus*), referring to Augustus,[63] as if her relationship with Caesar had already been established before Augustus took her in. If this was the case, then Octavian's reunion with his family at the Temple of Vesta in July 43 would have been another way of preserving the memory of Caesar. By using the temple in this way, Octavian was also linking his safety and that of his family with the larger safety and welfare of all Romans. He again could advertise himself as Rome's savior.

Octavian and the Popular Assemblies (August 43 BC)

Despite the backing of his army and the renown of his victory at Mutina, Octavian required the power and prestige that only the Roman people could confer through an enactment of the popular assemblies. He, therefore, focused his attention on election to the consulship, official sanction of his adoption, and a trial of the conspirators, before reconciling with Antonius and Lepidus. Octavian's adherence to the formal procedures of the Republican constitution was another indication of the manner in which Republican political institutions were gradually being transformed to accommodate monarchical power, as they came to serve the purposes of a powerful individual.

Octavian's principal objective, as I stated earlier, was to be elected to the consulship. He could not expect to be elected for the consulship of 42 since Caesar had already seen to the election of these magistrates, D. Brutus and L. Munatius Plancus, and both were still alive.[64] His only hope was to take the place, as *consul suffectus*, of one of the two fallen consuls for 43. The exact procedure for the election of a *consul suffectus* is not entirely clear from our sources. If only one consul needed to be replaced, then his colleague had the power to convene the *comitia centuriata* and preside over the elections. If, as was the case in 43, both consuls had died, then an *interrex* was appointed by the senate to preside over the elections (Liv. 4.7.10). Dio states that, since it was not possible to appoint an *interrex* for this purpose, with so many patrician magistrates absent from the city, two men were appointed instead to act as consuls for the elections (Dio 46.45.3). It is not known who were chosen or how, but it was an unprecedented procedure that would have perhaps tainted the outcome of the election. Octavian then departed the city—perhaps stationing himself on the Janiculum, where state funds had been collected and were being guarded[65]—just long enough for the consular elections to be held and to learn their inevitable result: the election of himself and his relative, Q. Pedius, as his colleague. Dio scoffs at Octavian's brief departure from the city on the grounds that it was a specious display of humility that masked the reality of his power. But we should keep in mind that Dio was likely thinking in terms of his own experiences, which were within the frame of the Principate, and he understood how the power and charisma of the *princeps* could be felt even in his absence. Octavian was a product of the Republic, and here he was following established Republican political procedure. Appearances in politics are important, and it is possible that Octavian's departure—really no more than a gesture—helped assuage the fears of the populace.

It is also important to remember that Caesar had begun to exercise his influence over elections in 49 (for 48), over which he presided as dictator. In subsequent years, his influence became more direct as he acquired the power to appoint the higher magistrates and in fact had done so for the years 44–42. Recently, then, from the perspective of those voting in the consular elections in July 43, such elections had not been held, and Romans had not had the opportunity to exercise this important right of citizenship. In other words, elections in recent years had been but a ghost of the Republican past. But at the same time we cannot claim that under Octavian's vigilance this important political institution returned to a pristine state in which the outcome of the elections was a clear and indisputable expression of popular will. We are not told, for instance, if there were other candidates for election, although it is hard to believe that any could be found to challenge the candidacy of Octavian himself and another man handpicked by him, especially with Octavian's army at the gates; we also do not know who voted. Can we expect that the municipal aristocracy made the journey to Rome to vote with Octavian's army? If so, would they have dared to vote for another candidate, if one was available? Octavian exhibited an adherence to the formal political procedures of the Roman Republic, but the integrity of the election was clearly undermined—and perhaps already had been by Caesar's overweening influence. Yet Octavian's desire to be elected consul shows that these ceremonies still conferred power and prestige even if their integrity was suspect. By being elected consul, Octavian equaled the status of his two rivals, Antonius and Lepidus.

Following his second entry into the city, Octavian convened a meeting of the *comitia curiata* for the purpose of sanctioning, officially and finally, his adoption into the Julian *gens*, which Caesar had included as a provision in his will. Octavian's adherence to form in this instance seems perhaps superfluous since (as I have argued in earlier chapters) he had spent the previous fourteen months acting as Caesar's heir whenever the opportunity presented itself. He had not required a *lex curiata* to sponsor games or erect a statue in Caesar's honor, or to attempt to display Caesar's *sella* and diadem in the theater. The soldiers had already claimed to be his "inheritance" (see chap. 6). Yet Octavian continued to seek formal sanction for his adoption through this increasingly antiquated assembly of the people.

The tradition of the *comitia curiata* has been well established, and only a spare outline is necessary here.[66] It was made up of thirty *curiae*, obsolescent divisions of the Roman citizen body, ten each coming from the three original tribes of Rome: Tities, Ramnes, and Luceres. It originally elected kings and later sanctioned the *imperium* of the higher magistrates. It usually met on the Capitolium under the presidency of the consul or, for religious purposes such as the sanctioning of wills and adoptions, under that of the Pontifex Maximus. In the late Republic, the *comitia curiata* had ceased to meet in its original form. Instead, thirty lictors, one representing each of the thirty *curiae*, met and voted as necessary. There are but few recorded instances of its meeting in this period, the most famous of which was under C. Caesar in 59 for the purpose of transferring P. Clodius Pulcher to a plebeian family so that he could stand for the tribunate and fulfill his political ambitions (Dio 38.12.2). Since the purpose of the meeting was to transfer Clodius to a plebeian family, Caesar was presumably presiding as Pontifex Maximus, but our sources do not say.

The tradition of the meeting of the *comitia curiata* that sanctioned Octavian's adoption is so meager that we are left with more questions than answers. All we are told is that, after the law was passed, Octavian finally fulfilled an important term of Caesar's will, namely his bequests to all Roman citizens (Dio 46.48.1). Octavian had been lavish with cash donatives to his troops, especially in the autumn of 44 when he was visiting Caesar's veteran colonies in an effort to find military backing for his stand against Antonius, but he had not yet disbursed the funds to all Roman citizens that Caesar's will had called for.

It is not clear who would have presided since the Pontifex Maximus, M. Lepidus, installed perhaps soon after Caesar's murder,[67] was in Gaul. Perhaps Q. Pedius, the newly elected suffect consul, could have played this part. It was an important rite of passage for Octavian, who required this *lex* in order for his adoption to be legitimate in a traditional sense, but, if his colleague had conducted the ceremony, it is possible that it would have appeared to be nothing more than a sham. Where did the meeting take place? Since meetings of the curiate assembly were rare in any case, would this have appeared to be a revival of an arcane ceremony?

Octavian, invested with the powers of the consulship and officially sanctioned as Caesar's heir, now turned his attention to punishing the murderers of Caesar.[68] The amnesty reached at the Temple of Tellus just after the Ides of March had long failed in one of its principal objectives, namely, to protect the conspirators. This amnesty, nonetheless, had been decreed by the senate, and it could be undone only through constitutional forms. In August 43, in the face of Octavian's forces, many of the conspirators' supporters were cowed or had fled the city; the senate declined to oppose him. Nevertheless Octavian endeavored to make the punishment appear as legitimate as possible; in order to do so, his colleague, Q. Pedius, passed a law condemning the conspirators to banishment. A day was declared for trial by public proclamation, and, despite the absence of the defendants, Octavian himself presided over a special trial (*quaestio extraordinaria*) in which the conspirators' guilt was put to the vote. L. Cornificius and M. Agrippa were chosen to prosecute Brutus and Cassius, respectively. There was a visible, if ultimately feeble, show of opposition. When a herald mounted the Rostra to summon Brutus to trial, the crowd that had gathered to witness the ceremony groaned aloud, and many senators bowed their heads in silent support of the conspirators (Plut. *Brut.* 27.4–5). All jurors were compelled to record their votes. Only P. Silicius Corona, who was seen weeping at the trial, voted for acquittal; his effrontery, forgiven at the time, was punished later through proscription.[69] A senatorial decree was undone by a ceremony of popular politics.

We have already discussed how frequently such trials became highly politicized ceremonies in the late Republic, when politicians used them as venues to demean opponents and exalt themselves.[70] The location for these trials was often the Temple of Castor, the site of Octavian's *contio* in November 44. Another possibility was the praetor's tribunal in the Forum. A speech before the crowd gathered around the tribunal (the *corona*) was customary in such cases. In this instance, the newly elected consul stood in the Forum and presumably reproached the conspirators in absentia as the duly allotted jurors and crowd looked on. This trial provided another opportunity at a different venue for Octavian to enact his new authority—this time as prosecutor in a criminal trial. But did this trial look like a legitimate criminal proceeding, or more like a "kangaroo" court, whose outcome was predetermined? In this case, form took precedence over substance. This was a show trial, the purpose of which was to quench the thirst of Caesar's veterans for vengeance while allowing Octavian to appear before the people as Caesar's legitimate heir, exactor of vengeance, and dispenser of justice.

Conclusion

The rivalry between Octavian and Antonius became more intense in the autumn months of 44 as they competed for the support of Caesar's veterans. Whatever power they gained from their visits to Caesar's colonies had to be legitimated back in Rome, often in ceremonies before the people. In the absence of Octavian and Antonius, the senate began to regain some stature, but its first achievement of the new year was to decree rare honors for Octavian, thus confirming what the army had already decided. In a similar vein, Cicero's triumphal procession was a demonstration of the people's attempt to reclaim some influence over events increasingly taking place away from Rome.

Octavian's assiduous adherence to form upon his return to Rome demonstrates again a Roman aristocrat's need to be seen performing the appropriate rituals and procedures before the Roman people. It further shows that these forms continued to carry weight at least in the eyes of Octavian, who found them necessary as he endeavored to embark on a political career, beginning with a consulship, even as the political structures of Rome were transforming to accommodate monarchy. Octavian's public image was now nearly complete: he returned to Rome with his troops after a significant victory, a *triumphator*, although not officially sanctioned by the senate; he was elected to the consulship, was officially adopted into Caesar's family, and presided over a criminal trial in which his father's murderers were banished from Rome. All that was left was to accommodate the other supporters of Caesar, restore order, and bring an end to this period of civil conflict.

8

The Performance of Politics in the Triumviral Period

Opposition and Consolidation

The previous five chapters focus on a relatively brief chronological period—the twenty months or so between Caesar's assassination and the formation of the Second Triumvirate—in which we examined public ceremonial against a backdrop of political developments. This approach has enabled us to see how such ceremonies reflected, advanced, or hindered the struggles for power that arose after Caesar's assassination. Our procedure will now have to change somewhat, since each of the next two chapters covers a much larger chronological period—first the Triumviral period (ca. 43–27 BC) and then the Augustan Principate (27 BC–AD 14)—rendering impossible a detailed narrative that discusses every ceremony that occurred; rather we will have to focus on larger patterns of such displays of power and consider how they reflect the great transformation in the polity of Rome and its empire.

The Triumviral period continued the process of transition already begun in the dictatorship of Caesar from the shared power that characterized the Republic to the burgeoning monarchy of the Principate.[1] Through public ceremonial the triumvirs displayed their unity of purpose and shared political ambitions as well as their extraordinary and unprecedented powers. They also could advertise peace and reconciliation, harmony and prosperity, as the salutary byproducts of their regime. Despite their great power, however, the triumvirs did not have full control over public ceremonial. Those opposed to the triumvirs, a long list that included L. Antonius, brother of the triumvir, Sextus Pompeius, the female relatives of the proscribed, and, at times, portions of the urban populace, voiced their outrage and demonstrated their opposition at public ceremonies as well. After M. Antonius departed for the east to engage the Parthians, our attention will be focused on Octavian, who distanced himself from his colleague and displayed his power without rival at public ceremonies. Throughout this period, the rivalries among the triumvirs, their attempts at reconciliation, opposition to the triumvirate, and popular demonstrations—that is, much of political activity—occurred at public ceremonies before the urban populace at Rome.

The Return of the Triumvirs (November 43 BC–early 42 BC)

The return of the triumvirs marked the beginning of a new era in Roman politics, but what would characterize this new era and how the triumvirs would use their power were still uncertain. In the first months of the triumvirate, the triumvirs tried to underscore the benefits of their regime at public ceremonies, but clues that foreshadowed the coming civil conflict were frequently visible. The presence of the legions in the city, the proscriptions of the triumvirs' enemies, which led to the exile or death of many distinguished Romans, and the performance of women in politics all indicated a social order in upheaval.

The new division of power that Antonius, Octavian, and Lepidus had negotiated away from the city of Rome had to be legitimated in the city itself. The triumvirs returned with their armies intact. They entered the city separately over the course of three days, Octavian first, followed by Antonius and then Lepidus, each one accompanied by a bodyguard and a legion of soldiers. The order in which they returned was significant, for in the first triumviral edict that announced and initiated the proscriptions the triumvirs were listed in order of age and priority of consulships held (46, 44, and 43 BC, respectively)—Lepidus, Antonius, Octavian.[2] Since Lepidus entered the city last of the three, his two colleagues became part of the crowd that received him, thus increasing the prestige of his return. Lepidus had also been instrumental in forging the agreement that resulted in the Second Triumvirate, in fact acting as intermediary between the other two, who had recently been on opposite sides at the battle of Mutina. Lepidus was chosen for the consulship of 42 BC, presumably as a sign of, and perhaps a reward for, the *concordia* that he had helped effect.

The return to Rome of a victorious *imperator* had become a ceremony for the enjoyment of the city populace as early as the middle Republic (see chap. 1). In the late Republic, those returning from exile borrowed the ceremony in order to transform a time of ignominy into a moment of glory (see chap. 1). In most cases, the returning citizen (whether general or exile) was greeted by a throng of wellwishers at the gates of the city and escorted to temples for a sacrifice and then to his home. The acclaim of the urban populace redounded to the glory of the returning citizen. When the triumvirs returned, the people changed their attire as a visible sign of the new era of *concordia*, and sacrifices were decreed in their honor (Dio 47.2.1–2; cf. App. *BC* 4.7.27–30). Our sources otherwise tend to underscore the presence of soldiers in the city, which was contrary to the Republican constitution but nonetheless had occurred frequently during the civil wars.[3] At this time, however, the military presence was more widespread and systematic. The deployment of military standards and troops throughout Rome in strategic locations demonstrated the triumvirs' control of the city through the physical occupation of its public spaces. If the triumvirs had indeed created *concordia*, they did so through civil war and conflict—a fractious foundation for a long-lasting peace.

The display of military might provide the backdrop for the triumvirs' constitutional acts, even when they made an outward show of respecting the sovereignty of the Roman people. P. Titius (*tr. pl.* 43) immediately convened a *contio* to promulgate a bill (*rogatio*) calling for the creation of a new magistracy to oversee the settlement of the present civil conflict; this new office was to be held jointly by the three returning generals for a period of five years, terminating on 31 December 38 BC. Appian states that this *rogatio* became a *lex* contrary to custom when the usual waiting period (*trinum nundinum*) between promulgation of a bill and its success or failure by vote in the *comitia tributa* was ignored; it passed into law on the day it was promulgated.[4] It is possible that Caesar's legislative procedure during his dictatorship set the precedent for the triumvirs' unconstitutional act. More to the point was the practical consideration that the conspirators were recruiting and training soldiers in the east, which necessitated a speedy confirmation and legal sanction of the triumvirs' private agreement. Dio (47.2.2) adds that the triumvirs demanded that the people petition them to act; thus, they would appear to be taking on their extraordinary powers through a mandate from the people. This is the way politics was supposed to work: magistrates were beholden to the will of the people. In this case, however, a ceremony that traditionally was an enactment of popular sovereignty became a specious pretext for the establishment of extraordinary powers. This was a ceremony turned on its head.

The proscriptions soon followed, and the scene of military might was replaced by the horror of heads adorning the Rostra.[5] This was a manifest indication that the triumvirs had taken control of one of the most important locations in the city, but the same question dogs us here, namely whether the Rostra Caesaris is meant or the old Rostra near the Comitium (see fig. 3). Ultimately, it probably matters little since, in either case, the message being communicated would have been roughly the same. If the remains had been placed on the Rostra Caesaris, then the statues of Caesar in his incarnation as savior of Roman citizens—also evoking perhaps the memory of the *Clementia Caesaris*—would have stood in stark contrast to the remains of the victims of his successors' less moderate victory. These remains would have underscored the new topography of the Forum and thus proclaimed a posthumous victory of Caesar against his political enemies. The sight of these severed heads on the old Rostra, if anything, would have had an even greater impact, especially if it was in the process of being dismantled when Caesar was killed. For this Rostra, as I argued earlier, was emblematic of the dying Republic, and many of those killed in the proscriptions, in particular someone like Cicero, were also representatives of this bygone age. Their remains on the old Rostra would have demonstrated visibly the end of the Republic. But at the same time, it would have provided only a clouded view of what the next era would be like. It told of the victory of Caesar and his supporters and the punishment of his (and their) enemies, and, through the transformation of the topography of the Forum, initiated by Caesar himself, this sight spoke of the end of the era of shared power, but what lay ahead was less clear.

At the end of 43, while the proscriptions continued but at a less frenzied pace, the consuls designate for 42, L. Munatius Plancus and M. Aemilius Lepidus, held triumphs on 29 and 31 December.[6] There are several triumphs attested for the Triumviral period, but in no instance is it entirely clear precisely how these triumphs were awarded. As we discussed earlier, in the early Republic, triumphs apparently were awarded jointly by the senate and people, although there are a few instances of the people conferring triumphs against the wishes of the senate.[7] A few months before these triumphs, Cicero had enjoyed an escort of the people to the Capitolium that he termed a triumph (see chap. 7). The triumph was a national drama that symbolized civic harmony and consensus, even though it was often awarded only after much contention. But in the late Republic, the civil wars changed the celebration of many triumphs.

In the Triumviral period, it is generally assumed that those who celebrated a triumph did so only by permission of one or more of the triumvirs, especially since most of the generals in this period were allied to the triumvirate, although it is not clear what procedure, if any, was followed. Was the senate compelled to pass a decree, or the *comitia* to vote? Such compulsion would only belie the consensus that the triumph was supposed to symbolize. The only direct evidence we have for the conferral of a triumph in the Triumviral period is of limited usefulness. In a passage describing the triumph of L. Antonius (which we will discuss at greater length later in this chapter), Dio claims that Lucius initially received no support for his triumph, but, after soliciting and receiving the permission of Antonius' wife, Fulvia, to celebrate one, "everyone voted for it" (Dio 48.4.3). The verb Dio uses here could describe either voting in the public assemblies or in the senate, but it at least shows that the triumvirs sought senatorial or popular approval when they awarded triumphs. Whether or not we can accept the story of Fulvia's involvement at face value is not clear. It is certainly true that Fulvia had long involved herself in politics through her marriages to eminent politicians, P. Clodius, C. Curio, and finally M. Antonius.[8] In general terms, then, the story is credible, but the mechanics of it—that is, precisely how Fulvia managed to bring about Lucius' triumph—are less clear.[9]

The triumphs of Plancus and Lepidus were ostensibly for victories in Gaul and Spain, but, amid the conferral of extraordinary powers on the triumvirs and the trials of the proscriptions, the memories of these foreign wars probably faded into the background. Moreover, part of Lepidus' success was due to his negotiations with Sextus Pompeius, for which he had received a *supplicatio*.[10] Cicero's letters around the time of the battle of Mutina attest to the centrality of Lepidus and Plancus to Cicero's hopes for the senate's renewed supremacy in a restored Republic,[11] and it is possible that they were chosen to celebrate triumphs and hold the consulship for 42 as a symbol of the consolidation and *concordia* that the establishment of the triumvirate would bring. The building program in which each *triumphator* engaged following his triumph is testimony to the kind of symbolism that these triumphs were intended to reflect. Lepidus began or continued construction of Caesar's new voting enclosure, the Saepta. This makes sense considering his position as *magister equitum* in 44 and consul and triumvir in 42, when the triumvirs were honoring Caesar's memory in several ways, including the construction of a temple.[12] But the Saepta not only honored Caesar's memory; it was also a symbol of popular politics, a place where the people could express their will and demonstrate their fundamental power of conferring honors through elections. It was a monument, in other words, that looked back to the ideals and ideology of Republican politics. Plancus' building project also hearkened back to the Republic, for he restored one of the most ancient monuments in the Forum Romanum, the Temple of Saturn,[13] which housed the state treasury.

These triumphs, then, marked the end of the hostilities that culminated at the battle of Mutina, but they did so without specifically celebrating a victory over Roman citizens. Celebrations for victories in civil wars had occurred previously in the late Republic, but in every case the celebrants attempted to conceal the bloodshed of Roman citizens behind a veil of foreign war. Nonetheless, the reality of what had happened was still visible at the triumphs of Lepidus and Plancus. We are told, for instance, that the soldiers at both triumphs, marching behind their commanders, shouted that the two consuls had triumphed not over the Gauls but over the "Germans,"[14] punning on the Latin word *germanus*, which also means "brother," since both Plancus and Lepidus had used their influence to spare their brothers who had been among the proscribed.[15] Further, Lepidus published an edict that compelled residents of the city to take part in the sacrifices and feasting, or face the grim prospect of proscription themselves. As a result, the people only reluctantly escorted Lepidus in his procession to the shrines of the city (App. *BC* 4.31.132). This edict was a reminder that the triumphs of Lepidus and Plancus were the product not of civic harmony and consensus but conflict and civil war.

The triumphs of Lepidus and Plancus could not purge memories of the recent civil conflict. Similar memories arose later in their consulship through a remarkable *contio* convened by Roman women, who had lost husbands and sons and brothers in recent battles and were then required, pursuant to a law passed by the triumvirs, to contribute through debilitating exactions to the imminent war against Brutus and Cassius. Such political action by women was virtually without precedent and could only have served as a reminder of the dislocation and suffering caused by the proscriptions. This collection of *matronae* first sought relief through the triumvirs' womenfolk, Antonius' mother and wife and Octavian's sister. When, however, they were unable to obtain satisfaction, they went directly to the Forum Romanum and onto the Rostra, where the triumvirs were presiding over a public meeting. The people and the army stood aside and let them pass. Hortensia, daughter of the famous orator, Q. Hortensius, chosen as spokeswoman, delivered a speech on that day before an assembled crowd of Roman citizens, the triumvirs, and a portion of their armies.[16] The appearance of women in the Forum to challenge the authority of the triumvirs and bring to light the injustice of the proscriptions could only have undermined what the triumvirs were hoping to achieve, in particular rebuking the idea that they had produced civic harmony.

Hortensia's speech might have had greater effect because of the topography of the Forum, which was still in a state of transformation. The mere presence of women in the Forum was eloquent testimony to the harsh effects of such proscriptions, since they probably included in their number widows and bereft mothers and sisters. In more general terms, the unfinished nature of Caesar's building projects, the moving of the Rostra and the construction of a new senate house, might have underscored the instability of the regime that had just formed. The sight of the women standing on the Rostra, where just recently the heads of those executed had been displayed, was a vivid reminder of the emotional and financial costs of the proscriptions. Whether the Rostra was still so decorated we do not know, but the memory of the proscriptions was still fresh. The triumvirs were indignant and angry, but the use of force against these women would have been an inappropriate demonstration of their powers. Instead, they disbanded the meeting until the next day when they reconsidered their exactions and shortened the list of women who were required to pay. The unexpected appearance of these women in the Forum undermined the best efforts of the triumvirs to enjoy a smooth transition to power.

The ceremonies in this early phase of the Triumviral period reflected the uncertainty and instability of the time as the triumvirs attempted to establish their new political office. The ideals that they asserted—consensus and reconciliation, peace and harmony—were often undermined by the ceremonies themselves. The triumvirs strong-armed the *comitia tributa* into passing a law that sanctioned their extraordinary powers; thus, a ceremony of popular sovereignty was made to serve the will of the three men in power. The public grief and indignation of Roman women combined with the grisly sight of heads on the Rostra were stern indictments of the triumvirs' claims to be restorers of public order. If the conspirators had hoped to achieve harmony in public life, the ceremonies that marked the beginning of their time in power were reminders of the unconstitutional nature of their political position, which was as much a source of conflict as consensus.

The Perusine War and the Pact of Brundisium (January 41 BC–January 39 BC)

The next phase of the Triumviral period was more unsettled and even riotous as opposition to the triumvirs grew. L. Antonius, brother of the triumvir, clashed with Octavian over the settlement of veterans in Italy. Sextus Pompeius celebrated his success against Octavian's forces with a mock naval battle near the toe of Italy. The Pact of Brundisium, an agreement to end hostilities between Antonius and Octavian, was supposed to bring unity to those in power and peace to Rome, but riots in the city imperiled the lives of Antonius and Octavian, even as they tried to quell the unrest with a display of reconciliation and peace.

Octavian came into conflict with L. Antonius during the latter's consulship in 41. This rivalry, which ultimately exploded in war around the walls of Perusia, was kindled in the city of Rome through Lucius' engagement with public ceremonial. Lucius' consulship began with a triumph on the first day of January 41. The practice of having a triumph mark the beginning of a consulship became more common in the Triumviral period.[17] L. Antonius was awarded a triumph for an alleged victory over some Alpine peoples (*ex Alpibus*),[18] against whom he had never enjoyed a command (Dio 48.4.3–6). The enemy, it seems, only provided the pretext for a triumph that was intended to elevate Lucius' public stature. Lucius, probably in the *contio* that accompanied his triumph, compared himself to the great C. Marius, who had also triumphed on the first day of his consulship in 101 BC,[19] and whose name and image continued to resonate long after his death, as demonstrated by the brief rise to power of the pseudo-Marius Amatius following Caesar's assassination (see chap. 4). Lucius, however, scrupulously avoided the error of Marius, who had convened the senate while still dressed in triumphal garb (*ILS* 59). The mention of Marius was not merely an obscure reference to remote history; rather it was intended to provide Lucius with an advantage in his rivalry with Octavian, which hinged on the issue of the placement of veteran colonies in the Italian countryside, and the ultimate prize was primacy in Italy. Lucius had been a member of a commission charged with this duty since June 44 (Cic. *Phil.* 5.7). He probably felt that Octavian's involvement was an encroachment on his sphere of influence. The regions that rose up to challenge Octavian—Umbria, Etruria, and the Sabine country—had, in the first civil war, supported Marius' cause against Sulla. Thus, the contest between Lucius and Octavian was a manifestation of a larger sea of social unrest, which involved issues that had provoked the Social War.[20] Lucius' mention of Marius' name at this time might have broached these issues once again.

Lucius attempted to demonstrate his supremacy in this struggle for control of Italy by modifying a traditional feature of the Roman triumph, namely the display of crowns sent by conquered cities and peoples. In Lucius' triumph, the crowns were offered not by the conquered peoples, as was customary, but the Roman people, one from each of the voting tribes. But it is vital to keep in mind that at this time, in fact since the end of the Social War, the thirty-five tribes of Rome comprised not just the people of Rome but also the people of Italy, as enfranchisement spread to most of the allied cities. The display of these crowns recalls Lucius' statue near the Temple of Castor bearing an inscription calling him patron of the thirty-five tribes (Cic. *Phil.* 6.12) and was proof of Lucius' patronage of Italy. He thus preempted any attempt on Octavian's part to win control of the peninsula. That Octavian himself was engaged in this struggle for control of Italy is evidenced by an inscription calling him *patronus* of Samnium.[21] This discussion should make it clear that Lucius' triumph was not simply a celebration for a victory over some Alpine tribes, but rather it cut to the heart of the political issues current in this period, which ultimately concerned Lucius' struggle for power with Octavian.

The very conflict between the consul L. Antonius and the triumvir Octavian called into question the distribution of power among senior magistrates and the danger posed to traditional politics by the establishment of the triumvirate. This issue was raised more directly at a *contio* later in Lucius' consulship (the precise chronology is uncertain). Lucius hastened to Rome with his troops and was received at the gates of the city by one Nonius, who immediately handed over the troops under his command.[22] Still in military dress, he harangued the people in a *contio* at an unknown location. Since Lucius later had to effect a special dispensation to be absent from the city to begin a war (probably through a *lex* voted on in the *comitia tributa*), it is likely that he addressed the people within the Pomerium, probably at the Temple of Castor where the voting took place. He appeared in military dress, unusual for a civilian *contio*, as Dio points out (48.13.5), and claimed that Octavian and Lepidus would be punished and that M. Antonius would exchange his portion of the triumvirate for the consulship, thus bringing to an end this period of unlawful rule and restoring the traditional magistracies.[23] Those present cheered Lucius' speech and saluted him *imperator* (App. *BC* 5.30.118; cf. Dio 48.13.5).

The acclaim of the people failed to carry Lucius home as victor. He and his forces were finally defeated near Perusia in early spring 40 BC. Hostilities between the triumvirs bubbled up once more, but after much political maneuvering they reconciled and struck an agreement, usually termed the Pact of Brundisium in the fall of that year.[24] Thereafter Antonius and Octavian returned to a discordant and riotous Rome, participated in several ceremonies that demonstrated their renewed friendship and advertised the peace and harmony that their reconciliation would effect.[25] The twin *ovationes* that M. Antonius and Octavian celebrated and the elections that they called should be understood in this context of contention, rivalry, and popular protest, during which the lives of the triumvirs were in peril.

Many of the traditional public festivals and games on the Roman calendar continued to be celebrated in the Triumviral period. Some (unsurprisingly) promoted the images and interests of the triumvirs. M. Agrippa was instrumental in the promotion of Octavian's image through public entertainment and at times acted as a kind of intermediary to the people. Following his part in the Perusine War, M. Agrippa returned to Rome and celebrated the *Ludi Apollinares* as praetor urbanus in 40.[26] The *Ludi Apollinares* occurred in Caesar's birth month, and (as we discussed earlier) it is possible that he took a personal interest in their production before his death.[27] In fact, the triumvirs had declared Caesar's birthday a holiday, compelled everyone to take part in the celebration, and moved it earlier in the month so that it would not conflict with the *Ludi Apollinares*.[28] Agrippa's games included the *Lusus Troiae*, performed by noble youths. The attested occurrence of the *Lusus Troiae* closest to Agrippa's rendition was at Caesar's games following his quadruple triumph in 46, his own revival after Sulla's revival in 81.[29] In both of these instances, before Agrippa's production, the *Lusus Troiae* was performed in conjunction with a triumph or with victory games. The tradition of the origin of the *Ludi Apollinares* also associates them with victory,[30] and it is possible that Agrippa exploited this connection following Octavian's victory in the Perusine War. Further, the performance of the *Lusus Troiae* in conjunction with the *Ludi Apollinares* was a celebration of the Julian *gens*, and, since they came so soon after Caesar's birthday, this month was rife with celebrations in memory of Caesar. Octavian never failed to advertise his family connection to Caesar, but it is possible that he called on Agrippa to make this connection more explicit, since in this year the inscription *Divi Filius* first began to appear on his coins.[31]

The most intriguing ceremony of the opposition around this time was held outside the city of Rome. Sextus Pompeius produced a mock naval battle in fall 40 BC to celebrate his supremacy on the sea and humiliate Octavian's lieutenant, Salvidienus Rufus, who had failed because of a storm to engage Sextus in battle. Rufus' failure was a factor in forcing the triumvirs to negotiate with Sextus, who enjoyed as a consequence a victory of a sort. The only previous mock naval battle occurred at Caesar's triumph in 46 (Suet. *Jul.* 39.4), and spectacles of this type remained rare in the imperial period because of the expense and logistics of putting them on.[32] Although the real naval battle had never happened, Sextus produced a lavish spectacle that pitted wooden boats against those made of leather, mocking Rufus' scheme, which involved using leather boats to cross the straits.[33] This "battle" took place in full view of his opponents on the opposite shore. Sextus' reenactment of a battle, like Caesar's, was associated with victory and triumph, but it was unusual in that, unlike the mock naval battles of the imperial period, the battle depicted was not really "historical" in the sense that it was a reenactment from a more remote past. Rather it depicted a battle that never took place and was put on for the benefit of those who would have been participants if it had. It did not celebrate a shared victory over a common enemy, as those of the imperial period would, but it was intended to demonstrate Sextus' superiority over his enemies—it was divisive, not unifying, and it perhaps showed that the *concordia* that the Pact of Brundisium was supposed to foster could only be short-lived.

Following the conclusion of this pact, Antonius and Octavian returned to Rome, probably in October, to attempt to repair the damage done by the hostilities in Italy, first the Perusine War and then the activities of Sextus Pompeius. The pair celebrated *ovationes*, which became symbolic of the peace that they consistently advertised.[34] These *ovationes*, like the triumph of L. Antonius in January 41, demonstrate the continuing evolution of these kinds of ceremonies in the late Republic. The *ovatio*, which had long been known as the lesser triumph in the middle Republic in particular, became a convenient option for the senate when it did not wish to award a triumph, but its conferral was much rarer than the triumph proper.[35] I argued earlier that Caesar's *ovatio*, held in conjunction with the *Feriae Latinae* in January 44, downplayed military victory[36] and instead celebrated peace, *concordia*, and reconciliation. Antonius and Octavian celebrated no victory at all, only reconciliation. And they made this clear by advertising the *ovationes* as celebrating *pax*, as duly recorded in the *Fasti*.[37] *Pax* had become an important symbol in the late Republic, especially in the uncertain months after Caesar's assassination when civil war appeared imminent.[38] When the two triumvirs proclaimed peace, they were hearkening back to the precedent set by Caesar's *ovatio* and also to a symbol of importance to the urban *plebs*. The people cheered the news of the reconciliation in the hopes that they too would enjoy the benefits of this peace (Dio 48.31.2). This ceremony demonstrated that the triumvirate remained intact despite the squabbles that arose as a result of Octavian's rivalry with L. Antonius, and that it would be a vehicle of peace, not a harbinger of yet more civil war. There was no Roman ritual designed specifically to celebrate *pax*, but the *ovatio* traditionally celebrated a victory of a certain type: one that was "bloodless" and "dustless"; it was, in other words, a ceremony that could be—and was on this occasion—adapted to suit the purposes of Antonius and Octavian.

If peace was the objective of these *ovationes*, they failed, for the city remained unsettled despite the presence of the triumvirs. Rioting persisted and even increased around the persons of Octavian and Antonius. The rioting had begun as a result of the breach between M. Antonius and Octavian caused in part by the war in Perusia and the excessive burdens on the people of Italy in the form of taxation and veteran settlements. The naval maneuvers of Sextus Pompeius in the Mediterranean, which disrupted the grain supply to Rome, caused near famine conditions and threw the city further into turmoil. Crowds came to Rome to vent their anguish and frustration, congregating at the temples and in the Forum and winning the sympathy of those resident in Rome (App. *BC* 5.12.48–50). The famine caused additional riots as the urban *plebs* used the traditional ploy of closing the shops and then forced the magistrates from the city (App. *BC* 5.18.73). Following the siege of Perusia, the rioting only worsened (App. *BC* 5.67–68; Dio 48.31.5–6). When the war with Sextus Pompeius dragged on, the people began to demand a settlement, usually at public ceremonies (Dio 48.31.4; cf. App. *BC* 5.67), still an important venue for the expression of popular sentiments. As a demonstration of their displeasure at the triumvirs, a crowd gathered in the circus, probably at the *Ludi Plebeii* in November 40, and cheered the statue of Neptune, on the grounds that it represented Sextus Pompeius, who had become accustomed to donning a sea-blue chlamys instead of the purple toga of a Roman commander and calling himself the son of Neptune.[39] This acclaim for Sextus is one of the few attested instances of the urban *plebs* acknowledging the political imagery and propaganda of one of the contestants for power. When Octavian refused to allow this statue to be displayed at a subsequent set of games, the people hurled stones at the magistrates, driving them from the Forum, and pulled down the statues of Octavian and Antonius (Dio 48.31.5; Suet. *Aug.* 16.2). At some point amid the riots, Octavian, it seems, attempted to convene a *contio* in the Forum (the precise location is not known) but was pelted by stones before he had a chance to defend his actions in a speech. With no opportunity in such a tumult to address the crowd with words, he tore his clothing presumably in an effort to show that he was suffering as the people were.[40] When Antonius came down the Sacra Via to rescue his colleague, the crowd stoned him as well. The triumvirs were forced to resort to summoning military support from outside the city to disperse the crowd and retake control of the city. The soldiers violently suppressed the rioters, Antonius with difficulty rescued Octavian, and finally calm was restored.

Following this period of rioting, the triumvirs remained in the city, first to celebrate the festival vowed at Philippi (Dio 48.32.4), and second to preside over new elections. The victory at Philippi, symbolically at least, brought an end to the Republic with the defeat and death of two of its foremost advocates, M. Brutus and C. Cassius (App. *BC* 4.138.580). It was also the greatest victory of the two leaders of Caesar's supporters, the result of their cooperation and the united strength of the forces at their command. The festival was intended to bring this period of civil unrest to a close by celebrating victory through *concordia*.

At the close of the year 40, Antonius and Octavian removed the praetors and consuls from office and replaced them with new ones, through appointment, it seems, rather than election in the *comitia*.[41] This is indicative of the changing nature of Roman elections, first under Caesar's dictatorship and then under the triumvirate.[42] Particularly characteristic both of Caesar's dictatorship and the period after his assassination was a marked diminishment of comitial activity, especially the elective assemblies. There were instances when a return to normalcy seemed to be in the offing, such as the praetorian elections in July 43 (as Cicero's letters attest), but these proved to be only illusory.[43] Octavian's election as suffect consul in 43, which may not have been a true expression of popular will, and subsequently the elective powers of the triumvirs demonstrated clearly that Caesar's control of the *comitia*, however this should be characterized, had become in the hands of his successors a permanent feature of the Roman constitution. We discussed earlier what effect the appointment of M. Lepidus and L. Plancus as consuls for 42 might have had on the minds of the electorate. In 39 the triumvirs appointed the consuls for the next eight years on the very day that elections were to be held, a frontal assault on popular sovereignty.[44] Other elections in this period are infrequently recorded in our sources. The removal of magistrates from office and new appointments were part of the reconciliation and consolidation of the triumvirs recently effected in Brundisium.[45] These new appointments also would ensure that no consul would challenge the triumvirs in the manner of L. Antonius. But the procedure involved in making these appointments, bypassing, as it did, the popular assemblies of the Roman Republic, declared openly that this consolidation did not include the Roman people, who had to look on as magistrates were chosen for them.

This reconciliation was further celebrated through the triumphs of one of the new appointees for the year 39. L. Marcius Censorinus (*cos.* 39) celebrated his triumph[46] on the first day of his consulship, as had L. Antonius two years before. Closer parallels were the triumphs of Plancus and Lepidus, both of which occurred in December 43, on the eve of their shared consulship. Those triumphs, as I discussed above, were intended both to mark the end of civil war and the proscriptions and, at the same time, begin the new era of the triumvirate. Not enough is known about Censorinus' triumph to draw firm conclusions. It was an opportunity for the triumvirs to celebrate a new era of *concordia*, which was a product of their recent meeting in Brundisium and became manifest through their appointment of the consuls.[47]

Amid the unrest in the streets of Rome, Censorinus' triumph reaffirmed the commitment of Antonius and Octavian to their extraordinary office and amicable relations.

The Consolidation of the Triumvirate and the War with Sextus Pompeius (Summer 39 BC–September 36 BC)

Many of the ceremonies in this phase of the Triumviral period celebrated the successes of the triumvirs and their subordinates. The voices of the opposition were muted but not completely silent. The existence of the treaty of Misenum, which was struck in the summer of 39, is an indication that Sextus Pompeius could not easily be disposed of. Other interests were at stake as well. But after the battle of Naulochus, where Sextus was defeated, Octavian returned to Rome without rival in Italy and received a number of extraordinary honors that prefigured the Principate. The process of consolidation began to proceed more briskly.

Our sources relate an anecdote describing Octavian's *clementia* and demonstrating how the triumvirs were beginning to take control of public ceremonial. A woman named Tanusia hid her husband, T. Vinius, in a chest at the house of a freedman, Philopoemen, in the hopes that everyone would think that he had already been killed. She then waited for a public festival, which a relative was sponsoring, and arranged through Octavia that Octavian alone of the triumvirs would enter the theater. She then informed Octavian what she had done and produced the chest and her husband from it. When Octavian discovered what had happened, he rewarded the freedman, one T. Vinius Philopoemen, with equestrian status.[48] Is this story plausible? I believe it is in the larger context of the recent agreement pardoning the proscribed.[49] Octavia's role as intermediary between Tanusia and Octavian is intriguing. By this time, in the year 39, her status had risen, especially since she served as the bond that held the triumvirate together through her marriage to Antonius.[50] The drama of Vinius and Philopoemen, played out so strikingly in the theater, was a visible demonstration of the tangible benefits accruing from the recent treaty with Sextus and further marked an end to the proscriptions. The theater had long been used for the expression of political sentiments in the Roman Republic, both on the part of performers on stage and members of the audience (see chap. 1). We do not hear of Octavian's complicity in planning or carrying out the demonstration, although it clearly redounded to his benefit. One advantage of the theater was that it was a more controlled environment in which to attempt to communicate with the people. Octavian's recent adventures with the crowd on the streets of Rome might have convinced him of this. In any event, the message was clear: one phase of the rule of the triumvirs was over, the proscriptions had ended, and clemency would now prevail.

The previous example is an indication that the triumvirs still could not fully control public performances. Other ceremonies that took place around this time offer evidence in a similar vein, even when the performers were the triumvirs' political allies. We will begin our discussion with two triumphs: the first celebrated by P. Ventidius Bassus (*cos. suff.* 43) over the Parthians in 38 and the second by Cn. Domitius Calvinus from Spain in 36. We should also bear in mind the triumph of L. Marcius Censorinus, which we discussed at the end of the previous section. My argument there was that Censorinus' triumph was an indication of the solidarity and unity of the triumvirs, especially since it followed so closely their reconciliation at Brundisium. In other words, the purpose of Censorinus' triumph first and foremost was to communicate a message for the triumvirs while the honor accorded Censorinus was of secondary importance. The evidence for the later two triumphs (mentioned earlier), however, suggests that the honorand, even when he received his command as a *beneficium* of the triumvirs, could put on a celebration that showed his independence from those in power. This is not to suggest that the interests of the triumvirs were not at stake at these triumphs, but rather that such ceremonies cannot be understood as communicating a message that was strictly in favor of or in opposition to the triumvirs. In other words, we cannot always assume that these ceremonies served only one purpose and communicated only one message.

Images of war in the east were conveyed to Rome in this period partly through the exploits of P. Ventidius Bassus, who was awarded a triumph to celebrate his victory over the Parthians.[51] Ventidius owed his early political advancement to his friendship with Caesar and later served on Antonius' side at the battle of Mutina, even raising two legions of soldiers on his own.[52] As part of the settlement that resulted from the formation of the second triumvirate, he was awarded a suffect consulship to replace Octavian in late 43 (App. *BC* 4.2.6). He also served with L. Antonius during the Perusine War and then fled to M. Antonius when Octavian proved victorious (App. *BC* 5.31–33, 35, 50). Dio explains that Ventidius' victory over Pacorus, the Parthian leader, caused a rift between subordinate and commander, so much so that Antonius removed Ventidius from command out of jealousy and refused to employ him again later, even though Antonius was awarded thanksgivings and a triumph (which he never celebrated) as a result of his lieutenant's victory.[53]

Ventidius' triumph was awarded no doubt as a result of his relationship to

Antonius.[54] In this period, as we have already seen, the traditional avenues to power and prestige in Rome—the holding of political office, triumphs, *ovationes*, even public entertainment—increasingly were personal favors of those in power, most notably, of course, Octavian and Antonius.[55] All of the honorands in the triumphs under discussion were subordinates of Antonius or Octavian. But does this mean that Ventidius' triumph could only have served the interests of the triumvirs, Antonius in particular?

Ventidius celebrated his triumph on 27 November 38 BC.[56] It is hard to believe that this date was a mere coincidence, for it marked the fifth anniversary of the *Lex Titia* that conferred on Antonius, Octavian, and Lepidus extraordinary powers that were about to expire on the last day of 38. Opposition to the triumvirate had been ardent at times in previous years, both in Rome and in Italy, and Sextus Pompeius continued to be a source of hope for those opposed to the triumvirs down to his defeat in 36. In the east, moreover, Antonius was then enjoying, at best, mixed success. He had consistently failed to achieve his ultimate objective of avenging the disaster at Carrhae and recovering the standards that a Roman army under the command of M. Crassus had lost to the Parthians in a humbling defeat. Dio informs us that Antonius even falsified his dispatches to Rome by emphasizing his successes and ignoring his reverses. Rumor and gossip let the truth be known, but Octavian refused to acknowledge publicly Antonius' misstatements concerning his campaign in the east, allowing instead sacrifices and festivals to be held in Antonius' honor, for the young Caesar was suffering similarly in his war against Sextus Pompeius.[57] Soon after Ventidius' triumph, in the early part of 37, the consul Agrippa declined to celebrate the triumph that he had been awarded, on the grounds that such a celebration would have been inappropriate at a time when his commander was enjoying so little success.[58] This was a time of political uncertainty: the triumvirs' powers were about to expire, and there was no clear indication of what would happen next; the prestige of Antonius had been compromised by his failures in the east. Under these circumstances, it would have been natural for Antonius to mask his failures behind the celebration of Ventidius' triumph and thus re-assure the populace of Rome that he was still very much in power.

Other aspects of this triumph also suggest that Antonius' interests would have been at the forefront. Antonius' absence from Rome when Ventidius celebrated his triumph meant that there could not have been an army to accompany Ventidius' *quadriga* into the city, since the troops in the east had been transferred to the command of Antonius upon the dismissal of Ventidius. It is unlikely that Antonius would have risked sending any legions to Italy for fear of losing them to Octavian. The presence of troops was traditionally required for a triumph to be conferred in the first place. The absence of the army from Ventidius' triumph reminded the spectators that this triumph was due ultimately to the authority and good will of Antonius.

Other aspects of the tradition of Ventidius' triumph suggest that Antonius' interests were not the only ones at stake. Dio tells us that Ventidius' reputation increased because he celebrated the triumph on his own, since (as stated earlier) Antonius never returned to Rome. There is also the story of Antonius' jealousy of Ventidius' success, although the depth of his jealousy is a matter of dispute in our sources.[59] A coin minted by Ventidius, which was in all probability struck in the east in commemoration of his victories in 39, suggests a cause of this ill will between subordinate and commander.[60] The head of Antonius decorates the obverse, demonstrating Ventidius' allegiance to the Antonian cause. The reverse inscription (P. VENTIDI PONT. IMP) shows that Ventidius received the acclamation of his soldiers, a customary prerequisite for the triumph, and the probable date of the minting of the coin shows that the acclamation took place before Antonius had even departed Athens for the east. This hastily made celebration of Ventidius' victories over the Parthians, before the *imperator* Antonius had even arrived on the scene, might have caused the ill will to which our sources refer.

Whether Antonius was truly jealous of Ventidius or not is of less importance than the fact that the story exists in our tradition, for it likely arose because Ventidius returned alone to celebrate a triumph for a war in which Antonius had only met with failure. This story also shows that Ventidius' triumph, rather than celebrating Antonius' part in this campaign, might have proved to be only a reminder of Antonius' failure. In other words, our tradition attempts to detach Ventidius' triumph from the influence of Antonius. All of this is only suggestive, but what it suggests is that Ventidius enjoyed a triumph that celebrated mainly his own glory with only partial reference to the *imperator* under whose auspices the battle was fought and the victory won.

Ventidius' background and career provide a further indication of whose interests might have been at stake in Ventidius' triumph. He was of Italian stock, descended from the soldiers of Italia who fought against Rome in the Social War, and he found success in a political career in the rapidly changing political climate of the late Republic. Ventidius can be classed with C. Asinius Pollio (*cos.* 40), a Marrucinus, whose grandfather had fought on the side of Italia, and Q. Poppaedius Silo, a Marsian, who served with Ventidius in the Parthian War and was descended from one who was active in the *Bellum Italicum*.[61] His rise to prominence, however, was stunning, not only because he was the first Roman to celebrate a triumph for a victory over the

Parthians but also because he achieved a triumph even though he himself had once been led captive as a young boy in the triumph of Pompeius Strabo (*cos.* 89).[62] By celebrating a triumph over the Parthians, Ventidius succeeded where all other Romans had failed. The anecdote about his boyhood, and his connection to the Social War, made his career emblematic of the rise of those of Italian stock to positions of power in the Roman Republic. Furthermore, it is possible that this anecdote found its way into our tradition through the speech that Ventidius delivered before the people on the occasion of his triumph. As it turns out, this composition was the work of another distinguished *municipalis*, the historian Sallust,[63] who, after Caesar's assassination, chose retirement and the study of history over the battlefield of Roman politics. Sallust, like Ventidius, came from Italian stock and was swept to power along with Caesar, who had successfully garnered support from many *municipia* in the war against Pompeius. The career paths of Sallust and Ventidius diverged when Ventidius maintained an active role in politics through adherence to Antonius, and Sallust abandoned the Rome of the triumvirs. How far Sallust's bitterness at his abrupt retirement from politics might have crept into the speech he composed for Ventidius is unclear. But he could be responsible for the attempt to detach Ventidius from Antonius and emphasize instead his Italian roots and remarkable career.

Another example of a similar kind of independent action was the triumph of Cn. Domitius Calvinus (*cos.* 53, 40). He was an enigmatic character[64] who appears as tribune of the *plebs* during the contentious consulship of Caesar and Bibulus (59 BC), siding with the latter. His later career was tainted by scandal after he was elected to the consulship of 53 amid charges of electoral malfeasance.[65] He was apparently Caesar's choice for *magister equitum* for the year 43 but disappears following Caesar's assassination; he reappears on the side of the triumvirs at Philippi and in 40 as the consular colleague of C. Asinius Pollio. Calvinus was awarded a triumph for his victory in Spain, despite the fact (we are told) that Octavian was *imperator*.[66] Dio relates this story in the larger context of a passage on C. Asinius Pollio's success and triumph over the Parthini in Illyricum, in which he also informs us that the triumvirs regularly awarded triumphs to their subordinates. Pollio celebrated his triumph almost immediately, it seems, but Calvinus' triumph was postponed for three years.[67] The simplest explanation for this postponement is that, despite his victory, Calvinus' presence was still required in Spain.[68] It is also possible that he postponed his triumph so as not to overshadow Octavian, the *imperator* under whose auspices he won his victory, acting in concert with M. Agrippa, who declined to hold a triumph at the beginning of his consular year (37), just two months after Ventidius celebrated his triumph.[69] But the timing of Calvinus' triumph in July 36[70] might have been equally ill suited to Octavian's public image, for he was preparing for his final confrontation with Sextus Pompeius, when a victory celebration—any victory celebration—was premature.

It is probably an overstatement to suggest that Ventidius' triumph is evidence for the persistence of the opposition to the triumvirate among the *municipia* of Italy—an opposition that flared up most notably during the Perusine War.[71] That pockets of resistance did exist in Rome is evidenced by the aedileship of the obscure M. Oppius.[72] M. Oppius was one of those proscribed in the early days of the triumvirate, who rescued his father from execution in a fashion that became Aeneas-like in our tradition. He was elected to the aedileship of 37, perhaps in July 38. When he tried to resign the office with pleas of poverty, the Roman people took up a collection to ensure that he could remain in office (App. *BC* 4.41.173; Dio 48.53.4–5). In the theater, the spectators[73] threw coins to Oppius in such quantities that he became a wealthy man. Appian tells us further that the craftsmen built for him, free of charge, whatever he needed for the execution of his duties as aedile (although it is not clear what is meant). Oppius' election to the aedileship indicates that free elections still existed, if only for the junior magistracies. But there were no candidates for the aedileship in the following year, which means that the triumvirs either did not succeed in filling the office or that it was becoming too expensive to hold. Dio's account of the election of M. Oppius, a man who suffered under, but survived, the proscriptions of the triumvirs, also shows that the people could use the *comitia* as a form of protest to decry the diminishment of comitial activity after the triumvirs took control of elections to the senior magistracies.

Another indication of Oppius' popularity was the demonstration at his funeral.[74] A crowd of people lifted his body on their shoulders and carried it to the Campus Martius for burial. Such expressions of grief occurred only rarely in the late Republic, and only for those who enjoyed great popularity. Such tributes were also usually politically partisan in nature, the most famous of which took place at the funerals of Clodius in 52 and Caesar in 44. The conveyance of the corpse, whether to the Forum for the traditional *laudatio* or to the Campus Martius or elsewhere for cremation or burial, was often an act of popular protest against the current political power structure. Therefore, based on what we know about such events, it is probable that M. Oppius' funeral also was a form of political protest and, combined with his aedileship, is an indication that a portion of the Roman people viewed him as a symbol of opposition to the triumvirate.

The preceding discussion shows how action independent of the triumvirate, and even in opposition to the triumvirate, manifested itself in the public ceremonies of the period. The anticipated expiration of the first five-year term of the triumvirate brought Antonius back to Italy for another meeting with Octavian and a new settlement that would endure for the next five years. This meeting took place at the foot of Italy, this time in Tarentum in spring 37, at which the triumvirate was renewed for another five years and the dispensation of provinces reaffirmed.[75] Antonius, who had temporarily allied himself with Sextus Pompeius as a foil to Octavian, now abandoned the former in view of his renewed friendship with the latter and returned to the east. The political rivalry that developed between Sextus and Octavian, as was the case with other political rivalries in our period, was played out in public ceremonies. We have already seen how Sextus remained in the consciousness of the urban *plebs*, a portion of which, to the embarrassment of Octavian, cheered the appearance of Neptune's statue at games in the circus on the grounds that this statue represented the absent Sextus.[76] The long-sought defeat of Sextus, and the deposition of M. Lepidus from the triumvirate, which followed soon thereafter, marked a turning point in Octavian's career; his prestige and power increased, and the ceremonies that he put on were intended to make this known.

After his victory over Sextus Pompeius at Naulochus in September 36, Octavian returned to Rome and celebrated his victory with several appearances before the people.[77] He declared the civil wars to be at an end and peace to have been established on land and sea. He also claimed that he would restore the Republic, thus promising the end of the triumvirate and a restoration of traditional political procedure. This declaration,[78] along with the themes of peace and conquest, played a part in establishing Octavian's status as champion of the people. Octavian had suffered through periods of great unpopularity, especially in the aftermath of the Perusine War; at the same time, Sextus Pompeius, mainly through the memory of his father, seems to have been regarded as a great popular hero. With the defeat of Sextus, Octavian may have hoped to take his place.

Our sources state that Octavian's return precipitated a number of extraordinary honors for him conferred by the senate and people of Rome.[79] The provision that he could accept or reject them as he saw fit was an overt acknowledgment that there was as much glory in declining such honors as in the honors themselves.[80] In an unprecedented display of public affection, the senate and people, wearing garlands, processed beyond the gates of Rome to greet him upon his return[81] and escorted him to the temples and then to his house. We have discussed how returns of commanders were a form of ceremony. In this case, the modification of this tradition to include an escort for the returning *imperator* conferred even greater honor on Octavian. Octavian's return was commemorated by the erection of a statue atop a column decorated with beaks of ships. This statue depicted Octavian in the dress that he wore when he returned (App. *BC* 5.130.541). Moreover, on this column was an inscription bearing Octavian's declaration that through his victory he had brought the civil wars to an end and established peace on land and sea.[82]

Following his return, Octavian delivered two speeches, the first to the senate, the second to the people in a *contio*, operating very much within the traditional institutions of the Republic. We are told that Octavian addressed the people outside the Pomerium (Dio 49.15.3), but the precise location is unknown. Returning generals often addressed the senate at the Temple of Bellona,[83] which was also equipped with a *rostra* and could be used for a *contio*.[84] But if Octavian hoped to appear as champion of the people, the Circus Flaminius (see fig. 1) would have been a better location for a *contio*, for both the recent and remote history of this monument made it an important popular political symbol. The speech that he delivered upon his return to Rome detailed his achievements throughout his entire administration (App. *BC* 5.130.539; cf. Dio 49.15.3), thus publicly acknowledging that he viewed his victory as marking the end of one period of his career. Octavian nowhere explicitly states what he viewed as the beginning of this same period, although the formation of the triumvirate in November 43 is a strong possibility, for that marked the beginning of the process of avenging Caesar's murder, or, in more general terms, of purging the state of the triumvirs' enemies. This process culminated in the defeat of Sextus, who represented the last of the "Republican" forces who had opposed Caesar's dictatorship. Moreover, the defeat of Sextus and deposition of Lepidus, along with Octavian's declared intentions of restoring the Republic, meant that the extraordinary office of triumvir was no longer needed and thus this period of his career could be brought to a close.

Finally, on the Ides (thirteenth) of November 36, Octavian celebrated an *ovatio ex Sicilia* for his victory over Sextus Pompeius. His choice of an *ovatio*, instead of the more prestigious triumph, is understandable in light of the changing nature of this ceremony in the late Republic. Caesar's *ovatio* in January 44, held in conjunction with the *Feriae Latinae*, set the precedent. Antonius and Octavian followed suit by using the *ovatio* to celebrate the Pact of Brundisium in 40 and so recorded it in the *Fasti*. They also celebrated, as Caesar had before them, the beginning of a new era, one that was marked by a renewed harmony between the triumvirs and made evident by the cooperative appointment of consuls for the coming years. It is probable that Octavian used his *ovatio* in a similar way, since his speech upon his return showed that he viewed these celebrations as marking the end of one phase of his career and the beginning of another.

The date of Octavian's *ovatio* is also significant because 13 November marked the midpoint (of a sort) of the *Ludi Plebeii*, the games held annually from the period 4–17 November, which were of especial importance to the Roman *plebs*.[85] Traditionally, the plebeian aediles shared the burden, and the prestige, of putting on this festival, but in this year, no aediles had been elected because of a lack of candidates. Dio informs us that their duties were performed by the praetors and tribunes of the *plebs* (Dio 49.16.2), but none is known for this year. The failure to fill the aedileship seems to follow logically on the election of M. Oppius to the aedileship in 37, which he accepted only begrudgingly due to poverty. But it is incredible that poverty would have precluded all from becoming candidates. In any event, on the Ides of November, as part of the *Ludi Plebeii*, a feast of Jupiter was held, probably at the temple on the Capitolium, which served as a day of respite between the *ludi circenses* and the *ludi scaenici*.[86] In other words, Octavian seems to have planned his *ovatio* to be held in the middle of an important festival, when the city would likely be crowded, but on a particular day when there were few other distractions to draw attention away from his celebration. The lack of a plebeian aedile to sponsor these games cleared the way for Octavian to stand without rival in the gaze of the people.

In this phase of the Triumviral period, the triumvirs' subordinates celebrated triumphs that spoke to the interests of commander and subordinate alike, while the ceremonies involving the obscure M. Oppius showed that opposition to the triumvirate still existed. Once the reconciliation between Antonius and Octavian took root and helped produce the victory over Sextus Pompeius, Octavian was without rival in Italy, which was reflected in his glorious return to Rome following that victory and the extraordinary honors conferred on him. His declaration that he had established peace on land and sea was an empty claim, as events unfolded, but it reflected the optimism of these ceremonies before war with Antonius was in the offing.

Actium and Victory (33 BC–January, 27 BC)

Octavian's return, his speeches, and finally his *ovatio* might have proclaimed a new era of peace, but this claim became a tangible reality only through the program of tax and debt relief that Octavian implemented in order to ease the financial burdens shouldered by landholders throughout Italy during the course of the war with Sextus (App. *BC* 5.130.540; Dio 49.15.3). These ceremonies reflected Octavian's public image as champion of Italy and provided the necessary grounding for undertaking an unpopular and perilous war. This was part of the consolidation of Italy that would culminate in the oath of loyalty sworn in Octavian's name and his revival of the Fetial ceremony before the campaign against Antonius and Cleopatra commenced. The preparations for war focused on Octavian's exploitation of his primacy in Italy, which he had won through the war in Perusia and victory at Naulochus.

The tangible benefits of Octavian's peace were also in evidence during Agrippa's aedileship in 33—a crucial time for Octavian, between his victory over Sextus Pompeius and the final confrontation with Antonius. The political importance of Agrippa's aedileship has long been acknowledged by scholars,[87] and it is not necessary to rehearse all the details here. Certain issues, however, merit discussion in order to place Agrippa's aedileship in its proper historical and political context. The aedileship was a magistracy, as we have already seen, that went unfilled in the year 36, and none is known for the years 35 and 34. We can infer from the incomplete evidence that comes down to us that, by the time Agrippa became aedile, the office had been held only infrequently in previous years,[88] and it is possible that Agrippa held the office without a colleague in 33.[89] Fifty-nine days of Agrippa's aedileship were set aside for public entertainment, including another revival of the *Lusus Troiae*. This was also the number of days traditionally set aside for all the major *ludi* in a given year—the *Megalenses*, *Ceriales*, *Florales*, *Apollinares*, *Romani*, and *Plebeii*. If we are to assume that Agrippa sponsored all these games as curule aedile,[90] then he must have usurped the duties of the plebeian aediles (if there were any) and the praetor urbanus. This is a further argument for the contention that Agrippa was sole aedile in this year. A sole aedileship was unusual and perhaps even unprecedented, but it provided Agrippa with the opportunity to sponsor games without having to share the prestige with a colleague,[91] although he seems to have done so by means of the traditional games and festivals and so within the parameters of the civic calendar.

Agrippa's tenure of the aedileship, a junior magistracy, was also unusual in that he had previously held the two senior magistracies, the praetorship (in 40), and the consulship (in 37). Agrippa held the aedileship out of sequence presumably because it was politically expedient to do so,[92] for, in this way, Agrippa could promote the interests of Octavian before the populace of Rome. Agrippa had previously done this in similar ways, both with his sponsorship of the *Ludi Apollinares* as praetor urbanus in 40, and as consul in 37, when he declined a triumph that could have caused Octavian some political embarrassment.[93]

The aedileship was an especially appropriate magistracy through which Agrippa could attempt to promote the interests of Octavian before the urban populace because its traditional duties dealt with all manner of public life in the city (Cic. *Leg.* 3.7). Agrippa's aedileship was remarkable for the breadth and spectacular nature of his expenditures, the funds for which he drew entirely from his own resources.[94] In Agrippa's aedileship, even the mundane duties of repairing and restoring public buildings, roads, and sewers became a spectacular display when he sailed through the newly cleaned Cloaca Maxima into the Tiber River (Dio 49.43.1; Plin. *Nat.* 36.104). Agrippa's brief voyage through the main sewer of the city demonstrated the extent and thoroughness of his public works projects.[95]

Agrippa's aedileship was even more remarkable for the largesse that he conferred on the people. He distributed olive oil and salt free of charge and opened up the baths (up to 170 in number) to the public. He showered tickets on the spectators in the theater, which could be redeemed for food and clothing. He even hired out barbers so that their services would be available to the people (Dio 49.43.3). Romans traditionally allowed their hair to grow long during periods of mourning, and with the suffering caused first by the proscriptions and then by wars in Italy and Sicily, it is possible that many Romans continued to maintain such an appearance. It is also true that the populace of Rome remained devoted to the memory of Sextus Pompeius, who had been killed probably at the end of 35.[96] Octavian sponsored games to mark the event—whether to honor his life or celebrate his death is not clear (Dio 49.18.6–7). Sextus' popularity endured, as was evidenced at the games sponsored by M. Titius, the man responsible for his execution. When Titius attempted to put on games in Pompeius' theater (date unknown), the crowd cursed and drove him from the building (Vell. 2.79.6). It is possible that a period of public mourning for Sextus' death still endured. By rendering the services of barbers available to the public, Agrippa might have been encouraging the Roman people to adopt an appearance that was consistent with an atmosphere of celebration.

The question remains whether Agrippa's aedileship advanced the political goals of Octavian. Most scholars contend that the Roman people could not have remained unaffected by Agrippa's lavish displays of generosity and the marked improvement to the urban amenities of Rome for which he was responsible.[97] Direct evidence is scarce. The only contemporary extant source is Horace, who states that Agrippa received applause for his efforts (Hor. *Serm.* 2.3.182–86). But opposition to Octavian took the form of rioting in the streets in 31, when the imminent campaign against Antonius and Cleopatra necessitated new and burdensome exactions from the people.[98] In our period, Octavian's relationship with the people of Rome was rarely without difficulties. They seem to have sincerely embraced Octavian only once, when he returned following his victory at Naulochus with the promise of peace and the hope that the civil wars were at an end. Whether this promise and hope were realistic under the political circumstances is another matter—in hindsight they clearly were not. It is perhaps best to describe the resistance and opposition to Octavian as not following a discernible trend or pattern, but rather as existing in "pockets," which flared up when the burdens of war were intolerable and subsided when the hope of peace seemed real. Agrippa's aedileship was another attempt to revive such hope, but with Antonius in the east mustering his forces war must have seemed inevitable.

Octavian prepared the way for the final confrontation with Antonius and Cleopatra by representing the imminent war as a great contest of Roman values against the dangers of foreign influences. He did this in three ways: first, he obtained Antonius' will from the Temple of Vesta and publicized its damning contents at a meeting of the senate and then in a *contio* before the Roman people (Dio 50.3.4); he declared war ostensibly against Cleopatra through the revival of the ancient Fetial ceremony; and, finally, he persuaded Italian *municipia,* the senate, and the people of Rome to swear an oath of allegiance to him (Aug. *Anc.* 25.2). The contents of Antonius' will and the oath of allegiance to Octavian need not detain us here,[99] other than to point out the oath's symbolic importance to Octavian, who used it to create an image of himself as champion of Roman and Italian interests against a foreign queen and her Roman paramour. This oath made a statement: it marked the successful culmination of Octavian's efforts to build a base of support among the Roman people and the *municipia* and *coloniae* throughout Italy. It is possible that the Fetial ceremony communicated a similar message.

In October 32 BC members of the senate, outfitted for war in military cloaks, processed to the Temple of Bellona where Octavian, as *fetialis*, ceremonially declared war on Antonius and Cleopatra near the Temple of Bellona (Dio 50.4.5). As part of the ceremony several religious formulae had to be uttered in specific contexts (Liv. 1.32.5–14); one invoked Jupiter and Janus Quirinus; then the officiant asked each senator in turn whether he favored war until a majority was reached. (Whether a quorum of senators was required for the vote to be valid is not known.) The officiant then took a bloody spear that was kept in the temple and hurled it over a small column (the *columna bellica*) located in front of the temple into ground that was regarded as enemy territory. Thus war was declared.

One hypothesis has it that this ceremony was an invented archaism on the part of Octavian for the purpose of his declaration of war against Cleopatra.[100] It is the aim of this section to test this hypothesis. Such a test is possible only by analyzing the significance of Octavian's rendition of the Fetial ceremony in 32 through a discussion of the tradition of its establishment and historical evolution. According to tradition, the Fetial ceremony originated in the Regal Period, specifically the reign of Ancus Marcius, and evolved in the historical period.[101] The performance of this ceremony itself was part of a larger pattern of religious archaism that continued into the Principate of Augustus.[102] The Fetial college had already been the subject of a revival of interest in the 130s BC, at a time when Romans were looking to preserve the purity of their ancestral religion in the face of the contamination of foreign cults.[103] This notion might also have been on Octavian's mind in 32, as he was also making a symbolic stand on behalf of traditional Roman religious practices in the face of unseemly foreign influences. The ceremony as a whole was obviously important for Octavian's purposes, since it could serve to mask the reality of the civil wars that Octavian claimed already to have brought to an end in 36.[104] He could do so by representing the coming campaign against Antonius and Cleopatra as one against a foreign enemy. Thus, implicit in the Fetial ceremony was a confirmation of Octavian's status as champion of Roman and Italian interests; in this way, it acted in conjunction with the statement of the oath sworn on Octavian's behalf. More generally, the Fetial ceremony also could have functioned as a way for Octavian to declare publicly that, in contrast to his enemy, he would adhere to the traditional values of Rome as embodied in such ceremonies.

Even more important is the possibility that Octavian was himself responsible for a revival of interest in the Fetial college during the Triumviral period, of which his performance in 32 was part. J. Reynolds has argued that the θεμιστῆρες mentioned in a decree of the senate concerning the people of Aphrodisias (probably dating to 39 BC) must be a Greek rendering of *fetiales*. She further suggests that the consuls mentioned in the document were to exhort the *fetiales* to perform a ceremony that ritually validated the treaty between Rome and Aphrodisias.[105] If she is correct, then Octavian might have prepared the way for his performance in 32 by exhibiting an interest in the ceremonial activities of the Fetial college as early as 39. Reynolds' arguments, therefore, lend some support to the hypothesis of Rüpke and Wiedemann that the Fetial ceremony for declaring war, or at least elements of it, was an invented archaism—invented by Octavian—for the purposes of declaring war against Cleopatra.

There are only two attested instances of the Fetial ceremony from the historical period: the one under discussion and that of Marcus Aurelius in AD 178, prior to his campaign on the northern frontier (Dio 72.33.3). Even though our only source for Octavian's observance of this ceremony, the historian Dio, does not actually state that Octavian hurled a spear on this occasion, the earliest sources for this rite date to the Augustan Principate, and it stands to reason that this revival of interest as expressed in these sources was due to Octavian's performance in 32. Wiedemann has argued that the rite of spear throwing in particular was the element of the ceremony that Octavian invented, and it is worth considering why he may have done so. Rüpke has remarked that in both attested instances from the historical period (cited earlier), it was the eventual leader in the war who performed the ritual and not another member of the Fetial college.[106] In other words, the ritual of spear throwing seems to sanction the leadership of the general who is about to lead his troops into battle.

It is possible, then, that the rite of spear throwing served as confirmation of Octavian's status as leader in the war against Antonius and Cleopatra and, by extension, champion of Roman and Italian interests. Some evidence can be brought to bear to support this conclusion, but it is admittedly indirect. Varro, in his lost treatise *Calenus*, also speaks of the ritual of spear throwing, but he does so in the context of military commanders who performed this rite *ominis causa* when they were preparing an area to pitch camp.[107] In other words, Octavian might have introduced the spear throwing ceremony to Rome as a way of providing a more generic kind of religious sanction to his war against Antonius and Cleopatra (so Wiedemann). I would take this argument one step further: Varro refers to the commanders who performed this ritual as *duces*, a term not normally used of Roman commanders with *imperium*. Octavian's legal status in 32, after the second five-year period of the triumvirate had expired,[108] has long been a point of contention among scholars.[109] As Linderski has shown, the oath that was sworn after the declaration of war points to his status as *dux privatus*,[110] that is, as a military leader "elected" to military command against Antonius and Cleopatra by acclamation and consensus. This is a title that Octavian embraced before he began to call himself *princeps*, but even in a later period we still see it used.[111] One wonders if the Fetial ceremony, in particular the spear throwing rite, could have drawn attention to the extralegal status of Octavian at this time.[112] If so, it could have provided a public and ritual-based legitimation of his position.[113]

Even if we are correct in concluding that Octavian invented the spear throwing rite for the purpose of his declaration of war against Antonius and Cleopatra, we still do not know whether Octavian's audience on this occasion would have perceived, and consequently disapproved of, the artificiality of Octavian's performance, or whether they believed that they were witnessing the revival of an ancient ceremony. If the evidence of the oath sworn on Octavian's behalf is any indication, which occurred soon after the declaration of war, then the Roman people appeared convinced that Octavian was the man to lead the Roman forces against Cleopatra and further that he deserved their full support as sanctioned by the oath. On the other hand, the abiding support for Antonius in the senate even on the eve of Actium showed that Octavian was still an object of suspicion, and the Fetial ceremony seems to have done little to undermine Antonius' support.

Following his victory at Actium, Octavian returned to Rome in August 29 BC and held a number of ceremonies to celebrate his recent successes, not only the end of civil war but also his victories in Gaul and Illyricum. His return, triumph, and accompanying public entertainment reiterated certain familiar themes, while at the same time introducing new ones. This celebration marked the conclusion of the civil wars and the advent of peace as well as the beginning of a new regime that was advertised as being the restoration of the old order. Octavian was forced to operate within specific parameters defined by Republican traditions, but he was still able to reshape the political landscape by his novel combination of longstanding ceremonies, which reflected the nature of his new power.

A theme that carried through many of Octavian's ceremonies was the advent of peace. Two longstanding but rarely performed ceremonies dramatically drew attention to the end of war. Tradition held that the doors of the Temple of Janus remained open in times of war and closed when no Roman troops were in the field. On 11 January 29,[114] these doors were closed for only the third time in Roman history.[115] The first closing occurred during the reign of king Numa Pompilius (Liv. 1.19.3), whose reign was marked by peaceful accomplishments in the domestic sphere; the second in 235 at the close of the First Punic War.[116] That the closing of this temple's doors was symbolic of peace dates back at least to Piso (writing in the second half of the second century), and, if he is preserving an accurate tradition, back to the First Punic War. In any case, this tradition predates Octavian, who thus cannot be responsible for inventing it wholesale. It is curious, however, that at no other time in Roman history were the doors of the temple closed, even though other times were as free of war as after the First Punic War. Octavian revived a tradition from the remote past and a ceremony that had long before slid into obsolescence for the purpose of advertising his victory and its glorious benefits. The ceremony was of especial interest to him because one of the Fetial formulae he uttered to declare war on Antonius and Cleopatra required the invocation of Janus Quirinus (Liv. 1.32.9). Thus, the ceremonial closing of the doors of this god's temple brought an end to the hostilities that Octavian had solemnly opened in October 32 BC through the Fetial ceremony.

Since the closing of the doors of the Temple of Janus had not occurred for two centuries when Octavian had the ceremony performed, those present would have been witnessing a ceremony never before seen. Unless instructions for the ceremony survived in dusty annalistic scrolls, Octavian would have had to invent it. Who were the officiants at this ceremony? In a passage describing the opening of the doors of this temple as part of the process of declaring war, Vergil has a consul in the dress of an augur (*Quirinali trabea*) and in Gabine fashion (*Gabino cinctu*) perform the ceremony (*Aen.* 7.601–15). It is probable, then, that the consuls would have supervised the closing of the doors in 29. At the beginning of the year, the two consuls were Octavian himself (for the fifth time) and Sextus Appuleius, who was replaced later in the year by Valerius Potitus (Dio 51.20.1; 21.1). Octavian did not arrive until midsummer, leaving Sextus to oversee closing the doors of the temple. Other aspects of the ceremony are unknown. Was there a sacrifice? The utterance of a religious formula? A speech? Octavian might have had some scope for creative invention while claiming that the ceremony dated back to the reign of Numa.

At about the same time, the *augurium salutis* was taken,[117] which Suetonius includes in a list of ancient ceremonies, along with the *Diale flamonium*, *sacrum Lupercale*, and the *Ludi Saeculares* and *Compitalicii*, that Augustus restored to prominence (Suet. *Aug.* 31.4). Dio provides the most details about this ceremony (Dio 37.24). It was carried out each year on the day when no army was preparing to leave the city for campaign or was already in the field. Hence, it became associated with the respite from hostilities and peace. Dio describes this ceremony in the context of Cicero's consulship (63 BC) (cf. Cic. *Div.* 1.105), the only other attested instance in the Republic besides the taking of it by L. Aemilius Paullus in 160.[118]

The two ceremonies just mentioned—the closing of the doors of the Temple of Janus and the *augurium salutis*—were intended to demonstrate peace, and they would have done so more effectively if they had been performed at the same time, as Dio's statement implies. There is a topographical connection that should also be noted. In the context of the ceremonies described above, Janus is referred to, both by Augustus and by Suetonius, as Janus Quirinus. Janus was a numinous deity who inhabited doorways and openings and whose temple was located on the Palatine hill.[119] Quirinus, whose temple was on the Quirinal hill, oversaw the assembled citizenry and became associated with the deified Romulus. The shrine of Salus was located on the same hill in the vicinity of that temple.[120] It is not clear from our sources where the *augurium salutis* was taken, but a good guess would be the shrine of Salus on the Quirinal hill. The association of Salus and Janus became clearer when Augustus erected statues of these deities, along with Pax and Concordia, and required that Romans worship them together on 30 March.[121]

The ceremonies that spoke of peace laid the groundwork for Octavian's triumph in that they turned the people's attention away from the horrors of civil war to the prospect of peace, just as Octavian was preparing to celebrate a victory in civil war. Octavian had already anticipated the ill will inherent in such a celebration when he attempted to characterize Antonius as "un-Roman" in order to build support for the war against him, but Antonius still had supporters in Rome in 32, on the eve of the Actian campaign. Octavian therefore tried to direct the public's gaze away from Antonius and toward Cleopatra, in part by reviving the ancient Fetial ceremony for declaring war. Foregoing the triumph was not an option, since there was the expectation that he would celebrate one already decreed for his victories in Illyria. Failure to celebrate a triumph for his victory over Antonius, as difficult as this was, could have been seen as an admission that the campaign itself was unjust. Octavian had to tread carefully as he prepared and then celebrated his triumph.[122]

Octavian's return to Rome set the stage for his triumph and allowed him to introduce the themes that he wished to underscore. In preparation for Octavian's return, statues and inscriptions of Antonius were removed or effaced and honors bestowed on his conqueror, including having the Vestal Virgins, senate, and people, along with their wives and children, go out to meet him (Dio 51.19.2–3), an honor that he ultimately declined (Dio 51.20.4). The consul Valerius Potitus, representing the senate and people of Rome, performed the unprecedented act of sacrificing on the occasion of Octavian's return. Octavian praised his lieutenants, and especially Agrippa, for their services, perhaps at a *contio*.[123] The *municipia* of Italy offered gold crowns in celebration of Octavian's victory, reminiscent of those crowns at L. Antonius' triumph in January 41 and perhaps intended to signal the final consolidation of the peninsula under a new leader. As we discussed earlier, such offers of gold crowns were customarily made by vanquished city-states as a sign of obedience to their new conquerors. Unsurprisingly, Octavian declined this honor, since his victory signified the triumph, not the conquest, of Italy.

Octavian's triumph took place over the course of three days (13–15 August), the first devoted to his victories in Illyricum, the second to Actium, and the third to Alexandria.[124] Triumphs lasting more than one day became more common in the late Republic, beginning with Sulla's triumph over Mithridates in January 81 and including Cn. Pompeius' triumph in 61, the third in his illustrious career. Caesar's triumphs in 46 surpassed them all, since he celebrated four in sequence, thus "trumping" his rival, Pompeius. Octavian's triumph, therefore, was consistent with the pattern of the military dynasts of the late Republic, but by celebrating only three triumphs and doing so on successive days he showed no desire to emulate Caesar. In fact, Octavian shared the first triumph over several Illyric peoples with C. Carrinas, the son of a man who had been proscribed under Sulla (Dio 51.21.5–6), thus underscoring the theme of reconciliation. At the same time, however, the joint triumph of Octavian and Carrinas was a reminder that the latter had won his victories under the auspices of the former, who was in the unique position of being supreme commander.

The difficulties of commemorating a victory in a civil war also are in evidence in Octavian's triumph. Octavian did choose to celebrate a triumph for his victory at Actium, unlike Caesar who never celebrated a triumph for his victory at Pharsalus, but Octavian attempted to minimize the Actian triumph by celebrating it between the two other triumphs, both of which were clearly over foreign enemies.[125] When it came to commemorating his triumphs for posterity, Octavian (and then Augustus) was still more ambivalent. He states explicitly in his *Res Gestae* that he celebrated three curule triumphs, but he does not name the vanquished. In the *Fasti Barberiniani*, only the victories in Dalmatia and Egypt are mentioned.[126] Octavian intentionally omitted mention of Actium on the monument that recorded his victories as if to remove, if only partially, the memory of his victory from the public record.[127]

Octavian, then, was careful not to underscore his victory in civil war, but he did alter the form of the ceremony in a manner that placed him at the center of power. According to custom, the *triumphator* entered the city in his chariot behind the magistrates and senate, as a sign of deference to their authority and an acknowledgment that it was only with their approbation and consent that he had been conferred a triumph. Keeping the *triumphator* in his place was an important signal that the triumph was a celebration for all of Rome, and it demonstrated that the *triumphator*'s power was the result of the consensus of Rome's political leaders. The triumphal procession, then, inscribed a political consensus of a particular type: one that centered on the senate and magistrates. Octavian, by contrast, had the magistrates for the year follow his chariot, along with the senate, rather than march in front of it (Dio 51.21.9). This was one way that Octavian could demonstrate that his position in the state was supreme, exalted above even his colleague in the consulship, who was relegated to a position behind Octavian's chariot. Moreover, Octavian included in his *pompa* only those senators who had participated in his victory, thus excluding Antonius' supporters. Tiberius, Livia's son and the future *princeps*, and Marcellus, Caesar's nephew, were seen leading the trace horses on either side of Octavian's *quadriga* (Suet. *Tib.* 6.4). This was not unprecedented—family members of the *triumphator* often accompanied the *quadriga*—but they were given greater prominence in the new marching order. Reconciliation and clemency were appealing ideals, but in this instance, at least, Octavian seems to have rejected them in favor of a show of his own supremacy. Through the marching order in his triumphal procession, Octavian was able to remind his audience of the benefits that accrued to those who were willing partners in the new regime and elevated members of his family to prominence. Thus, he created and displayed a new political consensus—with himself at the center.

In a similar way the traditional distribution of the spoils of war brought Octavian to the center of power and elevated members of his family. A traditional component of a triumph was the display of the spoils of war and a distribution of cash to the soldiers. Since Caesar's dictatorship a donative to the citizen body was expected as well. Octavian's material benefactions underscored the prosperity that the Roman world would enjoy under his regime and demonstrated further that the Roman people would share in this prosperity. In his Alexandrian triumph, he brought the royal treasures of Egypt to Rome, which introduced so much wealth to the city that interest rates immediately dropped (Suet. *Aug.* 41.1). We can only speculate on the psychological or emotional effect that the visible display of this wealth might have had on those who were present at Octavian's triumph, but if the economic impact was immediately felt, then it would have been clear that Octavian's regime brought with it the promise of stability and prosperity.[128] Octavian had previously taken advantage of the terms of Caesar's will to distribute cash benefactions to the Roman people (see chap. 6). On the occasion of his triumph, he demonstrated how the Roman people could share in the new prosperity by distributing four hundred sesterces apiece to all adult males. He gave the same amount to children in the name of his nephew, Marcellus (Dio 51.21.3; cf. Suet. *Aug.* 41.2), blurring the distinction between a public distribution and a private benefaction and further binding the next generation of Roman citizens to his family. He thus demonstrated that the source of this prosperity was the house of Octavian, who was now the universal patron of the Roman people.

Closely connected to Octavian's triumph were the dedications of two important structures bearing the name of Octavian's family, the Temple of Divus Julius and the Curia Julia.[129] On 18 August Octavian dedicated the former, which had been begun by the triumvirs in January 42, in part as a way of marking the beginning of their campaign against the conspirators;[130] ten days later, on 28 August, Octavian dedicated the latter, probably begun by Caesar himself in 44 and part of his larger scheme for remaking the Forum Romanum. The Curia also housed the altar of Victory, which came from Tarentum and was decorated with the spoils of Octavian's victory in Egypt. Included in the building of the new Curia was the Temple of Minerva, also known as the Chalcidium.[131]

The ceremonies put on to commemorate the dedication of the Temple of Divus Julius were triumphal in character but simultaneously celebrated the Julian *gens* and members of Octavian's own family. There were notable "firsts" in Octavian's games. A hippopotamus and rhinoceros, both seen for the first time in Rome, were displayed and then slain in a *venatio* (Dio 51.22.5). In a battle of prisoners of war, "Dacian" soldiers were made to fight against "Suebi." It is not clear if this was intended as a reenactment of a historical battle, or if Octavian simply made use of the prisoners of war from his own campaigns. In either case, such a battle could distract attention from the civil war by demonstrating that there remained enemies in the world against whom Romans could vent their anger. I argued earlier that Sextus Pompeius' mock naval battle off Sicily in 40 BC might have had a divisive effect, since it depicted a battle from civil war and mocked the plan of the opposing admiral, Salvidienus Rufus, in full view of those on the opposite shore who would have participated in the real battle had it taken place. Sextus' *naumachia* was not the kind of show that would heal the wounds of war and foster renewed harmony and peace. By contrast, Octavian's arranged battle between foreign enemies, Dacians and Suebi, could have had a unifying effect on those in attendance by focusing their attention on foreign enemies.[132]

The structures whose dedication Octavian was celebrating all bore the name Julia and honored his adopted family. One ceremony did so as well. Octavian sponsored another revival of the *Lusus Troiae* performed by boys of the patrician order with Tiberius leading the contingent of older boys. This time their elders also participated in a similar kind of equestrian performance (Suet. *Tib.* 6.4; cf. Dio 51.22.4). The presence of the nobility, young men and older, celebrated the place of the aristocracy in Rome. It is probable that those participating were staunch supporters of the new regime, demonstrating the rewards of loyalty. The presence of Tiberius, Octavian's stepson, in a prominent role underscored once again the importance of Octavian's family at the center of this new order.

Conclusion

The triumvirate advertised itself, legitimated its new powers, and celebrated consolidation, *concordia,* and peace to a large degree through the traditional ritual framework of the ceremonies of popular politics, over which they enjoyed an almost unrivaled control. Triumphs mostly were celebrated by those who had received the expressed approval of the triumvirs; festivals and games, when we hear of them in detail, were sponsored by the triumvirs or their agents; appointment of magistrates partly replaced free elections. Yet the continued existence of these ceremonies in our period at times encouraged action independent of, and perhaps even in opposition to, those in power. The theater and streets of Rome were still places for popular protest, as happened before and after the siege of Perusia; even one of the proscribed, M. Oppius, could be a candidate for popular election. Pockets of resistance persisted down to the battle of Actium. The Roman people depended on, and, it seems, continued to trust in, the ceremonies of political power, even when they were being manipulated by the triumvirs. At times the endurance of these ceremonies in the face of a drastically changing political power structure seems to disguise the meaning of events. For instance, in his *contio* in fall 36, especially if it was held in the Circus Flaminius, Octavian addressed the Roman *plebs* in a fashion similar to *popularis* politicians of the late Republic. Yet the nature of his *ovatio,* the circumstances of his victory, as well as the extraordinary honors bestowed upon him, made it clear that the political landscape of Rome had changed. Further, one characteristic of the events surrounding the battle of Actium and Octavian's victorious return to Rome was the revival of old ceremonies—the Fetial ceremony, closing the doors of the Temple of Janus, the *augurium salutis,* the *Lusus Troiae*—in the service of the new regime. Even the marching order of the venerable triumph was modified to accommodate the new leader and inscribe a new political consensus. All of this demonstrated that a monarchy could arise in Rome only within a traditional Republican political framework.

9

The *Princeps* as Performer

Creating Court Ceremony

When Augustus on his deathbed compared his life and career to the performance of a mime, even extending the metaphor with a request for applause as he left the stage,[1] he acknowledged that his actions as *princeps* were highly performative—that is, self-conscious, represented actions that took place in the gaze of the Roman people. This metaphor also demonstrates an awareness of the highly visible and ceremonial nature of the exercise of political power in Rome. This idea of *princeps* as performer seems to have grown out of the notion that in dealing with the *plebs urbana* it was not so much what one gave to them but rather how it was given.[2] Thus, showmanship, performance, and ceremony became the cornerstones of the Augustan Principate. The context of the *princeps*' performance is best understood in the larger scheme of Roman history between the Triumviral period and the consolidation of the power of the *princeps*. As a way of marking the end of the Second Triumvirate, and thus distancing himself from the proscriptions, debilitating exactions, and civil war that had become common in this period, Augustus claimed to have restored public affairs to the senate and people of Rome in 28 and 27 BC.[3] In order to signal this change further in the eyes of the Roman populace, the *princeps* made a great show of handing the *fasces* over to his colleague in the consulship of 28, M. Agrippa—an indication that the traditional powers of the consuls would be shared between the two colleagues.[4] Whatever extraordinary powers Augustus received in the period of his great consolidation (27–23 BC) ostensibly remained within the framework of the traditional institutions of the

Roman Republic. Nevertheless, the evidence is clear that to those living at the time there was no doubt about who would settle disputes that arose in the provinces or grant favors to loyal allies; in other words, there was no doubt in whose hands power resided in the Roman world.[5] Augustus adapted the requirements of Roman Republican traditions and values to his own needs for political self-preservation and dynamic displays of power, thus creating the novel form of government that we call the Principate. Roman Republican ceremonial remained important to Augustus, yet it, too, had to be modified to fit the requirements of the new *princeps*. In effect, these traditional Republican institutions, through which the people had long expressed their will and exercised their power, were reshaped to form one element of the court ceremony of the Principate. This transformation took time—it was evolutionary rather than revolutionary. Part of the process (as we have seen) was initiated by Caesar and continued under the triumvirate.

In this chapter, we will discuss the completion of this process of transformation by examining public ceremonial under Augustus. The length of the chronological period under discussion renders impossible a complete narrative of events and the role of all ceremonies in them. Our approach, therefore, will be to apply the typology of Roman Republican ceremonial, as established in the first chapter, to the Augustan Principate—to overlay the framework from chapter 1 onto the ceremonies of the Principate in order to identify more effectively the areas where change was most dramatic and also to see where the tensions were: where Augustus had to modify the existing ceremonies for his own purposes. Four main themes will emerge from this discussion: first, the theme (or opposing themes) of continuity with and change from the Republic; second, the effect that the changing topography of the city had on ceremony and politics; third, Augustus' use of public ceremonial to celebrate his family, introduce its members into public life and eventually designate a successor; fourth, the use of ceremony to retell history. Finally, Augustus understood the necessity of controlling these ceremonies of popular politics, demonstrating that the support of the Roman people formed one cornerstone of his Principate. This discussion, within the limits of a single chapter, cannot be exhaustive, and there will inevitably be gaps. It is my hope, however, that it will point the way to further research.

Oratory before the People

Public oratory was one of the defining aspects of the politics of the Roman Republic, and we have seen that it remained the principal means of communication between the political elite and the Roman people in the months after Caesar's assassination. Cicero was an influential force in the politics of late 44 and early 43 partly because of his mastery of the art of oratory. It is not surprising that this defining aspect of the Republic underwent a profound change in the imperial period. Tacitus, for instance, in his *Dialogus de Oratoribus* has one of his interlocuters, Messala, decry the state of oratory in his own day under the reign of the first Flavian emperor, Vespasian (*Dial.* 28–41), blaming changes in the system of education that produced the decline of Roman *virtus*. That Tacitus and others were so concerned about the state of oratory as a profession in their times demonstrates that it remained an integral part of the aristocratic ethos and hence of public life. A praiseworthy characteristic of an emperor was his *eloquentia*, and he was expected to be his own spokesman,[6] which demonstrates that he too adhered to this ethos. Augustus, for instance, was said to have written out every speech he ever delivered to the senate or to the people in a *contio*, whether civilian or military,[7] an indication not only of Augustus' level of preparation for public speaking, but also that *contiones* did in fact continue to be held in his reign. One question is whether the emperor appropriated, even monopolized, the *contio* as a ceremony of power, to the exclusion of others.

Since one of the most visually evocative aspects of public oratory in the Roman Republic was the location of the speech—its "stage"—it is necessary to finish our discussion of the transformation of the topography of Rome, which was finally completed by Augustus, before we can consider specific examples of *contiones* in the early Principate. Throughout this study we have attempted to chart the transformation of the topography of the principal venue for public oratory, the Forum Romanum, during the period under discussion. During the Principate, under the influence of Augustus, the topography of Rome was further transformed (see fig. 4). No region of the city was left untouched, it seems, nor any edifice.[8] The new topography of the city, furthermore, was symbolic of Augustus' restoration of Republican institutions, for his description of this restoration in an edict was filled with the imagery of building: "As far as I am concerned, I hope that the Republic will be allowed to stand safe and secure in its own place [*sedes*] and that I reap the benefits of this accomplishment, which I am striving for, namely that I be called the founder of the best state and when I die that I take with me the hope that the foundation [*fundamenta*] of the Republic, which I have laid, will remain in its own footprint [*vestigium*]" (Suet. *Aug.* 28.2). In his own view, as expressed in this edict, Augustus' ambitious building program was a symbolic reconstruction of the Republic: the *urbs* was the physical framework on which the *res publica* rested and through which it flourished.[9]

One of Augustus' first tasks after Actium was to complete the new topography of the Forum Romanum that Caesar had initiated. The dedication of the Curia Julia topographically marked the end of an era by completing the new orientation of the Forum, with the Curia, a symbol of senatorial prerogative and power—indeed, a symbol of the Republic itself—turned to face the new Rostra Caesaris. I argued in chapter 2 that Caesar's moving of the Rostra to the west end of the Forum and reconstruction of the Curia created a new orientation for the Forum by focusing the gaze of both senate and people toward the speaker standing on the Rostra. The removal of the Rostra away from the Curia separated the orator topographically and symbolically from the senate's influence. This new topography was underscored by the new sight line that was created between the new Rostra on the west end of the Forum and the Regia on the east end, which served as the headquarters of the Pontifex Maximus. A second *rostra* at the east end of the Forum would have made the new sight line clearer, but it is uncertain if Caesar built one.[10] In any event, this new sight line was further underscored in August 29 through the dedication of the Temple of Divus Julius, built on the site of the cremation of Caesar's body, immediately in front of the Regia, where a column had been erected in his honor by supporters soon after his death. The *rostra* of this temple, which corresponded topographically to the Rostra Caesaris across the Forum, was decorated with the beaks of ships captured at the battle of Actium.[11] The new topography of the Forum hinted at a redefined distribution of political power under the Principate.

We can now turn to a discussion of specific examples of *contiones*. The first occurred soon after Octavian took the title of Augustus and is part of a transitional phase in the development and consolidation of Augustus' power. A tribune of the *plebs*, whose name is variously given as Sextus Pacuvius or Apudius, addressed the senate, advising that body to dedicate itself to Augustus after the fashion of Spaniards—apparently meaning that senators should devote their lives to him.[12] Augustus, who was present, attempted to restrain Pacuvius, but the latter went out to the crowd standing nearby, presumably in the Forum, and asked that they dedicate themselves to Augustus in the same manner. He then went throughout the city street by street making his request known. Pacuvius later told a crowd that he intended to name Augustus his heir with a standing equal to that of his own son.

Pacuvius addressed the Roman people on two occasions—both likely in the form of *contiones* in the Forum Romanum. Since we know that Pacuvius also sponsored a bill conferring the honorific title of Augustus on Octavian (Macr. 1.12.35), we can surmise that the occasion for one of these *contiones* was the promulgation of that bill. Pacuvius' movement through the city is reminiscent of late Republican tribunes, who often attempted to gather popular support by mustering the *magistri* of the *collegia* in the neighborhoods (*vici*) of the city.[13] It is not clear whether we should view Pacuvius' actions as a first attempt on Augustus' part to acquire control of the neighborhood and guild organizations. Certainly later, Augustus reorganized the city and established rules for the election of neighborhood magistrates.[14]

We can only make some educated guesses as to how the new topography of the Forum that we described earlier, the setting for much of Pacuvius' activity, might have affected the *contiones* in question. I suggested that through his actions on this occasion Pacuvius might have appeared to be a revolutionary tribune of the *plebs* from the late Republic—a Clodius or a Cornelius, perhaps even a Gracchus. The speeches that he gave, however, were effusive in their support of the new *princeps*. We also do not know the precise location of his speeches within the Forum. If the senate meeting that Pacuvius attended had been held in the new Curia Julia, then it is probable that he delivered these speeches from the new Rostra. If so, the new Curia Julia was to his left, the Basilica Julia to his right, and he was facing the temple erected in honor of Augustus' deified father. Some of the changes to the topography of the Forum were sufficiently recent that his audience would probably have remembered how it looked before the changes had been made. Pacuvius' actions might have been reminiscent of revolutionary tribunes, but the words and the setting of his speeches made him appear more a mouthpiece for the new regime. Later in the Principate, the people made their grievances known to the *princeps* through the tribunes of the *plebs*, who acted in a sense as their elected representatives (Dio 55.9.10). Pacuvius' actions in support of the *princeps* and the topography of the Forum provided the people with the opportunity to reflect on the changes that Augustus made in the political power structure, despite his best efforts to underscore continuity with the Republic. The very magistracy that Pacuvius held showed that some of the institutions of the Republic still existed, and Pacuvius' actions showed that they could still be employed in a similar fashion, but the power that loomed behind Pacuvius' actions—and in fact was the cause of those actions—was ultimately the power of the *princeps*. The *contiones* of Pacuvius showed continuity with the past but one that was not unbroken.

The activity of Pacuvius as well as Dio's comment that Augustus employed the tribunes of the *plebs* as intermediaries between the *princeps* and the people indicate that Augustus may have wanted to communicate with the Roman people through agents, that the tribunes would act as his spokesmen. In fact, there is more evidence to suggest that Augustus used *contiones* to communicate directly with the Roman people and that they responded directly to him. Promulgation of new legislation is a case in point. One of the most important purposes of a *contio* in the Republic was to inform the people of the contents of a bill (*rogatio*) and to allow speeches for and against the proposed legislation.[15] Dio informs us that Augustus enacted many laws in his Principate but describes only briefly his procedure. He did not act on his sole authority, but rather often brought his proposals before the tribal assembly in advance so that he could correct any provisions of which the people disapproved (Dio 53.21.3). This sounds like a *contio*, but with a speech only in support of the proposal followed by the response of the people. The single attested instance of Augustus promulgating legislation—his laws on marriage and procreation, enacted in 18 BC—does not include a description of any *contio* connected to it. We are told only that he promulgated these laws from the Rostra in the Forum Romanum (Sen. *Ben.* 6.32.1). Pacuvius' actions are probably indicative of the procedure before Augustus had fully consolidated his power. A passage that describes in some detail a law promulgated by T. Quinctius Crispinus (*cos.* 9 BC)—establishing penalties for those who interfere with the city's water supply—has nothing to say about any preceding *contio*. Moreover, the only record of opposition to legislation enacted by Augustus or, for that matter, by anyone else, occurred not before the law was passed, in the form of debate in *contiones*, but only after.[16]

This is not enough evidence on which to base far-reaching conclusions. The existence of Quinctius' law indicates that Augustus was not the exclusive *rogator* of laws and therefore was probably not the exclusive *orator* at legislative *contiones* (on the passage of legislation in the Principate, see the discussion later in this chapter). He apparently did not bar others of senatorial rank from this particular means of access to the *plebs urbana*. Yet the apparent lack of debate in legislative *contiones* allowed little opportunity for brilliant oratory, the like of which characterized the late Republic. Instead of the people witnessing a debate between two magistrates (or a magistrate and distinguished *privatus*), as had customarily occurred in the Republic, the people responded directly to a proposal by the *princeps* or by another magistrate. If this indeed was the case, the legislative *contio* without any debate or discussion had the appearance of a ceremony of approval, the people's sanction of the emperor's authority, and as such it bore only a superficial resemblance to its Republican ancestor. Yet its mere existence showed an adherence to the ideal of popular sovereignty, even if the distribution of political power in Rome had clearly changed.

Other types of *contiones* showed more clearly this new distribution of power. One example was Augustus' refusal to take up the *fasces* of dictator in 22 BC in response to the pleas of the people, an offer that had perhaps been sanctioned by a law passed in the tribal assembly.[17] A few background remarks are necessary. Following his recovery from a serious illness, Augustus made a new settlement that consolidated his power and made more permanent his position as *princeps*. Augustus took up the consular *fasces* for the eleventh time in January 23 BC and a few months later resigned the office. His resignation allowed him to acquire two other, arguably more significant, powers: tribunician power for life and proconsular *imperium*.[18] Later in this year, or early in the next, M. Primus was put on trial for making war outside his province of Macedonia. At different points in his trial, he claimed in his own defense that Augustus and Marcellus had granted him permission to undertake this war. Augustus appeared at the trial without having been summoned and, in response to a question posed by the presiding praetor, denied Primus' claims. The defense counsel, L. Murena, testily asked Augustus to explain his presence, to which Augustus replied that he was there for the public good. Some jurors nonetheless voted for Primus' acquittal. A plot arose against Augustus, led by one Fannius Caepio and allegedly including Murena. All the conspirators were tried and convicted in absentia and later executed.[19]

Dio describes the year 22 as a time of pestilence and famine. The people congregated around the senate house, threatening to burn it down if the senate did not offer up a decree conferring the dictatorship on Augustus.[20] Such crowd activity around a meeting of the senate was a frequent occurrence in the periods of unrest during the late Republic.[21] And as they had done previously, the people demanded the aid of a champion. The people took up the twenty-four *fasces* symbolizing the dictatorship and presented them to Augustus, demanding that he accept. The *princeps* formally rejected this offer, probably at a *contio* in the Forum, and accepted in its stead a grain commission.

The presentation of the *fasces* by the people was a symbolic gesture made more significant as a result of recent events—namely, Augustus' resignation of the consulship in 23. This gesture on the part of the Roman people showed what Augustus lost when he resigned the consulship: the outward demonstration of authority and power through the display of the *fasces* in the city.[22] How the people obtained the *fasces* for the purposes of this *contio* is not known, nor can we determine whether or to what extent Augustus was involved in its planning or execution. Nonetheless, the crowd's actions showed the senate in no uncertain terms the perils that the state might undergo should the people's champion be removed. After the intrigue involving Caepio and Murena earlier in the year, such a demonstration played into Augustus' hands.

Whether Augustus' *contio* was fully planned or not, it made for high drama, for he declined the dictatorship by kneeling down and pulling back a fold of his toga to reveal his breast (Suet. *Aug.* 52; Dio 54.1.4). M. Bibulus (*cos.* 59) made a similar gesture at the assembly in which Caesar enacted controversial legislation during their consulship, demonstrating his willingness to sacrifice his life for the good of the Republic (see chap. 1). Caesar also is known to have made a similar gesture just before his assassination. While overseeing construction of his new forum, Caesar offended the senate by refusing to rise when its representatives came offering additional honors. Realizing the offense that he had caused, he shouted to his friends, pulling back his toga to reveal his throat and challenged anyone to kill him.[23] This gesture of baring one's throat has the imagery of sacrifice. In Bibulus' case, the gesture showed his willingness to die for his cause, thus bringing shame and ignominy on Caesar, his political enemy. Caesar, on the other hand, was trying to show his vulnerability, that he was mortal and not a god, despite the extraordinary honors accorded him by the senate. It was thus a gesture of humility. If this gesture had come to signify self-sacrifice for the good of the state, Augustus created a great show of declining the dictatorship, even adopting a (Republican?) gesture others were known to have used. (Whether anyone in his audience would have remembered Caesar's use of this gesture or Bibulus', for that matter, is impossible to say—our sources certainly do not.) Even with this gesture of humility, however, this *contio* showed the extent of Augustus' power—his power to refuse an honor offered by the Roman people. This ceremony established a clear hierarchy of deference by placing a limit on the honors that Augustus would accept from the people.[24]

A *contio* could also show the power of the *princeps* when it was used to introduce a potential successor, thus reflecting the new political reality of monarchy. The question of Augustus' successor had to be resolved through public ceremonial, but, since the novelty of the Principate meant that no ceremony existed for naming a successor to a monarch, Augustus was compelled to modify existing ceremonies to accommodate the requirements of monarchy. The *contio* was one such ceremony. When Augustus finally settled on Tiberius as his successor and had the adoption duly sanctioned by a *lex curiata* in the Forum (Suet. *Aug.* 65.1), he convened a *contio* and swore an oath that he had adopted Tiberius for the good of the state (*rei publicae causa*) (Suet. *Tib.* 21.3). Monarchical succession was sanctioned through Roman Republican ceremony. Thus, Augustus set a precedent that other emperors followed.[25]

It is worth noting, as a final point, that Augustus, after seeing a crowd at one of his *contiones* wearing dark clothing (*pullati*), forbade such attire for all those attending such a meeting. He punctuated his remarks with a quotation from the *Aeneid* (1.282): "Romans, masters of the world, the toga'd race."[26] *Pullati* is an adjective used to describe those wearing the dark clothing associated with mourning (Juv. 3.213) and the lower orders of society.[27] In the late Republic, the *tunica pulla* was worn with the Greek *pallium*, a form of dress perhaps associated with artisans that Cicero criticized in Verres but defended in C. Rabirius; it later became fashionable.[28] Augustus' "dress code" for *contiones*, similar to his requirements for the crowd in the amphitheater (Suet. *Aug.* 44.2), indicated his desire to restore traditional Roman fashion to public life (as Suetonius states) and to afford a more uniform appearance to the crowds at public ceremonies. If he indeed required that all attendees wear a toga, as the quotation from the *Aeneid* implies, then this would have restricted *contiones* to those of citizen status.[29]

The evidence for *contiones* under Augustus, fragmentary though it is, suggests that Augustus was the predominant but not exclusive orator at public meetings.[30] We should, however, allow for the possibility that Augustus' preeminent position in the state naturally drew the attention of historians, and consequently our historical tradition is replete with his exploits to the detriment of others. *Contiones*, nonetheless, were a means of communication with the Roman people that remained in use under the Principate for a variety of purposes, ranging from the more traditional promulgation of laws to Augustus' refusal of the dictatorship, and finally to the innovative presentation of Augustus' successor. The apparent absence of debate at those *contiones* that introduced new legislation, as well as Augustus' use of the *contio* for announcing a successor, suggests that even a ceremony as firmly rooted as the *contio* in the Roman Republican ideal of popular sovereignty could become a ceremony of monarchical power. But this in no way lessens the importance of the *contio* under the Principate, for it still showed one basis of Augustus' power—the principle of communication with the people through public oratory.

Electoral and Legislative Assemblies (*comitia*)

One of the main questions regarding the popular assemblies under Augustus is whether or not they constituted a true expression of popular will. Augustus was the principal but not exclusive *rogator* of legislation especially after 23 BC, and he clearly exercised some influence on elections, particularly through the principle of *commendatio*, whereby he recommended candidates for the highest magistracies, the praetorship and consulship, although there is evidence that the remaining positions were still contested.[31] If our sources present a slightly conflicted view on this issue, it is because Augustus understood the importance of performance, of demonstrating ceremonially the power of the people through the enactment of the ceremonies that symbolized popular sovereignty. The power of Augustus hinged not on his ability to arrest the expression of popular will, but in controlling its flow by means of these ceremonies.

The electoral assemblies are a case in point. They certainly felt Augustus' influence, but not to the point where he completely orchestrated elections and determined their outcome. Part of this ambivalence is reflected in the changing topography of Rome. The construction of the Saepta Julia, the voting enclosure for elections of the *comitia tributa* and *centuriata*, was planned by Caesar and completed and dedicated by Agrippa in 26 BC. The very name of this structure, as was the case with the Curia Julia and the Temple of Divus Julius, evoked the memory of Caesar and his family, which now was the leading family of the Roman aristocracy. The Saepta stood on the eastern side of the Campus Martius, its own eastern side bounded by the Via Flaminia, and just south of the complex of buildings connected with Agrippa and his family (see fig. 4).[32] It opened, and thus was oriented, to the north, away from the Capitolium and Forum Romanum and toward the complex of monuments associated with Augustus—his mausoleum and the Horologium with the Ara Pacis and obelisk (although the latter two monuments were completed much later). Augustus had restored (*reficere*) the Via Flaminia from the city to Ariminum in 27 BC (Aug. *Anc.* 20.5), and this restoration probably included a repaving and perhaps a widening of the road to accommodate the new structures planned and, in the case of the Saepta, already begun. The existence of a new structure and in essence a new topography, for the purposes of convening the electoral assemblies, signaled a change in the nature of these assemblies, although how they were to change was unclear. The display of a rhinoceros in the Saepta during a *venatio* celebrating the dedication of the Temple of Divus Julius in August 29,[33] before the Saepta itself was dedicated and before an election is attested, redefined the relationship between the governed and the elite, the latter now dominated by the *princeps*.

One of the many examples of Caesar's arrogance that the historical tradition records is the cavalier way in which he dealt with the electoral assemblies. We are told, for instance, that, when a consul died at the end of December 45 BC, Caesar appointed a suffect consul in his stead, who held office for only a few hours (see chap. 2). This story was retold to show how Caesar's excessive power encroached upon and thus curtailed popular sovereignty as exercised in these assemblies. That Augustus learned this lesson can be seen in his treatment of the popular assemblies during his reign, but this does not mean that he could completely mask the reality of his power. First, he was always present at elections (presumably when he was in Rome) until AD 8, when ill health forced him to absent himself (Dio 55.34.2). Second, when he did attend, he made the circuit of all of the tribes in the company of his candidates and asked (*supplicabat*) the people for their support in customary fashion.[34] By doing so, Augustus adhered to one of the principles of popular sovereignty in the Roman Republic, namely the act of asking the people for their support, which is especially evident in the word itself that was used to describe a piece of legislation proposed before the people (*rogatio*). A candidate was similarly required to ask for the people's votes, as were those who were campaigning on his behalf. Finally, we are also informed that Augustus voted in his tribe as though he was one of the people (Suet. *Aug.* 56.1). Augustus' behavior at elections, both in the manner that he canvassed for his candidates and in the way that he voted, was that of a typical Roman citizen, and this reflects an ideal of the *princeps* that became more important in a later age: his *civilitas*.[35] One cannot deny, however, that Augustus' presence at the campaigns of his candidates greatly increased their chances of success in the coming election—his influence (*auctoritas*) was supreme (Aug. *Anc.* 34.3), and his candidates' success further enhanced his power and influence. Moreover, his candidates were often members of his own family, since election to office was a necessary step in a political career. Marcellus and Tiberius were both allowed to stand for office at an earlier than customary age.[36] Such special favors were also granted to Augustus' grandsons, Gaius and Lucius Caesar. On the one hand, Augustus avoided outwardly disdaining or violating the sovereignty of the people through the exercise of this power. On the other, one wonders how the sight of Augustus campaigning for his candidates or voting in his place in his tribe would have appeared to the electorate. Did he look like a Roman aristocrat of Republican times earnestly lending his support to a friend or exercising his right as citizen to vote? Or did he look like a monarch performing an ancient ceremony that had lost its real meaning?

Augustus' acceptance of the grain commission in lieu of the dictatorship in 22 BC seems not to have been sufficient to settle the minds of the electorate in these years. Based on Dio's account of the consular elections of 21 and 19, it appears that Augustus attempted to distance himself from the electoral assemblies and place them once again in the hands of the people. The elections for the year 21 were first contentious and then riotous. Dio claims that one of the consulships was being held in reserve for Augustus (54.6.2), although he had publicly relinquished this magistracy in the previous year. It is not clear by whom the consulship was being held or under whose authority. Since Augustus repeatedly declined the office, we must assume that the Roman people insisted on voting for him, in the same way that they attempted to confer the dictatorship on him. Augustus, moreover, had already departed for Sicily by this time, in his capacity as grain commissioner and later journeyed to Greece, thus distancing himself from the squabbling in Rome. M. Lollius, perhaps his hand-picked candidate (*candidatus Augusti*), was elected to one consulship while Q. Lepidus and L. Silvanus vied for the other (Dio 54.6). Unrest continued after Augustus refused to intervene and Lepidus was eventually declared the victor. Augustus dispatched Agrippa to Rome to quell the unrest in the city.

The consuls for the year 20 were elected and entered office without incident (Dio 54.7.4), but in 19 an electoral dispute similar to the year 21 recurred. C. Sentius (again, perhaps the *candidatus Augusti*) was elected to the first consulship without incident, and Augustus again refused the position held open for him. Two lictors were dispatched to seek his intervention, and he evaded future unrest by appointing one of these lictors, Q. Lucretius, to the consulship (Dio 54.10.2).

The actions of C. Sentius Saturninus (*cos.* 19) and the brief career of M. Egnatius Rufus provide some evidence for the ambiguities in Augustus' position and the opportunities available to rise politically in traditional Republican fashion (i.e., without the support of the *princeps*). Rufus used the reputation and wealth that he had gained for himself in his aedileship through the activities of his slave fire brigade to attain the praetorship contrary to law. This presumably means that he allowed no time to elapse between his aedileship and praetorship. The year of his aedileship is uncertain. Dio (53.24.4–6) discusses his activities in the context of the year 26,[37] but Velleius' account (2.91.3) more accurately places Rufus' attempt at the consulship in 19 BC. It has recently been suggested that Rufus was striving for a suffect consulship for the remainder of 19 and not the consulship for the following year.[38] His aedileship therefore would have been in 21 BC and his praetorship in 20. When Rufus tried to stand for the suffect consulship for 19 BC, C. Sentius, who was the consul presiding over the elections, refused to allow him to become a candidate and threatened not to report him as victor even if the people voted him in (Vell. 2.92.4). Sentius also wins the praise of Velleius for refusing to allow some whom he thought unworthy to become candidates for the quaestorship.

Sentius' actions seem to have had the backing of Augustus. I suggested above that he probably had been the *candidatus Augusti* when he was elected to the consulship, and Velleius informs us that the *princeps* was also opposed to Rufus' candidacy. The reasons for Augustus' opposition are not hard to guess. First, he probably believed that Rufus was unworthy of the office.[39] Furthermore, if Rufus achieved the consulship, he would have done so through demagoguery, thus challenging the *princeps'* supremacy among the urban *plebs*. Augustus might have been especially fearful of Rufus' tactics in achieving his popularity; that is, Rufus seems to have acted through the neighborhood associations that had been so important in organizing collective action in the late Republic.[40] Sentius' selection of candidates for the quaestorship also bears the marks of Augustus' influence, for it is probable that Augustus already was planning his second purging of the senate to take place in the following year.[41] Election to the quaestorship still meant entry into the senate, and unworthy candidates would simply have to be purged from the senate at some future date. Sentius' actions were a preemptive strike and served the same purpose as the purging of the senate in the next year.

The extent of Augustus' influence and intervention in these elections and others in the Principate is unclear, although it is curious that, at least for a time, he continued to be considered a possible candidate for the consulship. The source of the unrest appears to be the people who refused to elect even some of Augustus' handpicked candidates. The electoral unrest of these years prompted the *princeps* to find a traditionally Republican solution to a traditionally Republican problem: in the next year, he enacted a law on electoral bribery. The fact that Augustus was compelled to pass another law in 8 BC dealing with the same issue—one that required candidates for office to leave a deposit that would become forfeit should they engage in bribery to secure election (Dio 55.5.3)—shows that his first solution was imperfect; it is also an indication of continued contested elections—perhaps beguiling the expectations and testing the patience of the *princeps*.

A law sponsored by the consuls of AD 5 altered the procedure at electoral assemblies under Augustus. The *Lex Valeria Cornelia* is known to us only through its mention in the bronze tablet found at Heba in Etruria (the so-called *Tabula Hebana*) containing honors conferred upon Germanicus, the emperor Tiberius' nephew and adopted son, who died in AD 19.[42] This law called for the creation of ten new centuries, five each named for Augustus' two recently deceased grandsons, C. and L. Caesar, consisting of members of the higher orders of Roman society, the senatorial aristocracy and equestrians. These centuries formed a select assembly that with their votes "destined" candidates for the two highest Republican magistracies, the consulship and praetorship. The slate of candidates thus established—two candidates for the consulship and twelve for the praetorship—were then voted on by the full assembly. This procedure known as *destinatio*, and how it relates to *creatio* (formal election), remains highly controversial. One theory holds that these new centuries functioned essentially as the *centuria praerogativa* in elections under the Republic, by setting an example that other centuries were expected to follow.[43] Under this theory, other candidates excluded from the slate offered by the select assembly could still be voted in by the full assembly. A second theory maintains to the contrary that the full assembly was required by law to vote in the slate of candidates offered by the select assembly of senators and *equites*.[44]

Whatever the case, it is clear that the select assembly's vote conferred enormous prestige on its slate of candidates, which the full assembly might have viewed as binding. The presiding official at the assembly was required to read off the names of each of the candidates voted on by the centuries named for C. and L. Caesar, thus reminding the assembled of the honors paid to the deceased as well as connecting the chosen candidates closely to the one-time heirs of the *princeps*, to the imperial family, and ultimately to the *princeps* himself.[45] In this sense, the procedure of *destinatio* had a similar effect as the *commendatio* of the *princeps*: not legally binding, perhaps, but virtually impossible to ignore.

Whether the electoral reforms instituted by the *Lex Valeria Cornelia* constituted an infringement on popular sovereignty as traditionally exercised in the Roman Republic is not entirely clear. The answer ultimately depends on the related question of whether the people's votes ever really counted in the elections under Augustus. At least early in his reign, Augustus seems to have been content with a supervisory role, allowing the assemblies to meet and vote as long as they did so in an orderly fashion, and sponsoring legislation to curtail electoral malfeasance when the circumstances called for it. But even at an early stage, the *commendatio* of the *princeps* was authoritative and perhaps decisive: we hear of no *candidatus Augusti* who failed to be returned at an election. In such an electoral climate, what change did the institution of *destinatio* bring? The principal importance of this new procedure was the prominent role of members of the senatorial aristocracy and equestrian order in it. This has to be understood as part of a larger process under Augustus of carefully distinguishing the place and function of each of the orders of society. This process was most visibly in evidence in the arranged seating at the theater and amphitheater, a longstanding custom that Augustus revived as part of his public entertainment (Suet. *Aug.* 44). The crowd at a spectacle, carefully arrayed in their seats, was a visible symbol of the harmony in Roman society under the *princeps*.[46] In a similar way, a slate of candidates chosen by the votes of senators and *equites* in a select assembly was a public demonstration of the consensus between the *princeps* and the two higher orders of Roman society.[47] The full assembly's election of these candidates legitimated the procedure and gave the final stamp of approval on the product of this consensus.

We can now turn to the legislative assemblies under Augustus. In the late Republic, the *comitia tributa* had begun to encroach on the traditional sphere of influence of the centuriate assembly by voting on laws conferring extraordinary commands on the great dynasts, although, as we have seen, there is some evidence to suggest that Caesar may have begun to employ the centuriate assembly as a legislative body as well (see chap. 2). There is no evidence that Augustus continued to use the centuriate assembly in this fashion, in which case he was distancing his own practice from that of the tradition of the classic Roman Republic and perhaps also from Caesar's reforms. The tribal assembly, in strengthening and legitimating Augustus' position, as evidenced by the *lex* conferring tribunician power on Augustus for life in 23 BC, all but dismantled the Republic.[48] It is also probable that this assembly passed a *lex* conferring tribunician power on M. Agrippa,[49] thus legitimating Augustus' choice of successor.

Our earlier discussion of *contiones* by necessity touched on the sphere of legislative assemblies. We cited, for instance, Dio's description of Augustus' legislative procedure, to inform the people of his proposal in advance and modify it if they objected (53.21.3). Dio goes on to describe the *consilium* of senators who acted as Augustus' advisers in legislative (among other) matters. This whole procedure could be viewed as an attempt on Augustus' part to accelerate the legislative process. By employing a *consilium* of senators, he received senatorial sanction for his proposed legislation without requiring a debate in the full senate. Caesar, it seems, also favored a more efficient procedure, for he was known to have used the power of his dictatorship at times to enact laws by decree rather than through the tribal assembly.[50] Further, his long absences from the city during his dictatorship necessitated a more efficient procedure. Cicero accused M. Antonius of dispensing with the traditional three market day waiting period (the so-called *trinum nundinum*) between promulgation of a *rogatio* and a vote on it in the assembly for some of the laws passed during his consulship in 44 (Cic. *Phil.* 5.8; see also chap. 5). Furthermore, when the triumvirs returned to Rome in November 43 to have their friendly arrangement legitimated by the *comitia tributa*, they also ignored this waiting period (App. *BC* 4.7.27). Legislative procedure later in the Triumviral period is unclear. In all of the instances cited, political instability, at times even civil war, necessitated a more efficient procedure.

Three examples from the Principate will provide some evidence for the development of legislative procedure, although no one procedure, it seems, prevailed in this period. In the previous section, we discussed the activity of Sextus Pacuvius, who in 27 BC addressed the people in *contiones* in support of Augustus' new position. He also passed a law, in accordance with a *senatus consultum*, renaming the month of Sextilis after Augustus.[51] The procedure that Pacuvius, the *rogator* of this legislation, and the senate followed in this instance bears a greater resemblance to procedure under the classic Roman Republic, with a tribune sponsoring legislation in accordance with the authority of the senate. No doubt, Augustus would have wanted his new power to be cloaked in traditional garb as far as was possible under the extraordinary circumstances that faced him. The procedure that Dio describes—the presentation of the proposal to the people in advance and modifying it as necessary—probably came into being later in the Principate, especially after Augustus had received tribunician power for life (in 23), which allowed him unfettered access to the legislative assembly.[52]

Augustus' famous legislation on marriage and adultery, enacted in 18 BC, provides an example of procedure somewhat closer to Dio's description. Augustus promulgated these laws first while standing on the Rostra in the Forum.[53] The only objections on record against any of the laws enacted during Augustus' reign were to this legislation, but they were apparently voiced only after the laws were enacted. Again, there is no evidence of debate and discussion in *contiones* preceding the voting on these laws. In accordance with the objections voiced, Augustus emended these laws (Suet. *Aug.* 34; and above), but it is not clear what procedure Augustus was required to follow in order to do so.

A law sponsored by T. Quinctius Crispinus (*cos.* 9 BC) provides an example of yet another procedure. This law was promulgated from the *rostra* on the Temple of Divus Julius (see fig. 3), and the people voted on it while assembled in the area in front of the temple. The first voter in the first tribe, Sextus Virro, son of Lucius, of the Sergian tribe, is duly recorded in the *praescriptio* of the text of the law,[54] in accordance with Republican custom. The existence of this law shows that Augustus was not the exclusive *rogator* of legislation in this period, even after 23 BC. The absence of a tribune is a bit curious, since this magistracy supplied the principal *rogatores* of laws under the Republic, especially in the classic Republic, until the reforms of Sulla perhaps allowed curule magistrates this privilege. Pacuvius' law in 27 shows that tribunes could act as *rogatores* early in Augustus' Principate. If Quinctius' law is evidence of a new procedure under Augustus, we can surmise that the *princeps* did not allow tribunes to sponsor legislation as a way of weakening their influence on the *plebs urbana*.[55] The tribunes' new duties, along with the aediles, included oversight of the new *regiones* of the city. The privilege and power of enacting legislation was restricted to the *princeps*, by virtue of his tribunician power, and the consuls, many of whom owed their positions to imperial favor and could be counted on for their loyalty to the emperor. If indeed the consulship was the only magistracy allowed to sponsor legislation, then this exclusive privilege would have lent some prestige to an office that had diminished in importance as an inevitable result of the growing power of the *princeps*.

The location of the promulgation and voting on this law is worthy of notice. Even though many aspects of the enactment of this legislation reflected Republican tradition, including the custom of the first voter, the location of the voting place, in front of the Temple of Divus Julius, was a reminder of the unique status of Augustus' family within the social and political context of Rome.[56] The area in front of this new temple was roughly coterminous with the area in front of the Temple of Castor, where voting took place under the Republic. Hence, Augustus did not establish a new polling place for the legislative assembly, but it had a new orientation toward the Temple of Divus Julius rather than the Temple of Castor.

The procedure in electoral and legislative assemblies indicates a similar distribution of power as at *contiones*. The electoral unrest in the years immediately following Augustus' resignation of the consulship proved that Augustus was indispensable and served as a warning to the senatorial aristocracy that they would remove him at their peril. An electoral campaign with Augustus canvassing for his candidates and the election itself with Augustus voting in his tribe shows how a traditional Republican ceremony came to be an enactment of the emperor's power and prestige. Elections involving his stepsons and grandsons further had dynastic implications. Whether Augustus could have orchestrated the popular unrest that arose in the late 20s BC cannot be known. But it clearly played out to his political advantage, for the Roman people let it be known that their champion was Augustus.

Augustus seems to have established a procedure for legislative assemblies that assured the passage of his laws so that he could avoid the embarrassment of a defeat. If consuls were the only other sponsors of bills aside from the emperor himself, their legislative success also redounded to his prestige, since they were his handpicked political allies. Further, their participation in the legislative process was an important component of the consensus that Augustus hoped to achieve, one that included the senatorial aristocracy as well as the people. In this period, the popular assemblies, hallmarks of a democratic constitution and ceremonies of popular sovereignty, became displays of the kind of power that underpinned the Augustan Principate—one that had at its roots a broad-based consensus.

Public Entertainment (*Ludi* and *Munera*)

In previous chapters, we have seen how public entertainment could be used as a venue for communicating political messages to the populace and in turn for the expression of popular will. Other scholars have demonstrated the continued importance of public entertainment in the Principate as a means of formulating the public image of the *princeps*, both as benefactor of the people through the funding and production of games and as the recipient of their petitions at the theater, circus, and later the amphitheater.[57] Augustus tried to distance himself from Caesar, who reportedly passed the time at festival games by reading and responding to correspondence and petitions. Suetonius tells this story to contrast Caesar's behavior at the games with Augustus' as reflections of their attitudes toward the spectacles that amused the masses (Suet. *Aug.* 45.1). As with the story about Caesar's exploitation of the popular assemblies, this anecdote expresses a truism about how to display one's autocratic power. Augustus' *Res Gestae* offer clear testimony to the frequency and lavishness of public entertainment under his Principate (*Anc.* 22–23; cf. Suet. *Aug.* 43). These games demonstrated the enormous wealth of Augustus, who was now the richest man in Rome, and his willingness to share his wealth with the Roman people—an indication of his *liberalitas*. In this sense, he was motivated by much the same sensibilities as a magistrate of the Roman Republic. On the other hand, the political reality of Augustus' position, as we have already seen, not only required that he be more than a Roman magistrate but also afforded him the opportunity to do so. *Contiones* and *comitia* allowed Augustus to display his *civilitas* and *auctoritas*—important aspects of his public image—but they were limited to the present moment. By contrast, Augustus could use games to present himself as an integral part of the continuum of Roman history; in fact, he was the linchpin that joined the glorious Roman past with its hopeful future. Furthermore, by sponsoring festivals himself, or in the names of his sons and grandsons, or again by offering to finance the productions of others, the *princeps* made himself indispensable to many cult practices. His role in public entertainment combined with his membership in the four major priestly colleges made him the center of religious activity.[58] By virtue of his extraordinary religious position, the *princeps* also became the central figure in the Roman calendar, following to a certain degree the precedent established by Caesar. Augustus' birthday, for instance, became a cause for celebration, first spontaneously by the aediles in 20 BC, and then as a permanent holiday on the Roman calendar.[59] Finally, Augustus used public entertainment as an occasion to introduce members of his family to public life. Already in 29, at the games celebrating the dedication of the Temple of Divus Julius, Augustus sponsored the *Lusus Troiae* where his stepson Tiberius led a division of noble youths (see chap. 8). This practice only increased during the Principate.

In earlier chapters, we discussed how Caesar's memory became bound up with many of the traditional festivals on the Roman calendar (see chaps. 2 and 3). Augustus followed the same practice. Following his new settlement in 23 BC that consolidated his power and made more permanent his position as *princeps*, Augustus ceremoniously, and perhaps not a little ostentatiously, resigned the consulship in this year on the occasion of the *Feriae Latinae*. He chose this festival for his resignation because it took place outside the city, and therefore he could not be prevented (presumably by the people) from doing so (Dio 53.32.2–6). This festival involved the most ancient and prestigious families of the Roman nobility, as Caesar's celebration demonstrated, and (I argued in chapter 2) had become symbolic of their power and importance in Roman society. It was the appropriate occasion, then, for Augustus to lay down the consulship and thus make this prestigious office available once again to members of the nobility. This tone and atmosphere of compromise was further advertised through the selection of the consuls for this year, for Augustus chose in his stead as suffect consul L. Sestius, a former quaestor and admirer of M. Brutus, who preserved images of the tyrannicide and pronounced eulogies in praise of him (53.32.4). This almost seems too much to be credible.[60] Perhaps his connection to Brutus was underscored, even exaggerated, so that Augustus could demonstrate further the *concordia* that now existed between senate and *princeps*. Sestius' colleague, Cn. Calpurnius Piso, a more intriguing figure, was a scion of a noble family. He also had supported the tyrannicides and then removed himself from public life.[61] The offer of a consulship ended his long retirement. Both consuls were chosen because of their pasts and their connections to the heroes of the Republic—Piso especially because of his family name. This was a symbolic gesture on the part of Augustus intending to show that senate and *princeps* could coexist in the new Rome. It is possible that the *Feriae Latinae* set in high relief the new *concordia* that would be one of the defining symbols of this new era.

In the early years of the Principate, Augustus endeavored to take control of the religious festivals and especially the public entertainment associated with them. The magistracy customarily responsible for the production of games associated with the traditional Roman festivals was the aedileship. We have already seen how burdensome this office had become in the Triumviral period and that it seems to have remained vacant or only partially filled on several occasions.[62] We hear of similar difficulties in the early years of Augustus' reign, as potential candidates for the aedileship claimed poverty as an obstacle to holding the office (Dio 53.2.2). Augustus responded in two different ways to these vacancies. First, he transferred some of the responsibilities for sponsoring public entertainment from the aediles to the more senior magistrates, the consuls and praetors. Thus, Augustus could control the production of games, which, like the sponsorship of popular legislation, was a way that an enterprising politician could challenge the supremacy of the *princeps* among the urban populace. Augustus forestalled this threat to his prestige and power by putting games in the hands of magistrates who ultimately owed their positions and their *dignitas* to his patronage,[63] in much the same way that he seems to have restricted the sponsorship of legislation to himself and only the most senior magistrates. A more immediate response to the vacancies in the aedileship was to assign to this magistracy two members of the imperial household, Tiberius and Marcellus, who held the office in 25 and sponsored games to mark the founding of Augusta Emerita (Dio 53.26.1). Two years later, Marcellus was responsible for some splendid games in Rome, probably the *Ludi Romani*.[64]

One of Augustus' most pressing tasks in the consolidation of power was to ensure that the form of government that he had created would endure after his death. We have already discussed the culmination of this process in the adoption of Tiberius and Augustus' presentation of him to the Roman people in a *contio*. Augustus' illness in 23 BC might have encouraged him to begin to plan the process of designating a successor. The role of public entertainment in this process, both as a means for Augustus to introduce a potential successor into public life or advertise a relationship of importance, was already in evidence in the Triumviral period, when Augustus frequently shared the spotlight with M. Agrippa.[65] This continued in the Principate with the creation, for instance, of a festival celebrating Augustus' victory at Actium, which the *princeps* held jointly with his partner.[66] The games sponsored by Marcellus and Tiberius afforded them a similar opportunity to stand in the public gaze. In fact, Augustus' affection for Marcellus and the games that the latter put on as aedile gave rise to popular talk about the nephew and son-in-law succeeding the *princeps*.[67] Augustus later brought his will into the senate to demonstrate that he had not chosen a successor (Dio 53.31.1), but the successful games of Marcellus are evidence that such events under the Principate came to be viewed as ceremonies of succession.

Marcellus' death solidified Agrippa's position. The bestowal of tribunician power on Agrippa made his claim even more secure. At the beginning of the year 17, Agrippa announced the birth of a second son, Lucius, whom Augustus immediately adopted along with his older brother, Gaius, thus establishing them as eventual successors (Dio 54.18.1). Dio tells us that Augustus did this in part to forestall the threats to his person, but it is probable that the *princeps* was initiating arrangements that would ensure a smooth transition of power when the time came for a successor to take his place. At about this time, Augustus sponsored the *Ludi Saeculares*, a revival of a set of games that celebrated the future prosperity of Rome (discussed in detail later in this chapter). There is no direct evidence that Augustus used these games especially to advertise the succession of his young grandsons, beyond the prominent presence and active participation of their father, Agrippa, yet the concurrence of both events—an adoption that established a plan of succession and thus a future after Augustus as well as a festival that called for the future prosperity of the city of Rome and its empire within the first months of this year—were meant to allow Romans now to look to the future with equanimity and hopeful expectations. In other words, the celebration of the *Ludi Saeculares* confirmed the promise of tranquility that Augustus made known through the adoption of his grandsons.[68]

Later in the Principate, members of the imperial household took an active role in the sponsorship of games. After the death of Marcellus, Augustus' stepsons, Tiberius and Drusus, were the focus of attention before his grandsons came of age. Tiberius and Drusus were allowed, by decree of the senate, to represent Augustus in the sponsorship of gladiatorial combat on the occasion of the dedication of the Temple of Quirinus, which he had rebuilt (Dio 54.19.5; cf. Aug. *Anc.* 19.2). This was a temple that had associations with the demigod Romulus and later with the divinity of the dictator Caesar, and, for the latter reason in particular, seems to have become important for Augustus and his family. With these considerations in mind, it was appropriate for Augustus to delegate to members of his own family the sponsorship of games that celebrated the dedication of this temple. Drusus also held games in his capacity as praetor in 11 BC (Dio 54.34.1). If entertainment sponsored by members of the *princeps*' family came to be viewed as ceremonies of succession, then Tiberius' and Drusus' games were a way for Augustus to demonstrate how he had secured Rome's future.

Augustus took up the consulship in 2 BC primarily for ceremonial reasons, so that he could oversee the dedication of the Temple of Mars Ultor (see fig. 4) and the introduction of his grandson Lucius into public life.[69] By this time, Gaius and Lucius had become the focal point of Augustus' plans for the succession, and they, along with their brother, Agrippa Postumus, were partly responsible for sponsoring the games that marked the dedication of the Temple of Mars Ultor.[70] Octavian vowed this temple on the battlefield of Philippi, where he sought and finally attained vengeance for the murder of Caesar. In 20 BC following Augustus' diplomatic triumph over the Parthians and the recovery of the Roman standards, the temple, still unbuilt, again received notice as a possible repository for these standards.[71] The forty-year delay between avowal and dedication of the temple remains something of a mystery, but it did allow Augustus to redirect the force of the god's vengeance (and his own) away from the conspirators at Philippi and toward enemies of the empire in the east,[72] in a manner similar to the Fetial ceremony on the eve of the battle of Actium. Already by 20 BC and certainly by 2 BC, when Augustus had consolidated his power, the conspiracy that ended Caesar's life was a memory conjuring images of civil war that the *princeps* would rather have suppressed. By establishing the Temple of Mars Ultor as the repository of the standards recovered from the Parthians and making it central to the topography of triumphal ceremonies, Augustus effectively changed the meaning of this structure from civil war monument to symbol of world conquest.

This temple was also a monument that blurred the distinctions between the public and private sides of the imperial family. Augustus tells us that the temple was built on private ground (*privato solo*) (*Anc.* 21.1), yet it was clearly the venue for many public ceremonies. This temple, along with the Forum Augustum, of which it was part, was associated not only with the Julian *gens*, whose most famous members, beginning with Aeneas, were commemorated with honorific statues but also with all distinguished men (the *summi viri*)—past heroes of Roman history who conquered and triumphed and eventually annexed territory to the Roman Empire. It thus placed the family of Augustus within the larger scheme of Roman history.[73] The importance of this monument in Augustus' imperial ideology is evidenced by his own words in an edict preserved by his biographer: "He stated that this [i.e., the statues of the *summi viri* in the portico of his forum] was a device whereby he himself, while he was alive, and future emperors of succeeding ages would be required by the people to follow the example set by the lives of those famous men."[74] This edict expressed Augustus' vision of a Roman future that was closely tied to and dependent upon its past heroes, who provided guidance and counsel through the memory of their achievements and mode of life.

The *Ludi Martiales*, along with the *Ludi Saeculares*, are the only two sets of games mentioned by name in Augustus' *Res Gestae*. Unlike the latter, which only were to be revived every century or so, the former were to be held on an annual basis under the supervision of the consuls for the year. The games included several lavish spectacles at different venues throughout the city. Chariot races (*ludi circenses*) were held in the Circus Maximus, under the sponsorship of Gaius and Lucius; the *Lusus Troiae* was performed once again, with Agrippa Postumus taking part as one of the leading youths; gladiatorial combat was put on in the Saepta Julia; a *venatio* of lions took place in the Circus Maximus; a mock naval battle between "Persians" and "Athenians"—a reenactment of the battle of Salamis—took place on the *stagnum Augusti;*[75] and finally, the Circus Flaminius was flooded for a *venatio* of crocodiles. These games served a dual purpose: first, they were put on to celebrate the dedication of the Temple of Mars Ultor and the Forum Augustum; second, they marked the departure from Rome of Gaius, as he set out to stabilize the eastern frontier.

Augustus' words in this edict spoke only in the most general terms of "emperors of future ages" (*insequentium aetatium principes*), not specifically of who might actually succeed him at that time. But if this edict was published around the time of the dedication of the temple and forum, which seems likely, then the dedication of these monuments and the games established to celebrate it would have provided a larger context for the interpretation of his words. For instance, if Gaius and Lucius, when they presided over the games in the Circus Maximus, did so by themselves—that is, in the absence of Augustus—then they would have had unimpeded access to the people. As they stood in the imperial box (*pulvinar*) at the Circus Maximus, which the *princeps* constructed for himself and his family,[76] the Roman people might have thought that they were looking at two of the future emperors of which Augustus had spoken in his edict. Their visible presence, in turn, bound the future of the Julian *gens*—indeed of all of Rome—closely with its past.[77]

These games also served as a send-off for Gaius as he departed for his eastern campaign, and the imagery of conquest expressed the promise of a successful return and triumph.[78] The games included two *venationes*, one of lions in the Circus Maximus, the other of crocodiles in a flooded Circus Flaminius. The hunt was traditionally associated with the triumph, and the display of exotic animals from distant lands and their subsequent slaughter were symbolic of Rome's imperial majesty.[79] In this case, the two different kinds of animals involved also required different venues.[80]

The final spectacle was a reenactment of the battle of Salamis, pitting condemned criminals dressed up as "Athenians" against appropriately attired "Persians" (Dio 55.10.7; Ov. *Ars* 1.171–72). Such *naumachiae* were also closely associated with triumphs. In fact, the first one attested was held in conjunction with Caesar's triumph in 46 BC.[81] Thus, this naval battle continued the imagery of conquest in anticipation of Gaius' departure. Syme has argued that the purpose of this mock battle was to demonstrate Augustus' role as defender of the Hellenic tradition and protector of Greeks against barbarian invaders.[82] Zanker has suggested it hearkened back to the battle of Actium and represented again this victory as one of west over east, civilization over barbarism.[83] My suggestion is that this spectacle looked both to the past and the future at once, for in it time was compressed; in other words, the past and the future converged on the present. But if this mock battle was intended to anticipate the successful conclusion of Gaius' campaign—to demonstrate, in effect, how his success would be an echo of the successes of Greeks over barbarians, or west over east, from history—then it stands to reason that the defeat of the "Athenians" at the hands of the "Persians" would have not only reversed the outcome of history but also offered a foreboding omen that would have clouded Gaius' departure. For this reason, it seems to me that Augustus would have wanted to ensure the "Athenians'" victory, because this would have created the appropriate context for Gaius' departure and, at the same time, demonstrated the emperor's ability to recreate history on a lavish scale for the entertainment of the residents of the capital.[84]

These ceremonies of succession exhibited the underlying theme of the place of Augustus and his family in the larger context of Roman history—how Augustus was the linchpin between Rome's glorious past and its equally prosperous future. This theme had already been more carefully articulated by Augustus' sponsorship of the fifth celebration of the *Ludi Saeculares* in 17 BC, a festival that occurred only once a century to mark the passage of one great age and the dawn of the next. In the inscription that records the preparations and execution of these games (*acta*), the consul C. Silanus proposed that unmarried people be allowed to attend since no one would be present a second time (*CIL* 6.32323.55–57). These games were truly a once-in-a-lifetime experience.

Even though Augustus was constrained by tradition and custom, the length of a *saeculum* and the manner in which such *saecula* were counted afforded him some flexibility within certain parameters in determining in what year the festival was to be carried out. He chose 17 BC for the celebration of this festival presumably because he thought it was an appropriate year to mark the transition from one *saeculum* to the next.[85] We should view Augustus' celebration of the *Ludi Saeculares* in 17 BC as an important part, if not the culmination, of a series of events that advanced the consolidation of his power. The advent of peace in the west and the east through his conquest and settlement of Spain in the Cantabrian wars and the return of the Roman standards from Parthia, the establishment of *concordia* between the *princeps* and the aristocracy by virtue of his relinquishing the consulship, further the "physical" revival of Rome through the reconstruction of the Republican landscape and the construction of new imperial buildings, and finally the moral revival of Roman character through the enactment of Augustus' marriage legislation set the stage for a brighter future for the Roman people that the *Ludi Saeculares* were designed to celebrate. Ten years had elapsed since he accepted the title of Augustus, and his power was now virtually unchallenged.

The promise of Rome's future prosperity was a theme frequently expressed at these games. On the second night of the *ludi*, Augustus spoke a prayer, documented in the *acta* (*CIL* 6.32323.92–99), that the gods preserve the victory, health, and well-being (*valetudo*) of the Roman people and increase their power in the future. Horace echoed these sentiments in the *Carmen Saeculare*, the hymnal anthem of these games, sung by a chorus of young men and women of Rome on 3 June (*Saec.* 61–68). At the same time, Rome's future prosperity was contingent upon the revival of traditional Roman religion and moral values, which had suffered under the civil wars. This ideal was expressed through the very celebration of these *ludi*, since the college of priests charged with their production, the *Quindecimviri*, seems to have lacked many members in the difficult times of the late Republic.[86] The active participation of this college in this rendition of the games was an indication of its renewed importance under the Augustan Principate and by extension the revival of traditional religion. At the same time, Augustus incorporated himself and his family (*domus et familia*) into the prayer alongside the Roman people (*CIL* 6.32323.99), thus declaring his role and that of his family in Rome's future prosperity.[87]

Augustus' objective was not a simplistic revival of the past, which would not have been possible in any case because Rome was now the capital of a worldwide empire, but rather a revival of the values of early Rome within the context of Imperial Rome. Whether such a revival of Roman character was actually possible cannot be known. But what was important for Augustus was to find ways to demonstrate that it had already taken place, and he did this in part through the passage of his laws on marriage and adultery beginning in 18 BC. The idea was to build a prosperous future on the foundation laid by the past.[88] Such a revival could also be demonstrated abstractly and symbolically through the topography of the *Ludi Saeculares*, the myriad rites of which occurred throughout the city of Rome and called attention to Augustus' building program, which revived the spirit of Republican Rome within the context of a new imperial capital. On the first evening of the celebration, for instance, following a sacrifice in Greek fashion, plays were performed on a makeshift stage with no provisions for seating,[89] presumably in an effort to recreate such performances at an earlier celebration of the *Ludi Saeculares* before the advent of permanent stone theaters in Rome. This revival of the past had even greater force in the present topography of Augustan Rome, where reminders of the city's status as capital of a world empire were everywhere visible. The precise location of these performances is not known, but the implication of the *acta* is that they took place near the Tarentum, where the sacrifice had been performed, in that part of the Campus Martius that is closest to the bend in the Tiber River—between the Corso di Vittorio Emanuele and the Lungotevere.[90] Such performances in this context not only brought together present and past, but with construction on the Theater of Marcellus (dedicated in 13 or 11 BC [see fig. 4]) in the southern Campus Martius already begun,[91] these performances might even have gestured toward the future. One could argue that the topography of Augustus' new Rome might have had the same effect on anyone walking in and around the city at any given time. I would suggest, however, that the *Ludi Saeculares* were especially evocative of the past and anticipatory of the future and thus were conducive to the kind of effect that Augustus was perhaps hoping to achieve—namely, a demonstration that his Rome was the link between Rome's glorious past and its prosperous future.

Another way that Augustus evoked the past at this festival was to organize another performance of the *Lusus Troiae*. Octavian already put this ancient ritual to good use in the Triumviral period as a way to celebrate his adoptive family. Under the Principate, it became a more permanent feature of those festivals that were especially important to the *princeps'* family. We have already discussed the performance involving Tiberius in 29 BC; at the games marking the dedication of the Theater of Marcellus, the performance featured his grandson, Gaius (13 BC, according to Dio 54.26.1). Finally in 2 BC, at the dedication of the Temple of Mars Ultor, the *Lusus Troiae* again was held.[92] At the performance at the *Ludi Saeculares*, it is probable that none of Augustus' heirs took part, since Tiberius and Drusus were both too old (and probably not in Rome), and Gaius and Lucius were still too young.

In celebrating the *Ludi Saeculares*, Augustus paused in the consolidation of his power in order to reflect on the transformation of Rome that his Principate had begun to effect. This transformation was contingent upon the revival of past ideals in preparation for a hopeful and prosperous future. In order for Augustus to achieve his objectives, he had to raise the historical consciousness of those who called him *princeps*. The *Ludi Saeculares* were an important part of this process, which had actually begun a few years earlier in 20 BC, when an important addition was made to the Forum Romanum. Attached to the south side of the Temple of Divus Julius was a triumphal arch bearing Augustus' name (see fig. 3). On one pillar were inscribed the consular *Fasti*, an annual listing of all Romans who had achieved the highest magistracy since the beginning of the Republic. On the other pillar were inscribed the *Fasti Triumphales*, comprising a list of all those who had ever processed into the city in triumph, beginning with the victory and triumph of Romulus himself, the founder of Rome. The public display of the consular *Fasti* demonstrated a clear continuity with the past of Rome, a cornerstone of Augustus' claim to have restored the Republic. The fact that this display was made so soon after Augustus had relinquished the consulship, thus restoring that magistracy to the senatorial aristocracy, further demonstrated Augustus' role in maintaining the institutions of the Republic. The display of the triumphal *Fasti* similarly demonstrated a continuity with the past—in particular the connection of Augustus as *triumphator* to the great military victors and conquerors from Rome's glorious past. At the same time, however, the list came to a perfunctory end with the triumph of L. Cornelius Balbus in 19 BC, thus abruptly concluding the customary conferral of triumphs under the Republic. If Balbus' name filled the last available space on the pillar, then even those who saw the list in 19 BC would have known that a change was in the offing, but it is unlikely that they would have been able to guess precisely how the conferral of triumphs would change without an explanatory announcement from the *princeps*. It is possible that Augustus himself had not thought through completely what changes he would implement. In any event, the appearance of both *Fasti* would have brought those Romans who visited the Forum face-to-face with their past, perhaps raising in the process their historical consciousness.

Public entertainment in Augustus' hands was transformed from the Republican display of *liberalitas*, often intended to garner votes in upcoming elections, to monarchical ceremony where members of the imperial family were on display and his successors could stand in the public gaze. Moreover, Augustus could use a special set of games like the *Ludi Saeculares* to paint a picture of his place and the place of his regime within the larger context of Roman history. He desired to show that his regime combined the moral values of Republican Rome, as revived through his marriage laws and the restoration of traditional Roman religion, with the peace and prosperity recently won through the Cantabrian wars and negotiated settlement with the Parthian Empire, to direct the Roman people to a safe, secure, and prosperous future. Public entertainment under Augustus never entirely lost its

Republican form, which enabled the *princeps* to channel his power through traditional means, yet the content and substance of that same entertainment had such a historical breadth and depth that it provided Augustus' power with the sheen of timelessness. Augustus might die, but the political power invested in the Principate would endure.[93]

Triumphs

Perhaps more than any of the other types of ceremony that we have considered thus far, triumphal celebrations served the needs of the *princeps* and the imperial family and came to form the court ceremony of the Principate, as these celebrations gradually came under the control of Augustus. Just as the *princeps* was the principal *rogator* and *orator* in dealing with the Roman people and the principal sponsor of public entertainment, so too was he the principal winner of military glory and renown. Augustus established a hierarchy of victory celebrations incorporating the new triumphal honors (*ornamenta triumphalia*) with the traditional Republican ceremonies of the *ovatio* and triumph proper. Thus, he seems to have wanted to reserve the triumph proper as a rare celebration, limited only to the most glorious victories won by members of the imperial family. The *princeps* himself never celebrated a triumph after his magnificent triple triumph of August 29 BC. We are told that Augustus was generous in his conferral of triumphs in the early years of his reign,[94] but M. Licinius Crassus' failure to attain the *spolia opima* in 27 BC following his conquest of the Bastarnae and slaying of their king Deldo perhaps was a harbinger of things to come when Augustus eventually exercised complete control over the triumph.[95]

In 19 BC, following the triumph of L. Cornelius Balbus, son of the Spaniard who rose to power through his association with Caesar, triumphs for those outside the imperial family abruptly ended, and this was clearly demonstrated for all to see by the *Fasti Triumphales* on the Arch of Augustus in the Forum, as we mentioned in the last section.[96] After 19 BC the triumph and related ceremonies, such as the departure and return, were completely in Augustus' hands. In 20 BC Augustus set a precedent of sorts after recovering the Roman standards lost at Carrhae. This "victory" over the Parthians, if such it could be called, was a bloodless one at best—a diplomatic triumph, not a military one. The senate seems to have concurred when they decreed an *ovatio* for Augustus,[97] thus reserving the triumph proper for the celebration of a true military victory. Agrippa had a role to play in this process as well, since he declined triumphs offered him on several occasions, beginning in his first consulship of 37 and again in 19. His final refusal in 14 seems to have helped establish the precedent of conferring triumphal honors (*ornamenta triumphalia*) in place of the triumph proper.[98] Augustus later demonstrated his control over such ceremonies when he reduced to triumphal honors the triumph proper decreed by the senate in 12 BC for Tiberius' part in pacifying Pannonia (Dio 54.31.4). He did this perhaps in an effort to maintain the prestige of the triumph proper, since the senate, in this instance, decreed one for Tiberius even though he had not defeated the enemy in a pitched battle. It is also possible that Augustus was trying to prevent Tiberius from achieving such an honor early in his career, for a few years later, following Tiberius' victory in Pannonia, Augustus allowed him to celebrate an *ovatio* (Vell. 2.96.3; Dio 55.2.4), still holding in reserve the triumph proper.

The new rarity of triumphs under Augustus is in evidence after Balbus celebrated his in 19, for the next triumph was not awarded until 9, but even then it had to be canceled when the honorand Drusus unexpectedly died. His funeral (which we will discuss later in this chapter) became his triumph. The hiatus between triumphs in Augustus' Principate was a long one, perhaps the longest in Roman history, and one can only wonder how this hiatus might have affected the spectators and the performers when it finally ended. In 9 BC, when Drusus was consul, the stage was set for the first "imperial" triumph, and it was Drusus himself, not Tiberius, who was to be the celebrant.[99] It was arranged that the *Feriae Latinae* be repeated in order that Drusus could celebrate his triumph during that festival. Unfortunately, Drusus died while on campaign and the plans had to be set aside (Dio 55.2.5). Nonetheless, the planned celebration of Drusus' triumph in conjunction with the *Feriae Latinae* seems to be part of a larger pattern that dates back to the Triumviral period. At that time, and also early in the Principate, it became increasingly common for triumphs to be celebrated on the occasion of the new year. The triumphs of M. Aemilius Lepidus and L. Munatius Plancus on the last day in December 43, of L. Antonius in January 41, and of L. Marcius Censorinus in January 39 are attested examples of this larger pattern. Furthermore, the senate, as if to codify this practice, in 25 decreed that Augustus could wear the triumphal garb on the first day of each year.[100]

We should also note the importance of the *Feriae Latinae* in this context. This festival was not a new year's celebration per se, but it occurred at the beginning of each year by this period and traditionally inaugurated the military campaigning season. Caesar, I believe, transformed the meaning of this festival when he merged the celebration of an *ovatio* with the *Feriae Latinae* in January 44, thus combining a celebration of peace and *concordia*, especially that of the senatorial aristocracy, with the beginning of a new era. Augustus did likewise when he resigned the consulship in 23. The *Feriae Latinae* was also appropriate, then, as an occasion for celebrating the first imperial triumph, since this triumph would also have marked the beginning of a new era—one in which the *princeps* and his family ceremonially moved to the center of power. But this is only part of the story of this ceremony. If the *Feriae Latinae* had become symbolic of reconciliation and harmony—especially between the *princeps* and the most important aristocratic families—then the coincidence of the triumph and this festival could also serve as a reminder of the nature of *concordia* under the Principate. This ideal was now dependent upon the power of the *princeps* and the willingness of the aristocracy to acknowledge that power while relinquishing some of its own.

After the death of Drusus preempted his triumph, the first imperial triumph to be performed as planned was that of Tiberius in 7 BC, the first to be celebrated in the twelve years since L. Cornelius Balbus had done so. Tiberius celebrated his triumph, as was now almost traditional, on the first day of his first consulship for a victory in Pannonia (Dio 55.8.2). He treated the senate to a banquet on the Capitolium while his mother, Livia, did the same for prominent Roman women at an unspecified location. Tiberius' triumph was distinguished from that of Balbus not only because he was a member of the imperial family, but because he was also a scion of a prominent patrician family of the Republic. We can only speculate on the effect this ceremony might have had on a populace that had not seen one for a number of years, but Augustus' purpose in taking control of the dispensation of triumphal honors was partly to restore the triumph to its former prestige and glory, following a period of degradation when the criteria for awarding a triumph were less stringently observed. Under these circumstances, Tiberius' nobility might have been reassuring, since it would show that the *princeps* was symbolically returning the triumph to the senatorial aristocracy.

Augustus' principal innovation to the traditional Roman victory celebrations was the establishment of a hierarchy of honors under which the triumph proper became the exclusive privilege of members of the imperial family. During the long hiatus between the last "Republican" triumph of Balbus and the first imperial triumph of Tiberius, Augustus underscored this innovation by awarding an *ovatio* and triumphal honors but delaying the decree of a triumph proper, thus further heightening the sense of anticipation for the triumph once it finally was awarded. The triumph bestowed great power and prestige on the honorand, but much of it was now inseparable from the glory of the emperor himself, who was commander-in-chief of the Roman army. Further, the conferral of the triumph, once the right of the senate and people of Rome, transferred into the hands of the emperor, who became the bestower of honors and the prestige that these honors conferred.

Departures and Returns

We have already discussed the importance of the triumph proper to the court ceremony of Augustus. Did the accompanying ceremonies of the departure (*profectio*) and return (*reditus* or *adventus*), so important in the Republic for spontaneous and planned displays of popular favor, also become the exclusive privilege of members of the imperial family?[101] Augustus' construction of the Temple of Mars Ultor altered the topography of departures and returns and further associated these ceremonies with the public image of the *princeps*.

In 9 BC, following the death of Drusus, Augustus first declined to enter the city lest he be required to perform the customary ceremonies honoring his achievements; he even delivered a *laudatio* in Drusus' honor in the Circus Flaminius (Dio 55.2.2; cf. Tac. *Ann.* 3.5.1; see also the discussion later in this chapter). He waited until the beginning of the next year, and, when the new consuls entered office, Augustus made his ceremonial entry into the city, delivering the laurel wreath symbolizing victory to the Temple of Jupiter Feretrius, rather than Jupiter Capitolinus (Dio 55.5.1). Dio acknowledges the change in ceremony but does not explain the reason for it. He goes on to tell us that Augustus, still in mourning at the loss of Drusus, declined to celebrate his victory with a triumph, instead leaving the sponsorship of gladiatorial combat to the consuls for the year. Perhaps Jupiter Capitolinus was associated too closely with the ceremony of the triumph, which Augustus was unwilling to celebrate at this time. In any event, Augustus' ceremonial entry into the city at the beginning of the new year in 8 BC was closely connected with the triumph, which in turn had evolved into a kind of new year's celebration in this period. Both contributed to the development of the imperial *adventus*, which became more explicit under Augustus, especially as cities began to mark the beginning of their new year with the arrival of the emperor.[102]

After 2 BC the Temple of Mars Ultor (see fig. 4) became a central structure in the rituals associated with victory, not only as the repository for the standards recovered from the Parthians but also as the starting point for a general setting out to the provinces and the first destination upon his return to the city (Dio 55.10; cf. 54.8.3), thus transforming the location and movement of ceremonial departures from and returns to the city of Rome under the Principate.[103] Following the dedication of the temple, and the inaugural celebration of the *Ludi Martiales* (described earlier), the first *profectio* was that of Augustus' grandson, C. Caesar, in preparation for his campaign against the Parthians. By this time, Tiberius had withdrawn to Rhodes, perhaps to leave a clear field for Gaius and Lucius,[104] who recently had been adopted by Augustus and apparently established as heirs to his power. Our only source for this *profectio,* a few lines from Ovid's *Ars Amatoria* (1.181–228), must be used with caution, yet it at least expresses the tenor of the celebration and adumbrates the hopes and expectations of the spectators present by anticipating the form that Gaius' expected triumph would take. For our purposes, it is sufficient to point out that Gaius' *profectio* must have acquired special meaning, not only since he was the first to depart from the Temple of Mars Ultor but also because his departure anticipated another campaign against the Parthians. By being the first to depart from this temple, and thus the first to use it for one of its expressed purposes, Gaius' *profectio* became a ceremony of succession because this monument celebrated the place of the family of the *princeps* in the long and glorious history of Rome. If Ovid's account is credible, then the youthful age of Gaius was a matter of some concern, but such concerns might also have been a reminder of his adoptive father's youthful start to his career, not to mention the other young commanders in Rome's history—Scipio, Flamininus, and Pompeius Magnus, whose statues adorned the *exedrae* of the Forum Augustum. Gaius' *profectio* in 2 BC underscored the link with the past and the hope for the future to which Augustus' edict (quoted earlier) and the games celebrating the dedication of these structures had already alluded. Spectators were gazing at a possible successor to Augustus and the continuation of the new form of government, an embodiment, if you will, of the future of political power in Rome. At the same time, Gaius emerged from the Temple of Mars Ultor, passing through the Forum Augustum, which contained not only an image of Augustus in a *quadriga,* very much a symbol of victory, but also statues of famous members of the Julian *gens* and many of the great *triumphatores* of Roman history. Gaius on this occasion was manifestly part of a continuum of commanders, the makers of Roman history, and his departure anticipated similar glory for himself.

The following years were not kind to Augustus' plans for the succession, and the promise of future glory expressed in the ceremonies surrounding the dedication of the Temple of Mars Ultor largely went unfulfilled. The premature deaths of Augustus' grandsons—Lucius in AD 2 and Gaius two years later—forced him to recall Tiberius from exile in Rhodes to take on the mantle of successor. Some of Tiberius' achievements have already been noted, but it was only in AD 9, upon his victorious return from Germany, that he participated in a lavish ceremony of succession—one that was likely carefully planned by the *princeps*.

The ceremony in question began with Tiberius' return to the city in AD 9. The return of a victorious general from the provinces anticipated, even more than his departure (*profectio*), the hoped-for triumph. Many of Augustus' returns to the city were greeted with great fanfare. To commemorate his return in October 19 BC, for instance, an arch was decreed to Fortuna Redux and a festival established, which served to transform one particular return to the city, a rather ephemeral event, into a recurring celebration (Aug. *Anc.* 11). By the time of Tiberius' return from Germany he was heir designate, and the ceremonies associated with his return express this most clearly. Augustus himself went out to greet Tiberius upon his return to the city, accompanied him to the Saepta Julia, and there presented him to the people. Tiberius and Augustus sat on a raised platform, flanked by the two consuls and accompanied by the senate (Suet. *Tib.* 17.2; Dio 56.1.1). This was a sight that showed clearly where the balance of power lay. The consuls, chief magistrates of the city, were present, but they were clearly figures of secondary importance at the sides of the *princeps* and his heir designate.

The use of the Saepta on this occasion also shows the dynamic relationship between *princeps* and *plebs* and therefore can shed light on the evolving role of the *plebs* in the new government. Since Tiberius was returning from the northern provinces, his route likely would have taken him down the Via Flaminia, past many monuments of importance to the Augustan regime, including the Ara Pacis and Horologium complex and the family mausoleum, and hence within easy reach of the Saepta. But the Saepta was probably chosen for this ceremony not only because of its topographical convenience. This ceremony sanctioned the principle of succession by legitimating the successor to Augustus in the eyes of the people. The triumph itself was an important ritual for celebrating victory and military glory, but traditionally the triumph was preceded by the *triumphator's contio*, in which he detailed his exploits to the people at a venue outside the Pomerium, customarily during the Republic in the vicinity of the Temple of Bellona. In this instance, the venue was the Saepta perhaps because of its importance as a symbol of popular sovereignty: the heir designate in his moment of glory returned to the acclamation of the people in a venue where this kind of acclamation had especial legitimacy, where it conferred a specific kind of power: it was the closest Tiberius could come to being elected the next *princeps* of Rome.

The planned celebrations for Tiberius' victory were postponed when word reached Rome that P. Varus' troops had been destroyed in the Teutoberg Forest. These celebrations are, nonetheless, indicative of the way in which an elaborate ceremony could be used to establish an order of succession. Tiberius, the returning general and heir designate, was awarded a triumph and an arch in Pannonia, as was the *princeps*. Germanicus, son of Tiberius' brother, Drusus, made the announcement of victory and was awarded the lesser distinction of triumphal honors; at the same time, he was given the rank of praetor with the privilege of casting his vote first among ex-praetors, immediately after the consulars, thus establishing his place in the traditional political hierarchy of the Roman Republic. Tiberius' son Drusus was given the privilege of attending meetings of the senate, although not yet a senator, and of voting before the ex-praetors. All of this to a man who had played no part in the campaign (Dio 56.17; cf. Vell. 2.121.2–3). The honors conferred showed each man in order of proximity to the *princeps* and perhaps were an indication also of proximity to the throne. Augustus, I believe, used this triumph as an opportunity to demonstrate the stability of the Principate, although recently discombobulated by the disaster in the Teutoberg Forest, by showing three candidates in a grand ceremony of succession who were qualified to serve as *princeps*.

Departures and returns were an important complement to triumphs and triumphal honors. The central importance of the Temple of Mars Ultor to these ceremonies placed Augustus and his family at the center of military activity and the glory that was won thereby. The departures and returns involving members of the imperial family became ceremonies of succession, culminated by Tiberius' last return to Rome, which occasioned a distribution of triumphal honors to members of Augustus' family that illustrated a hierarchy of succession.

Funerals

The Roman aristocratic funeral evolved during the late Republic into a potentially riotous and divisive ceremony that both reflected and exacerbated the volatility of the times. Under Augustus aristocratic funerals became rarer, it seems, as the *princeps* developed the imperial funeral. The imperial funeral was based closely on its forbears, with modifications to accommodate the changes in the topography of the Forum and, for Augustus' funeral, the city of Rome. In the early years of his reign, we are told that Augustus was lavish with his conferral of public funerals (Dio 54.12.2), although none is attested in our sources, aside from those for members of the imperial family,[105] which became models for Augustus' own funeral.[106]

The funeral of Augustus' sister, Octavia, must be given priority in this discussion, only because Dio provides specific details about it (Dio 54.35.4–5) that will allow us to draw firmer conclusions about the other funerals in this period and, finally, to show that Augustus' funeral was the culmination of a long process. After Octavia died in 11 BC, Augustus arranged to have her body, shrouded by a curtain, lie in state in the Temple of Divus Julius.[107] Dio states that the origin of the custom was unknown to him, after eliminating the possibility that it had to do with religious prohibitions owing to Augustus' position as Pontifex Maximus or censor.[108] It is possible that its origin in fact resides in Caesar's funeral, where his body was shrouded in order to hide the wounds that he had received.

We discussed earlier the new topography of the Forum and how it affected the *contiones* of the Roman people. A specific type of *contio*, the *laudatio* at the funeral of a member of the imperial family, became part of the changing funeral ritual in this period. Those whose funerals were put on in our period, namely, Octavia and Augustus himself, and possibly M. Agrippa, Drusus, and C. Marcellus, were honored with obsequies in which the *rostra* on the Temple of Divus Julius figured prominently. The use of this temple as a place to display the corpse was unusual. Customarily, the body of the deceased lay in state in the *atrium* of his own home. In the case of Agrippa's funeral, we are told only that Augustus allowed the body to lie in state "in the Forum"; perhaps the Temple of Divus Julius was also meant (see fig. 3).[109] In any event, this temple was appropriate for a number of reasons. In general terms, its use for this purpose demonstrates the importance of Octavia (and perhaps Agrippa), a member of the imperial family, as a public figure. Further evidence for this can be found in the period of public mourning decreed for her death and the fact that senators changed their dress. This temple, however, had an especial appropriateness to funerals, since it could trace its origins to the funeral of Caesar, was situated on the ground that had become consecrated through the efforts of his supporters, and thus was closely connected to the passage of Caesar from the world of the mortal to that of the divine. Neither Octavia nor Agrippa achieved divine status in the same manner that Augustus did,[110] but the display of Octavia's body, and probably Agrippa's, in the Temple of Divus Julius connected them to the cult of Caesar.

The speeches in praise of Octavia took place in unprecedented fashion and underscored the sight line across the Forum that first Caesar's and then Augustus' new topography had created. Two *laudationes* were delivered instead of just one. Drusus, the brother of Tiberius, delivered one from the Rostra, meaning the Rostra Augusti at the west end of the Forum. Augustus himself delivered the other, probably from the *rostra* of the Temple of Divus Julius, since we know that at Augustus' funeral Tiberius delivered a *laudatio* from that location, while his son Drusus read something from the Rostra Augusti (Dio 56.34.4; Suet. *Aug.* 100.3). The two *laudationes* in honor of Octavia, then, would have required the two orators to face each other across the Forum. It is also probable that Augustus delivered his *laudatio* over the body of his sister (as he did at Agrippa's funeral), in which case Octavia's body must have been moved from inside the Temple of Divus Julius to its *rostra*.

Just two years later, the death of another member of the imperial family was mourned. The funeral of Tiberius' brother, Drusus, occurred in 9 BC, the year of his consulship and planned triumph. He was both a descendant of a distinguished patrician family, the Claudii, whose roots stretched back to the early Republic, and a military hero whose exploits on the battlefield had already earned him a triumph that was supposed to have been held in this year.[111] This funeral, very much like a triumph, as Seneca informs us (*funus simillimum triumpho; Dial.* 6.3.1), perhaps in part replaced the triumph that Drusus never held and thus combined elements of both types of ceremony. Drusus had been campaigning in Germany when he fell ill. Augustus dispatched Tiberius, who found his brother near death. He accompanied the body back to Rome at the head of a procession that consisted first of centurions and military tribunes of the legions until they reached winter quarters, at which point the leading men (probably the *decuriones*) of each city in turn conveyed his body to Rome (Dio 55.2.1; Suet. *Tib.* 7.3).

Once in Rome Drusus was honored with a *pompa* and *laudatio* that were now becoming established traditions of imperial funerals. The lavish *pompa* included the *imagines* of both the Julian and Claudian *gentes*,[112] despite the fact that Drusus had never been formally adopted by Augustus.[113] For the purposes of his funeral at least, Drusus was treated as a member of the family. This funeral also afforded Augustus the opportunity to stress the unity of the two distinguished families, whose fame and glory was personified by the deceased.

The double *laudatio* that by now had probably become familiar from the recent funerals of Agrippa and Octavia were also spoken in Drusus' honor, but the location of one of the speeches was altered by necessity. Augustus delivered his eulogy in the Circus Flaminius, while Tiberius delivered a second one from the Rostra in the Forum. Dio explains that Augustus, who had been away on campaign, could not enter the Pomerium and perform the customary rites of his return until his period of mourning was complete (55.2.2). This necessity likely altered the entire topography of the funerary procession. A small fragment of Augustus' *laudatio* survives, in which he expresses his hopes in a prayer that Drusus' life will serve as a model for his sons (i.e., Gaius and Lucius) and that the gods will grant them as glorious a death.[114] This statement only makes sense if Gaius and Lucius were present, along with other members of the imperial family as well as the *imagines*, as was traditional in a funeral. A *laudatio* was also traditionally delivered over the body of the deceased. We are explicitly told that this was the case for the second *laudatio* which Tiberius delivered in the Forum.[115] Thus, it is possible that Drusus' funerary *pompa* started in the Circus Flaminius, where Augustus delivered his *laudatio*, and then proceeded to the Forum, where Tiberius delivered his. If so, then it began at the location of the mustering point of a Roman triumph. Could this procession have also gone through the Porta Triumphalis? This seems unlikely since a decree of the senate was required for this honor to be accorded to Augustus upon his death, and we do not hear of one for Drusus' funeral. But the route of the procession in any case, from the Circus Flaminius to the Forum, might have been one way for Augustus to honor Drusus with a form of posthumous triumph and thereby prompted Seneca's remark about the similarity of his funeral to a triumph.

The development of the imperial funeral as a ceremonial type continued with the death of Augustus. We should bear in mind, too, that Augustus, among the documents left at his death, provided instructions for his own funeral, not at all unusual for a Roman aristocrat. The existence of these instructions, however, did not preclude a debate in the senate, in which various senators rivaled each other in proposing unprecedented honors for the deceased *princeps* (Tac. *Ann.* 1.8; Suet. *Aug.* 100.2). We must assume that the senate simply appended the new honors moved by its members to the original instructions left by Augustus, thus creating, in the end, a ceremony that combined both. Finally, Augustus' successor, Tiberius, published an *edictum* instructing the populace of Rome not to attempt to burn Augustus' body in the Forum, as they had with Caesar's, but rather to allow it to be cremated in the Campus Martius, where a place had been designated (Tac. *Ann.* 1.8.5).

Augustus' body was conveyed by night from Nola, where he had died, with the *decuriones* of each *municipium* or *colonia* taking it in turn until it reached Bovillae. Here they handed it over to members of the equestrian order, who then conveyed it into the city and eventually to the vestibule of Augustus' home (Suet. *Aug.* 100.2; Dio 56.31.2), where it was presumably put on display in the *atrium*, as was traditional from Republican times, although we should note the variation in the funerals of Agrippa and Octavia, discussed earlier. It is curious that Augustus seems to have refused an honor for himself that he had bestowed upon his sister and son-in-law. On the day of the funeral, Augustus' body was hidden in a coffin underneath a bier made of ivory and gold with coverlets of purple and gold, apparently similar to the display of Octavia's body. Three images of Augustus were carried in the funeral procession, each apparently originating at a different location in the city. The magistrates-elect for the coming year carried the first image, made of wax and depicting the *princeps* in the costume of a *triumphator*, presumably from his home on the Palatium (Dio 56.34.1). A second image of Augustus made of gold was carried from the Curia Julia, presumably by members of the senate, although we are not told so explicitly. The third image showed Augustus in a triumphal chariot, but we are not told where it originated. Perhaps it emerged from the Forum Augustum, where an image of Augustus in a *quadriga* was permanently situated. Trailing behind these images of Augustus were the ancestral busts of members of Augustus' family and many of the great Romans of history, all the way back to Romulus himself, with the exception of Julius Caesar, whose divine status precluded his participation in a procession of mere mortals. Also included in this procession was an image of Pompeius Magnus, along with images of all of the peoples he added to the Roman Empire.[116] All three images of Augustus, it seems, converged at some point, with Augustus' body on the gold and ivory bier coming up behind.[117]

Dio's account of this procession is not without its difficulties. He describes first the bier of ivory and gold and then the three images of Augustus. Behind these, he states, came the images of Augustus' ancestors and famous Romans from history, including Romulus and Pompeius Magnus. Behind these images, in turn, came all of the things he mentioned previously. "All of the things mentioned previously" must mean the bier of ivory and gold, for Dio mentions nothing else. It also makes sense that Augustus' body would have come last in the procession.

As we have seen, Augustus' funerary *pompa* was replete with triumphal imagery—an aspect of his funeral that was not entirely innovatory.[118] In Augustus' *pompa*, there were two images depicting Augustus as *triumphator*, one traditionally garbed in triumphal dress, the other in a *quadriga*, for which there was no precedent. There were also the images of famous Romans (*summi viri*), including both the first *triumphator* of Roman history, Romulus, and the great conqueror from the last generation of the Republic, Pompeius Magnus. It is likely that Dio has recorded in his account the images that began and ended the parade of *summi viri*. Romulus would undoubtedly have been the first in such a parade, and there was no conqueror after Pompeius, save for Caesar, whose image, we are told, was not present.[119] After Actium all conquest and annexation of territory to the empire was done by the *princeps* himself or under his auspices. In the senate debate following Augustus' death, L. Arruntius proposed that placards bearing the names of the nations Augustus had conquered be carried in the procession (Tac. *Ann.* 1.8.3). If this motion was enacted by senatorial decree, then Augustus' accomplishments would have been inscribed in close juxtaposition to the accomplishments of the other great conquerors of Roman history. And if the enumeration of his conquests at his funeral matched the one that appears in the *Res Gestae* (25–33), his supremacy in this sphere would have been unquestioned.

The presence of the three images altered and embellished the usual topography of the funerary *pompa* in a manner that was unprecedented. What follows is a possible topography of this procession, but it is by no means the only one. It presupposes that Dio's account preserves the correct marching order of the three images of Augustus in the procession: first, the one of wax; second, the one of gold; and third, the one in the *quadriga*. We also know that, at some point, the three images converged to form one procession that eventually culminated at the Rostra in the Forum. The first image of Augustus, carried by magistrates already elected for the coming year, likely proceeded from his house on the Palatium through the Forum Romanum and to the Curia Julia, where it was joined by the second image of Augustus, perhaps depicting the *princeps* in his role as senator and accompanied by members of the senate. This was in contrast to the martial image associated with the garb of the *triumphator*. The origin of the third image of Augustus is something of a mystery, since Dio fails to inform us where it originated, although he does state that the parade of ancestral images trailed behind the second and third images. It is my belief that both the image of Augustus in the *quadriga* and the ancestral images emerged from the Forum Augustum. This monument was associated with Augustus' military victories, as evidenced by the permanent image of Augustus in a *quadriga* that was housed there. What's more, it contained, in its *exedrae*, statues of distinguished members of the Julian *gens* and other famous Romans (the *summi viri*), especially those who had held triumphs. It seems natural that such a procession as Dio describes, filled as it was with the imagery of triumph and conquest—including not only an image of Romulus, the first *triumphator* in Roman history, but also that of Pompeius Magnus, along with those of the peoples that he had conquered—would come from the structure that housed the standards recovered from the Parthians, which was the starting point for generals embarking on their campaigns and their destination upon their return. In other words, they emerged from the structure that was a memorial to the very imagery just described.

If this was the case, then the larger procession, including the first and second images, accompanied both by the magistrates-elect and other members of the senate, marched the short distance to the Forum Augustum, where it was joined by the image of Augustus in the *quadriga* and the images of his ancestors and the *summi viri* of Roman history. At this point, things get a bit murkier. It is unlikely that the procession, once it reached the Forum Augustum, would have reversed itself and turned back to the Rostra in the Forum. Rather, it makes more sense if the procession then marched down the Argiletum, perhaps as far as the Mons Oppius, and made the turn south once more toward the Palatium and the Forum where Augustus' bier, perhaps accompanied by living members of his family, including the two funeral speakers, could join it. If the bier did join the procession at this late stage, then its journey was a short one, from the vestibule of Augustus' home to the Rostra Augusti in the Forum (see fig. 4).

Once the procession reached the Rostra, Drusus, Tiberius' son, made a proclamation, while standing over Augustus' bier.[120] It is not clear precisely what his speech consisted of, although in the speech of Tiberius that followed, as Dio records it, Tiberius contrasts his own speech in praise of Augustus with that of Drusus, by saying that Drusus' speech contained words that were appropriately spoken privately and by members of Augustus' family, while Tiberius, pursuant to a senatorial decree, delivered a public speech.[121] This kind of double eulogy had already been used both at Drusus' and Octavia's funerals, as we have seen, although in those cases no distinction was made as to the content of the two speeches and how they might have differed.

Following the *laudationes*, the magistrates-elect for the coming year again took up the bier on their shoulders and marched in procession toward the Campus Martius where a pyre had been erected, accompanied by other members of the senate, the equestrian order, their wives, the praetorian guard, and, as Dio puts it, almost everyone else who was in the city at the time (Dio 56.42.1–2). The imagery of triumph and victory continued as the procession passed through the Porta Triumphalis, in accordance with a decree of the senate, perhaps also preceded by the statue of Victory from the Curia Julia and including placards listing the names of the nations that Augustus had conquered (Tac. *Ann.* 1.8.3). The precise location of the Porta Triumphalis is still a matter of dispute, but it is probable that it was located somewhere near the beginning of the route of the triumph, in the southern Campus Martius.[122] Thus, the procession to the pyre in the Campus Martius, probably located in close proximity to the mausoleum, began at the Rostra and proceeded down the Vicus Jugarius and eventually past the Theater of Marcellus, thus entering the Campus Martius from the south. At this point, the most likely route would have taken it around the base of the Capitolium to the Via Flaminia, which led to Augustus' mausoleum. This route would have taken the procession past many important Augustan monuments, beginning with the Theater of Marcellus but also including the Saepta Julia as well as the Horologium and Ara Pacis.

Augustus' body was finally placed on the pyre near his mausoleum, at which point priests marched around it, then knights, both those from the equestrian order and others, presumably cavalrymen, and finally heavily armed guards,[123] who tossed upon the pyre any rewards for victory that he had conferred upon them. Centurions set the pyre alight, and as it burned an eagle was released and made to fly aloft, a symbol of Augustus' divinity. This innovation to the traditional funeral ritual became a central part of imperial funerals from this time forward.[124] Livia remained at the site of Augustus' cremation for five days, accompanied by leading members of the equestrian order; at the end of this period, they gathered up his remains and placed them in the mausoleum.

There are three aspects of public ceremonial that have been implicit in much of our discussion of Augustus' funeral above: ceremony and dynastic succession; the effect of the changing topography of the city of Rome; and ceremony and history. It remains to bring a few points into greater relief. The presence of Tiberius as the principal *laudator* for Augustus was consistent with the traditional funeral ritual, in which the eldest son (in this case, adopted son) delivered the *laudatio* for the deceased. It also confirmed in part the arrangements that Augustus had made for the succession, which culminated in his adoption of Tiberius and the conferral of tribunician power on him. In this way, a traditional aristocratic ritual was modified to create a ceremony of succession, with Tiberius formally bidding farewell to Augustus so that he himself could take on the role of *princeps*. At the same time, the presence of Drusus as the second speaker, and the absence of Germanicus, who was on campaign in Germany, might have brought to light the rivalry to succeed Tiberius, which informed much of the early years of Tiberius' reign. Germanicus' absence was necessary, but it nonetheless might have called into question the line of succession that Augustus attempted to establish before his death.

The topography of Augustus' funeral also couples an adherence to tradition with added innovations. The basic topography connecting the Forum and Rostra with the Campus Martius became traditional, especially in the late Republic with the public funerals of Sulla and Caesar. If I am right, however, about the *quadriga* coming from the Forum Augustum, then the topography of the procession would have linked together spatially many of the most important monuments of Augustan Rome: Augustus' house and the adjacent Temple of Apollo, the Temple of Mars Ultor and Forum Augustum, the Curia Julia, the Rostra Augusti and Temple of Divus Julius, the Saepta Julia, Horologium, and Ara Pacis, and finally the Mausoleum Augusti. It is not that Augustus' funeral procession covered a greater distance than previous processions, but rather that many of the monuments that it passed bore the mark of the *princeps*' regime. In this sense, the procession confirmed Augustus' boast that he had found Rome a city of brick and left it a city of marble (Suet. *Aug*. 28.3).

The parade of *imagines* at Augustus' funeral also sheds light on the temporal aspect of ceremony. In this case, it served to validate Augustus' version of history. In addition to the traditional parade of *imagines* of members of his family (presumably the Julian *gens* is meant), there were also *imagines* of famous Romans, beginning with Romulus himself and including Pompeius Magnus. I suggested earlier that, in this way, Augustus' accomplishments on the battlefield were presented to the Roman people in close proximity to the accomplishments of the other great conquerors of Roman history. Thus, Augustus' place in history was secure. Furthermore, his own version of history, in which his adopted family, the Julian *gens*, takes center stage, as monumentalized in particular in the Forum Augustum, was played out in his funeral procession.

Augustus' funeral was the culmination of a process that transformed the aristocratic funeral into an imperial court ceremony. The imperial funeral was remade to reflect the changes in the topography of the Forum, with the Temple of Divus Julius in particular becoming an integral part of the ceremony. Further, the procession at Augustus' funeral linked ceremonially many of the most important monuments of Augustan Rome. The riotous and divisive ceremony of the late Republic, manifested most notoriously in the funerals of Clodius and Caesar, became under the Augustan Principate an exercise involving all strata of Roman society and the images of the most famous figures in Roman history, under the stewardship of Augustus' successor. They all converged to celebrate the life and career of the man who ended civil war and brought peace to the Roman Empire.

Conclusion

Out of the public ceremonial of the Roman Republic was forged the imperial court ceremony that celebrated the prestige and power of the *princeps* and his family. The distribution and sharing of power, the demonstration of which was so important in the public ceremonial of the Roman Republic, naturally came to center on the *princeps*. But court ceremony often revealed the ambiguities and complexities of Augustus' power, which were especially in evidence at electoral assemblies, when by virtue of *commendatio* and later *destinatio* he could see his chosen candidates through to election to high office. The creation of a select assembly responsible for "destining" candidates was a sign of Augustus' willingness to share power, but it equally demonstrated that the two higher orders of Roman society ultimately owed their allegiance to the *princeps*. Thus, these imperial ceremonies, as in the late Republic, were often harbingers of political consensus that adumbrated peace, stability, and prosperity, with the central figure now the *princeps*, without whom consensus could not exist. In a similar way, the spatial and temporal aspects of court ceremony demonstrated further the centrality of the *princeps*. The topography of Augustus' new Rome was ceremonially linked through the performances of the *princeps*, culminating in his funeral, which processed past many of the most important monuments of his regime. Court ceremony also often provided a link among past, present, and future, a public and performative demonstration of Augustus' place in Roman history.

Conclusion

Throughout this study, we have been concerned with the close relationship between power and public ceremonial in Roman politics. I have argued that public ceremonial in the late Republic and early Principate was not "mere ceremony," an inconsequential act with no effect on the politics of the time. Rather the ceremonies that we have discussed and analyzed demonstrate the fundamental dynamic of Roman politics, namely the distribution of power between elite and people. Roman aristocrats, for instance, justified their capacity and right to govern through their performance at a variety of ceremonies, through which they advertised the prestige of their families and their own accomplishments to the Roman people. But these performances were equally opportunities for the Roman people to express their collective will, some of which overtly acknowledged popular sovereignty. Public entertainment, for instance, showed off the great wealth and power of the sponsoring aristocrat, but shouts in the theater could undermine his prestige. Funerals celebrated the accomplishments of a distinguished statesman and his antecedents, but the rioting that often erupted at funerals in the late Republic was a manifestation of the people's acclaim or their derision. At a *contio*, a Roman aristocrat could display his ability to stir the emotions of the crowd through oratory, but the lowering of a magistrate's *fasces* at this same *contio* was a sign that his power was owed to the sovereignty of the Roman people—a power that was formally enacted through the people's vote in the assemblies.

One could argue that the electoral assemblies diminished in importance when Caesar began exercising his right of recommending candidates to the people for election to magistracies (*commendatio*), which set a precedent that first the triumvirs and then Augustus followed. However, the fact that these assemblies continued to meet even under the Principate, and that the *princeps* took control of the other ceremonies of popular politics, reveals that Augustus' power was based on the same ideology of popular participation that governed Roman politics in the late Republic.

At the root of the power displayed at these ceremonies was consensus, a harmony between all strata of Roman society. A magistrate at a public meeting, for instance, often backed by a recommendation of the senate, urged the cooperation of the people in approving or rejecting proposed legislation. The vote of the people in assembly was therefore the culmination of a process of consensus building and hence was itself an act of consensus. Other ceremonies similarly were an outward display of consensus: public entertainment required the sharing of scarce resources at religious festivals; the triumph was a national drama displaying booty and glory—the tangible and intangible benefits of military victory that an individual commander and his army brought back to Rome; the aristocratic funeral, especially as Polybius viewed it, celebrated shared ideals within the context of honoring the achievements of a distinguished Roman.

Consensus, a principal objective in Roman politics, was often elusive, however. The same *contio* we described above, part of the process of consensus building, also required debate that could divide the populace of Rome. The issues at stake often stoked the emotions that fired the engine of conflict. An assembly voting on a controversial law (e.g., Caesar's legislation in 59 BC) could be disrupted or violated by those desiring to thwart the vote. Political rivalries that flummoxed the conferral of a triumph could spill over into the performance of the triumph itself. These conflicts were frequently attempts on the part of an aristocrat to elevate his public standing or undermine the power of a rival. Thus, at the root of consensus and conflict were struggles over the distribution of power.

After Caesar's assassination, consensus remained an important objective, but it now centered on the preservation of Caesar's memory and the related issue of the fate of the conspirators. At the *contiones* in the days following Caesar's murder, the leaders of the opposing sides above all needed to be seen addressing the people, attempting to persuade the crowd, for it was this ability that conferred prestige and power. The two sides further began to formulate the rhetoric that would shape their public discourse in the months to come. Brutus' and Octavian's games in July, so closely juxtaposed in time, demonstrate most vividly the sentiments of the two sides. Brutus attempted to erase or ignore Caesar's memory as he reclaimed the *Ludi Apollinares* for the Republic. Octavian, after Amatius, was the most persistent in honoring the memory of the dead dictator, especially his insistence on displaying Caesar's *sella* and crown in the theater. Antonius strove for the middle ground and for a time was the best hope for a broader-based consensus until military conflict necessitated appeasement of Caesar's veteran soldiers, which put him directly at odds with Octavian.

In the Triumviral period and later the Augustan Principate, consensus began to coalesce around the figure of Octavian and then Augustus. This was a gradual and evolutionary process, slowed first by opposition to and rivalry among the triumvirs and then by the *princeps*' compromises with the senatorial aristocracy. Ultimately Rome was transformed with the establishment of a single ruler at the center of power. Augustus was quoted as saying that he had two wayward daughters whom he had to suffer, the Roman Republic and Julia (Macr. 2.5.4). His challenge as Rome's first citizen was to control Republican institutions that proved so unwieldy in the tumult and civil war of his formative years. Augustus attempted to bring under his control the popular assemblies, frequently centers of conflict in the late Republic, as a means to legitimate his regime. The brief career of Egnatius Rufus is an indication that elections were still being held, but the need for Augustus to supervise them in order to ensure the maintenance of public order shows how differently elections conferred public authority under the Principate. For now Augustus did not obtain the public authority of consul through these elections but rather a much less tangible distinction: the knowledge that he was the only Roman now who could quell the urban *plebs*. Elections also tended to focus on the *princeps*' handpicked candidates. Augustus' power was legitimate only with the consensus of the people as expressed at these assemblies. Elections still mattered, but the result—the kind of power that they enacted—was now different; they now evinced monarchy.

Other ceremonies demonstrate a similar imperial control. The Roman people were apprised in advance of Augustus' proposed laws, which apparently could be modified before a final vote to ensure passage. Public entertainment was sponsored by Augustus, members of his family, or magistrates who owed their prestige to his personal benefaction. There is no recorded instance of Augustus being embarrassed or humiliated in the theater, as so often happened to aristocrats in the late Republic. Triumphs, as well as the related ceremonies of departures and returns, often a source of political rivalry in the late Republic, were removed from the senatorial aristocracy and celebrated the achievements, and in some cases sanctioned the succession, of members of Augustus' family.

Two of the persistent themes of this study have been what I have called the spatial and temporal aspects of ceremony. The changing topography of

Rome in the period under discussion had a profound effect on the ceremonies of the time. The "incompleteness" of Caesar's modifications to the cityscape was an abiding reminder of the changes Roman politics was undergoing. The location of the conspirators' *contio* on the Ides of March, in the Forum on the Rostra that Caesar had built, reaffirmed the extent of Caesar's power, even as his murderers denounced him as a tyrant and celebrated his death. By contrast, when Octavian returned to Rome in May 44 and was presented to the people at a *contio,* he claimed his inheritance surrounded by reminders of Caesar. In November of that year, he exploited a statue of Caesar in the Forum for a dramatic gesture and oath that reclaimed Caesar's memory and spoke to his divinity.

After Augustus came to power, the rebuilding of Rome was complete, and many structures celebrated the *princeps*' adoptive family: a new senate house, the Curia Julia; a new voting place for the populace at Rome, the Saepta Julia; and a new cult center, the Temple of Divus Julius. These and other structures, like the Forum Augustum with the Temple of Mars Ultor and the mausoleum of Augustus, reconfigured public ceremonial. The Saepta Julia, despite its intended function as a voting place for the Roman electorate, became a venue for public entertainment and served as the destination for Tiberius upon his return in AD 9 from Germany, where he met Augustus, the magistrates, senate, and people of Rome as heir-designate to the *princeps*. The dedication of the Temple of Mars Ultor, which housed the standards recovered from the Parthians, provided Rome with a new ceremonial center, especially as the point of departure for military commanders as well as their first destination upon their return to the city, where they recounted their exploits and were awarded an appropriate victory celebration. The Temple of Divus Julius was a place of assembly for the vote on a law proposed by Quinctius (*cos*. 9 BC), perhaps preserving the memory of the crowd's action at Caesar's funeral. It is not known if this was a permanent function of the temple. Augustus also integrated this temple into the funeral rites of his family members and ultimately into his own funeral, as a place to display the body of the deceased and deliver a *laudatio*. The mausoleum of Augustus at the north end of the Via Flaminia was the new destination of funeral processions that passed in their course many other prominent Augustan monuments. Augustus' funeral procession ceremonially linked many of these structures.

The temporal aspect of public ceremonial had to do both with commemoration and history. Caesar, for instance, not only reformed the Roman calendar, but before his death he also inserted himself and his achievements into many of the public festivals on the calendar—the *Feriae Latinae* (especially in January 44), *Lupercalia*, *Parilia*, and *Ludi Apollinares*. All of these festivals had an origin deep in the Roman past, but, after Caesar, every iteration of these festivals came to commemorate his accomplishments. The history of these festivals was less important than the fact that they recurred at regular intervals, thus ensuring that Caesar would be commemorated as long as the Roman calendar endured. This commemoration became a reality after Caesar's death, as many ceremonies centered on the preservation of his memory (as we discussed earlier). Some of the festivals mentioned earlier were central in this process. At the *Parilia* in April 44, there was a celebration in honor of Caesar; Octavian moved the *Ludi Victoriae Caesaris* to July, and Antonius inserted into the *Ludi Romani* an extra day in honor of Caesar. At the *Ludi Apollinares*, the conspirators' last hope, Brutus' task was to reclaim these games for the Republic. Beyond these festivals, first Amatius, who ingratiated himself to the urban populace by claiming to be descended from Marius, was instrumental in preserving Caesar's memory in the early weeks after his death through the erection of a monument at the place of his cremation; then Octavian returned to Rome and became the principal preserver of Caesar's memory through his efforts to maintain the extraordinary honors decreed to his adoptive father.

In other ceremonies, a more important component was the use of the past, of history, to validate one's actions in the present and further to create a larger historical canvas on which to fix the present event. One such instance was the trial of Rabirius, in which a new form, or rather one that had been retrieved from the remote past (the procedure of *perduellio*, in this instance), underscored the historical importance of the issues at stake. This was a trial, as I argued earlier, in which the guilt or innocence of the defendant was secondary to the larger issue of the sanctity of the people's representative, the tribune of the *plebs*, even in the face of the autocratic authority of the senatorial aristocracy. Octavian's revival of the Fetial ceremony provided religious sanction to the imminent war against Cleopatra and Antonius, thus denying the unpleasant fact that another civil war was brewing.

A comparison of two *naumachiae*, those of Sextus Pompeius in 39 BC and Augustus in 2 BC, suggests another way of thinking about the temporal aspect of ceremony. When Sextus produced his mock naval battle at the toe of Italy, this form of entertainment was still comparatively unknown. The *naumachia* at Caesar's triumph in 46, pitting "Tyrians" against "Egyptians" was the only known precedent. Sextus eschewed a historical battle from the remote past and instead commemorated a battle that had not taken place, the one between his navy and the ships of Octavian's lieutenant, Salvidienus Rufus. Augustus, by contrast, chose to reenact one of the most famous naval battles in all of history, the battle of Salamis between "Persians" and "Athenians." Both *naumachiae* held a lesson for those watching. For Sextus' men, it was assurance that they would have won the battle had it been fought—that they were the superior force. Romans at Augustus' *naumachia*, which was performed as part of the sendoff for his grandson Gaius' campaign against the Parthians, could hope that this campaign would result in another victory of west over east. In other words, Augustus' *naumachia* had a historical depth that Sextus' *naumachia* lacked.

It would be an oversimplification to say that Augustus was the first to seek out legitimacy and confirmation of his power in the remote past. Caesar also revived the *Lusus Troiae*, exploited the *Feriae Latinae*, *Lupercalia*, and *Parilia*—all ancient ceremonies. But in the *Lupercalia*, for instance, when Caesar publicly declined the crown offered by M. Antonius, the remoteness of the ceremony's origin did little to deflect attention from the reality of Caesar's present power. In a similar way, Sextus' *naumachia* was fixed temporally in the present struggle between Sextus and the triumvirs. Augustus, more so than his contemporaries, threw off the shackles of the recent past and embraced the remote past. More importantly, through his use of ceremony for dynastic purposes to introduce potential heirs to the Roman people or sanction the accession of a successor, Augustus also gestured toward a stable and prosperous future. Augustus established himself as the linchpin between Rome's glorious past and its present. In his production of the *Ludi Saeculares*, for instance, Augustus partially recreated the past by using temporary theaters for some of the entertainment. These "traditional" theaters stood in close proximity to many of the new or newly refurbished buildings of Augustan Rome as a way of demonstrating visually how far Rome had advanced in one *saeculum*. Thus, the parade of images of famous Romans in the Forum Augustum, many of which animated his funeral procession, further established Augustus' place in Roman history. Under Augustus, ceremony was one way of showing how past, present, and future could be part of one long continuum of history.

I might be accused of being too enamored of forms. But it has been my contention that, in the politics of the late Republic and early Principate, form mattered. To say that form mattered more than content is to miss the point: form and content were inseparable. A ceremonial display of power was itself an enactment of power, and Roman aristocrats knew it. So did the Roman people. Perhaps this was the point of Augustus' last statement, with which we introduced this study, when he asked for applause as he left the stage of his life: his career as *princeps* was performance, but it was a performance that conferred great power. The trick, which he mastered, was how to display that power, never losing sight of the form that conferred it.

Notes

INTRODUCTION

1. By "Roman people" I mean all those who typically assembled at these events—a mixed crowd consisting of the city *plebs* (*plebs urbana*), including in the late Republic soldiers and veterans, freeborn, freed, and slaves, as well as members of the aristocracy and the equestrian order. See chapter 3 for more on the makeup of the crowd in the aftermath of Caesar's assassination. On the vocabulary used by ancient authors to describe the common people of Rome, see Yavetz 1969, 141–55; specifically on the distinction between *populus* and *plebs* in the late Republic, see Will 1991, 26–28.

2. Cic. *Off.* 2.44: *Nam si quis ab ineunte aetate habet causam celebritatis et nominis aut a patre acceptam, quod tibi, mi Cicero, arbitror contigisse, aut aliquo casu atque fortuna, in hunc oculi omnium coniciuntur, atque in eum quid agat, quemadmodum vivat inquiritur, et, tamquam in clarissima luce versetur, ita nullum obscurum potest nec dictum eius esse nec factum.*

3. Cf. Sal. *Jug.* 85.23: "the renown of the ancestors casts a light on the current generation; neither their vices nor their virtues are allowed to remain hidden."

4. On this topic in general, see Hölkeskamp 1987, 204–40; Earl 1967, 11–43; Meier 1966, 44–45.

5. For Roman politics and public life as theater, see Wiseman 1989, 151–55; cf. Castagnoli 1969, 63: "infatti i Fori erano il teatro dei più importanti atti della vita civile, politica, giudiziaria, di spettacoli ecc. . . ."

6. The symbolism of dress is also evident in the Roman custom of changing to dirty and disheveled clothing (*veste mutata*) in times of mourning; see, e.g., the senators and magistrates dressing in mourning to beseech the Roman people for Cicero's return from exile (Cic. *Red. Sen.* 31). On Roman costume in general, see Sebesta and Bonfante 1994.

7. "The great man was at his most visible as he went to or from his *domus*"; N. Purcell, s.v. "Forum Romanum (The Republican Period)," *LTUR* 2.325–36 (at 329).

8. For the public nature of Roman aristocratic houses, see Wallace-Hadrill

1994, 3–37; for the house as a center of emotion, see Treggiari 1999; for the house as part of the construction of an aristocrat's social identity, see Hales 2003, esp. 11–60. On the morning *salutatio*, see Hug, s.v. "salutatio," *RE* series 2, 1.2 (1920), 2060–72; Friedländer 1922, 1.228–30; Kroll 1933, 2.65–68.

9. By contrast homes could also advertise modesty. Following his return from Africa, C. Gracchus made a political statement by moving his residence from the Palatium to an area closer to the Forum where the poorer folk resided (Plut. CG 12.1); Caesar lived in the Subura before he was elected Pontifex Maximus (Suet. *Jul.* 46); Augustus' house, rather than being ostentatious, was lost among other aristocratic houses on the Palatium, perhaps to reflect his image of *primus inter pares* (Wiseman 1987, 405).

10. For a general treatment, see now Flower 1996.

11. Pliny *Nat.* 35.7. Cf. Cic. *Phil.* 2.68: Pompeius' house was adorned with *rostra* from pirate ships. On the subject of the display of spoils, see Rawson 1990.

12. E.g., Sp. Maelius, Sp. Cassius, L. Saturninus, and even Cicero; see Cic. *Dom.* 101. Cf. Bodel 1999b, 58–60, on the dismantling of structures connecting Cn. Piso's houses as punishment for his role in Germanicus' death.

13. See, e.g., Cornell 1995, 342.

14. This is a public manifestation of a more private social contract, that between the *patronus* and *cliens*. See Wallace-Hadrill 1989.

15. Hopkins and Burton 1983, 113. We should note that military service was also prerequisite for political office; Harris 1979, 11, citing Plb. 6.19.4.

16. I borrow the phrase from Gruen 1991, 251.

17. The work of Brunt 1971b, 1988, 1–92, esp. 12–32; and Millar (1998, and his preliminary studies, 1984a; 1986; 1989) have been especially influential. For a summary of the debate and more bibliography, see Jehne 1995, 1–9; Mouritsen 2001, 1–17; and, most recently, Ward 2004. For some notes of caution, see Gruen 1991; Harris 1990.

18. MacMullen 1980. But the primary sources indicate that these votes counted; see, e.g., Cic. *Planc.* 11: "For this is the position of free peoples and especially of this leading people, master and victor over all nations, that with its votes it can bestow or rescind whatever it wants from anyone; and it is our position, that is, those of us who are buffeted about in the storm and waves of the people, to endure without complaint the will of the people, to entice the support of those who are against us, maintain the support of those who are for us, placate those who are upset; if we do not believe that political office is worth it, we would not defer to the people; but if we strive for political office, then we have no business growing weary of begging them for it." On voting in elections, see now Yakobson 1999.

19. See Sallust's famous assessment, *Jug.* 63.6: *consulatum nobilitas inter se per manus tradebat*. "The senatorial aristocracy shared the consulship among themselves." Cf. *Cat.* 23.5–6.

20. Gelzer 1968b, 54–62. For another view, see Brunt 1982; Hopkins and Burton 1983. For a recent restatement of the traditional view, see Shackleton Bailey 1986; and Badian 1990, who has shown that approximately 90 percent of the consuls in the period under study were descendants of ex-consuls, demonstrating the small circle of men who ruled Rome. Both Shackleton Bailey and Badian concede that *nobilis* did not have a legal definition. For a summary of recent discussion, see Burckhardt 1990.

21. Brunt 1988, 30–32, 382–442; cf. Wallace-Hadrill 1989, 69.

22. *CAH*[2], 8.217. The expulsion of Latins and allies from Rome in 198 and 177 (Liv. 39.3.4–6; 41.8.6–12) is an indication of the seriousness of the problem.

23. *CAH*[2], 8.219.

24. Brunt 1971a, 381; cf. Brunt 1966.

25. Population estimates for this period are notoriously speculative; I generally follow the Brunt-Beloch model. See Beloch 1926; Brunt 1971a, 384. For a reassessment, and a much higher population estimate for Italy (on the order of 14 million), see now Morley 2001.

26. Taylor 1966, 105–6; cf. Gelzer 1968a, 100. Cf. also Millar 1989, 142–43, who argues that most modern analyses of the Roman political system attach too little importance to legislation; and Millar 1998, 7. Finally, Sandberg 2001 is now the most thorough discussion of the *comitia tributa* in the middle and late Republic. On extraordinary commands in general, see Gruen 1974, 534–43, who views them as less than extraordinary.

27. On the importance of the glory of war for the Roman aristocracy, see Cic. *Planc*. 60: *Etenim honorum gradus summis hominibus et infimis sunt pares, gloriae dispares*. "Indeed, the path to political office is the same for the most distinguished and least distinguished men, the path to glory is not." He goes on to state that of the approximately eight hundred consuls in Rome's history only a fraction can be said truly to possess *gloria: honorum populi finis est consulatus; quem magistratum iam octingenti fere consecuti sunt. Horum, si diligenter quaeres, vix decimam partem reperies gloria dignam*." The consulship is the pinnacle of the popular magistracies; nearly eight hundred men to date have achieved this office. Of these, if you examine carefully, scarcely one-tenth will you find worthy of glory." On these issues, cf. Harris 1979, 10–11.

28. Cic. *Sest*. 106: *Etenim tribus locis significari maxime de re publica populi Romani iudicium ac voluntas potest, contione, comitiis, ludorum gladiatorumque consessu*. "The Roman people can express their judgment and will about public affairs especially at three venues, the public meeting, popular assemblies and public entertainment."

29. Cic. *Att*. 2.19.3; see chapter 1.

30. *Att*. 14.3.2: *Tu si quid* πραγματικὸν *habes rescribe; sin minus, populi* ἐπισημασίαν-*et mimorum dicta perscribito*. "If you have anything about politics, write to me; if not, write about the applause of the people and actors' lines." Cf. Bollinger 1969; Abbot 1907, 49–56; Flaig 1995, 118–24; Parker 1999.

31. Nicolet (1980, 343–81) discusses these events under the rubric of "alternative institutions."

32. For a discussion of this process, see von Premerstein 1937; Gagé 1957. The story of the fall of the Republic is, in many ways, the story of the senate's failure to respond to the demands of those outside its order; cf. Brunt 1971b, 112–47. Cf. also Hobsbawm 1963, who discusses this phenomenon in a modern context, especially analyzing social movements in the nineteenth and twentieth centuries.

33. For the consequences of Marius' reforms, see Smith 1958; for a general treatment of the role of the army in politics, see Aigner 1974; Keppie 1984, 57–79; for a discussion of the army after Caesar's assassination, see Botermann 1968.

34. On Pompeius as world conqueror, see Nicolet 1991, 32, 37, 45. On his theater, see Hanson 1959.

35. Cf. the assessment of Yavetz 1969, 39: "Democracy did not exist in Rome,

but popular pressure did." In recent scholarship, the "democratic"model of the Roman Republican constitution has been articulated most vigorously by Millar (1998). The view that popular participation in Roman politics was rather an ideological construct can be found in Jehne 1995; Mouritsen (2001, 8–14), in his discussion of the debate, points out that both views articulate important aspects of Roman politics, but neither by itself is sufficient.

36. R. Graves' trans. (Penguin ed.). Suet. *Aug.* 99.1: *Supremo die identidem exquirens, an iam de se tumultus foris esset, petito speculo capillum sibi comi ac malas labantes corrigi praecepit et admissos amicos percontatus, ecquid iis videretur mimum vitae commode transegisse, adiecit et clausulam:* ἐπεὶ δὲ πάνυ καλῶς πέπαισται, δότε κρότον / Κα πάντες ἡμᾶς μετὰ χαρᾶς προπέμψατε.

37. Cic. *Brut.* 290: *ut qui haec procul videat, etiam si quid agatur nesciat, at placere tamen et in scaena esse Roscium intellegat.* "If one were to see all this from a distance, even if he does not know what's going on, he still would understand that it was pleasing, and he might think that a Roscius is performing."

38. On the orator's *corona*, see Frier 1985, 235–36.

39. On the Forum as theater, cf. also Cic. *Brut.* 6. We also know that orators could turn to actors for assistance in developing some of the skills so important to public speaking, such as physical movements (gestures) and voice intonation (as Cicero himself did [Plut. *Cic.* 5.4]), although Roman orators would have been quick to distinguish the two professions: Aldrete 1999, 53–54. On politics as theater in the Hellenistic world, see Chaniotis 1997.

40. *Comm. Pet.* 52: *Postremo tota petitio cura ut pompae plena sit, ut illustris, ut splendida, ut popularis sit, ut habeat summam speciem ac dignitatem. . . .*

41. Turner 1974, 23–59, esp. 37–42.

42. For a discussion of the change from the structural-functional approach to politics to politics as process or activity, see Swartz et al. 1966, 1–8. As these issues relate to classical antiquity, in particular to the Homeric epics, see Hammer 2002, esp. 20–29.

43. Geertz 1973, 448–53.

44. Turner 1986, 22.

45. Price 1984, 7–11.

46. Bell 1992, 204–5.

47. See, e.g., the mime performance directed at Pompeius Magnus at the *Ludi Apollinares* in 59 BC (Cic. *Att.* 2.19.3 and chap. 1).

48. E.g., the food riot at the *Ludi Apollinares* (Asc. 48C; Vanderbroeck 1987, 247) and *Ludi Romani* in 57 BC (Cic. *Att.* 4.1.6–7; cf. *Dom.* 6–7, 10–16, *Fam.* 5.17.2; Dio 39.9.2–3; Vanderbroeck 1987, 249), and the riot at the *Ludi Megalenses* in 56 (Cic. *Har.* 22–26; Vanderbroeck 1987, 253–54).

49. Cannadine 1987, 1–19, esp. 4–7.

50. Cannadine 1987, 19.

51. Shils 1965; Geertz 1977, 150–53.

52. I am influenced here by Davidson's discussion of the gaze in Polybius' narrative (1991, 18): "Historical action comes to resemble discourse, with events transformed into statements."

53. Cf. Feldherr 1998, 10.

54. Cornell 1991.

55. Rawson (1972 and 1985, 233–49) discusses the issues as they relate to the late Republic.

56. On the notion of "invented traditions," see Hobsbawm and Ranger 1983, 1; for its application to Roman history, see Flower 2000 on the *spolia opima*. I would add also, as possible invented traditions in this period, the *Lusus Troiae* and the performance of the Fetial ceremony by Octavian in 32 BC (for further discussion, see chap. 8).

57. Wiseman 1995, 137–38; cf. Flower 1995.

58. Wiseman 1986; Jaeger 1997, esp. 1–29; cf. also Edwards 1996.

59. Wiseman 1979; Vasaly 1993, 40–87.

CHAPTER 1

1. For a discussion of this simile and its connection to the concept of *auctoritas*, see Galinsky 1996, 20–24. For the Roman people compared to the sea, see Cic. *Rep.* 1.65.4.

2. Cf. Cic. *de Orat.* 1.31. For some famous exempla from Roman history of the power of oratory, see Cic. *Brut.* 54–56; cf. also Tac. *Dial.* 36.4.

3. On the audience reaction at *contiones*, and the pressure that a crowd could bring to bear on a speaker, see Laser 1997, 138–42.

4. *Röm. StR.*[3] 1.191–202; Humbert, s.v. "contio," D-S, 1.2, 1484–85; Liebenam, s.v. "contio," *RE* 4.1 (1901), 1149–53; Botsford 1909, 139–51; Taylor 1966, 15–33; Pina Polo 1996, 34–64, and 1995, 203–16; Mouritsen 2001, 38–62; for the *contio* as a ritual of consensus, see Flaig 1995.

5. The third type was the *contio* convened by a Roman general (*imperator*) to keep his soldiers apprised of the campaign or to inspire them with courage just before battle.

6. On the symbolic force of the *fasces*, see Marshall 1984.

7. Some instances of the breaking of *fasces* can be found in App. *BC* 1.15.65; Cic. *Pis.* 28 (cf. Dio 38.30.2); Cic. *Red. Sen.* 7; Dio 36.39.3.

8. Taylor 1971, 98–99.

9. See, e.g., Ter. *Hec.* 28–42.

10. Cicero, in fact, once accused the prosecutor in a case of ignoring the jurors and, in essence, performing for the crowd (*Flacc.* 69); cf. *Fin.* 4.74. M. Brutus claimed that he found it difficult to speak at trial once his *corona* had left him (Cic. *Brut.* 192).

11. Cic. *Man.* 52, 59; Dio 36.24.5–37.1; Plut. *Pomp.* 25–26.4; Asc. 72C; Liv. 99; Vell. 2.32.1–2. Vanderbroeck 1987, 224; Rotondi 1912, 371–72; Millar 1998, 80–81.

12. I follow here the reconstruction of Vanderbroeck (1987, 224) except where noted.

13. Perhaps at this point Q. Hortensius spoke as well, since we hear of his involvement from Cicero (*Man.* 52).

14. Vanderbroeck (1987, 224) believes that Roscius attempted to speak after the assembly had nearly voted to depose Trebellius.

15. Cic. *Att.* 1.16.4; on this trial, see Tatum 1999, 62–86.

16. The sources for the trials of Rabirius and the events surrounding them are Cic. *Rab. Perd.* (cf. *Att.* 2.1.3; *Pis.* 4); Suet. *Jul.* 12; Dio 37.26–28. Modern accounts

abound; especially useful are the brief remarks of Mommsen 1894, 4.458–59; Jones 1972, 40–44; Gruen 1974, 277–79; Rawson 1975a, 66–69.

17. The relationship between Marius and Saturninus is complicated. In 103 Saturninus passed legislation that benefited Marius' veterans (*MRR* 1.563), and in 100 sponsored a law that gave Marius power to grant citizenship in several colonies (*MRR* 1.575), lending credence to the assumption that they were political allies. But by the end of 100, Saturninus had clearly gone too far, since he had begun to use Marius' army for his own political ends, prompting Marius to join the *nobilitas* against the tribune; Badian 1964, 148. The ancient sources for these events are collected in Greenidge and Clay 1960, 105–10.

18. Rawson (1975a, 67) describes this as "splendid antiquarian play-acting of which it is tempting to suppose Caesar the author."

19. On orators' use of such "props," see Aldrete 1999, 27–29.

20. Cf. C. Marius' speech in which he implies that possession of *imagines* of one's ancestors was a hallmark of the old aristocracy that he was challenging (Sal. *Jug.* 85.38). On the *ius imaginum*, once thought to be a characteristic of the Roman *nobilitas*, see now Flower 1996, 53–59.

21. Cic. *Rab. Perd.* 15: *ex annalium monumentis atque ex regum commentariis.*

22. Liv. 1.26. 5–14 (with Ogilvie's note [1965, 114–15]). On *perduellio* in general, see Brecht 1938.

23. On the procedures of electoral and legislative assemblies, see Botsford 1909, 119–38, 201–316; Taylor 1966, 34–58; Staveley 1972, 121–216 (on electoral assemblies only); Nicolet 1980, 207–315; Mouritsen 2001, 63–89 (legislative assemblies), and 90–127 (electoral assemblies); for a discussion of the procedure involved in successive and simultaneous voting, see Fraccaro 1957; on elections and electioneering, see now Yakobson 1999; on public legislation, see Sandberg 2001; Paananen 1993; Bleicken 1975, 244–68.

24. Any slaves who might have been present to intimidate voters, as reportedly happened in the often tumultuous political circumstances of the period, would have been easily distinguished from the voting public; see, e.g., Vanderbroeck 1987, 233, 243.

25. We are informed of a lavish bribe offered to any century that received the lot for the consular elections of 54 BC (Cic. *Q.fr.* 2.15.4). Pompeius claimed that he heard thunder and dissolved the assembly after the *centuria praerogativa* returned his adversary Cato (Plut. *Cat. Mi.* 42.4).

26. Cic. *Agr.* 2.4. One estimate has the counting of votes taking approximately two hours for the election of two curule aediles. We can assume, then, that the counting of votes for the ten tribunes took much longer, which is perhaps why Cicero chose the tribunicial elections to begin his campaign for the consulship (Taylor 1966, 55–56).

27. Taylor and Broughton 1949; Linderski 1965.

28. E.g., Cicero announcing Murena's victory in the consular elections for 62 BC (*Mur.* 1). On the influence of the presiding magistrate at elections, see Staveley 1972, 209–11.

29. Cicero succinctly captures this sense in his metaphor of the secret ballot as the "living voice" (*vox viva*) of the Roman people (*Agr.* 2.4).

30. At the end of the Republic, about ninety magistracies had to be filled on an

annual basis (Hopkins and Burton 1983, 113, n. 99), which made voting in elections one of the most important privileges of the Roman citizen.

31. App. *BC* 2.17.64; Plut. *Pomp.* 52.1–2; *Cat. Mi.* 41; Dio 39.30.2; 31.1.

32. Violence also marred the aedilician elections in 55—Pompeius returned home with a blood-spattered toga (Plut. *Pomp.* 53.3; Dio 39.32.2; cf. App. *BC* 2.17.64); the consular elections of 54 (Asc. 20C; cf. App. *BC* 2.19.69–71); and the consular elections of 53 (Cic. *Mil.* 41, 43; Asc. 30C).

33. Twelve laws are attested from the tribunate of P. Clodius (58 BC), for instance, according to Rotondi 1912, 393–98.

34. The number of citizens who actually participated is disputed; see MacMullen 1980.

35. Cic. *Dom.* 79–80; cf. *Planc.* 35; Staveley 1969 with the additional support of Linderski 1973; cf. also Taylor 1966, 70–74; Nicolet 1980, 272.

36. The significance of the first voter is illustrated in Cicero's description of the assembly in March of 58 BC convened by P. Clodius to vote on legislation (the *lex de capite civis*) sending him into exile (*Dom.* 79–80). The first voter was a man named Fidulus (on his name see Shackleton Bailey 1976, 39), a henchman of Clodius' and probably selected by Clodius himself, as sanctioned by custom. One way for Cicero to demonstrate that the law sending him into exile was not representative of the will and desire of the Roman people was to castigate the first voter, who, in the act of casting his vote and then later having his name associated with the resultant *lex* in the inscription of the text of the law itself, came to symbolize the people's collective will by putting a name and face on an otherwise anonymous crowd. We should note that Cicero had his reasons for being suspicious of Fidulus' motives, for this was a man accustomed to spectacular demonstrations: he was seen two years later along with P. Vatinius (*tr. pl.* 59) dressed in the garb of mourning and entering the Temple of Castor on a feast day, perhaps with the intention of impugning the memory of the dictator Sulla, for whom the feast was being held (Cic. *Vat.* 31–32).

37. App. *BC* 2.10.35–11.41; Cic. *Vat.* 22; Dio 38.6.1–4; Liv. 103; Plut. *Caes.* 14.1–6, *Cat. Mi.* 32.2–4, *Luc.* 42.6, *Pomp.* 48.1–3; Suet. *Jul.* 20.1; Vanderbroeck 1987, 237; Gruen 1974, 397–99. We should bear in mind that Caesar's legislation in his consulship later came under attack by his political enemies, and for this reason it is likely that the historical tradition surrounding it contains vestiges of some of the charges laid by his enemies as well as the counterbalancing justification of his actions by his supporters. The historical tradition takes pains to show that Caesar followed customary procedure by first bringing his bill before the senate for approval, which it denied, and then introducing it to the people in the tribal assembly; he was also careful to avoid the pitfalls of previous agrarian legislation by calling for a commission of twenty to avoid creating a small faction of powerful individuals, and by insisting that he not be a member of the commission so that he would not be accused of promoting his own personal agenda (Dio 38.1.6).

38. Roman aristocrats subjected themselves to this kind of humiliation whenever they went out in public; some aristocrats avoided *contiones* when they thought the risks were too great, as Caesar did in 49 (Cic. *Att.* 10.4.8); for the theater as another venue for such humiliation, see the discussion later in this chapter.

39. Appian claims that Cato was "summoned" (ἐπιπεμφθείς) and then made his way to the Rostra, but it is not clear by whom (*BC* 2.11.40).

40. Dio 38.1.2; cf. Gruen 1974, 398.

41. The dictum is handed down by Livy (45.32.11): *vulgo dictum ipsius ferebant, et convivium instruere et ludos parare eiusdem esse, qui vincere bello sciret*. Cf. C. Marius' claims that he was accused of being vulgar and uncouth because he did not know how to put on a fine dinner party (Sal. *Jug*. 85.39).

42. For the increasing competitiveness among the aristocracy to outdo one another in putting on games, see Liv. 7.2.13; cf. Plin. *Nat*. 36.115–20.

43. On public entertainment in general, see Friedländer 1922, 2.1–162; Friedländer in Marquardt 1881–1885, 3.482–589; Wissowa 1912, 449–67; Bernstein 1998; on the concept of euergetism in the Greek world, see Veyne 1976, 185–373; on Roman games and euergetism, see 387–96. The theater in particular was a place for political spectacle; Dupont 1985, 30, calls the theater "le coeur véritable de la vie politique." See also Bollinger 1969; Abbot 1907; Parker 1999.

44. In an important passage in *de Officiis*, Cicero states that the aedileship was a much more attractive political office in his day because the aedile entertained the populace with games and in so doing had the opportunity to display his *liberalitas* (Cic. *Off*. 2.52–59). For Cicero's general feelings about public entertainment, see *Fam*. 7.1; *Mur*. 40. To show in particular the importance of games for political careers, Cicero cites the example of Mamercus, a wealthy man who failed to rise to the consulship because he shunned the aedileship entirely. He was doomed not only by his failure to entertain the people, a serious enough social blunder in itself, but more importantly by his refusal to share his great wealth—a clear abnegation of the Roman aristocratic ethos. Cicero's own career shows that he himself understood this political necessity, for he put on games—albeit only modest ones—during his aedileship in 69.

45. Suet. *Jul*. 10.1; cf. App. *BC* 2.1.3. D-G[2] 3.138–39.

46. The victory over the Cimbri: Vell. 2.43.4; Plut. *Caes*. 6.1; Suet. *Jul*. 11.

47. Suet. *Jul*. 10.1: *nec dissimularet collega Marcus Bibulus evenisse sibi quod Polluci: ut enim geminis fratribus aedes in foro constituta tantum Castoris vocaretur, ita suam Caesarisque munificentiam unius Caesaris dici*; Dio 37.8.2.

48. Scullard 1981, 196.

49. Cicero's mention of them shows that they were a regular part of the calendar by 70 BC (*Verr*. 1.31, with [Ascon.]'s note [p. 217St.]).

50. App. *BC* 1.99.464. If Sulla's games were in late October, it is curious that they conflicted with the Olympic games. Either he summoned the athletes to Rome in the summer (perhaps to train and prepare for his games) or Appian is confusing the *Ludi Victoriae* with another set of games in the summer (perhaps Sulla's celebration of a festival of Hercules [Plut. Sull. 35.1–2, although he mentions only a banquet]). Keaveney (1982, 191) connects the games with the banquet.

51. As Bernstein has recently argued (1998, 321–27).

52. On these issues, see Sumi 2002b.

53. Friedländer in Marquardt (1881–1885, 3.497), with sources cited in n. 4.

54. Before Sulla's games no *ludi votivi* in honor of a victory became fixed annual games (*ludi stativi*). Mommsen (1859) argued that the *Ludi Romani* in origin were *votivi*, which became permanent, but this has been shown to be unlikely; Versnel 1970, 101–4; cf. Michels 1967, 207–8.

55. Parker (1999, 168) paints a vivid picture of the Roman elite sitting in the

first rows of the *cavea* trapped between the declassé performers on stage and the lower orders of Roman society behind them.

56. Parker (1999, 167–68) calls this the "paradox of the gaze," demonstrating that Romans felt the need to be the "observed of all the observers" while at the same time trying to avoid the shame of making a spectacle of themselves.

57. Cic. *Att.* 2.19.3; Cameron (1976, 158–60) collects the evidence for such acclamations in the late Republic.

58. *Nostra miseria tu es Magnus* (Cic. *Att.* 2.19.3). The words came from a tragedy now unknown (Ribbeck 1897, 291). V. Max. 6.2.9 relates the same episode: *Diphilus tragoedus, cum Apollinaribus ludis inter actum ad eum versum venisset quo haec sententia continetur, "miseria nostra magnus es," derectis in Pompeium Magnum manibus pronuntiavit, revocatusque aliquotiens a populo sine ulla cunctatione nimiae illum et intolerabilis potentiae reum gestu perseveranter egit. eadem petulantia usus est in ea quoque parte: "virtutem istam veniet tempus cum graviter gemes."* "Diphilus the tragic actor in the course of a performance at the Apollinarian games came to a verse containing the following sentiment: 'To our misfortune, art thou great.'" He declaimed it with hands pointing at Pompeius Magnus; recalled by the people several times, without any hesitation he persistently by gesture accused Pompey of excessive and intolerable power. He used the same effrontery in another passage: 'But that same valour bitterly/in time to come shalt thou lament'" (Shackleton Bailey trans., Loeb ed.). Cicero's letter (cited earlier) makes it clear that Pompeius was not actually present in Rome for this performance, as Valerius claims, but in Capua (cf. Shackleton Bailey 1965, 1.62–63). For other dramatic lines that had political overtones, see Cic. *Sest.* 118–23; Suet. *Aug.* 53.1, 68; *Tib.* 45; *Galb.* 13.

59. Cf. Benner 1987, 98–99.

60. Cic. *Har.* 22–26; on these games in general, see Bernstein 1998, 186–206. On other occasions, food riots coincided with public entertainment: the *Ludi Apollinares* in July 57 (Asc. 48C); and the *Ludi Romani*, which were made to coincide with Cicero's return from exile in September 57 (Cic. *Att.* 4.1.6–7; *Dom.* 6–7, 10–16; *Fam.* 5.17.2; Dio 39.9.2–3); on food riots in general, see Virlouvet 1985.

61. There are two versions of this story—the one that Cicero retails here (*Har.* 24), which makes Scipio directly responsible for establishing the custom of arranged seating, and the other that he recounts in another speech (the *pro Cornelio*, for which we must rely on Asconius' comments [69C]); in the second version (which ultimately derives from Valerius Antias [cf. Liv. 34.44.5, 54.4]), A. Atilius Serranus and L. Scribonius Libo (*aed. cur.* 194), at the prompting of the censors, set aside seats for the senators for the first time at the *Ludi Romani*. Cf. Marshall 1985, 246–49.

62. Cicero states that what separated the most eminent Roman statesmen from the most humble was not access to political office (*honorum gradus*) but success on the field of battle (*gloria*), which was publicly celebrated in a triumph (*Planc.* 60 [the passage is quoted in note 27 in the introduction]). He goes on to state that of the approximately eight hundred consuls in Rome's history only a fraction can be said truly to possess *gloria*.

63. For *testimonia*, see Ehlers, s.v. "triumphus," *RE* 7A.1 (1939), 493–511; Marquardt 1881–1885, 2.582; Cagnat, D-S, s.v. "triumphus," 5, 488. On the origin of the *triumphus*, see Bonfante Warren 1970; Versnel 1970, 14–16. For possible reconstruc-

tions of the route of the triumphal procession, see Coarelli 1988, 365–66; Hinard 1985b, 233–34; Künzl 1988, 14–22, 33. Cf. also Favro 1994.

64. Livy's accounts of triumphs beginning ca. 300 BC contain a detailed accounting of the money each *triumphator* contributed to the city treasury (see, e.g., Liv. 33.23.7; 33.37.11; 34.46.2; 34.52.4–5; 36.40.12).

65. This is where we find the famous *veni, vidi, vici* of Caesar (Suet. *Jul.* 37.2). In Pompeius' triumph in 61, there were placards with the names of towns that he had conquered (Plut. *Pomp.* 45.2; cf. Plin. *Nat.* 7.98).

66. The prestige of Aemilius Paullus' triumph was dramatically increased by the presence of the Macedonian King Perseus in the *pompa* (Plut. *Aem.* 34.1–4; cf. Liv. 45.39.14).

67. Versnel 1970, 58–63.

68. See, e.g., Caesar's triumph (Suet. *Jul.* 49.4).

69. See Richardson (1975, 52–54), who has determined that the number of triumphs dramatically increased after 200, with many praetors celebrating victories; after 170 there was just as dramatic a decrease in triumphs, with the right being reserved solely for consuls, which leads to the conclusion that the senate tightened control over the triumph to the exclusion of praetors.

70. Plutarch (*Marc.* 22) describes the differences between a triumph and an *ovatio*. Cf. also Plin. *Nat.* 15.19; Serv. A. 4.543; Gel. 5.6.20–23.

71. Cic. *de Orat.* 2.195 (on M. Aquillius; cf. *MRR* 1.577); Plut. *Crass.* 11.6–11. On Crassus' *ovatio*, see also Marshall 1972.

72. See, e.g., Liv. 31.48; 38.44.9–50.3; 39.29.4–5.

73. Livy (33.23.8) states that Q. Minucius' (*cos.* 197) triumph on the Alban Mount was less prestigious because the funds to finance it were improperly appropriated from the treasury. On the triumph on the Alban Mount, see Brennan 1996.

74. In a speech of M. Servilius, who spoke in support of L. Aemilius Paullus' petition for a triumph to celebrate his victory over Perseus, Livy states that there were many commanders who triumphed on the Alban Mount after they had been denied a triumph proper in the senate (Liv. 45.38.4).

75. V. Max. 3.6.5; Piso, fr. 31 (*HRR*, Plin. *Nat.* 15.126).

76. *Inscr. Ital.* 13.1, 563.

77. V. Max. 2.8.7. Caesar faced similar challenges (see chap. 2).

78. Plut. *Sull.* 34.2. The phrase "savior and father" could be Plutarch's translation of the Latin *conservator* (or *liberator*) *et pater*, although we have no direct evidence that Sulla ever conferred on himself such titles. Cicero in the *Pro Lege Manilia* (30) does inform us that Sulla credited Pompeius with helping him free Italy during this civil war, and, even though Cicero is relating this story as part of his panegyric for Pompeius, the original statement makes sense only if Sulla considered himself to be primarily responsible for the liberation of Italy.

79. Versnel 1970, 385–89.

80. Cic. *Verr.* 2.5.40; Gel. 5.6.24–26; V. Max. 2.8. The Temple of Bellona lay near the Circus Flaminius (see fig. 2) but more importantly outside the Pomerium where it was possible for generals with *imperium* to attend a meeting of the senate (A. Viscogliosi, s.v. "Bellona, Aedes in Circo," *LTUR* 1.190–92; Richardson 1975, 57–58; cf. Bonnefond-Coudry 1989, 151–60).

81. A victorious general was required to satisfy a number of criteria before being

allowed to triumph. He had to possess *imperium* within the Pomerium; the victory had to be won while the general had the *auspicia;* see Versnel 1970, 164–95, for a detailed discussion of a *triumphator*'s need for *imperium* and *auspicium*. Moreover, his army had to be present (*deportatio exercitus*) to show that the war was indeed over and peace or conquest had been achieved. Later, other criteria may have been added, such as a minimum number of the enemy killed in battle (five thousand) (Gel. 5.6.20; V. Max. 2.8.1).

82. For instance, in 187, M. Aemilius Lepidus failed in his attempt to block the triumph of his longtime rival, M. Fulvius Nobilior (Liv. 39.4–5; cf. 38.43).

83. Q. Metellus Creticus apparently waited four years before triumphing in late May 62 (*Inscr. Ital.* 13.1, 85; Cic. *Pis.* 58; cf. Vell. 2.34.2 and 40.5).

84. The reason for the delay is not entirely clear. Caesar may have opposed it (*Schol. Bob.* 149–50St.; Nisbet 1961, 119–20).

85. In 449 the senate refused a triumph for L. Valerius Potitus and M. Horatius; it was put to a vote of the people and passed (Liv. 3.63.11: *Tum primum sine auctoritate senatus populi iussu triumphatum est;* D. H. 11.50; Zon. 7.19). Dionysius mentions the triumph of Servilius, who went ahead with the celebration despite the senate's opposition, led by his colleague Ap. Claudius (6.30.2; cf. 6.58.2). In 356 the senate also refused a triumph for C. Marcius Rutulus, the first plebeian dictator, but the people interceded (Liv. 7.17.9; cf. 10.37.6–12). See also the law for the triumph of Mam. Aemilius (437 BC) (Liv. 4.20.1; Rotondi 1912, 210) and the triumph of M. Camillus (367 BC) (Liv. 6.38.9; Rotondi 1912, 220). An exception is the law conferring a triumph on C. Flaminius (223 BC) (Plut. *Marc.* 4.6; cf. Liv. 21.63.2; Rotondi 1912, 248).

86. E.g., a law proposed by Ti. Sempronius Gracchus (*tr. pl.* 167 BC) that extended the commands of L. Aemilius Paullus, Cn. Octavius, and L. Anicius Gallus up until the day of their triumphs (Liv. 45.35.4; cf. Plutarch [*Aem.* 32.1], who states that the tribal assembly did vote on Paullus' triumph; Rotondi 1912, 285). There was also a law proposed by L. Sulla that allowed Pompeius to return to Rome to celebrate a triumph in 80 BC (Gel. 10. 20.10 [citing Sallust]; Rotondi 1912, 364).

87. In a speech he puts in the mouth of Cn. Manlius Vulso when the senate was debating the merit of his request for a triumph to celebrate a victory over the Galatians in 187 (38.47.1): *tribuni plebis antea solebant triumphum postulantibus adversari*. "Tribunes of the *plebs* previously were accustomed to oppose those who demanded triumphs."

88. Liv. 45.38.4 [M. Servilius advocating a triumph for L. Aemilius Paullus in 167]: *nemo L. Paullo magis eripere decus perfecti belli Macedonici potest quam C. Lutatio primi Punici belli, quam P. Cornelio secundi, quam illis, qui post eos triumphaverunt; nec L. Paullum minorem aut maiorem imperatorem triumphus faciet—, militum magis in hoc, universi populi Romani fama agitur*. "No one can wrest away from Lucius Paullus the honor of having completed the Macedonian war any more than one could do the same to Gaius Lutatius for the First Punic War, or Publius Cornelius for the Second, or similarly to those who triumphed after them. A triumph will not make Lucius Paullus any more or less of a commander—rather the reputation of the soldiers and of the whole Roman people is at stake." For the textual difficulty in this passage, see Briscoe 1986, 382–83.

89. Liv. 67; Plut. *Mar.* 12.7; cf. *ILS* 59.

90. Failure to adhere to these rules was considered unacceptable. For example, in

177 the success of A. Manlius Volso and M. Junius Brutus (both *coss.* for 178) against the Histri caused C. Claudius Pulcher (*cos.* 177) to fear that any chance for *gloria* in his province would be lost unless he moved quickly. He therefore departed Rome hastily under cover of night without vowing the usual vows or being attended by lictors in military dress (*lictores paludati*) (Liv. 41.10). Claudius arrived in the proconsuls' camp and insisted that they leave immediately for Rome. They responded that his *imperium* had no validity since he had not left Rome in a fashion befitting a consul departing for his province, and that they would obey his command only when he had uttered the appropriate vows and wore the appropriate dress. Claudius therefore returned to Rome and departed again, this time getting it right. In addition to being a religious ritual, a consular *profectio* was public ceremony, and one of Claudius' errors was not allowing the Roman people the opportunity to gaze upon his departure from the city. Cf. also Giovannini 1983, 17–19.

91. As Marshall points out (1984, 122).

92. Liv. 42.49.1–7. For a discussion, see Feldherr 1998, 9–12, 51–52; cf. also Rüpke 1990, 125–36.

93. Liv. 42.49.6; 45.39.11: *Consul proficiscens praetorve paludatis lictoribus in provinciam et ad bellum vota in Capitolio nuncupat; victor perpetrato <bello> eodem in Capitolium triumphans ad eosdem deos quibus vota nuncupavit, merita <dona portans> redit.* "A consul or praetor departing for a province and war attended by lictors dressed in military cloaks made vows on the Capitolium; as victor, after completing the same war, he returned in triumph to the Capitolium to the same gods to whom he had made vows, carrying obligatory gifts."

94. Liv. 34.52.2: *Ab Orico copiae omnes Brundisium transportatae; inde per totam Italiam ad urbem prope triumphantes non minore agmine rerum captarum quam suo prae se acto venerunt.* "All his troops were conveyed from Oricum to Brundisium; from there they went through all of Italy to the city practically in a triumphal procession with a column of captured treasure as long as the column of soldiers marching before their general."

95. For a study of the imperial *adventus*, see Lehnen 1997.

96. Cicero tells us it was customary for crowds to greet returning commanders (*Mur.* 68).

97. *Cat. Mi.* 39.1–3; Vell. 2.45.5.

98. During the war against Sertorius in Spain, Metellus Pius won a small victory that he decided to celebrate in grand fashion (Plut. *Sert.* 22.2–4). Cities honored Metellus' visits with altars and sacrifices. He was crowned with garlands and donned triumphal garb (*toga picta*) while he attended lavish banquets in his honor. Models or images of Victory, operated by a mechanical device, descended upon the guests and distributed golden trophies and wreaths. Choirs of boys and women sang hymns of victory in praise of him. In 71 BC Metellus was awarded an official triumph by the senate along with Pompeius and Crassus (Sal. *Hist.* 2.70R; cf. *MRR*, 2.104).

99. Plut. *Crass.* 16.4–8; App. *BC* 2.18.66; Dio 39.39.6–7. Cf. Cic. *Div.* 1.29–30. I disagree with Simpson (1938), who argues that many of the details of Crassus' departure as our later sources transmit them are unhistorical. For an argument against her thesis, see Ward 1977, n. 50, 285–86.

100. Cic. *Att.* 4.13.2: *Crassum quidem nostrum minore dignitate aiunt profectum paludatum quam olim aequalem eius L. Paulum, item iterum consulem. O hominem nequam!*

"They say that our friend Crassus left Rome in uniform with rather less *éclat* than his coeval L. Paulus, also Consul for the second time, in days gone by. What a rascal he is!" (Shackleton Bailey's trans. [1965, 4.105]).

101. Cic. *Sest.* 71; Marshall 1984, 122.

102. Cf. also Cicero's remarks in the senate about P. Clodius' return from Sicily (60 BC), which were in response to Clodius' claims in a *contio* (Cic. *Att.* 2.1.5).

103. Vell. 2.40.3: *Quo magis hoc homines timuerant, eo gratior civilis tanti imperatoris reditus fuit: omni quippe Brundusii dimisso exercitu nihil praeter nomen imperatoris retinens cum privato comitatu, quem semper illi astare moris fuit, in urbem rediit. . . .* "The return of so great a general as an ordinary citizen was all the more welcome because of the apprehensions which had been entertained. For, dismissing his whole army at Brundisium, and retaining none of his former power except the title of *imperator*, he returned to the city with only the retinue which regularly attended him" (trans. F. W. Shipley, Loeb ed.). Cf. Plut. *Pomp.* 43.3–4.

104. On Sulla's triumph, see earlier in this chapter and further Sumi 2002b.

105. Plut. *Pomp.* 43.2. Plutarch's version of this event is not without difficulties, for he claims that Crassus left "secretly," which would hardly constitute a highly visible performance, since no one would have been present to see him depart. Plutarch, however, then goes on to say that Crassus departed in this way in order to validate the rumors then flying in Rome that Pompeius aimed at absolute power. So it seems that Crassus wanted people to know that he had departed and why he had done so.

106. On the circumstances surrounding Cicero's exile, see Mitchell 1991, 127–43.

107. This is known as *squalor;* Lintott 1968, 16–20.

108. With the inscription, "To Minerva, Guardian of Rome." Plut. *Cic.* 31.6; Cic. *Leg.* 2.42; cf. *Fam.* 12.25.1.

109. On Cicero as savior, see his own account of a speech given by M. Crassus in February 61 (*Att.* 1.14.3).

110. On Metellus' return, see App. *BC* 1.33.149; Vell. 2.15.4. For comparisons of Metellus' return with Cicero's, see Cic. *Red. Sen.* 25, 37–38; *Red. Pop.* 6, 9–10; *Dom.* 82, 87; *Sest.* 37, 101, 130; Vell. 2.45.3; cf. Cic. *Dom.* 86, where Cicero compares his exile to that of K. Quinctius, M. Furius Camillus, and C. Servilius Ahala, all of whom rendered great services to the state and, after evoking the anger of the Roman people, endured exile but were eventually restored to their former positions in society.

111. See especially *Att.* 4.1.4–6; *Pis.* 51–52; cf. *Dom.* 64.

112. The consul P. Lentulus Spinther declared the day of Cicero's return to be his birthday (*Red. Sen.* 27–28).

113. The mss. of *Att.* 4.1.4 are unclear on the date; see Shackleton-Bailey 1965, 4.166–67.

114. Cic. *Red. Sen.* 28: *Itaque P. Lentuli beneficio excellenti atque divino non reducti sumus in patriam sicut non nulli clarissimi cives, sed equis insignibus et curru aurato reportati.* "Then it was that thanks to the signal, wonderful benefaction of Publius Lentulus I was not merely brought back to my country, as some illustrious citizens have been in the past, but carried home in a gilded chariot drawn by resplendent horses" (trans. Shackleton Bailey 1991, 19). Cf. *Red. Sen.* 39: *Italia cuncta paene suis umeris reportarit. . . .* "All Italy carried me back (in a manner of speaking) on their shoulders." Cf. *Dom.* 64.

115. For *testimonia,* see Mau, s.v. "Bestattung," *RE* 3 (1899), 350–59; E. Cuq, s.v. "funus," D-S, 2.2, 1386–1409. Cf. also Bodel 1999a.

116. See, e.g., the funeral of M. Flavius' mother (328) at which he distributed food to the people (*visceratio data*). He reaped immediate political dividends in the following year when he was elected tribune of the *plebs* in absentia (Liv. 8.22.3–4; cf. 39.46.2 for a similar distribution of food at the funeral of P. Licinius Crassus in 183); also, at the funeral of Aemilius Paullus (160) the people called upon him as their benefactor (εὐεργήτης) and savior (σωτήρ) (Plut. *Aem.* 39.8).

117. The funeral of Q. Metellus Macedonicus presents something of a Roman ideal: his four sons carried his bier, each of whom had achieved or would achieve the consulship (Vell. 1.11.7).

118. On the *imagines*, see Plb. 6.53.5–10 and Flower 1996. On the custom of actors impersonating the dead, see Diod. 31.25.2; Plaut. *Amph.* 458–59; Suet. *Vesp.* 19.2; Greg. Naz. *Orat.* 5. (*Contra Julianum* II) 18.33 (Migne, *PG* 35.688A); cf. App. *BC* 2.146.611; Sumi 2002a.

119. In origin, a *funus publicum* was an honor bestowed on a foreign dignitary, such as an ambassador or envoy, who died in Italy (Hug, s.v. "funus publicum," *RE* Suppl. 3 [1918], 530–32; for a list of public funerals, see Vollmer 1892; for the most recent discussion, see Wesch-Klein 1993). This practice ended when these ambassadorships became too numerous. Public funerals were also granted to important prisoners of war who died while in captivity—such as the Numidian king, Syphax (d. 203), and the Macedonian king, Perseus (d. 166). In Perseus' case, Valerius Maximus remarks that the Roman senate wanted to give him a funeral that befitted his regal status (V. Max. 5.1.1c). There was also a tradition that public funerals were granted to distinguished citizens who had died in poverty (e.g., P. Valerius Poplicola [d. 503 BC; Liv. 2.16.7] and Agrippa Menenius [Liv. 2.33.11; D. H. 6.96.3]).

120. E.g., Sulla's funeral (78 BC); App. *BC* 1.106.500.

121. Plut. *TG* 13.4–6. M. Seius (*aed. cur.* 74) was honored in similar fashion after he had facilitated the supply of grain to the city in time of famine (Plin. *Nat.* 18.16). The date of his funeral is not attested.

122. Serv. A. 6.861; Sumi 2002b.

123. Clodius' funeral as a whole seems to have been a ritual of inversion; Sumi 1997.

124. Plutarch goes so far as to describe the politics of this decade as a renewed struggle between the old Marian and Sullan "factions" (*Caes.* 6). This is probably an oversimplification, but there is some evidence that supports Plutarch's view of the politics of this decade. In 60 Faustus put on a *munus* in honor of his father, which was perhaps the Sullan "party's" reply to the revival of Marius' image. Faustus Sulla minted coins that depicted Bocchus handing over an abject Jugurtha to Sulla seated on a throne—the same scene that Sulla's signet ring bore. Grueber (*BMCRR*, no. 3824, p. 471) dates the coin to 62, shortly before or after Faustus' journey to Jerusalem in the company of Pompeius. Crawford (1974, no. 426.1), on the other hand, dates this coin to 56 as part of a series of coins that Faustus minted to honor his father and father-in-law Pompeius. The crucial piece of evidence is the image of the *lituus*, which, Crawford argues, is symbolic of Faustus' augurate of 57, and not his father's, and therefore, in his view, the coin must postdate 57. The year 62 is slightly better, but not crucial, for my argument. On the abiding influence of Sulla on the politics of this period, see Paterson 1985. Marius' importance can be seen as late as 44 through the rise of Amatius, the

man who claimed to be his grandson (Cic. *Att.* 14.6.1, 7.1, 8.1; App. *BC* 3.2.2–3.9; and for a discussion, see chap. 3).

125. Plut. *Caes.* 5.2; cf. Suet. *Jul.* 6.1; cf. Flower 1996, 124.

126. Vell. 2.43.4; Plut. *Caes.* 6.1; Suet. *Jul.* 11.

127. Many years later, during the war in Africa in 49, Caesar's kinship with Marius won him the trust of the descendants of Marius' veterans (*B. Afr.* 56.3; cf. 32.3 and 35.4 for the effect of Marius' name on his former clients). It is worth noting that when Amatius, the false grandson of Marius, first came to Rome he approached Caesar, citing a family connection (Cic. *Att.* 12.49.2; cf. Nic. Dam. 14.32–33 [*FrGH* 90, F128]); see also chap. 3. Moreover, Cicero's appraisal of Marius, his fellow townsman and *novus homo*, was uniformly positive, which in all likelihood helped foster this image of Marius as popular hero (*Leg. Man.* 47; *Cat.* 4.21; *Rab.* 27; *Sest.* 37, 38; cf. Carney 1960).

128. Dionysius claimed that this was a uniquely Roman convention (5.17.3); Plb. 6.54.1, with Walbank's commentary (1957, 1.737). See also Vollmer 1891; Kierdorf 1980; Koenen 1970.

129. Cic. *de Orat.* 2.341 (*brevitas nuda et inornata*).

130. Liv. 8.40.4; 27.27.13; Cic. *Brut.* 62.

131. This relationship was further advertised on a coin minted in 56 BC by a Marcius Philippus (exact identification unknown [Evans 1992, 139–40]). This coin depicts king Ancus Marcius on the reverse. Evans argues for a strong connection between this coin, the memory of Ancus, and Caesar's accomplishments, since this coin was minted a year after Caesar's conquest of Gaul was announced in Rome.

132. Suet. *Jul.* 6.1: '*Amitae meae Iuliae maternum genus ab regibus ortum, paternum cum diis immortalibus coniunctum est. nam ab Anco Marcio sunt Marcii Reges, quo nomine fuit mater; a Venere Iulii, cuius gentis familia est nostra. est ergo in genere et sanctitas regum, qui plurimum inter homines pollent, et caerimonia deorum, quorum ipsi in potestate sunt reges.* "'The maternal line of my aunt Julia arose from kings, her paternal line is conjoined with the immortal gods. For the Marcii Reges, my mother's family, are descended from Ancus Marcius; the Julii, my own family, from Venus. There is therefore in my family the inviolability of kings who have the greatest power among men, and reverence owed to the gods, who have power over kings.'"

133. In 129 BC Sextus Julius Caesar (*pr.* 123) issued coins showing the descent of the Julii from Venus (Crawford 1974, no. 258/1); in 103 L. Julius Caesar (*cos.* 90) did the same (Crawford 1974, no. 320/1).

134. It is also possible that when Caesar claimed descent from Venus, he was attempting to reclaim for the Julian *gens* their divine matriarch, whom Sulla had adopted as his patron deity following his victory over Marius. On Sulla's relationship with Venus, see Schilling 1954, 272–95; Keaveney 1983, 61–65. Sulla also revived the *Lusus Troiae* (Plut. *Cat. Mi.* 3.1), which was perhaps a further attempt to connect his own otherwise undistinguished family with the Aeneas legend and the legendary kings who founded Rome. On Caesar and Venus, see Schilling 1954, 301–24; Weinstock 1971, 15–18, 80–93.

135. Lintott (1967, 169) has remarked on the participation of the urban crowd in connection with the violence of the late Republic: "They [sc. the urban *plebs*] watched passively as the Catilinarians were led to execution, treating it as the performance of an aristocratic ritual, but they cremated Clodius in the senate house."

136. On Clodius' funeral, see Sumi 1997; on Caesar's funeral, see chapter 4 of this book.

137. Licin. 35.42–45 (Criniti); Vell. 2.21.4; Plut. *Pomp.* 1.2–3; Seager 1979, 5.

CHAPTER 2

1. Bibliography on Caesar is vast. See Gesche 1976; the standard biography is still Gelzer 1968a; see also the more recent work of Meier 1995. For the issues of particular interest in this chapter, see, above all, Yavetz 1969 and 1983. On the question of Caesar's popularity, see Yavetz 1969, 38–57, esp. 45. According to Yavetz, Caesar's policy consisted of "consolidation based on a body of supporters as heterogeneous in class as possible, among them the *plebs urbana*."

2. Yavetz's view is an important starting point (1969, 47–48): "Caesar did not introduce a new method of dealing with the *plebs* of Rome, but merely changed the standard. It was the scope that was remarkable, not the principle." He cites (48, n. 1) as one piece of evidence the dramatic increase in the number of pairs of gladiators that fought at a given *munus*, from three in 264 BC to 320 in Caesar's *munus* during his aedileship (65 BC) (Suet. *Jul.* 10.2; Plut. *Caes.* 5.9).

3. E.g., his prosecution in 77 or 76 BC of Cn. Dolabella on a charge of *repetundae* (Suet. *Jul.* 4.1; Damon and MacKay 1995), and his prosecution of C. Antonius in 76 (Asc. *Tog.* 84.C; cf. Plut. *Caes.* 4.2).

4. Sen. *Nat.* 5.18.4; cf. Yavetz 1983, 13.

5. A thorough discussion of modern views of Caesar can be found in Yavetz 1983, 10–57. My brief discussion here owes much to his longer one.

6. Adcock *CAH*, 9.739–40.

7. Ehrenberg 1964, 160.

8. Meyer 1922, 465–72. Meyer argues that Caesar strove for monarchy as a way to hang on to the power that he had gained through his victory over Pompeius. In this view, Pompeius was the real precursor to Augustus, while Caesar was but an interlude.

9. Alföldi 1951, 208

10. The quotation is from Syme 1959, 56, which owes much to Adcock *CAH*, 9.724; cf. also Rawson 1975b.

11. On this topic, see especially Gesche 1968; Vogt 1953; Weinstock 1971.

12. *Sest.* 143. Cf. the comparison of Romulus and Hercules in Liv. 1.7.15, where Livy claims that Romulus was striving for an immortality produced by courage (*immortalitas virtute parta*).

13. Plutarch relates Caesar's ultimate objectives of conquest in his Parthian campaign (*Caes.* 58.4–7).

14. For an imaginary view of the topography of Rome before the commencement of Caesar's building program, see Favro 1996, 24–41.

15. For a summary of the evolution of the Forum during the Republic, see N. Purcell, s.v. "Forum Romanum (The Republican Period)," *LTUR* 2.325–36; Coarelli 1992, 2.125–209; Bonnefond-Coudry 1989, 80–90.

16. Coarelli 1992, 2.234–35; Bonnefond-Coudry 1989, 168–76; Morselli and Tortorici 1989, 1.41–44. We should note, however, with Ulrich 1993, 71–72 (following Coarelli 1992, 1.153–54), that Caesar's forum project originally was planned to work around the old senate house.

17. On this question, see most recently P. Verduchi, s.v. "Rostra Augusti," *LTUR* 4.214–17; see also Coarelli 1992, 2.237–55; Richardson 1992, 336–37; Nichols 1877, 202–6.

18. Dio 43.49.1: καὶ τὸ βῆμα ἐν μέσῳ που πρότερον τῆς ἀγορᾶς ὂν ἐς τὸν νῦν τόπον ἀνεχωρίσθη, καὶ αὐτῷ ἡ τοῦ Σύλλου τοῦ τε Πομπηίου εἰκὼν ἀπεδόθη, "the Rostra which was in the middle of the Forum was moved to its present location and an image of Sulla and one of Pompeius were restored to it."

19. Perhaps on the steps leading from the Curia down into the comitium, as L. R. Taylor suggests (1966, 22–23).

20. Plutarch claims that C. Gracchus was the first to do this (CG 5.4). Elections were still held in the Comitium.

21. *Flacc.* 57: *Hic, in hac gravissima et moderatissima civitate, cum est forum plenum iudiciorum, plenum magistratuum, plenum optimorum virorum et civium, cum speculatur atque obsidet rostra vindex temeritatis et moderatrix offici curia, tamen quantos fluctus excitari contionum videtis!* Cf. Ulrich 1993, 74. On the association of *libertas* and the Rostra on a coin of Lollius Palicanus (45 BC), see Sear 1998, no. 86.

22. Taylor 1966, 21–25. Recent excavations have produced evidence to indicate that there was a restoration of the temple (known as Temple 1A) before the major rebuilding undertaken by L. Caecilius Metellus Delmaticus in 117 (for a full discussion of the Metellan renewal, see Nielsen and Poulsen 1992, 87–117). During the period of the Republic, the Temple of Castor passed through three phases: (1) the original temple is called Temple 1; (2) the first restoration, Temple 1A; (3) the second restoration, the Metellan temple. The most telling change was the removal of the front row of columns of the pronaos to make way for a tribunal (Nielsen and Poulsen 1992, 55; 80–86). Nielsen and Poulsen argue for a date of 164 since Aemilius Paullus was censor in this year, an office that usually administered public building projects, and he would have wanted to honor Castor and Pollux for their assistance at the battle of Pydna in 168 (1992, 86, following Steinby 1987, 167–69).

23. The tribunal of Temple 1A was ca. 11 m. wide and 6.50 m. in depth (Nielsen and Poulsen 1992, 84); the tribunal of the Metellan temple was ca. 21 m. wide and 7 m. deep (Nielsen and Poulsen 1992, 113).

24. Taylor 1966, 21–29. Raised platforms (*pontes*) led up to one side of the tribunal and down from the other so that voters could cast their votes.

25. See R. T. Scott, s.v. "Regia," *LTUR* 4.189–92.

26. On the Forum Julium, see Ulrich 1993; Morselli and Tortorici 1989; Westall 1996.

27. Morselli and Tortorici 1989, 15; Ulrich 1993, 73; Anderson 1984, 50.

28. Cf. Cic. *Att.* 4.16.8; 13.33a.1 (neither letter offers conclusive evidence; Ulrich 1993, 56–57, with n. 49 on p. 57); Castagnoli 1946, 284; Platner-Ashby 1929, 238.

29. Ulrich 1993, 66.

30. It was not until after his death that the triumvir M. Aemilius Lepidus broke ground for it in the Campus Martius; it was completed by M. Agrippa, who made it the eastern boundary of the complex of structures in the Campus Martius that resulted from his patronage and dedicated it as the Saepta Julia in 26 (Dio 53.23.1–2).

31. Cic. *Att.* 4.16.8: *Nam in campo Martio saepta tributis comitiis marmorea sumus et tecta facturi eaque cingemus excelsa porticu ut mille passuum conficiatur. . .* "As for the

Campus Martius, we are going to build covered marble booths for the Assembly of Tribes and to surround them with a high colonnade, a mile of it in all" (trans. Shackleton Bailey 1965, 2.115); cf. Dio 53.23.2. See also E. Gatti, s.v. "Saepta Iulia," *LTUR* 4.228–29. See figure 1 for the location of the Saepta Julia.

32. Taylor 1966, 47.

33. E.g., Suet. *Aug.* 43.4; Dio 55.8.5; 55.10.7.

34. Taylor 1966, 48; on Pompeius' theater, see Hanson 1959, 43–55. Cf. Wiseman 1992, 32–37, who argues that the new Saepta was meant to house a new map of the world commissioned by Caesar showing Rome's conquests. This would have made it a triumphal monument to rival Pompeius' theater, which had statues commemorating his many conquests.

35. Suet. *Jul.* 78.1; Nic. Dam. 22.78–79 (*FrGH* 90, F130); Plut. *Caes.* 60.4–8; Liv. 116; Dio 44.8; cf. App. *BC* 2.107.445–46.

36. Both temples were octastyle with ranks of closely spaced columns arranged on the façade and sides of the cella—a plan closely resembling the Vitruvian *peripteros sine postico* (Ulrich 1993, 74–75).

37. Ulrich 1993, 80.

38. Dio's statements are even less clear (43.47.1). For a brief analysis of the relevant issues, see Yavetz 1983, 127–32; a longer discussion can be found in Frei-Stolba 1967, 37–76.

39. Cic. *Fam.* 7.30.1; Suet. *Jul.* 76.2; *Nero* 15.2; Plut. *Caes.* 58.1–3; Dio 43.46.3.

40. Frei-Stolba 1967, 70–71. She bases this hypothesis on the evidence of Cic. *Fam.* 10.32.2, a letter from C. Asinius Pollio reporting the activities of Cornelius Balbus in Gades (in 43 BC). Balbus claimed to be following Caesar's example. Pollio reports that over the course of two days Balbus held elections (*comitia habuit*) for magistrates for the next two years. But Balbus did not actually hold elections, as Pollio goes on to report, but merely proclaimed as magistrates (*renuntiavit*) the candidates he favored (*quos ei visum est*).

41. For a brief overview of the procedure Caesar followed in enacting his laws, see Yavetz 1983, 58–59.

42. Taylor 1966, 104, citing primarily the law on Cicero's recall from exile as evidence.

43. Taylor 1966, 104.

44. Nic. Dam. 20.69 (*FrGH* 90, F130); Plut. *Caes.* 61.8; Suet. *Jul.* 79.1; App. *BC* 2.108.449; Dio 44.9.3.

45. Yavetz, on the other hand, maintains that Caesar used the *comitia tributa* because of his decisive influence there. In fact, there is no known case where one of his proposals was rejected (1983, 59, citing Cic. *Att.* 13.33a.1: '*Cave facias,*' *inquit* [sc. Varro], '*nam ista lex perferetur; vult enim Caesar.*' "Don't do it," he said. "The law will pass. Caesar wants it.").

46. For a discussion of legislative activity in the centuriate assembly down to the time of the Gracchi and a challenge of this traditional view, see Paananen 1993.

47. But see Paananen 1993, 26–36.

48. A preliminary study is Sandberg 1993. He more fully argues his case in Sandberg 2001.

49. Paananen 1993, 36–68, and his conclusions on 70. There is also the possibil-

ity that a dictator ruled by edict, himself proposing the rule of law, which was then designated a *lex*, even if it was not enacted in customary fashion through a vote in one of the popular assemblies.

50. Suet. *Jul.* 37; for the first four triumphs, cf. Nic. Dam. 8.17 (*FrGH* 90, F127), who adds that young C. Octavius appeared behind Caesar's chariot, resplendent in the garb of a commander, even though he had not participated in the war; App. *BC* 2.101–102; Dio 43.19.1–21.3; D-G² 3.550–54; Weinstock 1971, 76–79.

51. For the chronology of Caesar's triumphs and the games that followed, I adopt the thesis of Ramsey and Licht 1997, 183–84; for the days intervening between triumphal processions, see Suet. *Jul.* 37.1 (*interiectis diebus*).

52. Dio 43.24.4. Dio puzzles over the ceremony performed on this occasion. He describes it as a "ritual sacrifice" (ἱερουργία) but cannot explain the reason for it; he rejects the idea that it was in response to an oracle of any kind. We should note that Octavian was *pontifex* by this time and therefore would have been involved in the ceremony; on Octavian's pontificate, see chapter 5.

53. Dio 43.21.1–2. According to Dio this took place near the Temple of Fortuna constructed by Lucullus. Perhaps the Temple of Felicitas was meant (D-G² 3.552, n. 10; Jordan-Hülsen 1871, 1.2.486). Suetonius (*Jul.* 37.2) claims that Caesar was accompanied on this ascent by forty elephants bearing lamps, but this seems too lavish and spectacular, considering the omen Caesar had just received. If Suetonius is correct, this shows the height of Caesar's arrogance. It is possible that Suetonius and Dio are preserving two conflicting traditions—one positive, the other negative—about Caesar.

54. Dio 43.14.6; Nicolet 1991, 39–41.

55. Dio 43.14.3. Weinstock (1971, 68–75) has discussed at some length the symbolism of the white horses. Whether they were regarded as a divine or regal attribute is difficult to determine with any certainty; the most likely answer is that they were both. Another question, albeit equally difficult to answer, is whether Caesar "invented" the white horses and their attribution to Camillus. Certainly by the early Principate, white horses in a triumph seem to be a poetic convention. According to Tibullus (1.7.8), Messalla held a triumph with white horses in 27 BC; Ovid expected they would also appear in Tiberius' triumph over Germany (*Pont.* 2.8.50) and in C. Caesar's triumph over Parthia (*Ars* 1.214).

56. Flor. *Epit.* 2.13.88–89; Cicero also points out that Caesar never celebrated a triumph for his victory at Pharsalus (*Phil.* 14.23).

57. As he himself expressed (Cic. *Att.* 9.7C.1); on *clementia* as one of Caesar's cardinal virtues, see Weinstock 1971, 233–43.

58. T. Flamininus (Liv. 34.52.4) and L. Aemilius Paullus (Plut. *Aem.* 32–34; cf. Liv. 45.40) both celebrated triumphs lasting three days for their victories in the Macedonian wars; Sulla's triumph lasted two days (28, 29 January 81 BC) (Plin. *Nat.* 33.16; App. *BC* 1.101.473; Plut. *Sull.* 34.1–5); in September 61, Pompeius celebrated a triumph lasting two days (although there was enough booty for a third *pompa*) for his victories on three continents (Pomp. *Plut.* 45).

59. At Pompeius' triumph, there was a large trophy (perhaps a float? [Seager 1979, 78]) that bore an inscription indicating that it represented the entire inhabited world (*oikoumene*) (Dio 37.21.2–3).

60. D-G² 3.553. On the fame of Caesar's swiftness, see Cic. *Marc.* 5, who praises Caesar's speed in completing tasks (*celeritate conficiendi*); cf. his later statement

(describing Antonius' movements in Campania), *Aiunt enim eum Caesari<a>na uti celeritate* (*Att.* 16.10.1). Cf. also *Att.* 7.22.1, 8.9a.2, 9.18.2; Vell. 2.51.2; D-G^{2} 1.671, 723.

61. Suet. *Jul.* 35.2: *quem Mithridatis Magni filium. . . intra quintum quam adfuerat diem, quattuor quibus in conspectum venit horis, una profligavit acie*. For the date of the battle, see *Inscr. Ital.* 13.2, pp. 30–31, 190–91.

62. A further example of Caesar's historical consciousness is the trophy that he erected on the site of Zela, where he had defeated Pharnaces in 47, that stood in opposition to the trophy that Mithridates had erected on the same spot to celebrate his own victory over C. Valerius Triarius in 67; Dio 42.48.2; cf. Westall 1996, 115–17; as Westall states (116): "By his action, Caesar encouraged contemporaries and posterity to compare his victory of 47 with that of 67."

63. Suet. *Jul.* 39.4: *in minore Codeta* ("in lesser Codeta") is an emendation that most scholars accept for *in morem cochleae* ("in the shape of a shell"). For a discussion, see Coleman 1993, 50, with n. 5.

64. Fest. 50L; Haselberger 2002, 93. Dio fixes its location in the Campus Martius (43.23.4).

65. A parallel for Caesar's mock battle between Egyptians and Tyrians can be found in Book 7 of Chariton's *Callirhoe*, where the combined forces of Greeks and Egyptians routed the Persian fleet off the coast of Tyre. "The novel is set within an historical framework. . . the clash between Egypt and Persia seems to conflate the Egyptian offensive against the Persian Empire in 360 BC and Alexander the Great's attempt in 333 BC to plunder Phoenicia, where the Persian navy was based. The 'historical' context lends plausibility to the narrative; like Chariton's novel, Caesar's *naumachia* may reflect the same preference for verisimilitude over veracity" (Coleman 1993, 69; see also 73–74).

66. Plin. *Nat.* 2.93–94. Cf. Obseq. 68 (Rossbach); Weinstock 1971, 88–92.

67. On Sulla's games, see chapter 1.

68. The *Consualia* were associated with the rape of the Sabine women (Liv. 1.9.7), although the precise significance of this association is obscure (cf. Ogilvie 1965, 66; for an attempt to unravel the mystery through etymology, see Noonan 1990). Cf. E. Pottier, s.v. "Consus," D-S, 1.2, 1484; Wissowa 1912, 202–3; Latte 1960, 72. The *Equirria* were founded by Romulus (M. Schmidt, s.v. "Equirria," *RE* 6 [1909], 271–72; G. Bloch, s.v. "Equirria," D-S 2.1, 745–46).

69. Cf. Caesar's use of the *Parilia* to celebrate his victory at Munda (discussed later in chap. 2). On Caesar's connection with Rome's founder, Romulus-Quirinus, see Burkert 1962 and Weinstock 1971, 175–99.

70. Verg. *Aen.* 5.545–603. The most thorough discussion of the *Troia* remains Goebel 1852; cf. also Marquardt 1881–1885, 3.525–27; Wissowa 1912, 450; Weinstock 1971, 88–89.

71. Suet. *Jul.* 39.2; Dio 43.23.6. This equestrian performance is variously named in our sources: *ludicrum Troiae* (Tac. *Ann.* 11.11.2); *Troiae ludus* (Suet. *Aug.* 43.2); *Troiae lusus* (Suet. *Claud.* 21.3); *Troicus lusus* (Sen. *Troad.* 778); *Troiae decursio* (Suet. *Cal.* 18.3). See also Goebel 1852, 3–5, for testimonia.

72. Cf. Nicolet 1991, 33.

73. See, e.g., Livy's accounts of the triumphs in the second century BC (33.23.7;

33.37.12; 34.46.3; 34.52.11; 36.40.13; 37.59.6; 39.5.17; 39.7.2; 40.34.8; 40.43.7; 40.59.2; 41.7.3; 41.13.7; 45.43.7).

74. Dio 43.21.3. One is also reminded of Tacitus' epigrammatic assessment of Augustus' consolidation of power: *militem donis, populum annona, cunctos dulcedine otii pellexit. . .* (*Ann.* 1.2.1). "He enticed the soldiers with gifts, the people with bread, everyone with the allurement of peace." Livy (39.7.5) relates the story that after the triumph of Cn. Manlius (*cos.* 189) in 187 the senate, at the instigation of his friends, passed a decree setting aside some of the spoils of victory to be used to pay off a tax burden imposed on the people, but this did not constitute a direct cash payment to the people.

75. On this issue, see chapter 3.

76. Following his Spanish triumph in 45, Caesar fêted the people with two meals (*duo prandia*); Suet. *Jul.* 38.2: *Adiecit epulum ac viscerationem et post Hispaniensem victoriam duo prandia; nam cum prius parce neque pro liberalitate sua praebitum iudicaret, quinto post die aliud largissimum praebuit.* "He added a banquet and distribution of meat and, after his Spanish victory, two meals. For since he thought that first one had been produced sparingly and unbefitting his generosity, he offered a second more splendid one five days later." Cf. Gentili 1948, 136–41: *[C. Iulius Caesar dictator ex] | His[pania triumphum egit] | et popul[o in hortis trans Ti] | berim [duo prandia dedit].* "[Gaius Julius Caesar dictator led his] Span[ish triumph and offered two meals to] the people [in his gardens across the Ti]ber."

77. Dio, on the contrary, claims that Caesar did not allow the senator to fight, but many members of the equestrian order did (43.23.5).

78. Combat between aristocrats, like Laberius' performance, could symbolize the opportunity for political or social redemption in Caesar's Rome. For a discussion of freeborn citizens who chose the life of gladiators, see Wiedemann 1992, 108–14.

79. For a brief discussion, Gurval 1995, 24, n. 6. Note also Cicero's claim that a *supplicatio* was never decreed for a victory in civil war (*Phil.* 14.23–24).

80. Ov. *Fast.* 4.721–860; Var. *L.* 6.15; Prop. 4.4.73–78.; cf. Wissowa 1912, 199–201; Latte 1960, 87–88; Scullard 1981, 103–5.

81. Dio 43.42.3; for suspicions about the coincidence of the arrival of the news of victory, see D-G^2 3.580, n. 3; Weinstock 1971, 175–76. For the celebration of this festival in 44, a little more than a month after Caesar's murder, see chapter 4.

82. Ov. *Fast.* 4.837–44. In Ovid's version Romulus' aide, Celer, is responsible for Remus' death (cf. Liv. 1.7.2, with Ogilvie's note 1965, 54).

83. Hor. *Ep.* 7.17–20; cf. Luc. 1.95: *fraterno primi maduerunt sanguine muri.*

84. In this context, it is also worth noting that Caesar founded colonies at Corinth and Carthage (Dio 43.50.3–5), whose destruction in 146, which left Rome with no enemy in the Mediterranean, was regarded as one of the underlying causes of the civil wars of the late Republic (Sallust mentions only Carthage: *Cat.* 10.1–2; *Jug.* 41.2–5; *Hist.* fr. 1.11R; cf. Earl 1961, 13, 41–42).

85. Weinstock 1971, 175–99, explores these issues in some detail.

86. We would expect the curule aediles to be in charge of the *Ludi Romani* (Mommsen 1864, 2.53), but Broughton (*MRR*, 2.307) contends that no curule magistrates, with the exception of Caesar himself as consul, had been elected in this year (citing Dio 43.47–48).

87. Cic. *Att.* 13.45.1: . . . *plane* [sc. epistula] *declarabat illum ante ludos Romanos esse venturum. in qua extrema scriptum erat ut ad ludos omnia pararet neve committeret ut frustra ipse properasset;* cf. 13.46.2. On the dates of these games, see Ramsey and Licht 1997, 31, n. 21; *contra* Mommsen, *CIL* 1², pp. 328–29. Velleius claims that he returned to the city in October (2.56.3), but he may be confusing Caesar's triumph with his return.

88. Plut. *Ant.* 11.1: Ἐκ δ' Ἰβηρίας ἐπανιόντι Καίσαρι πάντες μὲν οἱ πρῶτοι πολλῶν ἡμερῶν ὁδὸν ἀπήντων, ἐτιμήθη δ' Ἀντώνιος ἐκπρεπῶς ὑπ' αὐτοῦ. κομιζόμενος γὰρ ἐπὶ ζεύγους διὰ τῆς Ἰταλίας Ἀντώνιονεἶχε μεθ' ἑαυτοῦ συνοχούμενον, ὄπισθεν δὲ Βροῦτον Ἀλβῖνον καὶ τὸν τῆς ἀδελφῆς υἱὸν Ὀκταουιανόν, ὃς μετὰ ταῦτα Καῖσαρ ὠνομάσθη καὶ Ῥωμαίων ἦρξε πλεῖστον χρόνον. "When Caesar returned from Spain, all the most important men traveled a journey of several days to meet him; Antonius was especially honored by him, by being allowed to share his chariot through Italy. Behind them came D. Brutus Albinus and Caesar's nephew Octavian, who later was called Caesar and ruled the Romans for a long time."

89. Deutsch 1928, 179, 199–200.

90. This requires that these *ludi* remained in late September/early October in 45 and were not moved to July, as some scholars have long thought. See now Ramsey and Licht 1997, 41–57, for a full discussion of the relevant issues.

91. Ramsey and Licht 1997, 43.

92. Dio 44.4.3; cf. Suet. *Jul.* 79.1. Weinstock 1971, 318–31.

93. Weinstock 1971, 326.

94. D. H. 4.49.2; Macr. 1.16.16–17; Latte 1960, 144; Cornell 1995, 294–95.

95. E.g., Cic. *Fam.* 8.6.3.

96. On the origin of the festival, see D. H. 4.49; Liv. 1.31.3; 5.17.2. Cf. also Wissowa 1912, 40, 124–25; Scullard 1981, 111–15.

97. *Lanuvinus magistratus;* Liv. 41.16.1. On the magistrates of Italian cities in general, see Gervasoni 1998.

98. E.g., Cornell 1995, 73–74.

99. It should be noted that there was a plebeian branch of the Servilii as well; Cornell 1995, 254, 447 n. 47.

100. We should also note that the senate decreed to build a temple to Concordia Nova in order to acknowledge Caesar's role in establishing peace in Rome (Dio 44.4.5).

101. Syme 1938.

102. Syme 1939, 94; cf. Bruhns 1978.

103. Tac. *Ann.* 11.25.2; Suet. *Jul.* 41.1; Dio 43.47.3.

104. *Inscr. Ital.* 13.1, p. 87.

105. *quod pacem cum M. Antonio fecit. . .* (*Inscr. Ital.* 13.1, p. 87); cf. Dio 48.16.1. See also chapter 8.

106. Gel. 5.6.20–21; cf. also D. H. 9.36.3, who tells us that the consul Manlius was awarded an *ovatio* for his victory over the Veii, which he won through negotiation.

107. Suet. *Jul.* 79.2: *Neque ex eo infamiam affectati etiam regii nominis discutere valuit, quamquam et plebei regem se salutanti, 'Caesarem se, non regem esse,' responderit. . . .*

108. Caesar's purpose on this occasion is much disputed, and various explanations

have been offered. I am largely in agreement with Zecchini 2001, 11–34. For explanations other than the one proposed here, see Meyer 1922, 520–23; Bianchi 1958; Rossi 1959, 44–49.

109. Cic. *Phil.* 2.85–87: *Sedebat in rostris collega tuus amictus toga purpurea, in sella aurea, coronatus. Escendis, accedis ad sellam <Lupercus>—ita eras Lupercus ut te consulem esse meminisse deberes—diadema ostendis. Gemitus toto foro. Unde diadema? Non enim abiectum sustuleras, sed attuleras domo, meditatum et cogitatum scelus. Tu diadema imponebas cum plangore populi; ille cum plausu reiciebat. . . . at etiam misericordiam captabas: supplex te ad pedes abiciebas. . . .at etiam ascribi iussit in fastis ad Lupercalia C. Caesari, dictatori perpetuo, M. Antonium consulem populi iussu regnum detulisse, Caesarem ut noluisse.* "Your colleague was seated on the Rostra wearing the *toga purpurea*, on a golden chair, with a garland. You climb up, approach his chair as Lupercus—you were as much a Lupercus as you should have remembered you were a consul—you show a diadem. Groans throughout the Forum. Where did you get the diadem? You certainly did not pick up what someone else had tossed away; but you brought it from home, a carefully laid scheme. You kept trying to place the diadem on Caesar's head as the crowd groaned; then he kept rejecting it to their applause. . . you tried pity: as a suppliant you tossed it at his feet. . . . but he ordered it to be written in the *Fasti:* 'At the *Lupercalia*, Marcus Antonius consuls by order of the people offered Gaius Caesar, Dictator Forever, the kingship; Caesar declined.'" Cf. Nic. Dam. 21.71–75 (*FrGH* 90, F130); Plut. *Caes.* 61.1–7; Suet. *Jul.* 79.2; App. *BC* 2.109.456–58; Dio 44.11.1–3.

110. Cic. *Phil.* 5.38: *Semper ille* [sc. M. Aemilius Lepidus] *populum Romanum liberum voluit maximumque signum illo die dedit voluntatis et iudici sui, cum Antonio diadema Caesari imponente se avertit gemituque et maestitia declaravit quantum haberet odium servitutis, quam populum Romanum liberum cuperet, quam illa quae tulerat temporum magis necessitate quam iudicio tulisset.* "Lepidus always wanted the Roman people to be free; the clearest indication of his desire and judgment he provided on that day when, as Antonius offered Caesar a diadem, he turned away and with a groan and a gloomy expression offered testimony to how deeply he hated slavery, how he wanted the Roman people to be free, and how he endured all that he had endured because of the exigencies of the times, not his own desire."

111. His identity is otherwise unknown; *MRR* 2.334.

112. Plut. *Ant.* 12.6. In his *Caesar* (60.6), Plutarch assigns this gesture to the moment when Caesar was presiding over the construction of the Temple of Venus Genetrix in his new forum. After receiving the senate and magistrates, who were coming to confer extraordinary honors on him, Caesar failed to rise. He also declared that the honors should be pared rather than increased. He soon realized that he had caused offense and, pulling back his cloak to reveal his throat, he invited his friends to offer a blow should they so desire it. M. Bibulus made a similar gesture when he was being attacked by Caesar's supporters in the mêlée surrounding Caesar's controversial legislation in their consulship in 59 BC (App. *BC* 2.11.39; Dio 38.6.2–3; see also chap. 1). Augustus mimicked this gesture in the spring of 22 BC when the people were clamoring for him to become dictator. He knelt down before them, threw back his toga to expose his neck and begged them not to force the dictatorship on him (Suet. *Aug.* 52); see further the discussion in chapter 9.

113. πίστιν ἐν ὀφθαλμοῖς μείζω παρασχὸν ὧν δι᾽ ὑποψίας εἶχον (21.75).

CHAPTER 3

1. Dio 47.25.3; Crawford 1974, no. 508/3; Sear 1998, nos. 215, 216; Cahn 1957. Coinage was only one way in which the conspirators represented themselves as tyrannicides. According to Dio, Brutus and Cassius received a hero's welcome in Athens in 42 and were honored with bronze statues erected next to those of Harmodius and Aristogeiton (47.20.4). They also claimed that the Republic existed wherever they were (Vell. 2.67.3), and the watchword at the battle of Philippi was *libertas* (Dio 47.43.1).

2. The main sources for the events between Caesar's assassination and the reading of his will are: Nic. Dam. 24.85–27.106 (*FrGH* 90, F130); Vell. 2.58–59; Plut. *Caes.* 66–67; *Ant.* 14, *Brut.* 17–19; App. *BC* 2.118–142; Dio 44.19–34; V. Max. 9.9.1. Cf. also D-G² 1.56–71; Becht 1911; Frisch 1946, 25–56; Alföldi 1953, 53–70; Gotter 1996, 21–29.

3. Dio 44.21.3. Appian names names (*BC* 2.119.500): P. Cornelius Lentulus Spinther (*cos.* 57), M. Favonius (*pr.* 49; *MRR* 2.257), M. Aquinus (*MRR* 2.300; 3.25), P. Cornelius Dolabella (*cos. suff.* 44), L. Staius Murcus (*MRR* 2.349), and a certain Patiscus (*MRR* 2.348). Plutarch also mentions a C. Octavius (*Caes.* 67.4), who may be C. Octavius Balbus, later proscribed and executed (*MRR* 3.151; Wiseman 1964, 124).

4. Two months later Cicero (*Att.* 14.19.1) hoped for a restoration of the constitution (*re publica constituta*), but he does not describe what this entailed; cf. Wistrand 1981, 5–6.

5. Cic. *Att.* 15.1a.2; on this *contio*, see also Motzo 1940; more generally on the speeches in the days after Caesar's assassination, see Gowing 1992, 228–34.

6. Plut. *Brut.* 18.11. But in his various *Lives*, Plutarch's accounts of the events after Caesar's murder are not consistent. For instance, in his Caesar he fails to mention any speech of Brutus on the Capitolium and places the *contio* in the Forum on 16 March (*Caes.* 67.7).

7. So Radin 1939, 154.

8. Dio 44.4.5; cf. Plin. *Nat.* 22.6–7; Richardson 1992, 336–37.

9. App. *BC* 3.50.202. Cf. Bonnefond-Coudry 1989, 44.

10. Cic. *Phil.* 6.12–13: *Aspicite illam a sinistra equestrem statuam inauratam, in qua quid inscriptum est? 'QUINQUE ET TRIGINTA TRIBUS PATRONO.' Populi Romani igitur est patronus L. Antonius. Malam quidem illi pestem! Clamori enim vestro adsentior. Non modo hic latro quem clientem habere nemo velit sed quis umquam tantis opibus, tantis rebus gestis fuit qui se populi Romani victoris dominique omnium gentium patronum dicere auderet?* (13) *In foro L. Antoni statuam videmus, sicut illam Q. Tremuli, qui Hernicos devicit, ante Castoris.* "Look at that gilt equestrian statue to the left. What's inscribed on it? 'The 35 tribes to their patron.' So Lucius Antonius is patron of the Roman people. A plague on him! I agree with your shouts. Is there anyone who had so much wealth and who had accomplished so much who would dare claim that he was patron of the Roman people, conqueror and master of all peoples, much less this criminal whom no one would want as a client?—(13) In the Forum, we see a statue of Lucius Antonius near the Temple of Castor, just as we see one of Quintus Tremulus, who conquered the Hernicans."

11. As Coarelli concludes (1992, 2.233–57, esp. 242).

12. This argument has a bearing on how I understand Brutus' *contio* on the Capitolium on 17 March (see the discussion later in this chapter).

13. Nicolaus also speaks of the conspirators' desire to "test" the magistrates and

the people (26b.99) at this *contio*, which implies that they had no foreknowledge of the content or tone of the speeches of Cinna and Dolabella.

14. Proof of the crowd's displeasure came to light two days later when Cinna was seen at the senate meeting at the Temple of Tellus dressed once again in the insignia of a praetor. He narrowly escaped an angry mob who caught sight of him, gave chase, and threw stones; he took refuge in a house, and the mob was ready to burn it down, but they were thwarted by M. Lepidus and his soldiers (App. *BC* 2.126.526–27). This was not the end of it. The crowd at Caesar's funeral mistook the tribune Helvius Cinna for the praetor Cinna. They tore the unfortunate Helvius Cinna to pieces and paraded his head around Caesar's makeshift bier in the Forum (V. Max. 9.9.1).

15. Dio 44.22.1. Velleius states only that Dolabella took up the *fasces* and insignia of consul before the senate meeting at the Temple of Tellus (2.58.3).

16. The consul put on the robes of office, presumably in the Forum, and then processed to the Capitolium with his friends where he was placed on his ceremonial seat of office (*sella curulis*) and supervised the sacrifice of oxen. He then convened the first senate meeting of the year, which was held in the Temple of Jupiter Optimus Maximus. We should note, however, that the descriptions of this ceremony in our sources and the scholarly discussion focus on the installation of a consul on 1 January, not on a suffect consul, as Dolabella was (Ov. *Fast.* 1.79–86; Marshall 1984, 133). Versnel (1970, 302–3) describes the ceremony of the installation of a consul on 1 January, following Mommsen (Röm. *StR*[3]. 1.615–18; cf. 1.414–16; Wissowa 1912, 126). It is not clear if a suffect consul underwent the same ceremony in every detail. One aspect of the ceremony—the convening of the senate for its first meeting of the year in the Temple of Jupiter Optimus Maximus—could not have taken place when a suffect was installed. Otherwise, one would expect the other aspects of the ceremony to have been in place.

17. Dio 43.14.3, although he does not give the total number of lictors.

18. Dio 44.4.3; Weinstock 1971, 106, 110.

19. Cic. *Pis.* 73; cf. *Marc.* 14 and *de Orat.* 3.167. Vergil calls the Roman people the *gens togata* (*Aen.* 1.282). As part of his longer discussion on proper delivery in oratory (*actio*), Quintilian describes in some detail the care that an orator should take over how he wears his toga (Quint. *Inst.* 11.3.137–49). Consequently, the changing of one's clothes to dirty and disheveled rags was intended to evoke the pity of onlookers (on this practice, see Lintott 1968, 16–20).

20. Appian and Dio often include such speeches as a way of analyzing the issues surrounding a significant historical development or the character of the speaker. For a comparison of speeches in Appian and Dio, see Gowing 1992, 225–45.

21. Cic. *Fam.* 12.22.2: *Spes tamen una est, aliquando populum Romanum maiorum similem fore.*

22. Crawford 1974, nos. 433/1 and 2. Brutus' mother, Servilia, was descended from Servilius Ahala (*Plut.* Brut. 1.5; Cic. *Phil.* 2.26; *Att.* 13.40.1). (For the story of Ahala and Maelius, see Cic. *Cat.* 1.1.3; Liv. 4.13–14.) For the mythology of Brutus' ancestry, see Evans 1992, 145–48.

23. The story of L. Brutus fostered other traditions as well. In the weeks leading up to the Ides of March, as Caesar's dictatorship was becoming increasingly intolerable, we are told that graffiti appeared on a statue of L. Brutus and on the praetor's tribunal of M. Brutus, chiding him for not measuring up to his distinguished ancestor (Plut. *Brut.* 9.5–7; App. *BC* 2.112.469; Dio 44.12.2–3; cf. Nic. Dam. 19.61 [*FrGH* 90, F130]).

24. App. *BC* 2.122.514; Powell (2002) argues further that Sextus adopted a strategy that evoked the career of his father.

25. Liv. 116; V. Max. 5.7.2; Suet. *Jul.* 79–80; Plut. *Caes.* 61.4–5; *Ant.* 12.7; App. *BC* 2.108; Dio 44.9.3, 46.49.2; cf. Vell. 2.68.4–5.

26. Tribunician power included the *ius auxili* and *provocatio*—the right to seek refuge with the tribune of the *plebs* and the right to appeal a magistrate's decision directly to the people—as well as the tribunician veto (*intercessio*); Mouritsen 2001, 10; cf. Raaflaub 1974, 173–74.

27. In Livy's famous account of the Decemvirate (3.33–42), the tragic story of Verginia (3.44–49), and the subsequent actions taken to guarantee protection of the people, we see the origins of these popular ideals. At this time, the *ius auxili* and *provocatio* were called bastions for the defense of freedom (*arces libertatis tuendae*). Cf. also the coinage of P. Porcius Laeca (dated 110 or 109 BC) on the reverse of which is a scene depicting a Roman warrior wearing a cuirass and armed with a sword, standing left, and placing his hand on the head of a togate figure; behind him is a lictor holding *fasces*. This depiction celebrated the *Lex Porcia de provocatione*, which gave a Roman citizen residing outside the city right of appeal in criminal cases (Crawford 1974, no. 301; cf. *BMCRR* 2.301, with n. 1).

28. Pina Polo 1996, 160–61.

29. For a discussion of *libertas*, see Wirszubski 1960; Brunt 1988, 327–34; Bleicken 1962; cf. Hellegouarc'h 1963, 549.

30. Cic. *Sest.* 103; cf. *Planc.* 11; Yakobson 1995.

31. Clodius' *lex de collegiis* in 58 overturned a senatorial decree of 64 severely restricting the formation of *collegia* and thus brought renewed freedom to the Roman people (Rotondi 1912, 393).

32. Yavetz 1969, 63.

33. Cic. *Att.* 8.13.2: *Multum mecum municipales homines loquuntur, multum rusticani; nihil prorsus aliud curant nisi agros, nisi villulas, nisi nummulos suos.*

34. Cf. Q. Metellus Scipio's propaganda in Utica in 46: he spoke only of the liberation of the senate and people without making any material promises (Dio 43.5.3–4; Gelzer 1968a, 267). Catilina, when he was exhorting his followers, made an appeal to freedom (*vindicamus in libertatem*), but they demanded more tangible rewards, and Catilina promised that they would receive them (Sal. *Cat.* 21.1).

35. Plut. *TG* 9.6: . . . κύριοι τῆς οἰκουμένης εἶναι λεγόμενοι, μίαν δὲ βῶλον ἰδίαν οὐκ ἐχόντες.

36. Cic. *Tusc.* 3.20.48.

37. Cic. *Att.* 10.4.8; App. *BC* 2.41.164; Dio 41.17.1–2.

38. Gel. 11.10.2–6; cf. Millar 1986, 8–9; Sal. *Jug.* 31.

39. *ORF*², fr. 28 (Gel. 15.12.4).

40. Cic. *Man.* 14–19. Cicero's speech against Rullus' agrarian legislation included similar rhetoric: the *rogatio* included a provision for selling off the *ager Campanus*, a fertile region that provided much revenue for the city. The passage of this bill, Cicero argued, would effectively dry up this important resource (Cic. *Agr.* 2.79–81).

41. For this meeting, see Cic. *Phil.* 1.31; *Att.* 16.14.1; App. *BC* 2.126–129; Plut. *Brut.* 19.1; Dio 44.22.3; Frisch 1946, 51–56; Bonnefond-Coudry 1989, 132–36.

42. Appian (*BC* 2.126.525) presumes that the Curia was available for this meet-

ing, although, as demonstrated earlier, it is likely that the Curia Hostilia had already been demolished and the Curia Julia not yet completed.

43. Dio 48.38.2. On the location of the home, see Suet. *Gram.* 15; cf. Serv. *A.* 8.361; Palombi 1997, 137–46; Richardson 1992, 378–79; Bonnefond-Coudry 1989, 132–36. Antonius had purchased this home at the auction of confiscated property that was held by Caesar (Cic. *Phil.* 2.62).

44. Bonnefond-Coudry 1989, 132. Other features of the temple are worth noting. Its construction was connected with the death of Sp. Cassius, who had been accused and later condemned of aspiring to monarchy (in 485) (Cic. *Dom.* 101; Liv. 2.41.11; D. H. 8.79.3; V. Max. 6.3.1b). According to one of the variant traditions, the Temple of Tellus was built on the site of Cassius' home on the occasion of its destruction by vote of the Roman people (D. H. 8.79.3; V. Max. 6.3.1b). Thus, the temple had associations with the concept of *libertas*. In fact, in a later period, when Sulla marched on Rome in 88, it was from this temple that Marius promised freedom to any slaves who joined him in resisting Sulla (Plut. *Sull.* 9.14). Another tradition of the vowing of this temple places it squarely in the context of the unification of Italy. Namely, that Temple of Tellus was vowed by P. Sempronius Sophus during a battle with the Picenes in 268, when there was an earthquake (Flor. *Epit.* 1.14.2). Since, however, there is weighty evidence that the temple was founded soon after the death of Sp. Cassius in 485, the vow of Sempronius most likely concerned the rebuilding of the temple, not its original construction (Richardson 1992, 378). What's more, according to Varro, there was a map or metaphorical representation of Italia on a wall of this temple (Var. *R.* 1.2.1).

45. Cic. *Att.*. 15.20.2: *Quod ais extrema quaedam iam homines de re publica loqui et eos quidem viros bonos, ego quo die audivi illum tyrannum in contione clarissimum virum appellari, subdiffidere coepi.*

46. Cic. *Att.* 14.11.1: *Cum [equidem] contionem lego de 'tanto viro', de 'clarissimo civi' ferre non queo.*

47. Motzo 1940, 136–41. *Contra* D-G[2] 1.419, who suggest rather that Cicero is referring to Antonius' *laudatio* at Caesar's funeral. But if Cicero had meant the *laudatio*, he likely would have referred to it as such (as he does elsewhere; *Phil.* 2.91), not as a *contio*.

48. From another letter of Cicero, in which he recounts a conversation with an unnamed Caesarian, he makes it clear that such praise of Caesar as a most distinguished man had become a theme (ὑπόθεσις) of the ideology of the Caesarians (Cic. *Att.* 14.22.1). This theme was repeated by C. Matius in his famous letter in defense of his own actions after the Ides of March (Cic. *Fam.* 11.28.5: *vir amplissimus*).

49. Antonius may have had a legitimate right to fear for his life since he barely escaped the mêlée on 15 March (Plut. *Brut.* 18.3; cf. 20.2; Dio 44.19.2). On the other hand, charges of assassination attempts were common in the late Republic, and they often provoked sympathetic reactions from the Roman people. Cicero wore a breastplate when he conducted the consular elections at which Catilina was a candidate. In 59 Vatinius allowed Vettius to speak in a *contio* at which he confessed to an assassination attempt against Caesar and Pompeius under the orders of Cicero, Bibulus, and Cato (Cic. *Vat.* 24). The people surrounded Caesar to protect him against possible attack. In 52, at one of the many *contiones* held to denounce Milo, Pompeius appeared

before the people and expressed his fear that an attempt would be made on his life (Asc. 38C). Later in the year, Antonius accused Octavian of plotting to assassinate him (Cic. *Fam.* 12.23.2; Nic. Dam. 30.123–24 [*FrGH* 90, F130]).

50. App. *BC* 2.130.544. For this oath among Caesar's other extraordinary honors, see App. *BC* 2.106.442.

51. Cicero (*Att.* 14.22.1) reports his conversation with some of Caesar's supporters who viewed Caesar's *clementia* as his undoing.

52. Roman generals, for instance, were expected to exercise mercy toward a conquered enemy; see, e.g., Anchises' statement of Rome's destiny to Aeneas: *parcere subiectis* (Verg. *Aen.* 6.853); the *clementia* of P. Scipio Africanus was legendary (Vell. 1.12.5).

53. Weinstock 1971, 235–36.

54. Cicero dubbed it "*clementia Corfiniensis*" (*Att.* 9.16.1). For Caesar *clementia* was an especially important virtue because it allowed him to distance himself from the example of Sulla, whose *crudelitas* was legendary, and from Pompeius, who even Cicero attests aspired to emulate Sulla (Cic. *Att.* 8.11.2; 8.16.2; 9.7c.3: *Gnaeus noster Sullani regni similitudinem concupivit*; 9.10.6; 10.7.1).

55. Sear 1998, no. 110, with his comments, p. 76.

56. Weinstock 1971, 241.

57. In Appian's account (*BC* 2.131.548), Lepidus states that he stood with Caesar on the Rostra "yesterday" (χθές), which was of course impossible since Caesar had been killed two days before this *contio* took place.

58. Taylor 1966, 46–47.

59. On the memory of the conspirators, see Rawson 1986.

60. Cic. *Fam.* 9.17.2 seems to corroborate this, in which Cicero expresses his concern that he might lose one of his villas. According to our sources, however, the bulk of Caesar's settlements took place overseas (*MRR*, 2.294).

61. Cf. Tac. *Ann.* 14.27.3, who describes this same mode of settlement. Cf. also Brunt 1971a, 294–300. However, the previous cultivators were not necessarily displaced, for, if they were owners, *possessores* (of *ager publicus*), tenants, or laborers, they might continue on as tenants or laborers under the new *coloni*.

62. App. *BC* 2.142.593. Cicero claims that this *contio* was well attended (*Phil.* 1.32; cf. sections 2 and 31).

CHAPTER 4

1. As Appian has Antonius remind Octavian at their first meeting (*BC* 3.18.68).

2. For the events covered in this chapter, see D-G^2 1.71–80; Becht 1911; Rice Holmes 1928, 1.2–12; Frisch 1946, 56–81.

3. Cf. Flor. *Epit.* 2.15.1: *Prima civilium motuum causa testamentum Caesaris fuit, cuius secundus heres Antonius, praelatum sibi Octavium furens, inexpiabile contra adoptionem acerrimi iuvenis susceperat bellum.* "The principal cause of the civil conflict was Caesar's will, since Antonius, named heir in the second degree, was enraged that Octavius had been preferred to himself, and he undertook an implacable war to show his opposition to the adoption of so cruel a young man." Florus is perhaps exaggerating the importance of Caesar's will as the cause of the civil war; nonetheless this shows the

importance of wills as expressions of the most intimate sentiments of the deceased (cf. Champlin 1991, 1). Caesar's earlier wills, down to the beginning of the first civil war, named Pompeius heir, which Caesar made a point of announcing to his soldiers in a *contio* (Suet. *Jul.* 83.1–2), no doubt to show how greatly he esteemed his former son-in-law and the depth of Pompeius' betrayal.

4. Cf. App. *BC* 3.19.72 (Antonius speaking to Octavian): "you imply that I also covet political mastery. This is not so, although I am regarded as not unworthy of it. You imply too that I resent not being Caesar's heir, yet you admit my descent from Heracles is quite good enough for me."

5. Cf. Deutsch 1928, 199; although we should note the testimony of Nicolaus, who states that Caesar treated young Octavius as his son on more than one occasion (8.17 and 11.24 [*FrGH* 90, F127]).

6. According to what Balbus told Cicero (*illum hereditatem aditurum*) (Cic. *Att.* 14.10.3). Nicolaus (18.54 (*FrGH* 90, F130) tells us that as soon as Octavius heard of his adoption, he was determined to accept the inheritance, despite the admonition of his stepfather, Philippus (cf. App. *BC* 3.11.36–37).

7. On the knotty issue of testamentary adoption, see Champlin 1991, 144–46; Weinrib 1967; Schmitthenner 1973, 39–44; Syme 1982; Kunst 1996. I follow here the views of Champlin.

8. Champlin 1991, 145–46.

9. The best discussion of Caesar's funeral remains that of Weinstock 1971, 346–55.

10. On the date, see D-G[2] 1.417.

11. This was an honor reserved for a man who had performed a signal service to the state, although there were apparently no concrete criteria for its bestowal. Hug, s.v. "funus publicum," *RE* Suppl. 3 (1918), 530–33; Vollmer, 1892; Wesch-Klein 1993 collects some later examples; see also Flower 1996, 96, with n. 28.

12. Nic. Dam. 17.48 (*FrGH* 90, F130). This practice was not unusual; e.g., Scipio Africanus (Liv. 38.53.8) and Augustus (Suet. *Aug.* 101.4; Dio 56.33.1) planned their own funerals. See also Trimalchio's funeral (Petr. 71); although this is satire, the humor is effective only if Trimalchio was thought to be parodying Roman aristocrats. Cf. Champlin 1991, 169.

13. According to M. Brutus, Philippus later lent less support to Octavian than did Cicero (Cic. *ad Brut.* 1.17.5, dated to the year 43).

14. Toynbee 1971, 44.

15. The assassins abandoned Caesar's body where it had fallen, and some loyal slaves conveyed it home (App. *BC* 2.118.498; Nic. Dam. 26.95–97 [*FrGH* 90, F130]; Suet. *Jul.* 82.3); in Nicolaus' version, many people were witness to the slaves as they carried the body to Caesar's house, and lamentations could be heard in the city.

16. In 52 Clodius' body was used in a similar way, especially before his funeral, when his wife, Fulvia, dramatically displayed the wounds that had caused his death, stirring the emotions of the crowd that had gathered (Asc. 32C).

17. Picard 1957, 226. The passage that he cites as evidence for a *pulvinar* in Caesar's honor (Dio 44.6.4), however, does not explicitly mention this honor.

18. The Domus Publica, the headquarters of the Pontifex Maximus, is another possibility, but it is more likely that his body was taken to his villa across the Tiber—a safer place immediately after the assassination—and remained there until his funeral.

19. On *imagines* in general, see Flower 1996.

20. In the *pompa* at Augustus' funeral, there was no bust for Caesar on display since he was a god (Dio 56.34.2); see chapter 9. Also in the *exedrae* of the Forum Augustum, where statues of famous members of the Julian *gens* resided, Caesar was also absent. His place was with Venus and Mars, in the very cella of the temple (Zanker 1988, 211).

21. Cic. *Att.* 14.10.1: *Meministine te clamare causam perisse si funere elatus esset? At ille etiam in foro combustus laudatusque miserabiliter servique et egentes in tecta nostra cum facibus immissi.*

22. Cic. *Phil.* 2.91: *Tua illa pulchra laudatio, tua miseratio, tua cohortatio; tu, tu, inquam, illas faces incendisti, et eas quibus semustilatus ille est. . . .* For the meaning of *cohortatio* as "incitement to anger," see *Rhet. Her.* 3.24.

23. Suet. *Jul.* 84.2. Cf. D-G[2] 1.417–20; Syme 1939, 98, n. 1; Yavetz 1969, 68–69; *contra* Frisch 1946, 60–61; Kennedy 1968.

24. Appian perhaps is preserving in his account the version of the *laudatio* that Suetonius knew.

25. The body apparently remained hidden from view at this point; see App. *BC* 2.147.612.

26. In Dio's version of Antonius' *laudatio* (44.49.4), the consul refers dramatically to the robe at the end of his speech, and we can imagine him punctuating these remarks by holding the robe aloft on the end of a spear.

27. Cicero studied under a Greek named Apollonius Molon, whose theories on oratory Cicero himself never mentions, but Quintilian's description of him suggests that he (i.e., Apollonius) was an Asianist, albeit a moderate one, and judging from what Cicero says in the *Brutus* this Apollonius seems to have influenced him chiefly in the area of delivery (Plut. *Cic.* 4.5–7; Quint. *Inst.* 12.6.7; Cic. *Brut.* 316).

28. App. *BC* 2.146.611: ἐμὲ δὲ καὶ τούσδε περισῶσαι τοὺς κτενοῦντας με. . . . Suetonius mentions this line as well, but he puts it in the mouth of an actor who was performing during the funeral games for Caesar (*Jul.* 84.2: *Men' servasse, ut essent qui me perderent*), but, from what we know, there were no funeral games for Caesar until perhaps those sponsored by Octavian in July (see chap. 5).

29. Suet. *Vesp.* 19.2. As befitted an emperor, the actor who portrayed him was an *archimimus*, the leader of a troupe of mimes. More generally on the phenomenon of funerary mimes, see now Sumi 2002a.

30. Dio's account (44.35.4) contradicts Appian's in that he claims that one of Antonius' first acts during the funeral was to display the corpse with all its wounds.

31. Dio 56.42.3 (on the eagle at Augustus' funeral); cf. Hdn. 4.2; Price 1987, 56–57, 60.

32. Cicero used this custom against Antonius, when he accused him of being overly influenced by actors (*Phil.* 2.62; cf. Sal. *Jug.* 85.39).

33. Cf. Tac. *Ann.* 1.8.6, who describes an edict of Tiberius forbidding for Augustus' funeral (AD 14) the kind of mob violence that had erupted at Caesar's funeral.

34. Cf. Clodius' funeral (Asc. 33C); also, Pliny describes the funeral of one M. Seius (*aed. cur.* 74): *Seius. . . supremo die populi umeris portatus in rogum est* (*Nat.* 18.16); for other instances of such an honor, see Plut. *Num.* 22.1; *Aem.* 39.8; Luc. 8.732.

35. App. *BC* 2.148.615. Pompeius Rufus implied in a *contio* that Pompeius might

deserve to be buried on the Capitolium (Asc. 51C). M. Marcellus (*cos*. 51) was returning to Rome from Mytilene in 45 when he was treacherously murdered in Athens. Ser. Sulpicius Rufus attempted to honor him with burial within the city limits, but the Athenians refused (Cic. *Fam*. 4.12.3). Cf. Lintott 1974, 70, n. 97 (with bibliography). He points out that the honor of burial within the city limits was similarly practiced by Greek hero cults to honor the founders and benefactors of cities.

36. One could argue that the tradition surrounding Poplicola's life is largely mythology, and therefore his funeral and burial can hardly be regarded as a precedent for Caesar's. However, these myths of early Rome helped form opinion in the late Republic. Valerius Antias is one annalist likely responsible for bringing this tradition to a late Republican audience, especially as regards the *gens Valeria*, which tends to dominate his narrative (Ogilvie 1965, 12–16; Walsh 1961, 121).

37. For notice of his death, see Liv. 2.16.7; for burial near the Velia, see D. H. 5.48.3; Plut. *Publ*. 23.5 (Plutarch also records the interesting custom of this branch of the Valerian *gens*: all of Poplicola's descendants were given the honor of being buried near the Velia, but none actually were; instead, when a member of this family died, the body was conveyed to this place, and a lighted torch was placed under the bier for an instant to indicate that he had the right to burial there but was refusing it); cf. Richardson 1992, 140. One of the laws of the Twelve Tables later prohibited burial within the city limits.

38. On their appearance after the battle of Lake Regillus, see Cic. *N.D*. 2.6; 3.11; D. H. 6.13.1–3; V. Max. 1.8.1; Plut. *Cor*. 3.5–6; *Aem*. 25.2–3; Flor. *Epit*. 1.5.4.

39. Dio 44.50.4; App. *BC* 2.147.614; Suet. *Jul*. 85; Plut. *Caes*. 68.2.

40. Yavetz 1969, 69.

41. Frisch 1946, 63.

42. On these events, see Yavetz 1969, 58–74.

43. He is variously called Amatius (Liv. 116), Herophilus (V. Max. 9.15.1), or Marius (Cic. *Att*. 14.6.1).

44. Cic. *Att*. 14.6.1, dated 12 April, provides the first testimony of his presence in Rome. He was more of a concern to Cicero at this time than Octavius: *Nam de Octavio, susque deque. exspecto quid de Mario; quem quidem ego sublatum rebar a Caesare*. "[A]s far as Octavius is concerned, it is neither here nor there. I am awaiting news about Marius—I thought Caesar had removed him."

45. On the use of the *collegia* for these purposes, see Vanderbroeck 1987, 112–13, 167–69; Tatum 1999, 25–26, 117–19, 146; Benner 1987, 65–71; Nippel 1995, 82.

46. Suet. *Jul*. 85. It should be noted that Amatius does not appear in Suetonius' account. It is possible that Suetonius was relying on official imperial records, from which the role of Amatius had been utterly excised. Cicero (*Att*. 14.15.1) also calls this monument a *columna*, but Brutus and Cassius (*Fam*. 11.2.2) refer to it as an altar (*ara*). On this monument, see Weinstock 1971, 364–67; Taylor 1931, 83–85.

47. See figure 2. Figure 3 shows the Temple of Divus Julius, which was constructed at the approximate location of the *columna Caesaris*.

48. Cic. *Att*. 14.5.1. Precisely what they were conspiring to do, and who their leaders were, is not mentioned, although it is possible that Amatius was responsible for this as well, since Caesar's freedmen would have turned to a leader who could claim a special tie with the dead dictator.

49. Yavetz 1969, 71.

50. Cic. *Phil.* 1.5; App. *BC* 3.3.6; V. Max. 9.15.1: *iussu patrum necatus in carcere*; cf. Cic. *Att.* 14.8.1. Appian claims that Antonius did this to protect the conspirators, which fits with his general policy of supporting the amnesty (Frisch 1946, 64).

51. The use of troops became a common means of crowd control during this period (Nippel 1995, 83). Appian further asserts that the *plebs* demanded that the magistrates dedicate an altar to Caesar and, in place of Amatius, offer the first sacrifices (*BC* 3.3.7).

52. Cic. *Att.* 14.11.1; Motzo 1940.

53. These games had been used for political demonstrations previously under the supervision of P. Clodius (Cic. *Har.* 22–26); see also chapter 5.

54. See Canetti 1962 for a modern analysis of crowd behavior; cf. Sumi 1997 for an attempt to apply this analysis to an ancient crowd.

55. This dilemma shows through in Cicero's letters (e.g., *Att.* 14.6.2).

56. Cic. *Fam.* 11.1. There is no general agreement on the dating of this letter. Groebe (D-G[2] 1.411–14) opts for 16 March; Schmidt 1884, 334–37, argues for the morning of 17 March before the meeting at the Temple of Tellus, which Decimus does not mention. Shackleton Bailey 1977, 2.463–64, too, prefers 17 March, but immediately after the senate meeting at the Temple of Tellus. All seem too early. Before the senate meeting, the conspirators remained together on the Capitolium, making such a letter unnecessary. Immediately after the meeting, the amnesty agreed upon created an atmosphere of calm (albeit briefly), while the reconciliation was celebrated at a *contio* (see chap. 3). Watt (1982, 340), with whom I am in agreement, proposes a date no more than a few days after Caesar's funeral (which took place around 20 March). Frisch 1946, 69–71, dates this letter to April.

57. Cicero mentions a meeting between Antonius and the conspirators in a letter dated 12 April (*Att.* 14.6.1); another letter (dated 16 April) implies that Antonius was cooperating with the conspirators (*Att.* 14.8.1).

58. Cic. *Att.* 14.5.2 [dated 11 April]; 14.6.1 [dated 12 April].

59. Cic. *Att.* 14.7.1 [relating a conversation Cicero had with Paulus on 14 April].

60. The later sources provide no more detailed account of the conspirators' departure from Rome. All describe their sudden departure as a response to the anger of the urban *plebs* (Plut. *Brut.* 21.1; App. *BC* 3.6.18; Dio 44.51.4).

61. This is an inference from Dio (43.51.3), who states that Caesar created, in addition to the existing four aediles (two curule and two plebeian), two plebeian aediles who took their titles from Ceres.

62. Rice Holmes 1928, 1.191; see chapter 5 for a full discussion.

63. Cic. *Att.* 14.14.1; 14.19.3; cf. Dio 45.6.4; for the young Cicero's support of Caesar, see also *Att.* 14.17.3.

64. Lamia was involved in the preparations for the *Ludi Romani* in September of 45 BC (*Att.* 13.45.1). Cicero also mentions a *munus* that Lamia was eager to sponsor during his aedileship, but it is not clear if he is referring to these or other games (*Fam.* 11.17.1).

65. Cic. *Att.* 14.19.3: *De coronatis, cum sororis tuae filius a patre accusatus esset, rescripsit se coronam habuisse honoris Caesaris causa, posuisse luctus gratia; postremo se libenter vituperationem subire quod amaret etiam mortuum Caesarem.*

66. Weinstock 1971, 367.

67. This was much to the delight of Cicero (*Att.* 14.15.1; cf. *Att.* 14.16.2; *Fam.* 12.1.1), who feared that this popular furor eventually would be dangerous to the conspirators. Cicero refers to this episode frequently in his letters (e.g., *Att.* 14.17a; 14.19.1; cf. 14.18.1).

68. Richardson 1992, 377–78, following mainly Liv. 6.20.12.

69. Nippel 1995, 9–10; Thommen 1989, 187–88.

70. E.g., C. Atinius Labeo Macerio (*tr. pl.* 131) threatened to throw from the Tarpeian rock the censor Q. Metellus, who had stricken his name from the list of senators in the previous year (Cic. *Dom.* 123; Liv. 59; Plin. *Nat.* 7.143; cf. *MRR*, 1.500–501); M. Livius Drusus (*tr. pl.* 91) threatened the same against Servilius Caepio (*pr.* 91?) (Auct. *Vir. Ill.* 66.8 and 13; cf. Cic. *Dom.* 120; Plin. *Nat.* 28.148; *MRR*, 2.24, n. 5).

CHAPTER 5

1. For the events in this period, see D-G² 1.81–90; Becht 1911 (until 1 June; for events from 1–30 June, see Ehrenwirth 1971, 5–44); Rice Holmes 1928, 1.13–18; Syme 1939, 98–117; Frisch 1946, 63–92.

2. Suet. *Aug.* 8.1; Quint. *Inst.* 12.6.1. Nic. Dam. 3.4 (*FrGH* 90, F127) puts his age at nine for his first public speech but does not mention the occasion.

3. Suet. *Aug.* 8.1; Nic. Dam. 4.8 (*FrGH* 90, F127) puts his age as fourteen when he assumed the *toga virilis;* for the date of the ceremony, see *CIL* 10.8375.

4. Nic. Dam. 4.9 (*FrGH* 90, F127): περιβλεπόμενος δ' ὑπὸ παντὸς τοῦ δήμου.

5. Most scholars accept the year 48 for Octavian's election to the pontificate, e.g., Beard, North, and Price 1998, 1.186; Southern 1998, 12–13; Gardthausen 1891, 1.48. The exception is Broughton (*MRR* 2.292), who puts it in 47.

6. Beard, North, and Price 1998, 1.135–36.

7. Szemler 1972, 21–24; Wissowa 1912, 501–23.

8. Nic. Dam. 5.13 (*FrGH* 90, F127). Another tradition had it that Octavian was *magister equitum* in this year (App. *BC* 3.9.30; Dio 43.51.7; Plin. *Nat.* 7.147). But Gardthausen showed that it was possible especially for the later Greek sources to confuse the Greek terms for the two offices (1891, 1.48), and Gesche (1973) has argued convincingly that Octavian was not Caesar's master of horse. On the office of *praefectus urbi* in general, see *Rom. StR*³, 1.661–74. On the expansion of this office under Caesar, see Dio 43.48.1–4; Yavetz 1983, 122–26. In 34 BC Octavian appointed sons of *equites* as prefects of the city for the Latin festival (Dio 49.42.1).

9. Cf. Dio 43.48.2; *Rom. StR*³, 1.664, 672. Yavetz avers that it was a "meaningless office" (1983, 124).

10. Nic. Dam. 8.17 (*FrGH* 90, F127): . . . τὸν νέον . . . υἱὸν ἤδη πεποιημένος.

11. The primary sources for Octavian's return are Nic. Dam. 18.51–57 (*FrGH* 90, F130); App. *BC* 3.10.35–12; Dio 45.3.1; cf. Vell. 2.60.1. Also, on Octavian's return, in addition to the scholarship cited here in n. 1, see Gotter 1996, 56–65; Southern 1998, 22–32.

12. Nic. Dam. 16.38 (*FrGH* 90, F130): ἀγνοεῖν γὰρ ἔφη καὐτὴ [sc. Atia] τἀπὸ τοῦδε ἐσόμενα· δεῖν δὲ ἤδη ἄνδρα γίγνεσθαι καὶ γνώμηι τε ἃ χρὴ φρονεῖν καὶ ἔργωι πράττειν ἑπόμενον τῆι τύχηι τε καὶ τοῖς καιποῖς.

13. Other sources confirm the basic outline of this narrative: Octavian crossed to Italy without full knowledge of the conspiracy and the political situation in Rome or, more importantly, of the contents of Caesar's will (App. *BC* 3.9.32; Dio 45.3.1–2).

14. Gotter 1996, 57.

15. Nic. Dam. 18.53 (*FrGH* 90, F130): ὁ δὲ Καῖσαρ ᾔδει μὲν ὑπ᾽ εὐνοίας ταῦτα παραινοῦντα, ἐγίνωσκε δὲ τἀναντία, μεγάλα ἐπινοῶν ἤδη καὶ φρονήματος μεστὸς ὤν, ποιούμενος δὲ ἴδια πόνον καὶ κίνδυνον ἢ ἀνδρῶν ἀπέχφειαν, οἷς οὐκ ἔμελλεν ἀρεστὸς φανεῖσθαι, <εἰ> τοσοῦδε ὀνόματος καὶ ἀρχῆς παραχωρήσειεν ὁτῳοῦν. . . . Cf. Hall 1923, 83.

16. As Syme noted (1939, 113); cf. Alföldi 1976, 9–11.

17. L. Cornelius Balbus and C. Oppius are two notables; on their efforts in Octavian's behalf, see esp. Alföldi 1976, 31–54.

18. These were the *coloniae* from which Octavian recruited soldiers in the autumn of 44 (Cic. *Att.* 16.8.1–2; cf. *Phil.* 2.102; Vell. 2.61.2; App. *BC* 3.40.165). Caesar settled a total of fifteen to twenty thousand veteran soldiers from his Gallic campaigns (Brunt 1971a, 322–26). Cf. Dio (45.12.2), who claims that most of Octavian's recruits came from Capua.

19. Gotter (1996, 64) suggests 6 or 7 May; Becht (1911, 56–57) dates his arrival to 8 or 9 May; Yavetz (1969, 73) suggests 11 May. The *terminus ante quem* of his arrival was 11 May since Cicero heard of his *contio* by this date (*Att.* 14.20.5).

20. Vell. 2.59.6 [Woodman's text]: *Cui adventanti Romam inmanis amicorum occurrit frequentia, et cum intraret urbem, solis orbis super caput eius curvatus aequaliter circumdatusque <vers>icolor arcus, velut coronam tanti mox viri capiti imponens, conspectus est;* "When Octavian arrived a large crowd of his friends met him, and when he entered the city, there was seen above his head the orb of the sun in a perfect circle and around his head a multi-colored arc, as though a crown was placed on the head of a man soon to be great." Cf. Plin. *Nat.* 2.98; Sen. *Nat.* 1.2.1; Suet. *Aug.* 95, who adds that the tomb of Caesar's daughter Julia was struck by lightning; Oros. 6.20.5; Obseq. 68 (Rossbach); Dio 45.4.4.

21. Preserved in Suet. *Aug.* 94.4; Dio 45.1.2.

22. Kleinstück 1932, 244; cf. Woodman 1983, 119.

23. Postdating Octavian's arrival to early May, as I have done, does not undermine Kleinstück's thesis. For the time of day when Octavian arrived, see Oros. 6.20.5; Obseq. 68 (Rossbach).

24. Liv. 116 fr. 47 (Serv. G. 1.472); see also Ramsey and Licht 1997, 99–107.

25. Gotter 1996, 64. The fact that L. Antonius and Dolabella had both recently given speeches at *contiones*, only one of which (Dolabella's) Cicero approved, might indicate a growing rivalry between the two men (Cic. *Att.* 14.20.2) and lend further credence to Gotter's suggestion.

26. Dio mentions a *contio* in the context of the games in honor of Venus Genetrix (20–30 July) and Octavian's aborted stand for the tribunate (undatable, but probably about the same time). In this *contio*, convened by the tribune of the *plebs* Ti. Cannutius, Octavian proclaimed amid other promises that he would honor his father's bequests to the people. Dio further claims that these bequests were only a pretext (πρόφασις) so that Octavian could address the people (45.6.3).

27. According to Appian (*BC* 3.14.49), Octavian entered the Forum attended by many friends and a large crowd, a display for which he had hoped and had even

encouraged. Dio, on the other hand, states that Octavian arrived with little fanfare and a small entourage (45.5.2), an example of the young man's political astuteness that belied his years. Thus, we do not know for certain who accompanied him, or in what numbers. Nonetheless, these divergent descriptions of Octavian's entry into the Forum are further evidence that such events were examined as indicators of a politician's motives and ambitions.

28. We shall discuss in chapter 7 the arrival of Octavian from Caesar's colonies in November, which happened to coincide with the *Ludi Plebeii*.

29. App. *BC* 3.28.105–6. On Critonius' aedileship, see Ryan 2000.

30. Taylor 1931, 87, n. 15; *MRR*, 2.322–23. *Contra* Hall 1923, 92, n. 3. Other possibilities are the *Ludi Apollinares* (6–13 July) and the *Ludi Florales* (27 April–3 May). The *Ludi Apollinares* can be eliminated immediately because they came under the jurisdiction of the praetor urbanus, which precluded the involvement of the aedile Critonius. The *Ludi Florales* were impossible too since we know that Antonius was away from Rome at this time and would not have been available to hear Octavian's appeal. Rice Holmes (1928, 1.190–91) asserts that Antonius departed Rome between 22–29 April. He was back in Rome by mid-May. Another suggestion is the *Ludi Martiales* (Alföldi 1953, 77), but these games were not instituted until much later (Ov. *Fast.* 5.597; cf. Weinstock 1971, 368; Bernstein 1998, 346, n. 207).

31. Wissowa 1912, 192–97; Latte 1960, 69–72, 101, 161–62; Radke 1965, 86–91.

32. Rice Holmes 1928, 1.191; Syme 1939, 116 n. 3. This hypothesis finds corroboration in a letter of Cicero's dated 22 May, in which he mentions another episode involving Caesar's *sella*, although he says nothing about the aedile Critonius (Cic. *Att.* 15.3.2); Shackleton Bailey (1967, 6.248) believes that Cicero is referring to the production of the *Ludi Ceriales* in April. But if we assume that Cicero was responding to Atticus' news about recent developments and not to something that had occurred a month previously, then the event under discussion must have taken place at a recent festival. But since none was on the calendar, we must assume the postponement of the *Ludi Ceriales*.

33. An analogous situation occurred in 216 BC, when, following the battle of Cannae (2 August), the streets of Rome were filled with so many mourners that an annual rite (*sacrum anniversarium*) in honor of Ceres had to be canceled (Liv. 22.56.4). Because of the date this could not be the *Ludi Ceriales*, but it is noteworthy that under extraordinary circumstances such rites could be canceled.

34. For Antonius' trip, see Cic. *Att.* 14.21.2 (dated 11 May).

35. Cic. *Phil.* 2.108: *Qui vero inde reditus Romam, quae perturbatio totius urbis! Memineramus Cinnam nimis potentem, Sullam postea dominantem, modo Caesarem regnantem videramus. Erant fortasse gladii, sed absconditi nec ita multi. Ista vero quae et quanta barbaria est! Agmine quadrato cum gladiis sequuntur; scutorum lecticas portari videmus. Atque his quidem iam inveteratis, patres conscripti, consuetudine obduruimus.*

36. Cic. *Phil.* 3.27; 5.21; the precise context is not clear. See the discussion later in this chapter.

37. Antonius' second return to Rome, in November of 44, was described by Cicero in much the same way (*Phil.* 3.3: *crudelis et pestifer reditus*; cf. *Phil.* 4.3).

38. Jos. *AJ* 14.10.10; cf. Cic. *Att.* 14.9.3, which contains a laconic remark about Balbus providing better news about Gaul (*idem Balbus meliora de Gallia*).

39. Cic. *Fam.* 11.1.4. Cicero frequently asked Atticus for news regarding Sextus

from the time he first left Rome on 7 April (*Att.* 14.1.2; 14.4.1; 14.8.2; cf. 14.13.2).

40. App. *BC* 3.8; Dio 45.9.3. For the date of the allotment of these provinces, see Frisch 1946, 72 (with n. 41), and Rice-Holmes 1928, 1.188–90; cf. also Schwartz 1898.

41. Dio 38.1–8; cf. Cic. *Att.* 2.16.2; 2.21.5.

42. We know from a letter of Cicero (*Att.* 15.4.2) that Atticus was to meet Cicero at Tusculum on 27 May and from there they would proceed to Lanuvium. (Atticus apparently arrived on 30 May [*Att.* 15.8.1].) From a later letter (dated 20 June), we also know that Cicero and Atticus met with the "heroes" at Lanuvium, and the former despaired because he felt that Brutus and Cassius were relying too much on Antonius for their safety (*Att.* 15.20.2; cf. Frisch 1946, 91). This despair may have been the result of a meeting of the conspirators with Cicero and Atticus at Lanuvium on 30 May to discuss their response to Antonius' continued position of authority. We have a letter from the conspirators to Antonius that can be dated to May, asking whether they would be safe in Rome when rumor had brought news of large numbers of troops gathering in the city. Word that the veterans were thinking of reerecting Caesar's altar was even more disturbing (Cic. *Fam.* 11.2.2; for the date of this letter, see Watt 1982, 1.341).

43. Trans. Carter 1996, 171, with n. 31; App. *BC* 3.30.117–18: ἐλθούσης δὲ τῆς κυρίας ἡμέρας ἡ μὲν βουλὴ τὴν λοχῖτιν ἐνόμιζεν ἐκκλησίαν συλλεγήσεσθαι, οἳ δὲ νυκτὸς ἔτι τὴν ἀγορὰν περισχοινισάμενοι τὴν φυλέτιν ἐκάλουν, ἀπὸ συνθήματος ἐληλυθυῖαν. καὶ ὁ δημότης λεώς, ἀχθόμενος τῷ Ἀντωνίῳ, συνέπρασσεν ὅμως διὰ τὸν Καίσαρα ἐφεστῶτα τοῖς περισχοινίσμασι καὶ δεόμενον.

44. Cic. *Phil.* 1.19; Yavetz 1983, 108–9.

45. The date of 2 June (a.d. IIII Non. Iun.) is confirmed by Cic. *Att.* 16.16C.2. An earlier letter, *Att.* 15.11.4, describes Cicero's appointment to Dolabella's staff on 3 June.

46. This is the approach adopted by Frisch 1946, 94–104. The secondary sources, as Frisch points out, are very little help in reconstructing the legislation that was passed since they often contradict each other or compress the events of several months into a short narrative. See also Rotondi 1912, 432–34.

47. Liv. 117; Rotondi 1912, 432.

48. Cic. *Att.* 15.12.2; cf. Sternkopf 1912a; Rotondi 1912, 433–34; Frisch 1946, 96.

49. The people of Buthrotum in Epirus had apparently failed to pay a levy in full and as a penalty their land—the land of Atticus' neighbors—had been scheduled for distribution under Caesar's colonization program. Cicero intervened; Atticus paid the outstanding sum out of his own pocket and received a favorable response from Caesar (Cic. *Att.* 16.16A.2–4), but apparently the issue had not been entirely resolved since Caesar's intervening death caused further trouble (Shackleton Bailey 1967, no. 243.1 (12.7.1), 304–5; Ramsey 1994.

50. Cic. *Phil.* 1.6: *Ecce enim Kalendis Iuniis, quibus ut adessemus edixerant, mutata omnia: nihil per senatum, multa et magna per populum et absente populo et invito. . . .*

51. Cic. *Phil.* 1.25: *Neglegimus ista* [i.e. the possibility of his legislation being vetoed by the tribunes of the *plebs*] *et nimis antiqua ac stulta ducimus: forum saepietur; omnes claudentur aditus; armati in praesidiis multis locis collocabuntur.*

52. Cic. *Phil.* 2.109: *Qui chirographa Caesaris defendisset lucri sui causa, is leges Cae-*

saris easque praeclaras, ut rem publicam concutere posset, evertit. Numerum annorum provinciis prorogavit; idemque, cum actorum Caesaris defensor esse deberet, et in publicis et in privatis rebus acta Caesaris rescidit. . . . leges alias sine promulgatione sustulit, alias ut tolleret promulgavit.

53. Cic. *Phil.* 3.27: *Etenim in contione dixerat se custodem fore urbis, seque usque ad Kalendas Maias ad urbem exercitum habiturum. O praeclarum custodem ovium, ut aiunt, lupum! Custosne urbis an direptor et vexator esset Antonius? Et quidem se introiturum in urbem dixit exiturumque cum vellet. Quid illud? Nonne audiente populo sedens pro aede Castoris dixit, nisi qui vicisset, victurum neminem?*

54. Cic. *Phil.* 5.21: M. *vero Antonium quis est qui civem possit iudicare potius quam taeterrimum et crudelissimum hostem, qui pro aede Castoris sedens audiente populo Romano dixerit nisi victorem victurum neminem? Num putatis, patres conscripti, dixisse eum minacius quam facturum fuisse? Quid vero quod in contione dicere ausus est, se, cum magistratu abisset, ad urbem futurum cum exercitu, introiturum quotienscumque vellet?*

55. Frisch 1946, 151, following D-G[2] 1.152.

56. The second statement, therefore, we will discuss at its appropriate place, in the middle of November, 44 BC. See chapter 7.

57. The quotation is not verbatim; Cic. *Att.* 15.22: *Hic autem noster Cytherius nisi victorem neminem victurum.*

58. Taylor 1966, 41, 108–9; Ulrich 1994, 101.

CHAPTER 6

1. On the events covered in this chapter, see D-G[2] 1.91–92, 103; Rice Holmes 1928, 1.18–23; Frisch 1946, 106–14; Ehrenwirth 1971, 44–67.

2. Cic. *Att.* 15.10: *ludos vero non facere! quid foedius?*

3. We hear of Atticus' possible involvement in these preparations in a letter of Cicero dated 15 June (*Att.* 15.18.2). Brutus requested that Cicero attend the games as a show of support and to lend them some dignity, but Cicero politely declined. In Cicero's mind, to attend these games would not have been "respectable" (*honestum*), because he had remained away from Rome since troops began to gather in the city, and to reappear suddenly just to attend some games would harm his public image (Cic. *Att.* 15.26.1).

4. On this, see Liv. 25.12; Macr. 1.17.25–30. Cf. J. Toutain, D-S, s.v. "Ludi Apollinares," 3.2, 1376–77; Friedländer in Marquardt 1881–1885, 3.500–501; Fowler 1908, 179–82; Wissowa 1912, 295; Latte 1960, 223; Scullard 1981, 159–60; Bernstein 1998, 171–86.

5. Cic. *Att.* 2.19.3; V. Max. 6.2.9; Nicolet 1980, 363–73, discusses this and other topical lines in the theater; cf. also Bollinger 1969.

6. Cic. *Att.* 2.19.3: *Caesar cum venisset mortuo plausu, Curio filius est insecutus. Huic ita plausum est ut salva re publica Pompeio plaudi solebat. Tulit Caesar graviter. Litterae Capuam ad Pompeium volare dicebantur. Inimici erant equitibus, qui Curioni stantes plauserant, hostes omnibus; Rosciae legi, etiam frumentariae minitabantur.* On this law, see Rotondi 1912, 374.

7. Plut. *Cic.* 13; Plin. *Nat.* 7.117. Since Cicero spoke from the Temple of Bellona, the theater in question must have been that of Apollo, which presumably stood near the Temple of Apollo in the Campus Martius (Platner-Ashby 1929, 15–16). If the

Theater of Apollo was the venue for theatrical entertainment on this occasion, the festival must have been the *Ludi Apollinares*.

8. Asc. 48C. Benner 1987, 98, 111–13; Vanderbroeck 1987, 248–49.

9. Garnsey 1988, 211.

10. Cic. *Sest*. 116–25. On these so-called *fabulae praetextae*, plays with historical themes and often contemporary political significance, see Zorzetti 1980, esp. 29–52 for bibliography; Wiseman 1995, 133–41; Flower 1995.

11. Cicero informed Atticus that he was planning to begin his canvass (*prensatio*) for the consulship on 17 July 65, one year before the elections for the consulship of 63 (*Att*. 1.1.1).

12. Cic. *Att*. 13.44.1; so argue Ramsey and Licht 1997, 25–40; their argument rests in large measure on reordering the sequence of letters in *ad Att*. Books 12–13. The traditional sequence, which most modern editions adopt, is based on the work of Schmidt 1893.

13. Cf. Ov. *Am*. 3.2.43–56 for his description of a *pompa circensis*.

14. On Brutus' preparations, see Plut. *Brut*. 21.4–6; App. *BC* 3.23.87; Dio 47.20.2 (who identifies Cassius as the sponsor of these games); cf. Cic. *Att*. 16.4.1. On the importance of exotic wild animals for festival games, see the correspondence of Caelius and Cicero (e.g., *Fam*. 8.9.3; 2.11.2).

15. Scullard 1981, 160.

16. Flower 1995, 175–76.

17. Crawford 1974, nos. 433/1 and 2; cf. Evans 1992, 145–48.

18. Cic. *Phil*. 1.36: *Quid? Apollinarium ludorum plausus vel testimonia potius et iudicia populi Romani parum magna vobis videbantur?* "What about the applause at the *Ludi Apollinares*—or should I say the testimony and judgment of the Roman people? Didn't you think that was enough?"

19. Gotter (1996, 271–72) dates this *contio* around 21/22 July, the first days of Octavian's games, but Ramsey (2001) has now shown that the *contio* must have taken place a few days earlier.

20. Cicero mentions this meeting in *Phil*. 1.8 and *Att*. 16.7.1. The latter passage contains no mention of the *contio*. For a full discussion of these two passages as well as the political situation at the time, see Ramsey 2001.

21. Dio (45.6.2–3) includes it in his narrative of events in the summer of 44 (cf. Plut. *Ant*. 16.5); Appian (*BC* 3.31.120) places it in the fall and states that Octavian did not stand for the office himself but supported a certain Flaminius.

22. Cic. *Att*. 15.2.3; cf. *Fam*. 11.28.6; Alföldi 1976, 96–97; Weinstock 1971, 368.

23. Ramsey and Licht 1997, 54–55.

24. See Ramsey and Licht 1997, 19–57, who cite the relevant bibliography.

25. Suet. *Aug*. 10.1; cf. Dio 45.6.4. Both mentioned men who apparently had some special responsibility for the *Ludi Victoriae*, perhaps members of the *collegium* that Caesar established to be in charge of these games (Plin. *Nat*. 2.93). For a discussion of these games, see Bernstein 1998, 327–48.

26. Nic. Dam. 28.108 (*FrGH* 90, F130): "Again, [Octavian] came forward with several friends and requested that Antonius allow him to set up the chair with the diadem for his father. Antonius made similar threats, if Octavian did not leave aside the

chair and diadem and stay out of trouble." Cf. Dio 45.6.5; App. *BC* 3.28.107. For modern arguments, see Rice-Holmes 1928, 1.18–19, n. 6; cf. Frisch 1946, 109.

27. Plin. *Nat.* 2.91–92; Manil. 1.892–95; Sen. *Nat.* 7.1.5; Serv. A. 10.272. There was, however, a comet sighted at the birth of Mithridates, which may have influenced Octavian (Just. 37.2.1–3; cf. Weinstock 1971, 371).

28. It is impossible to establish the chronology with certainty, but our sources indicate that this happened soon after the games concluded; Dio 45.7.1; Plin. *Nat.* 2.93–94: . . . *id insigne [sc. sidus] simulacro capitis eius, quod mox in foro consecravimus, adiectum est* (94). "This [star] was added above the head of his statue, which we soon dedicated in the forum." Cf. Suet. *Jul.* 88. The language of Pliny is ambiguous. Could he mean the Forum Romanum and not the new Forum Julium? It is possible, but Dio's statement is clear and the Temple of Venus Genetrix would have been the appropriate place for a statue that celebrated Caesar's divinity, since Venus was the divine matriarch of the Julian *gens*, and the games during which the comet appeared were in her honor (Ramsey and Licht 1997, 159, n. 3). On the ancient sources for this comet, see Ramsey and Licht 1997, 157–77.

29. Weinstock 1971, 370–84, has a long discussion, with bibliography.

30. Crawford 1974, nos. 281 (Roma), 418/2b (Mercury), 474 (Apollo), 480/26 (Venus).

31. Crawford 1974, no. 480/5a.

32. See, e.g., Scott 1941; Pesce 1933, 404. Crawford (1974, no. 480) provides only a relative chronology of this issue, along with those of L. Aemilius Buca, M. Mettius, and C. Cossutius Maridianus.

33. Weinstock 1971, 377–78.

34. Octavian did not begin to use the title *Divi filius* publicly until after Caesar's deification on 1 January 42. The *sidus Iulium* first appears on a coin minted by M. Agrippa (Crawford 1974, no. 534, p. 744). The title *Divi Filius* does not appear on coins until 36 BC (Crawford 1974, p. 744).

35. Cic. *Att.* 16.7.1; cf. *Phil.* 1.7–10,where he also outlines the events that led to his return to Rome. Gotter (1996, 271–72) attempts a chronology of the events in late July and early August.

36. This is Mommsen's suggestion (*Röm. StR*³, 1.202–9; 2.221–22).

37. Nic. Dam. 29.116–19 (*FrGH* 90, F130); cf. Plut. *Ant.* 16.6; App. *BC* 3.39.156 (cf. 3.30.115, where Appian describes an earlier reconciliation; he seems to be preserving a doublet in the tradition); Dio 45.8.2.

38. Octavian had several residences in his young life. After the death of his father (59 BC) and his grandmother, Julia (51 BC), he moved in with his mother, Atia, and stepfather, L. Marcius Philippus, who were living presumably in the family home of the Marcii on the Carinae (Hor. *Ep.* 1.7.48; Palombi 1997, 146). After Octavian came of age, he lived with his great-uncle Caesar until his return to Rome in the summer of 45, when he again took up residence on the Carinae, perhaps in the home of A. Manlius Torquatus, a supporter of Pompeius, who eventually fell at Philippi. (This is the hypothesis of Palombi 1997, 148–49.) After Caesar's assassination, Octavian moved nearer the Forum into the home once owned by C. Licinius Calvus Macer (Suet. *Aug.* 72.1; Palombi 1997, 147, 148; for the general location, see fig. 1). This house was adjacent to the "Ringmakers' stairs" (*Scalae Anulariae*), perhaps to be

equated with the *Scalae Graecae* on the northwest slope of the Palatium. (On the location of the *Scalae Anulariae*, see E. Papi, s.v. "Scalae Anulariae," *LTUR* 4.238–39; Haselberger 2002, 221).

39. Epstein 1987, 12–14.

40. Liv. 40.45.6–46.15; Cicero's mention of this reconciliation shows that these exempla from an earlier period in Roman history remained part of the political discourse of the late Republic (*Prov.* 20). Münzer (1999, 184) suggests that this reconciliation was staged, the result of a secret pact between the two families; cf. Scullard 1951, 180–81; *contra* Epstein 1987, 133 n. 10.

41. See chapter 7. We are also informed that Q. Cornificius began riding on an elephant whenever he dined out—even in Rome—as a way of drawing attention to his achievement of saving his soldiers during the war against Sextus Pompeius in 36 BC (Dio 49.7.6).

42. Botermann 1968, 27–32; Gotter 1996, 270–71.

CHAPTER 7

1. For the events covered in this chapter, see D-G^2 1.140–205; Rice-Holmes 1928, 1.23–46; Frisch 1946, 114–93; Ehrenwirth 1971, 67–99 (covering the period until 9 October).

2. Cicero expresses doubts about Antonius' devotion to Caesar's memory, which shows that the issue was current in the fall of 44 (*Phil.* 2.110).

3. Cic. *Phil.* 2.110; Rotondi 1912, 428.

4. Cic. *Fam.* 12.3.1 (to C. Cassius, dated 2 October): *Auget tuus amicus furorem in dies. Primum in statua quam posuit in rostris inscripsit 'parenti optime merito', ut non modo sicarii sed iam etiam parricidae iudicemini.* "Your friend's madness grows by the day. First, he erected a statue on the Rostra with the inscription: 'to our father for his great services.' Now not only are you judged murderers but also parricides."

5. For the title, see Cic. *Phil.* 13.23; Dio 44.4.4; Taylor 1931, 67; cf. Cicero's remark that the conspirators will now be judged not only murderers but also parricides (previous note).

6. We are told that Antonius, in fact, represented himself as Caesar's son, although it is not clear if he would have done so after the contents of Caesar's will were made public; see Cic. *Phil.* 2.71 (addressing Antonius): *Cuius* [sc. Caesaris] *tu imperatoris quaestor fueras, dictatoris magister equitum, belli princeps, crudelitatis auctor, praedae socius, testamento, ut dicebas ipse, filius, appellatus es. . . .* "You had been his quaestor when he was commander, master of horse when he was dictator, you provoked his war, authored his savagery, and shared in his plunder; you were named his son in his will, as you yourself claimed. . . ."

7. For an account of this *contio*, see Cic. *Fam.* 12.3.2; cf. *Fam.* 12.23.3. Following the fall of Perusia in 41, Cannutius was sacrificed at the altar of Caesar by Octavian (Dio 48.14.4).

8. Cic. *Att.* 16.15.3; App. *BC* 3.41–42; Dio 45.12.4–6.

9. App. *BC* 3.41.168. This temple, which stood just outside the Porta Capena, was vowed in the war with the Gauls (390) and dedicated by T. Quinctius Cincinnatus in 388 (Liv. 6.5.8; see also Richardson 1992, 244–45).

10. Weinstock 1971, 365–66, argues for the presence of a statue on this monu-

ment (365, n. 5), citing only the location of this *contio* and the oath sworn by Octavian as evidence.

11. Liv. 9.43.22. We know from Cicero that the statue was still standing in 44/43 (Cic. *Phil.* 6.13; cf. Plin. *Nat.* 34.23); in the same passage, Cicero mentions a statue of L. Antonius, brother of Octavian's rival, that stood in front of the temple, but we do not know when it was erected.

12. Octavian's route on this occasion is intriguing because it followed at least in part the route of the annual parade of Roman knights (*transvectio equitum*), which took place on 15 July (*Vir. Ill.* 32.3; S. Weinstock, s.v. "transvectio equitum," *RE* series 2, 6 [1937], 1278–87). This military parade, according to Dionysius, began at the Temple of Mars and proceeded through much of the city and past the Temple of Castor in the Forum (6.13.4). The Temple of Castor was an important element in this ritual because the Dioscuri, as gods of horses and horsemanship, were associated with the Roman *equites* (Albert 1883, 81–89; cf. also Dubourdieu 1989). Was Octavian intentionally trying to evoke the *transvectio equitum*? If so, what was his purpose? Octavian was a member of a prominent equestrian family from Velitrae who had only recently been given patrician status by the dictator Caesar (probably in 45 or the beginning of 44; Suet. *Aug.* 2.1; cf. *Jul.* 41.1; Dio 43.47.3; Plut. *Caes.* 58.1). Augustus himself evinced no shame at his equestrian birth and even boasted of it in his own writings, remarking that his father was the first member of his family to enter the senate (Suet. *Aug.* 2.3). However, for one who was still attempting to legitimate his adoption into the Julian *gens*, a patrician family, such a public acknowledgment—advertisement even—of his equestrian roots might have drawn attention to his humble birth at an inopportune time. In fact, Antonius had recently published an edict degrading Octavian's family (Cic. *Phil.* 3.15). Some of the details of Antonius' calumnies are preserved by Suetonius [*Aug.* 2.3]). On balance, it seems unlikely that Octavian would have purposely brought attention to his family lineage by evoking the *transvectio equitum*.

13. Cic. *Att.* 16.15.3: *Redeo ad rem publicam. Multa mehercule a te saepe* ἐν πολιτικῷ *genere prudenter, sed his litteris nihil prudentius. Quamquam enim †postea† in praesentia belle iste puer retundit Antonium, tamen exitum exspectare debemus. At quae contio! nam est missa mihi. Iurat 'ita sibi parentis honores consequi liceat' et simul dextram intendit ad statuam.* μηδὲ σωθείην ὑπό γε τοιούτου!

14. Gotter (1996, 102) understands Cicero's exclamation as a genuine compliment.

15. *OLD* s.v. "honor," 5.

16. *OLD* s.v. "honor," 2c.

17. Gesche (1968, 79–82) believes that Octavian's statement, as most scholars interpret it, was so bold and ambitious that the senate and Cicero would have balked at supporting him. She argues, instead, that we should understand the phrase *honores parentis* as referring to Caesar's *acta*. She is certainly correct to point out the boldness of the statement, and Cicero himself implies as much by his reaction to it, but Cicero chose to throw his support behind Octavian only because at this time he appeared to be the lesser of two evils.

18. *iuro* usually introduces indirect statement, although it can take *ut* + subjunctive (*OLD*, s.v. "iuro").

19. *CIL* 1^2.582; *Röm. StR*^{3}, 1.620–21, with n. 3 on p. 620; Crawford 1996, 1.193–208.

20. For Plancus, see, e.g., *Fam*. 10.6.2; 10.10; 10.12.5; 10.16.2; for Cornificius, see, e.g., *Fam*. 12.25.5; 12.28.2.

21. Dio 45.12.5. In Appian's version of this *contio* (*BC* 3.41.168–69), Cannutius spoke first, criticizing Antonius, and then Octavian followed with reminiscences of Caesar (ὑπεμίμνησκε) and an account of all that he himself had suffered from Antonius; this is what prompted his recruitment of soldiers as a bodyguard.

22. *CIL* 1².582: [*pro ae*]*de Castorus* (sic) *palam luci in Forum vorsus*.

23. Brutus and Cassius alluded to the possibility that this might happen in a letter to Antonius dated late May (Cic. *Fam*. 11.2.2; Weinstock 1971, 365). There is no direct evidence that this monument also included a statue of Caesar, but, under the circumstances, it is probable.

24. Cf. Gesche 1968, 79–82.

25. Dio 44.6.1: τήν τε τύχην αὐτοῦ ὀμνύναι. Cf. Taylor 1931, 67–68; Weinstock 1971, 212–14.

26. E.g., Plaut. *Capt*. 977; Ter. *Andr*. 289; Hor. *Ep*. 1.7.94; Weinstock 1971, 212.

27. Suet. *Jul*. 85. Cf. Weinstock 1971, 213–14.

28. It is possible that the location of Octavian's *contio* (the Temple of Castor) brought the issue of Caesar's divinity into greater relief. Castor and Pollux were demigods, heroes whose achievements in their lifetimes were so grand that they were raised to divine status (Cic. *Leg*. 2.19; Castor and Pollux appear as part of a list that includes Hercules, Liber, Aesculapius, and Quirinus; cf. Hor. *Ep*. 2.1.5–6). Moreover, the legend of Castor and Pollux was revived in the context of Pharsalus (Dio 41.61.4), and two figures clearly meant to evoke these deities were said to have appeared at Caesar's funeral (Suet. *Jul*. 84.3; see chap. 4). Thus, there was some connection between these deities and the figure of Caesar. How close this connection was is still not clear. If the very location of Octavian's *contio* could evoke the legend and image of Castor and Pollux (that is, without Octavian specifically alluding to them in the text of his speech, for which we have no evidence), then his oath and gesture, pointing to the altar of Caesar near the temple, might have drawn attention to the divine status of Caesar, who, like the twin deities, began life as a mortal and became a god.

29. On Octavian's gesture at this *contio*, see also Aldrete 1999, 30–31.

30. At least this was Cicero's reading of Octavian's intentions: "He clearly is looking to a war with Antonius and himself as leader" (*Att*. 16.8.1 [dated 2 or 3 November]).

31. The statue of Caesar on the Rostra wearing an oak wreath, the *corona civica*, which was awarded to a soldier who had saved the life of a Roman citizen in battle, was especially evocative of Caesar as savior of all Roman citizens (App. *BC* 2.106.441). (L. Gellius Poplicola [*cos*. 72] failed in his attempt to have the *corona civica* bestowed on Cicero after he had saved Roman citizens from Catilina [Cic. *Pis*. 6]). Caesar not only saved Romans with his victory; he also used the privileges of the victor with moderation, publicly refusing to follow the harsh and cruel precedent set by Sulla (Cic. *Att*. 9.7C.1). Caesar's *clementia*, then, was an abstraction of his role as savior. Finally, the well-being of Rome and all its citizens was dependent upon the life of Caesar (Cic. *Marc*. 25), and all Romans were required to swear an oath that they would consider his person inviolate. On Caesar as savior, see Weinstock 1971, 163–74.

32. Cic. *Phil*. 3.3: . . . *firmissimum exercitum ex invicto genere veteranorum militum*

comparavit patrimoniumque suum effudit: quamquam non sum usus eo verbo quo debui; non enim effudit: in salute rei publicae collocavit. Cf. *Fam*. 12.25.4.

33. Cic. *Phil*. 3.5: *Qua peste rem publicam privato consilio—neque enim fieri potuit aliter—Caesar liberavit*; "Caesar freed the Republic from this plague through private initiative, for it could not have happened otherwise." Cf. Cic. *Fam*. 11.7.2. Cf. also Aug. Anc. 1.1: *Annos undeviginti natus exercitum privato consilio et privata impensa comparavi, per quem rem publicam a dominatione factionis oppressam in libertatem vindicavi*. "At the age of 19 I recruited an army at private initiative and expense, through which I freed the Republic from the oppression of a faction." On the ideology of *privatus* in this passage, see Béranger 1958.

34. Var. *L*. 7.37; Liv. 45.39.11 (quoting M. Servilius); V. Max. 5.1.11; cf. Apul. *Apol*. 22; Wilson 1938, 100–101; H. Sauer, s.v. "paludamentum," *RE* 18.3 (1949), 281–86.

35. On the relationship of Octavian and his soldiers at this time, see Botermann 1968, 36–45. On the status of his soldiers, see Linderski 1984, 78–79.

36. The main difficulty is to reconcile the accounts of Cicero in *Phil*. 13.19 and Appian *BC* 3.45–46. Rice Holmes (1928, 1.199–200) attempts to do so (unsuccessfully, in my view). See also Frisch 1946, 151–55 (whom Botermann 1968, 48–49 [with n. 3 on p. 49] generally follows).

37. Cic. *Phil*. 3.15; cf. 13.19. Some of Antonius' charges are preserved in Suet. *Aug*. 2.3; 4.2.

38. Cic. *Phil*. 3.24; Sternkopf 1912a, 385–97; cf. also Schwartz 1898, 193–94.

39. Cic. *Phil*. 3.3; 4.3; 13.19; cf. *Fam*. 12.25.4. Appian (*BC* 3.45.184) calls Antonius' entry into the city "arrogant"; cf. Dio 45.13.5.

40. Appian (*BC* 3.66.269) states that there were frequent public meetings during this time.

41. Cic. *Phil*. 6.9; Cicero had made a proposal in the senate, ultimately voted down, that its members don their military cloaks (*saga*) in order to make manifest the troubling state of affairs (6.2, 16).

42. *Phil*. 4.1; 4.2; 4.8; 4.11; 4.16; 6.2; 6.9; 6.17; 6.19.

43. Richardson 1992, 205–6; cf. E. Tortorici, s.v. "Ianus Imus, Medius, Summus," *LTUR* 3.93–94.

44. On this concept, see Wallace Hadrill 1989. L. Antonius represented himself similarly at his triumph in 41 BC. See chapter 8.

45. Of Cicero's extant speeches, only eight (*Pro Lege Manilia*, *De Lege Agraria* 2 and 3, *In Catilinam* 2 and 3, *Post Reditum ad Populum*, and *Philippics* 4 and 6) were delivered in *contiones* before the people. Of these eight, only the speeches under discussion indicate that the audience responded to the orator's rhetoric with shouts or jeers.

46. For the events surrounding the battle of Mutina, see D-G[2] 1.205–65; Rice Holmes 1928, 1.47–71; Frisch 1946, 248–305.

47. App. *BC* 4.47.200; cf. *MRR*, 2.339.

48. See chapter 8. The praetor urbanus M. Caecilius Cornutus, who under normal circumstances would have been responsible for the *Ludi Apollinares*, was in charge of the city in the absence of the consuls and likely had more pressing concerns than this festival. Moreover, in July, when these games were traditionally held, news of Octavian's imminent arrival perhaps would have required their postponement or can-

celation. Cornutus committed suicide soon after Octavian took control of Rome in August (App. *BC* 3.92.381).

49. Cic. *Phil.* 14.12–13: *An si quis Hispanorum aut Gallorum aut Thraecum mille aut duo milia occidisset, illum hac consuetudine quae increbruit imperatorem appellaret senatus: tot legionibus caesis, tanta multitudine hostium interfecta—[dico] ita, inquam, hostium, quamvis hoc isti hostes domestici nolint—clarissimis ducibus supplicationum honorem tribuemus, imperatorium nomen adimemus? Quanto enim honore, laetitia, gratulatione in hoc templum ingredi debent illi ipsi huius urbis liberatores, cum hesterno die propter eorum res gestas me ovantem et prope triumphantem populus Romanus in Capitolium domo tulerit, domum inde reduxerit! Is enim demum est mea quidem sententia iustus triumphus ac verus, cum bene de re publica meritis testimonium a consensu civitatis datur*. Cf. Cic. *ad Brut.* 1.3.2.

50. E. Papi, s.v. "Domus: M. Tullius Cicero," *LTUR* 2.202–4.

51. Cic. *Phil.* 14.22–29, esp. section 23 in which he discusses the victories of Sulla and Caesar, among others.

52. A few of Pollio's letters to Cicero survive (*Fam.* 10.31–33); for Cicero's correspondence with Plancus, see *Fam.* 10.1–24 (these include Plancus' official dispatches as well); for his correspondence with Cornificius, see *Fam.* 12.17–30; for Lepidus' letters to Cicero, see *Fam.* 10.34–35.

53. On the effects of Marius' reforms, see Smith 1958, 11–69; for a discussion of the issues involved, see Gruen 1974, 365–84.

54. Octavian apparently never celebrated this *ovatio*, if indeed the senate awarded it; see now Keaveney and Madden 1983.

55. Cicero also viewed the praetorship as a less distinguished office, perhaps because Caesar had increased the number from eight to sixteen; in *Fam.* 10.26.2 he calls the praetorship a *magistratus levissimus et divulgatissimus*.

56. Rumors that Octavian desired the consulship had been around since early May (Cic. *ad Brut.* 1.4a.2; cf. 1.10.3).

57. Appian makes the comparison explicit (*BC* 3.88.365).

58. Cicero had frequently urged M. Brutus to bring his army to Italy for just such an eventuality (*ad Brut.* 1.10.1, 4; 1.9.3; 1.12.3; 1.14.2, etc.).

59. The Temple of Quirinus was also located here (F. Coarelli, s.v. "Quirinus, Aedes," *LTUR* 4.185–87), which had a tradition that was associated with the Julian *gens* and Julius Caesar. The story of Romulus and Proculus Julius is well established (Cic. *Rep.* 2.20; *Leg.* 1.3; Liv. 1.16, with Ogilvie 1965, 84–85; cf. D. H. 2.56), as is the connection between Caesar and Romulus-Quirinus (Weinstock 1971, 175–88; Burkert 1962). Moreover, a statue of Caesar in the Temple of Quirinus, erected probably in 45 (Cic. *Att.* 12.45.2; 13.28.3), bore the inscription "For a god unconquered" (Dio 43.45.3). Did Octavian exploit the connection between Quirinus and Caesar when he returned to Rome in July 43? An anecdote about his return that exists in our later tradition is suggestive. Following his election to the consulship, Octavian entered the Campus Martius and spied six vultures; later at a *contio* before his soldiers another twelve appeared (Dio 46.46.2–3; cf. the slightly different version in App. *BC* 3.94.388). This anecdote, however, is meaningless if it was a later invention. But it is possible that this anecdote was fixed in our tradition soon after the event occurred, and it was perhaps suggested by the topography of Octavian's return in which the Temple of Quirinus figured so prominently. Dio does state that Octavian himself acknowledged the comparison to Romulus and expressed his hopes that he would also achieve a kingship. But it is not clear when Octavian made this statement. It could have been as early

as the *contio* Dio mentions—bold words but spoken to a friendly audience. Certainly later Octavian became identified with Romulus and hence Quirinus, as a passage from Vergil attests (Verg. G. 3.27; cf. Serv. G. 3.27, and Thomas 1988, 44). He even for a time considered taking the name Romulus as a title before settling on Augustus (Suet. *Aug.* 7.2; Dio 53.16.7–8). Another possibility is that this tradition began only with the publication of Augustus' *Memoirs*, in which he could reflect on the events of his early career and aggrandize them in light of his ultimate victory. One would expect, however, that, if political considerations had persuaded him to decline (perhaps publicly) the name of Romulus in 27, they would also have discouraged a boastful account of the earlier event in his *Memoirs*, which he likely completed just a few years later (Yavetz 1984). We know that Octavian's return to Rome and election to the consulship were recorded in his *Memoirs* (Plut. *Brut.* 27.3). The evidence of Octavian making explicit the connection with Caesar and Quirinus during his return in 43 is inconclusive.

60. On Vesta, see Wissowa 1912, 156–61; Latte 1960, 108–11; Radke 1965, 320–35; Beard, North, and Price 1998, 1.52–53.

61. On Vesta and *salus*, see Cic. *Har.* 12; *Phil.* 11.24.

62. Ov. *Fast.* 4.949–54; Beard, North, and Price 1998, 1.191.

63. Ov. *Fast.* 4.949–50: *cognati Vesta recepta est / limine*. . . . "Vesta has been welcomed in her relative's home. . . ."

64. L. Munatius Plancus went on to hold the consulship along with the triumvir M. Aemilius Lepidus, who took the place of the fallen D. Brutus (for his death, see App. *BC* 3.98.407–8; Dio 46.53.3).

65. App. *BC* 3.94.387; cf. Alföldi 1958, 486–88.

66. Taylor 1966, 3–5; Botsford 1909, 168–200.

67. Lepidus was probably Pontifex Maximus by April of 44 BC, before his departure for Spain (Weigel 1992, 48). On the procedure of such elections, see Taylor 1942.

68. Liv. 120; Vell. 2.69.5; Plut. *Brut.* 27.4–5; App. *BC* 3.95.392–93; Suet. *Ner.* 3.1; *Gal.* 3.2; Dio 46.48; Bringmann 1996; Rotondi 1912, 435.

69. App. *BC* 3.95.393. Appian calls him Icelius when he describes his death (*BC* 4.27.118).

70. See Millar 1998; Gruen 1968, 157–84; see chapter 1.

CHAPTER 8

1. For an overview of this period of transition, see D-G² 1.265–370; Rice Holmes 1928, 1.72–186; Levi 1933, 2.1–186; Syme 1939, 187–312; Fadinger 1969; Millar 1973; Bleicken 1990; *CAH*² 10.1–69.

2. App. *BC* 4.8.31; cf. Plut. *Ant.* 21.1. Cf. also Palmer 1978, 315–16.

3. Nippel 1995, 78–84.

4. App. *BC* 4.7.27; Dio 47.2.1–2; the only evidence for the law's date of expiration is the *Fasti Colotiani* (*CIL* 1, p. 466); on this law, see also Rotondi 1912, 434–35; Fadinger 1969, 48–79.

5. On the proscriptions, see Hinard 1985a, 227–326; cf. also Canfora 1980, 430–35. More specifically, on the spectacle of executions and urban space, see Hinard 1987.

6. *Inscr. Ital.* 13.1, p. 87; Vell. 2.67.4; App. *BC* 4.31.132 mentions only the triumph of Lepidus.

7. Cf. Richardson 1975 and chapter 1.

8. On Fulvia's political career, see Babcock 1965; Delia 1991; Virlouvet 2001.

9. We should note that Fulvia was depicted as Victory on the obverse of several coins in this period, which shows another connection with military victory (Sear 1998, nos. 122, 126, 186, 321).

10. Weigel 1992, 50; cf. Cic. *Phil.* 3.23.

11. See, e.g., Cic. *Fam.* 10.6–24; 27, 34–35. On the correspondence between Cicero and Plancus, see Walser 1957. For the role of Plancus and Lepidus in the battle of Mutina, see Bardt 1909.

12. Shipley 1931, 17–18.

13. *CIL* 10.6087; cf. Suet. *Aug.* 29.5; *CIL* 6.1316; Shipley 1931, 16.

14. Vell. 2.67.4: *De germanis, non de Gallis duo triumphant consules.* "The two consuls triumphed over the 'germans,' not the Gauls."

15. Vell. 2.67.3; App. *BC* 4.12.45, 4.37.155–58; Dio 47.8.1.

16. The entire episode is described in some detail in App. *BC* 4.32–34; cf. also V. Max. 8.3.3; Quint. *Inst.* 1.1.6. Hortensia's speech became famous and continued to be read long after she died; a copy of it might have been available to Appian when he was composing the version that he included in his history. On Hortensia, see Peppe 1984, 17–50; cf. also Canfora 1980, 434–35. On Appian's reasons for including this episode in his account, see Gowing 1992, 260.

17. Lepidus and Plancus had triumphed in the last days of 43, on the eve of their consulship in 42. Later, in 39, L. Marcius Censorinus triumphed on the first day of his consulship (*Inscr. Ital.* 13.1, p. 87).

18. *Inscr. Ital.* 13.1, p. 87.

19. On Marius' triumph, see Greenidge and Clay 1960, 100.

20. Syme 1939, 208: "Denied justice and liberty, Italy rose against Rome for the last time." For a discussion of these issues as they relate to the Perusine War, see also Gabba 1971.

21. *ILS* 76: *C. Iulio C. f. Caesari imp. triumviro r. p. c. patrono d.d.*

22. The identity of this Nonius is unknown. He might be the Nonius Asprenas who was tribune in 44 (*MRR*, 2.325; 3.147–48) and so a former colleague of Lucius'.

23. Octavian adopted the theme of restoring the Republic as well later in the Triumviral period after he had disposed of Sextus Pompeius in 36 (cf. App. *BC* 5.132.548), and then when he became *princeps.* Suetonius claims that Augustus thought seriously about restoring the Republic (*de reddenda re publica*) on two occasions: the first came immediately after Actium and the second after a long illness, presumably in 23 or 22, but he never felt that it would be able to stand on its own (*Aug.* 28.1). Cf. Augustus' own words in his *Res Gestae*, where he makes the claim that the Principate constituted a return to Republican ideals (*Anc.* 34.1, 3).

24. For details, see App. *BC* 5.65.274–76; Dio 48.28.4; Gardthausen 1891, 1.210–23; Syme 1939, 217–20. For the chronology of the events surrounding the Pact of Brundisium, see Kromayer 1894.

25. This new *concordia* was advertised on the coinage of the period; Sear 1998, nos. 301–4, esp. no. 304.

26. Dio 48.20.2; for Agrippa's part in the Perusine War, see App. *BC* 5.35.139–40; on his praetorship in general, see Reinhold 1933, 21–27; Roddaz 1984, 61–63.

27. Cf. Ramsey and Licht 1997, 32–36; see chapter 6.

28. Dio 47.18.5–6. Caesar's birthday was on 12 July, and the *Ludi Apollinares* ran from 6 to 13 July. In order to avoid a conflict, the celebration of Caesar's birthday must have been moved back to the fifth (Cary 1917, 5.154, n. 1).

29. Suet. *Jul.* 39.2; Dio 43.23.6; for Sulla's production, see Plut. *Cat. Mi.* 3.1.

30. Liv. 25.12.15; Bernstein 1998, 171–86.

31. Sear 1998, no. 325; on this coin, the title appeared in its fuller form, including Caesar's *gens* name—*DIVI IVLI F*.

32. On *naumachiae* in general, see Coleman 1993.

33. Dio 48.18.2 and 19.1; such boats are attested by other sources; cf. Caes. *Civ.* 1.54.2; Plin. *Nat.* 4.104 and 7.206.

34. Even in Casinum a monument was erected to celebrate the reconciliation (a *signum concordiae*; *ILLRP* 562a).

35. On the *ovatio*, see chapter 1.

36. The *Fasti* mention only that Caesar celebrated his *ovatio* "from the Alban Mount" (*ex Monte Albano*); *Inscr. Ital.* 13.1, p. 87. See chapter 2.

37. *Inscr. Ital.* 13.1, p. 87: . . . *quod pacem cum* M. *Antonio fecit*.

38. E.g., App. *BC* 2.121.508; cf. Weinstock 1971, 256–69.

39. Dio 48.31.5; 48.48.5; Suet. *Aug.* 16.2; cf. App. *BC* 5.100.416–17; Hor. *Epod.* 9.7 (*Neptunius dux*); for the image of Neptune on Sextus' coinage, see Sear 1998, nos. 235, 236 (Crawford 1974, no.483/1 and 2). The date of issue is in dispute. Crawford (1974, p. 94) and Sear (1998, p. 139) both date the coinage prior to April of 43, since these coins omit the title *Praefectus classis et orae maritimae*, which was conferred on Sextus in that month, but see also Evans 1987, 111 with n. 31, who suggests a date after 38 BC. For Sextus and Neptune, see also Scott 1933, 30; Taylor 1931, 120–21; Wallmann 1989, 191. For a brief reassessment of the evidence, see Gowing 1992, 309–10. Another coin of Sextus also depicts Neptune; Sear 1998, no. 333 (dated 42 BC).

40. Dio 48.31.6. This was a common ploy to evoke sympathy; Lintott 1968, 16–21.

41. Dio 48.32.1; and when an aedile died on the last day of his term, they replaced him even for the last remaining hours (48.32.3). This anecdote sounds suspiciously like the episode in Caesar's dictatorship when he appointed a suffect consul to replace a consul who had died on the last day of his term (see chap. 2).

42. For a discussion, Frei-Stolba 1967, 37–86.

43. Cf. Cic. *Fam.* 11.16, 11.17, 12.29; and see chapter 7.

44. Dio 48.35.2–3; Appian claims that they were appointed for only four years (*BC* 5.73.313).

45. For instance, the Antonian Pollio gave way to the wealthy Spaniard, and Caesarian, L. Cornelius Balbus; Agrippa relinquished his praetorship, following his celebration of the *Ludi Apollinares* in July. *MRR* 2.378–80.

46. *Inscr. Ital.* 13.1, p. 87; Syme 1939, 231, 241.

47. See also the coinage struck at this time to celebrate the new settlement (e.g., Sear 1998, nos. 261–62).

48. Dio 47.7.4–5; App. *BC* 4.44.187; in this version, the freedman's name is Philemon; Suet. *Aug.* 27.2; cf. Hinard 1985, 548–49. For a discussion of this story, Gowing 1992, 257–58. On T. Vinius, see Wiseman 1971, no. 496; Syme 1962, 153.

49. According to Appian (*BC* 4.44.187), T. Vinius was kept hidden "until the treaty," which is probably a reference to the treaty of Misenum, struck in the summer of 39, which included a provision for pardoning the proscribed (Dio 48.36.3–4).

50. On this marriage, see Vell. 2.78.1; Plut. *Ant.* 31; App. *BC* 5.64.273; Dio 48.31.3. The wedding ceremony itself spoke of reconciliation between the two rivals, and could have been exploited for these purposes, but our sources record no details about it. It was also customary for women in Rome to approach the female relatives of those in power when seeking a favor, as Hortensia and her group of *matronae* did before they entered the Forum and addressed the triumvirs directly.

51. Vell. 2.65.3; V. Max. 6.9.9; Plin. *Nat.* 7.135; Plut. *Ant.* 34.8–9; Fro. *Ver.* 2.1.5 (123N); Gel. 15.4.4; Dio 49.21.3; Eutrop. 7.5; *Inscr. Ital.* 13.1, p. 87.

52. App. *BC* 3.66.270; cf. 3.72.297. On Ventidius' early career, see Dio 43.51.4–5; Gel. 15.4. For a general discussion of his career, see H. Gundel, *RE* series 2, 8 (1955), 795–816; Wiseman 1971, no. 474. For his exploits in this period, Gardthausen 1891, 1.228–33.

53. Dio 49.19–21.2; Plut. *Ant.* 34.4 (cf. the note of Pelling 1988, 211); on his earlier exploits in the east, see Dio 48.39.3–41.6; cf. App. *BC* 5.65.276.

54. The clearest evidence of this is a statement of Dio, who says that Ventidius did not receive any commendation from the senate for his initial successes in the east because he was not acting with independent authority (48.41.5), while Antonius received praise and thanksgivings (ἐπαίνους καὶ ἱερομηνίας).

55. On triumphs in particular, see Dio 48.42.4–5; cf. 49.42.3.

56. The date is in the entry in the *Fasti Triumphales* (*V Kal. Dec.*); *Inscr. Ital.* 13.1, p. 87.

57. Dio 49.32.2. It is possible that Dio was thinking of Ventidius' triumph in this context, but the text is not explicit.

58. Dio 48.49.4; Reinhold 1933, 29, accepts Dio's explanation. Agrippa also declined a triumph in 19 (Dio 54.11.6) and in 14 (Dio 54.24.7); the latter refusal set the precedent for the honor of *ornamenta triumphalia* at times to replace the triumph proper; see chapter 9.

59. Plut. *Ant.* 34.4 states that Ventidius stopped short of provoking Antonius' jealousy.

60. This coin has been the subject of a long dispute concerning its date and attribution. I follow here the argument of Buttrey 1960.

61. Syme 1938, 20–22.

62. Vell. 2.65.3; V. Max. 6.9.9; Plin. *Nat.* 7.135; Plut. *Ant.* 34.8–9; Gel. 15.4.4; Dio 49.21.3.

63. Fro. *Ver.* 2.1.5 (123N); Syme 1964, 223.

64. For a brief discussion of his career, see D-G^2 3.3–11; cf. Syme 1939, 234–35.

65. On this election, see Gruen 1969.

66. Dio 48.42.4–5. Calvinus' salutation as *imperator* was commemorated on coins that made no reference to the triumvir to whom he owed his command (Sear 1998, no. 342).

67. C. Asinius Pollio (*cos.* 40) was a Marrucinus from Teate—the heart of rebel Italy during the Social War (Syme 1964, 7 with n. 4)—whose grandfather was killed in the conflict. Pollio commanded Spain under Caesar in 44 and gave his allegiance to Antonius following the murder of the dictator. Following his consulship in 40, he

acquired a command in Macedonia through which he earned his success over the Parthini. (The exact sphere of his command remains a subject of controversy; see Syme 1939, 222–23; Bosworth 1972; Zecchini 1982, 1276–77; Woodman 1983, 192–96 on Vell. 2.78). His triumph took place on 25 October in 39 or 38 (the *Fasti* fail to give a year) (*Inscr. Ital.* 13.1, p. 87; cf. also Bosworth 1972, 466).

68. This is also the assumption of Broughton (*MRR*, 2.392, 397, 402), who includes Calvinus as promagistrate in Spain during the years 38–36 BC, although we have no sources to support this.

69. Dio 48.49.3. Agrippa was awarded a triumph for his successes in Gaul, where he earned the distinction of being only the second Roman to cross the Rhine for the purposes of war.

70. *Inscr. Ital.* 13.1, p. 87.

71. Syme 1939, 286–87; Gabba 1971.

72. For the little that we do know of him, see F. Münzer, s.v. "Oppius," *RE* 18.1 (1939), 739.

73. So Appian; Dio calls them "criminals" (κάκουργοι) and states further that they entered the theater wearing masks as if they were going to act in a play (48.53.5).

74. The chronology is uncertain; Dio says only that Oppius died "not much later" than his aedileship (48.53.5).

75. Dio 48.54.6. The renewal of the triumvirate was also advertised on the coinage of the period; Sear 1998, nos. 312–15.

76. Dio 48.31.5; cf. App. *BC* 5.100.416–17.

77. App. *BC* 5.130.538–43; Dio 49.15.1–3; Vell. 2.81.3. This victory was also celebrated through the issuance of coins a few years later (Sear 1998, no. 418).

78. On Octavian's attempt at restoring the Republic in 36 BC, see Palmer 1978.

79. Among the extraordinary honors decreed to him was the right to sit on the long bench of the tribunes and to enjoy their inviolability, thus acquiring tribunician power and sacrosanctity without actually being elected to the office. He was also given a house at public expense (Dio 49.15.1–3, 5–6).

80. Dio 49.15.3; cf. App. *BC* 5.130.541; Rich 1998, 71–72.

81. A possible point of comparison was the dispatch of senators and magistrates (including the tribunes of the *plebs*) to visit Augustus in Campania in 19 BC, when his absence from Rome resulted in electoral mischief. Augustus points out that this honor was unprecedented (*Anc.* 11–12.1; cf. Dio 54.10.2 and chapter 9).

82. This statue and inscription survived until Appian's day (App. *BC* 5.130.542); on Octavian's claim that he ended the civil wars, see Wallmann 1969, 268–74.

83. A. Viscogliosi, s.v. "Bellona, Aedes in Circo," *LTUR* 1.190–92, Richardson 1992, 57–58; for meetings of the senate here, see Bonnefond-Coudry 1989, 151–60.

84. Cicero held a *contio* here to quell a riotous crowd (Plut. *Cic.* 13.4); cf. Vanderbroeck 1987, 230. Discussed in chapter 1.

85. Bernstein 1998, 157–71; Scullard 1981, 197.

86. Scullard 1981, 197.

87. Reinhold 1933, 45–52; Roddaz 1984, 145–59.

88. From 42 to 34 only two aediles are known—Villius Annalis in 42 (*MRR*, 2.359) and M. Oppius in 37 (*MRR*, 2.396–97). The office was vacant in 36 (Dio 49.16.2) and then again in 28 (Dio 53.2.2). Cf. Reinhold 1933, 46.

89. So Frandsen 1836, 62–63, and Herzog 1887–1891, 121; *contra* Reinhold 1933, 48, n. 16, who claims that Agrippa's building program was such a laborious undertaking that it would have been impossible for him to bring it to fruition without a colleague. If, however, praetors and tribunes were able to take on the duties traditionally assigned to aediles in 36, it is probable that they could have done so in 33 as well, thus assisting Agrippa, who still might have remained technically the only aedile for the year.

90. Reinhold 1933, 48, with n. 16.

91. One possible precedent was the aedileship of C. Caesar in 65, when he sponsored such lavish games that his colleague, M. Bibulus, complained that the people would remember only Caesar's generosity (Suet. *Jul.* 10.1; Dio 37.8.2). This is discussed in chapter 1.

92. This was not unprecedented; see *Röm. StR*³, 1.537, n. 1; Kubitschek, s.v. "Aedilis," *RE* 1 (1894), 448–64, at 451.

93. On the *Ludi Apollinares*, Dio 48.20.2; on his refusal of the triumph, Dio 48.49.4.

94. Dio 49.43.1–4; Plin. *Nat.* 36.121; for a contemporary assessment, cf. Hor. *Serm.* 2.3.182–86. The later tradition concerning Agrippa's aedileship might owe something to his own memoirs (Plin. *Nat.* 36.121). Cf. Roddaz 1984, 147, n. 48; 153, n. 90.

95. With the proper conveyance, it is possible that this voyage took on a triumphal character, celebrating in the city of Rome Agrippa's naval victory at Naulochus. Agrippa, for his part in the victory, had received the unprecedented honor of a naval crown (Dio 49.14.4; Maxfield 1981, 75), but otherwise he had not had the opportunity to celebrate in Rome. He had not been awarded a triumph, presumably because it would have overshadowed Octavian's *ovatio*. In other ways, Agrippa seems to have kept the memory of this victory alive, for he added dolphins, which were sacred to Neptune, as lap-counting devices in the Circus Maximus (Dio 49.43.2). Sextus Pompeius had also represented himself as the son of Neptune, as we discussed earlier. Agrippa's purpose was not just to commemorate his victory but also to reclaim Neptune for Octavian. It should also be noted that Agrippa included dolphins as decorations on the friezes of his Basilica of Neptune; Shipley 1933, 84–85.

96. Hadas 1930, 159–60; for the date of his death, p. 160; see also D-G² 4.590.

97. See, e.g., Reinhold 1933, 51: "It is small wonder that Agrippa's popularity [citing Hor. *Serm.* 2.3.185–86 as evidence] and the popularity of the government of Octavian increased tremendously"; Rice Holmes 1928, 1.136: "[Agrippa's aedileship] doubtless increased the popularity of the government."

98. Dio 50.10.4–5. Dio informs us that freedmen were thought responsible for the rioting, which turned to arson; their summary punishment cowed freemen into complying with the exactions.

99. For more on the oath and its historical context, Syme 1939, 276–93. On Antonius' will, Johnson 1978; Sirianni 1984.

100. Rüpke (1990, 105–7) makes this claim, following the work of Wiedemann 1986, who has argued that the rite of spear throwing in particular was the element of the ceremony that Octavian invented.

101. The most complete ancient account of the evolution of this ceremony can be found in Serv. 9.52; cf. Liv. 1.32.5–14 with Ogilvie's note (1965, 127–29); Gel. 16.4.1

(quoting L. Cincius); Ov. *Fast.* 6.205–8; Fest. 30L. On the Fetial college in general, Marquardt 1881–1885, 3.415–27; Wissowa 1912, 550–54; Samter, s.v. "Fetiales," *RE* 6 (1909), 2259–65; Beard, North, and Price 1998, 1.26–27, 111–12, 132–34. Rawson 1973 expresses some doubts about the story as Servius tells it. For a general discussion about the changes in the Fetial ritual procedure, Rich 1976, 56–60, 104–7.

102. Millar 1973, 61.

103. Rawson 1973.

104. Dio 50.4.5. See also Volkmann 1958, 169–70; Kearsley 1999, 57; cf. Reinhold 1981/82, who discusses the propaganda campaign against Cleopatra.

105. Reynolds 1982, 39, 89–90. The ceremony in question is the one described by Livy (1.24.4–9).

106. Rüpke 1990, 106. We know very little about the activity of the Fetial college in the imperial period; see Lewis 1955, 138–39; Scheid 1978, 640.

107. Serv. A. 9.52; Wiedemann 1986, 483.

108. I accept the last day of December 33 BC as the end of the Second Triumvirate; see Girardet 1995, who discusses the most recent scholarship on this issue.

109. Girardet 1990 has the most thorough discussion with bibliographic data; Benario 1975, Lewis 1991, and Kearsley 1999.

110. Linderski 1984, 79–80.

111. Although, admittedly, it appears exclusively in poetry (Hor. *Carm.* 4.5.5; Ov. *Fast.* 1.613; 2.60; 5.145; 6.92). On the adoption of the title of *dux* by Octavian, see Syme 1939, 288, 311–12; von Premerstein 1937, 53; Béranger 1953, 47–49.

112. The ritual of spear throwing was also associated with Alexander, who performed a similar ritual upon his arrival in Asia (Wiedemann 1986, 483, citing Justin. 11.5.10). This was an appropriate evocation for Octavian since he was also embarking on a campaign in the east, and in fact Asia supplied Antonius and Cleopatra with much of their manpower and resources. It further removed the present campaign from the sphere of civil war and placed it firmly in that of foreign war and especially world conquest—another confrontation between the forces of the west against the east. In other words, the spear throwing simply confirmed the basic meaning and purpose of the ceremony as a whole. It is unclear, however, if the act of Octavian hurling a spear alone (that is, without some statement on Octavian's part) would have been sufficient to evoke, in the minds of his audience, the image and memory of Alexander.

113. One other point of interest in this ceremony, which has been neglected in other discussions, deserves our attention. The *columna bellica*, a small column located in front of the Temple of Bellona, was an important feature of the city's topography and figured in the Fetial ceremony (Ov. *Fast.* 6.205–8; Fest. 30L.: *Columella quae bellica vocabatur, super quam hastam iacebant, cum bellum indicebatur.* Platner-Ashby 1929, 131; E. La Rocca, s.v. "Columna Bellica," *LTUR* 1.300–301). According to Festus, the spear was hurled over this column before landing in the area of the Circus Flaminius, which had been designated enemy territory. If the column was already in existence when Octavian performed the Fetial ceremony in 32, it is hard to believe that the history surrounding this ceremony, as Servius relates it, would have been unknown. In other words, I believe that the existence of the *columna bellica* in 32 would be evidence for the existence of the tradition surrounding the Fetial ceremony, including the rite of throwing a spear into enemy territory. Thus, this rite could not have been a wholly invented archaism on the part of Octavian. If, on the other hand, the column did not

exist at the time of Octavian's performance, then Octavian would have had a freer hand to invent the details of the ceremony. Unfortunately, our sources do not provide clear enough testimony to decide the issue. We can only note that the oldest source to mention the *columna bellica* is Ovid, who, of course, is of Augustan date, and so he can only attest to its existence after Octavian but not before. On the other hand, if the *columna bellica* did not exist before Octavian, and Octavian himself did not erect it for his observance of the ceremony in or around 32, then Augustus must have erected it. But Augustus does not mention doing so among his many adornments in the city (*Anc.* 19–21).

114. *Fasti Praenestini* (*Inscr. Ital.* 13.2, p. 113); cf. Syme 1979, 189.

115. Aug. *Anc.* 13; Liv. 1.19.3; Vell. 2.38.3; Suet. *Aug.* 22; Dio 51.20.4. Brunt and Moore 1967, 54–55; Syme 1979. Augustus claims to have closed them three times in his own reign—the first time in 29, again in 25 following the pacification of Spain, and a third time the date of which is unknown. These famous closings of the doors were accompanied by Augustus' claim to have established a worldwide peace (*pace terra marique parta*) (Liv. 1.19.3; cf. *AE* 1977, no. 778 [dated 29 BC]).

116. Var. *L.* 5.165, quoting the historian Piso; Liv. 1.19.3; cf. Vell. 2.38.3. Both Varro and Livy state that the second closing happened in the consulship of T. Manlius Torquatus (*cos.* 235), but the First Punic War ended in 241, when A. Manlius Torquatus was consul. There may be a confusion over or corruption of the *praenomina*; cf. Ogilvie 1965, 94.

117. Dio 51.20.4; Beard, North, and Price 1998, 1.110–11, 188.

118. Plut. *Aem.* 39.5; Liegle 1942. The emperor Claudius had the *augurium salutis* taken in AD 49—the first time in seventy-five years, Tacitus informs us (*Ann.* 12.23.1 [with Ritter's conjecture])—while at the same time extending the Pomerium of the city, which Claudius undertook in order to draw attention to his expansion of the empire through his conquest of Britain, ultimately in imitation of Augustus, who conducted this ancient ceremony in his reign. It is equally probable that Claudius' taking of the *augurium salutis* was done in imitation of the founder of the empire.

119. The legend associated with the founding of this temple is consistent with the theme of peace. According to one tradition, Romulus and Titus Tatius founded this temple jointly to celebrate the union of their two communities (Serv. *A.* 1.291). Another tradition places the foundation of this temple in the reign of Numa (Liv. 1.19.1–4, with Ogilvie's note (1965, 93–94); cf. Plin. *Nat.* 34.33).

120. On Salus, see Thulin, s.v. "Salus," *RE* series 2, 1.2 (1920), 2057–59; for the location of the shrine, Cic. *Att.* 4.1.4; 12.45.2; Platner-Ashby 1929, 462; F. Coarelli, s.v. "Salus, Aedes," *LTUR* 4.229–30.

121. Ov. *Fast.* 3.881–82; on the concept of Salus, see Winkler 1995.

122. Gurval 1995, 19–36, discusses Octavian's triumph in some detail, with special emphasis on the difficulties of celebrating victory in a civil war; see also Gardthausen 1891, 1.471–77.

123. Dio states that this was done "as was customary" (ὥσπερ εἴθιστο) (51.21.2), which leads me to believe that it occurred in the context of the *contio* delivered by a returning general before the people outside the Pomerium, perhaps at the Circus Flaminius.

124. Aug. *Anc.* 4.1; Liv. 133; Vell. 2.89.1; Suet. *Aug.* 22; Dio 51.21.5–9; *Inscr.*

Ital. 13.1, p. 570; cf. Verg. *Aen.* 8.714–23. Coins were also minted to celebrate this triumph; Sear 1998, no. 416.

125. As Gurval notes (1995, 28).

126. Gurval 1995, 31–32, argues cogently against the possibility that the omission can be explained by a lacuna or a stonecutter's error.

127. We have discussed previously the difficulties facing those victors in civil wars (see chaps. 1 and 2).

128. Cf. Vell. 2.89.3–4 on the effect (whether imagined or real) of Octavian's victory and return to Rome.

129. Dio 51.22.1–2; Aug. *Anc.* 19.1; for a depiction of the Curia Julia on the reverse of a coin minted about this time, see Sear 1998, no. 421.

130. Dio 47.18.4; for the date of dedication, *Fasti Antiates*, *CIL* 1, p. 328; *Inscr. Ital.* 13.2, p. 497.

131. Dio 51.22.1–2; Aug. *Anc.* 19. On the transformation of the Forum Romanum in this period, see Zanker 1972.

132. Caesar sponsored a similar mock battle at his games in 46, but the combatants are not named in our sources (see chap. 2).

CHAPTER 9

1. Suet. *Aug.* 99.1; for a discussion, see the introduction to this book.

2. Yavetz 1969, 101–2, quoting Seneca (*Ben.* 2.6.1): *Idem est quod datur, sed interest quomodo detur.* "It makes no difference what is given but how it is given."

3. Aug. *Anc.* 34.1; cf. Adcock 1951.

4. Dio 53.1.1; cf. also Velleius' assessment (2.89.3): *Prisca illa et antiqua rei publicae forma revocata.* "The old traditional form of the Republic was restored." On the symbolic importance of the *fasces* as part of public ceremonial, see Marshall 1984.

5. Millar 1984b.

6. Tac. *Ann.* 13.3.2; Millar 1977, 203–12.

7. Suet. *Aug.* 84.1. A later source describes the variety of ways in which the emperor exercised his oratorical abilities, including addressing the people on a variety of issues in *contiones* (Fro. *Ant.* 1.5; cf. *Aur.* 3.1). Suetonius further states that Augustus occasionally employed a herald when his voice was inadequate to address a large crowd at a *contio* (*Aug.* 84.2).

8. A complete list can be found in Aug. *Anc.* 19–21.

9. On Augustus' building program, see Favro 1996, esp. 252–80 (an imaginary walk through Rome after Augustus' death); Sablayrolles 1981; Haselberger 2002.

10. That Caesar built one is implied in Livy's account of his funeral (116; cf. Platner-Ashby 1929, 287).

11. Dio 51.19.2. On this temple and its place in the Forum, see Zanker 1972, 12–14.

12. Dio 53.20.2–4; Dio gives two versions of this man's name, Sextus Pacuvius and Apudius. For the form of dedication that he advocates, see V. Max. 2.6.11; Caes. *Gal.* 3.22.1–3.

13. Vanderbroeck 1987, 112–14; for the *vici* under Augustus, MacMullen 1974, 67–69.

14. Suet. *Aug.* 30.1; Kienast 1982, 164–66; Bleicken 1998, 444–45.

15. These could become riotous affairs; see chapter 1.

16. Augustus' marriage laws, for instance, were perceived as going too far, and Augustus was forced in the face of opposition to amend them. Roman knights voiced their objections at festival games (Suet. *Aug.* 34.2).

17. Aug. Anc. 5.1: *Dictaturam et apsenti et praesenti mihi delatam et a populo et a senatu, M. Marcello et L. Arruntio consulibus non recepi.* "The dictatorship, which the senate and people had offered me both in my presence and in my absence in the consulship of Marcus Marcellus and Lucius Arruntius (22 BC), I did not accept." Cf. Rotondi 1912, 441–42.

18. Dio 53.32.5. On this settlement, see Kienast 1982, 86–92; Southern 1998, 120–25; Bleicken 1998, 350–53; Cuff 1973; on the tribunician power, see Béranger 1953, 96–106.

19. The events surrounding Primus' trial and Caepio's conspiracy are notoriously difficult to untangle, and the bibliography is large. The ancient sources are Vell. 2.91.2; Dio 54.3.2–8; Suet. *Aug.* 19.1. For modern scholarship, in addition to the works cited by Kienast 1982, 86, n. 72, see Raaflaub and Samons 1990, 425–26; Southern 1998, 120–21.

20. Dio 54.1.1–4; on the dictatorship, cf. Vell. 2.89.5.

21. Vanderbroeck 1987, 223, 249–50, 252.

22. Cf. Brunt and Moore 1967, 13.

23. Plut. *Caes.* 60.6; in his *Antony*, Plutarch changes the date and location of this gesture, placing it at the *Lupercalia* in February of 44, after Caesar had declined the diadem offered by the consul, and Lupercal, Antonius (Plut. *Ant.* 12.6). Sulla held a similar, albeit less theatrical, *contio* after he laid down his dictatorship (App. *BC* 1.104.484).

24. Augustus is known to have boasted as much about the honors that he declined as he did about those he accepted: e.g., the right to hold the consulship in perpetuity (*consulatum annuum et perpetuum*; *Anc.* 5.3), and the office of Pontifex Maximus, while M. Lepidus was still alive (*Anc.* 10.2).

25. Claudius showed off his son Britannicus at a *contio* (Suet. *Claud.* 27.2). More to the point, Galba announced his adoption of Piso at a *contio* (Suet. *Galba* 17; cf. Tac. *Hist.* 1.14–17), as did Nerva for his adoption of Trajan (Plin. *Pan.* 8.3).

26. Suet. *Aug.* 40.5: *Etiam habitum vestitumque pristinum reducere studuit, ac visa quondam pro contione pullatorum turba indignabundus et clamitans: 'en Romanos, rerum dominos, gentemque togatam!'*

27. Quint. *Inst.* 2.12.10; the presence of *pullati* at the speech that Quintilian is imagining here suggests, however, that Augustus' prohibition did not last. Cf. 6.4.6; Plin. *Ep.* 7.17.9.

28. Cic. *Verr.* 2.4.54–55; *Rab. Post.* 25–27; Heskel 1994, 134–35.

29. In other ways, Augustus attempted to control access to Roman citizenship. I am thinking in particular of his laws on manumission (e.g., the *Lex Fufia Caninia*; background for this law can be found in the remarks of D. H. 4.24.4–8; cf. Sherwin-White 1973, 327–28). On his policy regarding Roman citizenship in general, see Sherwin-White 1973, 225–36.

30. A cursory examination of the historical tradition for Augustus' successors shows a similar pattern. Virtually all attested *contiones* were convened and presided

over by the emperor. Exceptions include Claudius' provision that the praetor announce in a *contio* a public holiday whenever there was an earthquake; Suetonius informs us that in this way Claudius was reviving an old custom (*Claud.* 22.1). Also during the reign of Claudius, Valerius Asiaticus was accused of masterminding Gaius' murder and taking credit for it in a *contio* (Tac. *Ann.* 11.1.2). That both these exceptions date to Claudius' reign is perhaps noteworthy. Valerius Asiaticus' *contio*, whether or not he actually used it to take credit for Gaius' assassination, perhaps was part of the attempt on the part of the senate to "restore" the Republic before the praetorian guard proclaimed Claudius emperor.

31. Suetonius states only that Augustus revived the customary privilege of elections (*Aug.* 40.2: *comitiorum quoque pristinum ius reduxit*); cf. Dio, who states that Augustus not only recommended his own candidates but also had the power to veto certain candidates if he deemed them unfit for office (53.21.6–7). On elections under Augustus, see, above all, Frei-Stolba 1967, 87–129; also Levick 1967; Staveley 1972, 217–23; Tibiletti 1953; Jones 1955; see also the briefer remarks of Kienast 1982, 167–70; Bleicken 1998, 442–43.

32. Platner-Ashby 1929, 460–61; E. Gatti, s.v. "Saepta Iulia," *LTUR* 4.228–29.

33. Dio records the display of a rhinoceros and hippopotamus during these games but not the location (51.22.5); Suetonius records, in a passage concerning the spectacles sponsored by Augustus throughout his reign, the display of a rhinoceros in the Saepta (*Aug.* 43.4). It is probable that the two sources are describing the same occasion. In 7 BC Augustus sponsored gladiatorial combat here in commemoration of the anniversary of Agrippa's death (Dio 55.8.5). A *venatio* was also held here in 2 BC during the games that celebrated the dedication of the Temple of Mars Ultor (Dio 55.10.7).

34. Suet. *Aug.* 56.1: *Quotiens magistratuum comitiis interesset, tribus cum candidatis suis circuibat supplicabatque more sollemni.*

35. Wallace Hadrill 1982.

36. Marcellus was given the status of an ex-praetor and allowed to stand for the consulship ten years earlier than was customary (i.e., at age twenty three); Tiberius was allowed to stand for each office five years before the customary age (Dio 53.28.3), although the rules were flexible; Tiberius was quaestor in 23 BC at age eighteen, seven years before the customary age; see Sumner 1967, 422–24.

37. For an explanation of Dio's chronological error, see Manuwald 1979, 113–15; Millar 1964, 87–88.

38. Phillips 1997, 110–11, with n. 19 on 110; *contra* Badot 1973, 611–12, who puts Rufus' aedileship in 20 and his praetorship in 19, when he stood for the consulship of 18.

39. Jones (1955) argues that Augustus used elections to the higher magistracies in particular to control membership in his new aristocracy.

40. Badot 1973; Raaflaub and Samons 1990, 427–28. The precise chronology of Augustus' law suppressing the *collegia* is uncertain, but perhaps we should place it in the context of Rufus' activities; Rotondi 1912, 442–43, provisionally dates this law to 21 BC.

41. The first purging of the senate took place in 29/28 BC (Dio 52.42.1–7; Suet. *Aug.* 35.1–3, cf. 37). On Augustus' relationship with the senate, see Sattler 1960; Talbert 1984, 167, 196, 224, 262, 267, 298, 412, 423, 434, 488–89.

42. For a text of the *Tabula Hebana*, see Oliver and Palmer 1954 (also in Ehrenberg and Jones 1955, 94a).

43. This is the view of Tibiletti 1953, 28–47 (followed by Jones 1955, 37–38).

44. Frei-Stolba 1967, 123, with bibliography cited in n. 169; cf. also the remarks of Béranger 1957.

45. Frei-Stolba 1967, 125–27; Staveley 1972, 219.

46. Brunt 1961, 76–77.

47. Jones (1955) has argued that the number of "new men" (*novi homines*) increased after AD 5 and attributes the increase to the influence of this select assembly. Brunt (1961, 73) has countered that the increase is in fact overstated and actually begins in 5 BC, when Augustus began appointing suffect consuls.

48. Lintott 1999, 40.

49. That Agrippa held tribunician power is clear from Augustus' *laudatio* at his funeral, partially preserved on papyrus (Koenen 1970). Less clear is how this power was conferred. Koenen believes that it was conferred only by decree of the senate, but I am inclined to agree with Badian (1980/81, 99–101) that a vote of the people in the assembly was also necessary.

50. Yavetz 1983, 59.

51. Macrobius (1.12.35) includes the text of the *senatus consultum*; cf. Dio 53.20.2–4; Liv. 134. Rotondi 1912, 441.

52. Southern 1998, 122–23.

53. Sen. *Ben*. 6.32.1. On these laws more generally, see Csillag 1976.

54. Fron. *Aq*. 129: *T. Quin<c>tius Crispinus consul populum iure rogavit populusque iure scivit in foro pro rostris aedis Divi Iuli{i} p<r(idie)> <k(alendas)> Iulias, tribu<s> Sergia principium fuit, pro tribu{s}Sex.<–>L. f. Virro <primus scivit>*. "T. Quinctius Crispinus as consul lawfully proposed to the people and the people lawfully resolved in the forum before the rostra of the temple of the deified Julius on the day before the Kalends of July, the tribe Sergia was the first to vote, for his tribe Sex.<–> L. F. Virro <voted first.>" Text and translation can be found in Crawford 1996, no. 63, 2.795, 797.

55. Other laws that bear the names of consuls are the *Lex Fufia Caninia* (2 BC) and the *Lex Aelia Sentia* (AD 4) on manumissions (Rotondi 1912, 454–56), and the *Lex Papia Poppaea* on marriage (AD 9) (Rotondi 1912, 457–62). All other laws of the Principate after 23 BC bear the name of the *princeps*.

56. On this *rostra*, see Coarelli 1992, 2.308–24.

57. Yavetz 1969, 108; Cameron 1976, 157–92; Gilbert 1976, 71–100; cf. Bollinger 1969, 44–55.

58. For his religious offices see *Anc*. 7.3 and 10.2 (his election as Pontifex Maximus); for the *princeps* as a subject of vows see *Anc*. 9 and the object of sacrifice, 11. Augustus minted a coin in 16 BC depicting the emblems of the four major priestly colleges of which he was a member; *RIC* 1^2 69, nos. 367–68. Cf. *RIC* 1^2 73, no. 410, 13 BC; Beard, North, and Price 1998, 1.186.

59. The epigraphic calendars, which show how Augustus was celebrated, have been collected by Ehrenberg and Jones 1955, 44–55. On the celebration of his birthday in 20 BC, see Dio 54.8.5; praetors seem to have taken over the celebration by 12 BC (Dio 54.34.2). Augustus' birthday was permanently celebrated by *ludi circenses* beginning in 8 BC, following Tiberius' victory over some German tribes, for which he was

awarded a triumph (Dio 55.6.6). At the same time the *princeps* extended the Pomerium and allowed the name of the month Sextilis to be changed to Augustus (Dio 55.6.6–7).

60. Syme 1986, 41, refers to him as a "republican of a kind."

61. Tac. *Ann.* 2.43.2; Syme 1986, 368–69.

62. Jones surmises that the difficulty in filling the aedileship can be attributed to the fact that it was not a necessary step on the *cursus honorum*, and for that reason ambitious aristocrats bypassed it (1955, 32). But it seems to have been an important step in Marcellus' career, and the evidence of the Triumviral period indicates that the difficulties in filling the aedileship were not new to the Principate.

63. On the importance of praetors for the production of games see Dio 54.2.3–4; cf. also P. Servilius' magnificent *venatio* as praetor in 25 BC (Dio 53.27.6) and the games of Drusus' praetorship in 11 (Dio 54.34.1).

64. The fact that Marcellus seems to have held the aedileship in two separate years is another indication of the difficulties Augustus experienced in filling this magistracy. On Marcellus' games in 23 see Dio 53.31.2–3; cf. 53.30.2; Prop. 3.18; cf. Vell. 2.93.1.

65. In particular, Agrippa's games, first as praetor in 40 and then as aedile in 33 (see chap. 8).

66. In 28 BC (Dio 53.1.4). Augustus instituted this festival immediately after his return to Rome in 29 (Dio 51.1.2). In 16 Agrippa helped celebrate this festival in absentia as one of the *quindecimviri* (Dio 54.19.8).

67. Dio 53.31.1; cf. also Sen. *Dial.* 11.15.3; 6.2.3; Vell. 2.93; Tac. *Ann.* 1.3.1; *Hist.* 1.15.1–2. The issues surrounding Augustus' designation of Marcellus as successor have been discussed recently by Brandt 1995.

68. The active participation of Caracalla and Geta at the celebration of the *Ludi Saeculares* under Septimius Severus in AD 203 showed similarly the future of that dynasty; Birley 1972, 156–60.

69. His previous consulship of 5 BC occurred when Gaius donned the *toga virilis* (Dio 55.9.9).

70. Dio 55.10.1–8; Vell. 2.100.2; cf. Aug. *Anc.* 21.1.

71. The construction of a Temple of Mars Ultor on the Capitolium, as Dio states (54.8.3), remains a matter of dispute; for a recent discussion, see Rich 1998, 79–88.

72. Cf. Rich 1998, 88.

73. On the Forum Augustum as a historical record see Luce 1990.

74. Suet. *Aug.* 31.5: *commentum id se, ut ad illorum <vitam> velut ad exemplar et ipse, dum viveret, et insequentium aetatium principes exigerentur a civibus.*

75. On this *naumachia* see also Ov. *Ars* 1.171–74; Coleman 1993. For its location see Haselberger 2002, 179 (s.v. "naumachia").

76. Aug. *Anc.* 19.1; Humphrey 1986, 78–83.

77. Another reminder of the importance of Augustus' family in the history of Rome was the performance of the *Lusus Troiae* (Dio 55.10.7).

78. See the discussion of Gaius' ceremonial departure, later in this chapter.

79. On the symbolic meaning of such *venationes*, see Wiedemann 1992, 59–63.

80. Dio 55.10.8; possibly also at this exhibition, locals from Tentyra were on hand to net the crocodiles and display them to the spectators at closer quarters (Strabo 17.1.44; Toynbee 1973, 219; cf. Coleman 1993, 56).

81. Coleman 1993, 72.

82. Syme 1974, 15; cf. Bowersock 1984, 174.

83. Zanker 1988, 84.

84. My conclusions owe much to the discussion in Coleman 1993, 69–70, 72–73.

85. On the question of the *saeculum*, see Pighi 1965; Hall 1986. On the origin of the games, see Brind'Amour 1978; Coarelli 1993.

86. This inference is based on the list of *quindecimviri* provided by Lewis 1955, 86.

87. Cf. the vows undertaken on behalf of Augustus' well-being in accordance with a decree of the senate (*Anc.* 9) and the insertion of his name in the Salian hymn (*Anc.* 10.1).

88. Manilius Fuscus in a speech at a senate meeting in AD 204, in which he advocated the production of the seventh edition of the *Ludi Saeculares*, put on in imitation of Augustus' games, expressed this idea more explicitly: "You should, with all worship and veneration of the immortal gods, for the security and eternity of the empire, frequent the most sacred shrines, for the rendering and giving of thanks, so that the immortal gods may pass on to the future generations what our ancestors have built up and the things which, after previously conferring them on our ancestors, they have granted to our own times as well" (*CIL* 6.32326.21–25; trans. Birley 1972, 157).

89. *CIL* 6.32323.100: *Ludique noctu, sacrificio [co]nfecto, sunt commissi in scaena quoi theatrum adiectum non fuit, nullis positis sedilibus. . . .*

90. On the location of the Tarentum, see Coarelli 1997, 74–100, with fig. 9 on p. 86; Haselberger 2002, 240.

91. Haselberger 2002, 242.

92. Dio 55.10.7; cf. Vell. 2.100.2. Performances of the *Lusus Troiae* were not without incident in this period. According to Suetonius, Nonius Asprenas was injured in a fall from his horse (*lapsu debilitatum*) at one performance, for which Augustus conferred on him the hereditary name "Torquatus" along with a golden torque, but when Asinius Pollio's grandson broke his leg (date unknown), and Pollio afterward complained about it in the senate, Augustus put an end to the performances (Suet. *Aug.* 43.2). The performance in 2 BC is the last attested in the reign of Augustus.

93. So Tiberius in an edict that Tacitus records (*Ann.* 3.6.3): *Principes mortales, rem publicam aeternam esse.* "Emperors die; the Republic is forever."

94. Dio 54.12.2. Only seven triumphs are recorded between 28 and 19 BC in the *Fasti Triumphales* (*Inscr. Ital.* 13.1, p. 87).

95. Dio 51.24.4. Augustus also rebuilt a temple to Jupiter Feretrius, perhaps to show a special relationship with this deity (Nep. *Att.* 20.3; Aug. *Anc.* 19.2; Liv. 4.20.7; cf. D. H. 2.34.4; F. Coarelli, s.v. "Iuppiter Feretrius, Aedes," *LTUR* 3.135–36). One explanation for Augustus' refusal of Crassus' request was that Crassus was not consul and therefore did not engage in battle under his own auspices and win the victory from which the *spolia opima* were taken. This technicality made it impossible for him legitimately to claim the right to offer the *spolia opima* to Jupiter Feretrius. Dessau (1906) first offered this explanation, which Syme advanced (1939, 308, with n. 2). More recently, Rich (1996) has questioned this explanation and asserted instead that Crassus probably never laid claim to the *spolia opima*, perhaps out of fear of offending Octavian. It has recently been suggested, however, that the tradition of the *spolia opima* was "invented" in part by Augustus as a display of his supremacy (Flower 2000). This tradi-

tion, in some ways similar to Octavian's use of the Fetial ceremony in 32 BC, demonstrates further Augustus' desire to root his new form of government in rituals that were thought to be ancient.

96. Eck 1984, 138; on Augustus' changing attitude toward senatorial self-representation, see also Wallace-Hadrill 1986, 79.

97. Dio 54.8.3. It seems that Augustus declined to celebrate this *ovatio* (Rich 1998, 75–79).

98. In 37, Dio 48.49.4; in 19, Dio 54.11.6; in 14, Dio 54.24.7. L. Piso was awarded triumphal honors in 11 for a victory over the Bessi (Dio 54.34.7); in AD 6 Cornelius Cossus received triumphal honors for a victory over the Gaetulians (Dio 55.28.4); in the same year C. Sentius received the same for his victory over the Germans (Dio 55.28.6). On the origins of the *ornamenta triumphalia,* see Abaecherli Boyce 1942 and more generally Maxfield 1981, 101–9.

99. It is not clear whether Augustus was favoring Drusus over Tiberius, or whether it was the former and not the latter who had the better chance to succeed him. It is perhaps too early in Augustus' Principate to draw any firm conclusions about the succession, since in later years he showered the sons of Agrippa with special honors before their premature deaths compelled him, as the tradition tells it, to look to Tiberius once again.

100. The senate granted this honor to Augustus in conjunction with a triumph that he never celebrated (Dio 53.26.5).

101. On the imperial *adventus*, see Lehnen 1997.

102. Suet. *Aug.* 59; Alföldi 1980, 88–90.

103. On this monument and the forum of which it was part, see Zanker 1968 and 1988, 192–215; Anderson 1984, 65–100; Richardson 1992, 160–62; V. Kockel, s.v. "Forum Augustum," *LTUR* 2.289–95; Bonnefond 1987; La Rocca, Ungaro, and Meneghini 1995, 38–87; Evans 1992, 109–18; Flower 1996, 224–36; Galinsky 1996, 197–213.

104. On Tiberius' retirement and the reasons for it, see Vell. 2.99.2; Suet. *Tib.* 10; Bowersock 1984; cf. also Levick 1972.

105. Tiberius was praised for his willingness to attend funerals of prominent aristocrats and for sanctioning the revival of the custom of having the deceased publicly praised at these funerals (Suet. *Tib.* 32.1). For funerals under Augustus, see Flower 1996, 237–46; for imperial funerals more generally, see Arce 1988, esp. 35–57, and Price 1987.

106. Cf. Price 1987, 62.

107. We first observe the custom of concealing the body with a curtain in the context of M. Agrippa's funeral, which took place two years earlier (Dio 54.28.3–5).

108. It is possible that, by concealing the body in this way, Augustus was hoping to avoid the mob violence that the display of the deceased provoked at the funerals of Clodius and Caesar. It must be admitted, however, that the latter two funerals occurred at politically volatile times and both men died violent deaths.

109. Drusus' body also lay in state in the Forum (Dio 55.2.2).

110. Dio informs us that Augustus did not accept all the honors decreed for Octavia (54.35.5); perhaps this included divine status.

111. Dio 55.2.5; on Drusus' triumph, see the discussion earlier in this chapter.

112. Tac. *Ann.* 3.5.1; Flower 1996, 242–44.

113. Although in a speech to the senate Augustus did express his affection for Drusus by calling him an heir like his sons (*coheredem semper filiis*; Suet. *Claud.* 1.5).

114. Suet. *Claud.* 1.5: *similes ei Caesares suos facerent sibique tam honestum quandoque exitum darent quam illi dedissent.*

115. Tac. *Ann.* 3.5.1: *Circumfusas lecto Claudiorum Iuliorumque imagines; defletum in foro, laudatum pro rostris.* "The busts of the Claudian and Julian families surrounded the bier; [Drusus] was mourned in the Forum and eulogized on the Rostra."

116. Dio 56.34.2–3. An image of Pompeius can also be attributed to his relationship to Augustus. However, since Dio notes that images of the people that Pompeius conquered were also paraded (56.34.3), it seems to me that the emphasis was on Pompeius' role as conqueror, as one of the *summi viri*, not as a relative of Augustus.

117. For an imaginary reconstruction of Augustus' funeral, see Favro 1996, 252–55.

118. Sulla's funeral also bore a striking resemblance to a triumph (App. *BC* 1.105.493–106); Caesar's funeral procession included actors dressed in triumphal garb who impersonated the deceased (Suet. *Jul.* 84.4); Drusus' funeral procession may have closely followed the traditional route of a triumph.

119. For a general treatment of *imagines* in the Augustan Principate, see Flower 1996, 224–36.

120. Perhaps he read a text prepared by Augustus; Flower 1996, 244.

121. Dio 56.35.1. That Tiberius was acting in accordance with a decree of the senate, I infer from Dio's language (. . . δημοσίας τρόπον τινὰ φωνῆς ἡ γερουσία καλῶς ποιοῦσα ἠξίωσεν αὐτόν. . . .). "The senate acting well deemed [Augustus] worthy of a public eulogy of some sort."

122. Cic. *Pis.* 55; Jos. *BJ* 7.130. Coarelli 1988, 363–414 places it in the Velabrum at the end of the Vicus Jugarius; Platner-Ashby 1929, 418–19; cf. Versnel 1970, 132–63.

123. Dio 56.42.2. It is not clear if Dio means members of the praetorian guard or perhaps *vigiles*. A similar parade encircled Sulla's pyre (App. *BC* 1.106.500).

124. On the custom of *consecratio*, see Bickerman 1973 and Arce 1988, 125–57; cf. also Kierdorf 1986; on the symbolism of the eagle, see Arce 1998, 131–40.

References

Abbot, F. F. 1907. "The Theatre as a Factor in Roman Politics under the Republic." *TAPA* 38:49–56.

Abaecherli Boyce, A. 1942. "The Origin of *Ornamenta Triumphalia*." *CP* 37:130–41.

Adcock, F. E. 1951. "The Interpretation of *Res Gestae Divi Augusti* 34.1." *CQ* 45:130–35.

Aigner, Heribert. 1974. *Die Soldaten als Machtfaktor in der ausgehenden Republik*. Innsbruck: AMOE.

Albert, Maurice. 1883. *Le Culte de Castor et Pollux en Italie*. Paris: École française de Rome.

Aldrete, Gregory. 1999. *Gestures and Acclamations in Ancient Rome*. Baltimore, MD: Johns Hopkins University Press.

Alföldi, Andreas. 1951. "Die Geburt der kaiserlichen Bildsymbolik: Kleine Beiträge au ihrer Entstehungsgeschichte. 2. Der Neue Romulus." *MH* 8:190–215.

———. 1953. *Studien über Caesars Monarchie*. Lund.

———. 1958. "Der Einmarsch Octavians in Rom." *Hermes* 86:480–96.

———. 1976. *Oktavians Aufstieg zur Macht*. Bonn: Habelt.

———. 1980. *Die monarchische Repräsentation im römischen Kaiserreiche*. Darmstadt: Wissenschaftliche Buchgesellschaft.

Anderson, J. C., Jr. 1984. *The Historical Topography of the Imperial Fora*. Brussels: Latomus.

Arce, Javier. 1988. *Funus Imperatorum: Los funerales de los emperadores romanos*. Madrid: Alianza Editorial.

Babcock, Charles L. 1965. "The Early Career of Fulvia." *AJP* 86:1–32.

Badian, Ernst. 1964. "Marius and the Nobles." *Durham University Journal* 56 (n.s. 25):141–54.

———. 1980/81. "Notes on the *Laudatio* of Agrippa." *CJ* 76:97–109.

———. 1990. "The Consuls, 179–49 BC." *Chiron* 20:371–413.

Badot, P. 1973. "À propos de la conspiration de M. Egnatius Rufus." *Latomus* 32:606–15.

Bardt, Carl. 1909. "Plancus und Lepidus im Mutinensischen Krieg." *Hermes* 44:574–93.

Barton, I. M., ed. 1989. *Roman Public Buildings*. Exeter: University of Exeter Press.

Beard, Mary, John North, and Simon Price. 1998. *Religions of Rome*. 2 vols. Cambridge: Cambridge University Press.

Becht, Erich. 1911. *Regeste über die Zeit von Cäsars Ermordung bis zum Umschwung in der Politik des Antonius*. Dissertation. University of Freiburg.

Bell, A. J. E. 1997. "Cicero and the Spectacle of Power." *JRS* 87:1–22.

Bell, Catherine M. 1992. *Ritual Theory, Ritual Practice*. New York: Oxford University Press.

Beloch, K. J. 1926. *Römische Geschichte bis zum Beginn der punischen Kriege*. Leipzig: de Gruyter.

Benario, H. W. 1975. "Octavian's Status in 32 BC." *Chiron* 5:301–9.

Benner, Herbert. 1987. *Die Politik des P. Clodius Pulcher*. Stuttgart: Steiner.

Béranger, Jean. 1953. *Recherches sur l'aspect idéologique du Principat*. Basel: F. Reinhardt.

———. 1957. "La démocratie sous l'Empire romain: les opérations électorales de la *Tabula Hebana* et la *destinatio*." MH 14:216–40; repr. 1973, 209–42.

———. 1958. "L'accession d'Auguste et l'idéologie du '*privatus*.'" *Palaeologia* 7:1–11; repr. 1973, 243–58.

———. 1973. *Principatus. Études de notions et d'histoire politiques dans l'Antiquité gréco-romaine*. Geneva: Librairie Droz S. A.

Bergmann, Bettina, and Christine Kondoleon, eds. 1999. *The Art of Ancient Spectacle*. New Haven, CT: Yale University Press.

Bernstein, Frank. 1998. *Ludi Publici: Untersuchungen zur Entstehung und Entwicklung der offentlichen Spiele im republikanischen Rom*. Stuttgart: Steiner.

Bianchi, U. 1958. "Cesare ed I Lupercali del 44 a. C." *StudRom* 6:253–59.

Bickerman, Elias. 1973. "Consecratio." In *Le Culte des Souverains dans l'Empire Romain*, 3–25. Entretiens, Tome XIX. Geneva: Fondation Hardt pour l'Étude de l'Antiquité Classique.

Birley, A. R. 1972/1988. *Septimius Severus: The African Emperor*. New Haven, CT: Yale University Press.

Bleicken, Jochen. 1962. "Der Begriff der Freiheit in der letzten Phase der römischen Republik." *HZ* 195:1–20.

———. 1975. Lex Publica: *Gesetz und Recht in der römischen Republik*. Berlin: de Gruyter.

———. 1990. *Zwischen Republik und Prinzipat: Zum Charakter des zweiten Triumvirats*. Göttingen: Vandenhoeck and Ruprecht.

———. 1998. *Augustus: Eine Biographie*. Berlin: A. Fest.

Bodel, John. 1999a. "Death on Display: Looking at Roman Funerals." In *The Art of Ancient Spectacle*, ed. Bettina Bergmann and Christine Kondoleon, 259–81. New Haven, CT: Yale University Press.

———. 1999b. "Punishing Piso." *AJP* 120:43–63.

Bollinger, Traugott. 1969.Theatralis licentia: *Die Publikumsdemonstrationen an den öffentlichen Spielen im Rom der früheren Kaiserzeit und ihre Bedeutung im politischen Leben*. Winterthur: Hans Schellenberg.

Bonfante Warren, Larissa. 1970. "Roman Triumphs and Etruscan Kings: The Changing Face of the Triumph." *JRS* 60:49–66.

Bonnefond, Marianne. 1987. "Transferts de fonctions et mutation idéologique: le Capitole et le Forum d'Auguste." In *L'Urbs: Espace urbain et histoire*, 251–78. Rome: École française de Rome.

Bonnefond-Coudry, Marianne. 1989. *Le Sénat de la République Romaine*. Rome: École française de Rome.

Bosworth, A. B. 1972. "Asinius Pollio and Augustus." *Historia* 21:441–73.

Botermann, Helga. 1968. *Die Soldaten und die römischen Republik in der Zeit von Caesars Tod bis zur Begründung des zweiten Triumvirats*. Munich.

Botsford, G. W. 1909. *The Roman Assemblies*. New York: Macmillan.

Bowersock, G. W. 1984. "Augustus and the East: The Problem of the Succession." In *Caesar Augustus: Seven Aspects*, ed. Fergus Millar and E. Segal, 169–88. Oxford: Clarendon Press.

Brandt, H. 1995. "Marcellus 'successioni praeparatus'? Augustus, Marcellus und die Jahre 29–23 v. Chr." *Chiron* 25:1–17.

Brecht, C. H. 1938. *Perduellio: Eine Studie zu ihrer begrifflichen Abgrenzung im römischen Strafrecht bis zum Ausgang der Republik*. Munich: Beck.

Brennan, T. Corey. 1996. "Triumphus in Monte Albano." In *Transitions to Empire: Essays in Greco-Roman History, 360–146 B.C., in Honor of E. Badian*, ed. R. W. Wallace and E. M. Harris, 315–37. Norman: University of Oklahoma Press.

Brind'Amour, P. 1978. "L'Origine des Jeux Séculaires." *ANRW* 2.16.2:1334–1417.

Bringmann, Klaus. 1996. "Der Prozess gegen die Caesarmörder: Von der Amnestie zum politischen Schauprozess." In *Grosse Prozesse: Recht und Gerechtigkeit in der Geschichte*. Ed. Uwe Schultz, 32–40. Munich: Beck

Briscoe, John, ed. 1986. *Livius: Ab Urbe Condita Libri XLI–XLV*. Stuttgart: Teubner.

Bruhns, Hinnerk. 1978. *Caesar und die römische Oberschicht in den Jahren 49–44 v. Chr*. Göttingen: Vandenhoeck and Ruprecht.

Brunt, P. A. 1961. "The *Lex Valeria Cornelia*." *JRS* 51:71–83.

———. 1966. "The Roman Mob." *P&P* 35:3–27.

———. 1971a. *Italian Manpower (225 B.C.–A.D. 14)*. London: Oxford University Press.

———. 1971b. *Social Conflicts in the Roman Republic*. NewYork: Norton.

———. 1982. "*Nobilitas* and *Novitas*." *JRS* 72:1–17.

———. 1988. *The Fall of the Roman Republic and Related Essays*. Oxford: Clarendon Press.

Brunt, P. A., and J. M. Moore, eds. 1967. *Res Gestae Divi Augusti: The Achievements of the Divine Augustus*. London: Oxford University Press.

Burckhardt, L. 1990. "The Political Elite of the Roman Republic: Comments on Recent Discussion of the Concepts *Nobilitas* and *Homo Novus*." *Historia* 39:77–99.

Burkert, Walter. 1962. "Caesar und Romulus-Quirinus." *Historia* 11:356–76.

Buttrey, T. V. 1960. "The Denarius of P. Ventidius." *ANSMN* 9:95–108.

Cahn, H. A. 1957. "L'aureus de Brutus avec EID: MAR." In Bd. 2, *Actes*, of *Congrès international de numismatique*, ed. J. Babelon and J. Lafaurie, 213–17. Paris: Commission internationale de numismatique.

Cameron, Alan. 1976. *Circus Factions*. Oxford: Clarendon Press.

Canfora, L. 1980. "Proscrizioni e dissesto sociale nella repubblica Romana." *Klio* 62:425–37.

Cannadine, David. 1987. "Introduction: Divine Rites of Kings." In *Rituals of Royalty*, ed. David Cannadine and Simon Price, 1–19. Cambridge: Cambridge University Press.

Cannadine, David, and Simon Price, eds. 1987. *Rituals of Royalty*. Cambridge: Cambridge University Press.

Canetti, Elias. 1962. *Crowds and Power*. Trans. C. Stewart. London: Gollancz.

Carney, T. F. 1960. "Cicero's Picture of Marius." *WS* 73:83–122.

Carter, J. M. 1970. *The Battle of Actium*. London: Hamilton.

———. 1996. *Appian: Civil Wars*. London: Penguin.

Cary, Earnest. 1917. *Dio's Roman History*. 9 vols. Cambridge, MA: Harvard University Press.

Castagnoli, Ferdinando. 1946. "Atrium Libertatis." *RAL* 8.1:276–91.

———. 1969. *Topografia e urbanistica di roma antica*. Bologna: L. Capelli.

Çelik, Zeynep, Diane Favro, and Richard Ingersoll, eds. 1994. *Streets of the World, Critical Perspectives on Public Space*. Berkeley: University of California Press.

Champlin, Edward. 1991. *Final Judgments*. Berkeley: University of California Press.

Chaniotis, Angelos. 1997. "Theatricality beyond the Theater: Staging Public Life in the Hellenistic World." *Pallas* 47: 219–59.

Coarelli, Filippo. 1988. *Il Foro Boario*. Rome: Quasar.

———. 1992. *Il Foro Romano*. 2 vols. Rome: Quasar.

———. 1993. "Note sui ludi Saeculares." In *Spectacles sportifs et scéniques dans le monde étrusco-italique*, 211–45. Rome: École française de Rome.

———. 1997. *Il Campo Marzio*, vol. 1. Rome: Quasar.

Coleman, K. M. 1993. "Launching into History: Aquatic Displays in the Early Empire." *JRS* 83:48–74.

Cornell, T. J. 1986. "The Formation of the Historical Tradition of Early Rome." In *Past Perspectives: Studies in Greek and Roman Historical Writing*, ed. I. Moxon, J. D. Smart, and A. J. Woodman, 67–86. Cambridge: Cambridge University Press.

———. 1991. "Rome: The History of an Anachronism." In *City States in Classical Antiquity and Medieval Italy*, ed. A. Molho, K. Raaflaub, and J. Emlen, 53–69. Ann Arbor: University of Michigan Press.

———. 1995. *The Beginnings of Rome*. London: Routledge Press.

Crawford, M. H. 1974. *Roman Republican Coinage*. 2 vols. London: Cambridge University Press.

———. ed. 1996. *Roman Statutes*. 2 vols. BICS Supplement 64. London: Institute of Classical Studies.

Csillag, Pal. 1976. *The Augustan Laws on Family Relations*. Budapest: Akademiai Kiado.

Cuff, P. J. 1973. "The Settlement of 23 B.C.: A Note." *RFIC* 101:466–77.

Damon, Cynthia, and Christopher MacKay. 1995. "On the Prosecution of C. Antonius in 76 B.C." *Historia* 44:37–55.

Davidson, James. 1991. "The Gaze in Polybius' Histories." *JRS* 81:9–24.

Delia, Diana. 1991. "Fulvia Reconsidered." In *Women's History and Ancient History*, ed. S. Pomeroy, 197–217. Chapel Hill: University of North Carolina Press.

Deroux, Carl, ed. 1983. *Studies in Latin Literature and History*, vol. 3. Brussels: Latomus.

Dessau, Hermann. 1906. "Livius und Augustus." *Hermes* 41:142–51.

Deutsch, M. 1928. "Caesar's Son and Heir." *California Publications in Classical Philology* 9:149–200.

Dubourdieu, Annie. 1989. *Les origines et le développement du culte des Pénates à Rome*. Rome: École française de Rome.
Dupont, Florence. 1985. *L'acteur-roi ou Le théâtre dans la Rome antique*. Paris: Belles Lettres.
Earl, D. C. 1961. *The Political Thought of Sallust*. Cambridge: Cambridge University Press.
———. 1967. *The Moral and Political Tradition of Rome*. Ithaca, NY: Cornell University Press.
Eck, Werner. 1984. "Senatorial Self-Representation: Developments in the Augustan Period." In *Caesar Augustus: Seven Aspects*, ed. Fergus Millar and E. Segal, 129–67. Oxford: Clarendon Press.
Eder, Walter, ed. 1990/1991. *Staat und Staatlichkeit in der frühen römischen Republik*. Stuttgart: Steiner.
Edwards, Catherine. 1996. *Writing Rome*. Cambridge: Cambridge University Press.
Ehrenberg, Victor. 1964. "Caesar's Final Aims." *HSCP* 68:149–61.
Ehrenberg, Victor, and A. H. M. Jones, eds. 1955. *Documents Illustrating the Reigns of Augustus and Tiberius*. 2nd ed. Oxford: Clarendon Press.
Ehrenwirth, Ursula. 1971. *Kritisch-chronologische Untersuchungen für die Zeit vom 1. Juni bis zum 9. Oktober 44 v. Chr*. Munich: Ehrenwirth Verlag.
Epstein, David F. 1987. *Personal Enmity in Roman Politics, 218–43* B.C. London: Croom Helm.
Evans, Jane DeRose. 1987. "The Sicilian Coinage of Sextus Pompeius (Crawford 511)." *ANSMN* 32:97–157.
———. 1992. *The Art of Persuasion*. Ann Arbor: University of Michigan Press.
Fadinger, Volker. 1969. *Die Begründung des Prinzipats*. Berlin.
Favro, Diane. 1994. "Rome: The Street Triumphant; The Urban Impact of Roman Triumphal Parades." In *Streets of the World, Critical Perspectives on Public Space*, ed. Zeynep Çelik, Diane Favro, and Richard Ingersoll, 151–64. Berkeley: University of California Press.
———. 1996. *The Urban Image of Augustan Rome*. Cambridge: Cambridge University Press.
Feldherr, Andrew. 1998. *Spectacle and Society in Livy's History*. Berkeley: University of California Press.
Flaig, Egon. 1995. "Entscheidung und Konsens: Zu den Feldern der politischen Kommunikation zwischen Aristokratie und Plebs." In *Demokratie in Rom? Die Rolle des Volkes in der Politik der römischen Republik*, ed. Martin Jehne, 77–127. Stuttgart: Steiner.
Flower, Harriet. 1995. "*Fabulae Praetextae* in Context: When Were Plays on Contemporary Subjects Performed in Republican Rome?" *CQ* 45:170–90.
———. 1996. *Ancestor Masks and Aristocratic Power in Roman Culture*. Oxford: Clarendon Press.
———. 2000. "The Tradition of the *Spolia Opima:* M. Claudius Marcellus and Augustus." *ClAnt* 19:34–64.
Fowler, W. W. 1908. *Roman Festivals of the Period of the Republic*. London: MacMillan.
Fraccaro, Plinio. 1957. "La Procedura del voto nei comizi tributi romani." *Opuscula* 2:235–54.

Frandsen, P. S. 1836. M. *Vipsanius Agrippa: Eine historische Untersuchung über dessen Leben und Wirken*. Altona.

Frei-Stolba, Regula. 1967. *Untersuchungen zu den Wahlen in der römischen Kaiserzeit*. Zurich: Juris.

Friedländer, Ludwig. 1922. 10th ed. *Darstellungen aus der Sittengeschichte Roms*. 4 vols. Leipzig: Hirzel.

Frier, B. W. 1985. *The Rise of the Roman Jurists: Studies in Cicero's* Pro Caecina. Princeton: Princeton University Press.

Frisch, Hartvig. 1946. *Cicero's Fight for the Republic*. Copenhagen: Gyldendalske Boghandel.

Gabba, Emilio, ed. and trans. 1970. *Appiani Bellorum Civilium Liber Quintus*. Florence.

———. 1971. "The Perusine War and Triumviral Italy." *HSCP* 75:139–60.

Gagé, Jean. 1957. "Les clientèles triomphales de la République romaine." *RH* 218:1–27.

Galinsky, Karl. 1996. *Augustan Culture*. Princeton: Princeton University Press.

Gardthausen, Viktor. 1891. *Augustus und seine Zeit*. 2 vols. Leipzig: Teubner.

Garnsey, Peter. 1988. *Famine and Food Supply in the Graeco-Roman World*. Cambridge: Cambridge University Press.

Geertz, Clifford. 1973. "Deep Play: Notes on the Balinese Cockfight." 412–53. *The Interpretation of Cultures*. New York: Basic Books.

———. 1977. "Centers, Kings, and Charisma: Reflections on the Symbolics of Power." In *Culture and Its Creators: Essays in Honor of Edward Shils*, ed. J. Ben-David and T. N. Clark, 150–71. Chicago: University of Chicago Press.

Gelzer, Matthias. 1968a. *Caesar: Politician and Statesman*. Trans. P. Needham. Cambridge, MA: Harvard University Press.

———. 1968b. *The Roman Nobility*. Trans. R. Seager. Oxford: Blackwell.

Gentili, G. V. 1948. "Due nuovi frammenti dei Fasti consolari di Cupra maritima." *Epigraphica* 10:131–42.

Gervasoni, M. C. 1998. *Les Magistrats des cités italiennes de la seconde guerre punique à Auguste: Le Latium et la Campanie*. Rome: École Française de Rome.

Gesche, Helga. 1968. *Die Vergottung Caesars*. Kallmünz: Lassleben.

———. 1973. "Hat Caesar den Octavian zum Magister equitum designiert? Ein Beitrag zur Beurteilung der Adoption Octavians durch Caesar." *Historia* 22:468–78.

———. 1976. *Caesar*. Darmstadt: Wissenschaftliche Buchgesellschaft.

Gilbert, Rolf. 1976. *Die Beziehungen zwischen Princeps und stadtrömischer Plebs im frühen Principat*. Bochum: Studienverlag Brockmeyer.

Giovannini, Adalberto. 1983. *Consulare imperium*. Basel: Reinhardt.

Girardet, K. 1990. "Der Rechtsstatus Oktavians im Jahre 32 n. Chr." *RhM* 133:332–50.

———. 1995. "Per continuos annos decem (res gestae divi Augusti 7,1): Zur Frage nach dem Endtermin des Triumvirats." *Chiron* 25:147–61.

Goebel, A. 1852. *De Troiae Ludo*. Düren.

Gotter, Ulrich. 1996. *Der Diktator is Tot!* Stuttgart: Steiner.

Gowing, Alain. 1992. *The Triumviral Narratives of Appian and Cassius Dio*. Ann Arbor: University of Michigan Press.

Greenidge, A. H. J., and A. M. Clay, eds. 1960. *Sources for Roman History, 133–70 B.C.*, 2nd ed., rev. E. W. Gray. Oxford: Clarendon Press.

Groebe, Paul. 1893. *De legibus et SC. anni 710 quaestiones chronologicae.*

Gruen, Erich. 1968. *Roman Politics and the Criminal Courts, 149–78 B.C.* Cambridge, MA: Harvard University Press.

———. 1969. "The Consular Elections for 53 B.C." In vol. 2 of *Hommages à Marcel Renard,* ed. J. Bibauw, 311–21. Brussels: Latomus.

———. 1974/1995. *The Last Generation of the Roman Republic.* Berkeley: University of California Press.

———. 1991. "The Exercise of Power in the Roman Republic." In *City States in Classical Antiquity and Medieval Italy: Athens and Rome, Florence and Venice,* ed. A. Molho, K. Raaflaub, and J. Emlen, 251–67. Ann Arbor: University of Michigan Press.

Gurval, Robert. 1995. *Actium and Augustus: The Politics and Emotions of Civil War.* Ann Arbor: University of Michigan Press.

Hadas, Moses. 1930. *Sextus Pompey.* New York: Columbia University Press.

Hales, Shelley. 2003. *The Roman House and Social Identity.* Cambridge: Cambridge University Press.

Hall, C. M. 1923. *Nicolaus of Damascus' Life of Augustus: A Historical Commentary Embodying a Translation.* Smith Classical Studies no. 4. Northampton, MA.

Hall III, J. F. 1986. "The *Saeculum Novum* of Augustus and Its Etruscan Antecedents." *ANRW* 2.16.3:2564–89.

Hammer, Dean. 2002. *The Iliad as Politics: The Performance of Political Thought.* Norman: University of Oklahoma Press.

Hanson, J. A. 1959. *Roman Theater-Temples.* Princeton: Princeton University Press.

Harris, W. V. 1979/1985. *War and Imperialism in Republican Rome, 327–70 B.C.* Oxford: Clarendon Press.

———. 1990. "On Defining the Political Culture of the Roman Republic: Some Comments on Rosenstein, Williams, and North." *CP* 85:288–94.

Haselberger, Lothar, ed. 2002. *Mapping Augustan Rome.* JRA Suppl. Portsmouth, RI.

Hayne, Léonie. 1971. "Lepidus' Role after the Ides of March." *AClass* 14:109–17.

Hellegouarc'h, Joseph. 1963. *Le Vocabulaire latin des relations et des partis politiques sous la république.* Paris: Belles Lettres.

Herzog, Ernst. 1887–91. Vol. 2 of *Geschichte und System der römischen Staatsverfassung.* Leipzig.

Heskel, Julia. 1994. "Cicero as Evidence for Attitudes to Dress in the Late Republic." In *The World of Roman Costume,* ed. J. L. Sebesta and Larissa Bonfante, 133–45. Madison: University of Wisconsin Press.

Hinard, François. 1985a. *Les proscriptions de la Rome républicaine.* Rome: École française de Rome.

———. 1985b. *Sylla.* Paris: Fayard.

———. 1987. "Spectacle des exécutions et espace urbain." In *L'Urbs: Espace urbain et histoire,* 111–25. Rome: École française de Rome.

Hobsbawm, Eric J. 1963. *Primitive Rebels: Studies of Archaic Forms of Social Movement in the 19th and 20th Centuries.* 2nd ed. New York: Praeger.

———. and Ranger, T. 1983. *The Invention of Tradition.* Cambridge: Cambridge University Press.

Hölkeskamp, K.-J. 1987. *Die Entstehung der Nobilität.* Stuttgart: Steiner.

Hopkins, Keith. 1983a. *Death and Renewal.* Cambridge: Cambridge University Press.

———. 1983b. "Murderous Games." In *Death and Renewal*, 1–30. Cambridge: Cambridge University Press.

Hopkins, Keith, and Graham Burton. 1983. "Political Succession." In *Death and Renewal*, by Keith Hopkins, 31–119. Cambridge: Cambridge University Press.

Humphrey, J. H. 1986. *Roman Circuses: Arenas for Chariot Racing*. Berkeley: University of California Press.

Jaeger, Mary. 1997. *Livy's Written Rome*. Ann Arbor: University of Michigan Press.

Jehne, Martin. 1987. *Der Staat des Dictators Caesar*. Cologne.

———, ed. 1995. *Demokratie in Rom: Die Rolle des Volkes in der Politik der römischen Republik*. Stuttgart: Steiner.

Jones, A. H. M. 1955. "The Elections under Augustus." *JRS* 45:9–21; repr. 1960. *Studies in Roman Government and Law*. Oxford: Blackwell.

———. 1972. *The Criminal Courts of the Roman Republic and Principate*. Totowa, NJ: Rowman and Littlefield.

Jordan, Henri, and Christian Hülsen. 1871–1907. *Topographie der Stadt Rom in Altertum*. 2 vols. Berlin: Weidmannsche Buchhandlung.

Kearsley, R. A. 1999. "Octavian in the Year 32 B.C.: The S.C. *de Aphrodisiensibus* and the *genera militiae*." *RhM* 142:52–67.

Keaveney, Arthur. 1982. *Sulla: The Last Republican*. London: Croom-Helm.

———. 1983. "Sulla and the Gods." In vol. 3 of *Studies in Latin Literature and History*, ed. Carl Deroux, 44–79. Brussels: Latomus.

Keaveney, Arthur, and A. J. Madden. 1983. "An *Ovatio* for Octavian." *Phoenix* 37:245–47.

Kennedy, George. 1968. "Antony's Speech at Caesar's Funeral." *QJS* 54:99–106.

Keppie, Lawrence. 1984. *The Making of the Roman Army: From Republic to Empire*. Totowa, N.J.: Barnes and Noble Books.

Kienast, Dietmar. 1982. *Augustus. Prinzeps und Monarch*. Darmstadt: Wissenschaftliche Buchgesellschaft.

Kierdorf, Wilhelm. 1980. *Laudatio funebris: Interpretationen und Untersuchungen zur Entwicklung der römischen Leichenrede*. Beiträge zur klassischen Philologie, 106. Meisenheim am Glan: Hain.

———. 1986. "'Funus' und 'Consecratio'. Zu Terminologie und Ablauf der römischen Kaiserapotheose." *Chiron* 16:43–70.

Kleinstück, H. 1932. "Antike Beobachtungen zur meteorologischen Optik." *PhW* 52, nos. 35/38:238–44.

Koenen, Ludwig. 1970. "Die 'laudatio funebris' des Augustus für Agrippa auf einem neuen Papyrus." *ZPE* 5:217–83.

Kroll, Wilhelm. 1933. *Die Kultur der ciceronischen Zeit*. 2 vols. Leipzig: Dieterich.

Kromayer, Johannes. 1894. "Kleine Forschungen zur Geschichte des Zweiten Triumvirats [I–III]." *Hermes* 29:556–85.

Kunst, C. 1996. "Adoption und Testamentsadoption in der späten Republik." *Klio* 78:87–104.

Künzl, Ernst. 1988. *Der römische Triumph: Siegesfeiern im antiken Rom*. Munich: Beck.

La Rocca, Eugenio, Lucrezia Ungaro, and Roberto Meneghini. 1995. *I luoghi del consenso imperiale. Il foro di Augusto. Il foro di Traiano* I. Rome: Progetti Museali Editore.

Laser, Günter. 1997. "Populo et Scaenae Serviendum Est." *Die Bedeutung der städtischen Masse in der späten römischen Republik*. Trier: Wissenschaftlicher Verlag.

Latte, Kurt. 1960. *Römische Religionsgeschichte*. Munich: Beck.

Lehnen, Joachim. 1997. Adventus principis: *Untersuchungen zu Sinngehalt und Zeremoniell der Kaiserankunft in den Stadten des Imperium Romanum*. Frankfurt am Main: P. Lang.

Levi, M. A. 1933. *Ottaviano Capoparte*. 2 vols. Florence: La Nuova Italia.

Levick, Barbara. 1967. "Imperial Control of Elections in the Early Principate." *Historia* 16:209–30

———. 1972. "Tiberius' Retirement to Rhodes in 6 B.C." *Latomus* 31:779–813.

Lewis, M. W. H. 1955. *The Official Priests of Rome under the Julio-Claudians*. Rome: American Academy.

Lewis, Naphtali. 1991. "Rechtsfrage II: Octavian's Powers in 32 B.C." *LCM* 16:57–62.

Liegle, J. 1942. "L. Aemilius Paullus als Augur maximus im Jahre 160 und das Augurium des Heils." *Hermes* 77:249–312.

Linderski, Jerzy. 1965. "Constitutional Aspects of the Consular Elections in 59 B.C." *Historia* 14:423–42; repr. 1995:71–90.

———. 1973. "A. Gabinius A. F. Capito and the First Voter in the Legislative Comitia Tributa." *ZPE* 12:247–52; repr. 1995, 95–100.

———. 1984. "Rome, Aphrodisias and the *Res Gestae*: The *genera militiae* and the Status of Octavian." *JRS* 74:74–80; repr. 1995, 147–53.

———. 1995. *Roman Questions*. Stuttgart: Steiner.

Lintott, A. W. 1967. "P. Clodius Pulcher—*Felix Catilina?*" *G&R* 14:157–69.

———. 1968. *Violence in Republican Rome*. Oxford: Clarendon Press.

———. 1974. "Cicero and Milo." *JRS* 64:62–78.

———. 1999. *The Constitution of the Roman Republic*. Oxford: Clarendon Press.

Luce, T. J. 1990. "Livy, Augustus, and the Forum Augustum." In *Between Republic and Empire*, ed. K. A. Raaflaub and M. Toher,123–38. Berkeley: University of California Press.

MacMullen, Ramsay. 1974. *Roman Social Relations*, 50 B.C. *to* A.D. 284. New Haven, CT: Yale University Press.

———. 1980. "How Many Romans Voted?" *Athenaeum* 58:454–57.

Manuwald, B. 1979. *Cassius Dio und Augustus: Philologische Untersuchungen zu den Büchern 45–56 des dionischen Geschichtswerkes*. Palingenesia 14. Wiesbaden: Steiner.

Marquardt, Joachim. 1881–85. *Römische Staatsverwaltung*. 3 vols. Leipzig: Hirzel.

Marshall, A. J. 1984. "Symbols and Showmanship in Roman Public Life: The Fasces." *Phoenix* 38:120–41.

Marshall, B. A. 1972. "Crassus' Ovation in 71 B.C." *Historia* 21:669–78.

———. 1985. A *Historical Commentary on Asconius*. Columbia: University of Missouri Press.

Maxfield, V. A. 1981. *The Military Decorations of the Roman Army*. Berkeley: University of California Press.

Meier, Christian. 1966. *Res Publica Amissa*. Wiesbaden: Steiner (2nd ed. 1980. Frankfurt am Main: Suhrkamp).

———. 1995. *Caesar:* A *Biography*. Trans. D. McClintock. New York. (Orig. pub. in German, Berlin, 1982).

Meyer, Eduard. 1922. 3rd ed. *Caesars Monarchie und das Principat des Pompeius*. Stuttgart: Cotta.

Michels, A. K. 1967. *The Calendar of the Roman Republic*. Princeton: Princeton University Press.

Millar, Fergus. 1964. *A Study of Cassius Dio*. Oxford: Clarendon Press.

———. 1973. "Triumvirate and Principate." *JRS* 63:50–67.

———. 1977. *The Emperor in the Roman World*. Ithaca, NY: Cornell University Press.

———. 1984a. "The Political Character of the Classical Roman Republic." *JRS* 74:1–19.

———. 1984b. "State and Subject: The Impact of Monarchy." In *Caesar Augustus: Seven Aspects*, ed. Fergus Millar and E. Segal, 37–60. Oxford: Clarendon Press.

———. 1986. "Politics, Persuasion and the People before the Social War (150–90 B.C.)." *JRS* 76:1–11.

———. 1989. "Political Power in Mid-Republican Rome: *Curia* or *Comitium*?" *JRS* 79:138–50.

———. 1998. *The Crowd in Rome in the Late Republic*. Ann Arbor: University of Michigan Press.

Millar, Fergus, and E. Segal, eds. 1984. *Caesar Augustus: Seven Aspects*. Oxford: Clarendon Press.

Mitchell, T. N. 1991. *Cicero: Senior Statesman*. New Haven, CT: Yale University Press.

Molho, A., K. Raaflaub, and J. Emlen, eds. 1991. *City States in Classical Antiquity and Medieval Italy*. Ann Arbor: University of Michigan Press.

Mommsen, Th. 1859. "Die *Ludi Magni* und *Romani*." *RhM* 14:79–87; repr. 1864, 1.42–57.

———. 1864. *Römische Forschungen*, 2 vols. Berlin.

———. 1894. *The History of Rome*. 5 vols. Trans. W. P. Dickson. London: Richard Bentley and Son.

Morley, Neville. 2001. "The Transformation of Italy, 225–28 B.C." *JRS* 91:50–62.

Morselli, Chiara, and Edoardo Tortorici. 1989. *Curia, Forum Iulium, Forum Transitorium*. 2 vols. Rome: De Luca.

Motzo, R. B. 1940. "Le contiones di M. Antonio e di M. Bruto dopo la morte di Cesare." In *Studi di antichità classica offerti. . . a E. Ciaceri*, 136–43. Genoa.

Mouritsen, Henrik. 2001. *Plebs and Politics in the Late Roman Republic*. Cambridge: Cambridge University Press.

Moxon, I., J. D. Smart, and A. J. Woodman, eds. 1986. *Past Perspectives: Studies in Greek and Roman Historical Writing*. Cambridge: Cambridge University Press.

Münzer, Friedrich. 1999. *Roman Aristocratic Parties and Families*. Trans. T. Ridley. Baltimore, MD: Johns Hopkins University Press. Originally published as *Römische Adelsparteien und Adelsfamilien* (Stuttgart, 1920).

Nichols, F. M. 1877. *The Roman Forum: A Topographical Study*. London: Longmans.

Nicolet, Claude. 1980. *The World of the Citizen in Republican Rome*. Berkeley: University of California Press. Originally published as *Le Métier de citoyen dans la Rome républicaine* (Paris: Gallimard, 1976).

———. 1991. *Space, Geography, and Politics in the Early Roman Empire*. Ann Arbor: University of Michigan Press. Originally published as *L'Inventaire du monde: géographie et politique aux origines de l'Empire romain* (Paris: Fayard, 1988).

Nielsen, Inge, and Birte Poulsen. 1992. *The Temple of Castor and Pollux: The Pre-Augustan Temple Phases with Related Decorative Elements*. Rome: De Luca.

Nippel, Wilfried. 1995. *Public Order in Ancient Rome*. Cambridge: Cambridge University Press.

Nisbet, R. G. M. 1961. *M. Tulli Ciceronis: In L. Calpurnium Pisonem Oratio*. Oxford: Clarendon Press.

Noonan, J. 1990. "Livy 1.9.6: The Rape of the Sabine Women at the *Consualia*." CW 83:493–501.

Ogilvie, R. M. 1965. *A Commentary on Livy, Books 1–5*. Oxford: Clarendon Press.

Oliver, James H., and Robert E. A. Palmer 1954. "Text of the *Tabula Hebana*." AJP 75:225–49.

Paananen, Unto. 1993. "Legislation in the *Comitia Centuriata*." In Senatus populusque romanus: *Studies in Roman Republican Legislation*, ed. U. Paananen, K. Heikkilää, K. Sandberg, L. Savunen, and J. Vaahtera, 9–73. Helsinki: Helsinki University Press.

Palmer, R. E. A. 1978. "Octavian's First Attempt to Restore the Constitution (36 B.C.)." *Athenaeum* 56:315–28.

Palombi, Domenico. 1997. *Tra Palatino ed Esquilino: Velia Carinae Fagutal*. Rome: USPI.

Parker, Holt. 1999. "The Observed of All Observers: Spectacle, Applause, and Cultural Poetics." In *The Art of Ancient Spectacle*, ed. Bettina Bergmann and Christine Kondoleon, 163–79. New Haven, CT: Yale University Press.

Paterson, Jeremy. 1985. "Politics in the Late Republic." In *Roman Political Life, 90 B.C.–A.D. 69*, ed. T. P. Wiseman, 21–43. Exeter: University of Exeter Press.

Pelling, C. B. R., ed. 1988. *Plutarch: Life of Antony*. Cambridge: Cambridge University Press.

Peppe, Leo. 1984. *Posizione giuridica e ruolo sociale della donna romana in età repubblicana*. Milan.

Pesce, G. 1933. "Sidus Iulium." *Historia* 7:402–15.

Phillips, D. A. 1997. "The Conspiracy of Egnatius Rufus and the Election of Suffect Consuls under Augustus." *Historia* 46:103–12.

Picard, G. C. 1957. *Les Trophées Romains: Contribution à l'histoire de la religion et de l'art triomphal de Rome*. Paris: De Boccard.

Pighi, I. B. 1965. 2nd ed. *De ludis saecularibus populi Romani Quiritium libri sex*. Amsterdam.

Pina Polo, Francisco. 1995. "Procedures and Functions of Civil and Military *contiones* in Rome." *Klio* 77:203–16.

———. 1996. *Contra Arma Verbis*. Stuttgart: Steiner.

Platner, S. B., and Thomas Ashby, eds. 1929. *A Topographical Dictionary of Ancient Rome*. London: Oxford University Press.

Powell, Anton. 2002. "'An Island amid the Flame': The Strategy and Imagery of Sextus Pompeius, 43–36 B.C." in *Sextus Pompeius*, ed. Anton Powell and K. Welch, 103–33. Swansea: Classical Press of Wales.

Premerstein, Anton von. 1937. *Vom Werden und Wesen des Prinzipats*. Munich: Beck.

Price, S. R. F. 1984. *Rituals and Power: The Roman Imperial Cult in Asia Minor*. Cambridge: Cambridge University Press.

———. 1987. "From Noble Funerals to Divine Cult: The Consecration of Roman Emperors." In *Rituals of Royalty*, ed. David Cannadine and Simon Price, 56–105. Cambridge: Cambridge University Press.

Raaflaub, K. A. 1974. *Dignitatis Contentio*. Munich: Beck.

Raaflaub, K. A., and M. Toher, eds. 1990. *Between Republic and Empire*. Berkeley: University of California Press.

Raaflaub, K. A., and L J. Samons II 1990. "Opposition to Augustus." In *Between Republic and Empire*, ed. K. A. Raaflaub and M. Toher, 417–54. Berkeley: University of California Press.

Radin, Max. 1939. *Marcus Brutus*. London: Oxford University Press.

Radke, Gerhard. 1965. *Die Götter Altitaliens*. Munster: Aschendorff.

Ramsey, John. 1994. "The Senate, Mark Antony, and Caesar's Legislative Legacy." *CQ* 44:130–45.

———.2001. "Did Mark Antony Contemplate an Alliance with his Political Enemies in July 44 B.C.E.?" *CP* 96:253–68.

Ramsey, John, and A. Licht. 1997. *The Comet of 44 B.C. and Caesar's Funeral Games*. Atlanta: Scholars Press.

Rawson, Elizabeth. 1972. "Cicero the Historian and Cicero the Antiquarian." *JRS* 62:33–45; repr. 1991:58–79.

———. 1973. "Scipio, Laelius, Furius, and the Ancestral Religion." *JRS* 63:161–74; repr. 1991:80–101.

———. 1975a. *Cicero: A Portrait*. Ithaca, NY: Cornell University Press. Repr. 1983.

———. 1975b. "Caesar's Heritage: Hellenistic Kings and Their Roman Equals." *JRS* 64:148–59; repr. 1991:169–88.

———. 1985. *Intellectual Life in the Late Roman Republic*. Baltimore, MD: Johns Hopkins University Press.

———. 1986. "Cassius and Brutus: The Memory of the Liberators." In *Past Perspectives: Studies in Greek and Roman Historical Writing*, ed. I. Moxon, J. D. Smart, and A. J. Woodman, 101–19. Cambridge: Cambridge University Press. Repr. 1991:488–507.

———. 1990. "The Antiquarian Tradition: Spoils and Representations of Foreign Armour." In *Staat und Staatlichkeit in der frühen römischen Republik*, ed. Walter Eder, 157–73. Stuttgart: Steiner. Repr. 1991:582–98.

———. 1991. *Roman Culture and Society*. Oxford: Clarendon Press.

Reinhold, Meyer. 1933. *Marcus Agrippa: A Biography*. Geneva, NY: W. H. Humphrey Press.

———. 1981/82. "The Declaration of War Against Cleopatra." *CJ* 77:97–103.

Reynolds, Joyce. 1982. *Aphrodisias and Rome*. Monograph series, no. 1. London: Society for the Promotion of Roman Studies.

Ribbeck, Otto. 1897. 3rd ed. *Tragicorum Romanorum fragmenta*. Leipzig: Teubner.

Rice Holmes, T. 1928. *The Architect of the Roman Empire*. 2 vols. Oxford: Clarendon Press.

Rich, J. W. 1976. *Declaring War in the Roman Republic in the Period of Transmarine Expansion*. Brussels: Latomus.

———. 1996. "Augustus and the *spolia opima*." *Chiron* 26:85–127.

———. 1998. "Augustus's Parthian Honours, the Temple of Mars Ultor and the Arch in the Forum Romanum." *PBSR* 66:71–128.

Richardson, J. S. 1975. "The Triumph, the Praetors and the Senate in the Early Second Century B.C." *JRS* 65:50–63.

Richardson, L., Jr. 1992. A *New Topographical Dictionary of Ancient Rome*. Baltimore, MD: Johns Hopkins University Press.

Roddaz, J.-M. 1984. *Marcus Agrippa*. Rome: École française de Rome.

Rossi, R. F. 1959. *Marco Antonio nella lotta politica della tarda repubblica romana*. Trieste.

Rotondi, Giovanni. 1912. *Leges publicae populi romani*. Milan: Società Editrice Libraria. Repr. 1966. Hildesheim: G. Olms.

Rüpke, Jörg. 1990. *Domi militiae: Die religiöse Konstruktion des Krieges in Rom*. Stuttgart: Steiner.

Ryan, F. X. 2000. "The Type of the Aedileship of Critonius." *Hermes* 128:243–46.

Sablayrolles, R. 1981. "Espace urbain et propagande politique: L'organisation du centre de Rome par Auguste (*RG*, 19–21)." *Pallas* 28:59–77.

Sandberg, Kaj. 1993. "The *Concilium Plebis* as a Legislative Body during the Republic." In Senatus populusque romanus: *Studies in Roman Republican Legislation*, ed. U. Paananen, K. Heikkilää, K. Sandberg, L. Savunen, and J. Vaahtera, 74–94. Helsinki: Helsinki University Press.

———. 2001. *Magistrates and Assemblies. A Study of Legislative Practice in Republican Rome*. Rome: Finnish Institute.

Sattler, Peter. 1960. *Augustus und der Senat*. Göttingen: Vandenhoeck and Ruprecht.

Scheid, John. 1978. "Les prêtres officiels sous les empereurs julio-claudiens." *ANRW* 2.16.1.610–54.

Schilling, Robert. 1954. *La Religion Romaine de Vénus*. Paris: De Boccard.

Schmidt, Otto. 1884. "Zur Chronologie der Correspondenz Ciceros seit Caesars Tod." *NJbb. für Philologie* 129:331–50.

———. 1893. *Der Briefwechsel des* M. *Tullius Cicero: Von seinem Prokonsulat in Cilicien bis zu Caesars Ermordung*. Leipzig: Teubner.

Schmitthenner, Walter. 1973. 2nd ed. *Oktavian und das Testament Cäsars*. Munich: Beck.

Schwartz, E. 1898. "Die Vertheilung der römischen Provinzen nach Cäsars Tod." *Hermes* 33:185–244.

Scott, K. 1933. "The Political Propaganda of 44–30 B.C." *MAAR* 11:7–49.

———. 1941. "The *Sidus Iulium* and the Apotheosis of Caesar." *CP* 36:257–72.

Scullard, H. H. 1951. *Roman Politics, 220–150* B.C. Oxford: Clarendon Press.

———. 1981. *Festivals and Ceremonies of the Roman Republic*. Ithaca, NY: Cornell University Press.

Seager, Robin. 1979. *Pompey: A Political Biography*. Berkeley: University of California Press.

Sear, David R. 1998. *The History and Coinage of the Roman Imperators 49–27 BC*. London: Spink.

Sebesta, J. L., and Larissa Bonfante, eds. 1994. *The World of Roman Costume*. Madison: University of Wisconsin Press.

Shackleton Bailey, D. R. 1965–67. *Cicero's Letters to Atticus*. 6 vols. Cambridge: Cambridge University Press.

———. 1976. *Two Studies in Roman Nomenclature*. Atlanta: American Philological Association.

———. 1977. *Cicero Epistulae ad Familiares*. 2 vols. Cambridge: Cambridge University Press.

———. 1986. "*Nobiles* and *Novi* Reconsidered." *AJP* 107:255–60.

———. 1991. *Cicero: Back from Exile; Six Speeches upon His Return*. Chicago: American Philological Association.

Shatzman, Israel. 1975. *Senatorial Wealth and Roman Politics*. Brussels: Latomus.

Sherwin-White, A. N. 1973. 2nd ed. *The Roman Citizenship*. Oxford: Clarendon Press.

Shils, Edward. 1965. "Charisma, Order, and Status." *American Sociological Review* 30:199–213.

Shipley, F. W. 1931. "The Building Activities of the *Viri Triumphales* from 44 B.C. to 14 A.D." *MAAR* 9:7–60.

———. 1933. *Agrippa's Building Activities in Rome*. St. Louis, MO: Washington University.

Simpson, A. D. 1938. "The Departure of Crassus for Parthia." *TAPA* 49:532–41.

Sirianni, F. 1984. "Was Antony's Will Partially Forged?" AC 53:236–41.

Smith, R. E. 1958. *Service in the Post-Marian Roman Army*. Manchester: Manchester University Press.

Southern, Pat. 1998. *Augustus*. London: Routledge.

Staveley, E. S. 1969. "The Role of the First Voter in Roman Legislative Assemblies." *Historia* 18:513–20.

———. 1972. *Greek and Roman Voting and Elections*. Ithaca, NY: Cornell University Press.

Steinby, E. M. 1987. "Il lato orientale del Foro Romano." *Arctos* 21:139–87.

Sternkopf, W. 1912a. "Die Verteilung der römischen Provinzen vor dem Mutinensischen Krieg." *Hermes* 47:321–401.

———. 1912b. "Lex Antonia Agraria." *Hermes* 47:146–51.

Sumi, Geoffrey S. 1997. "Power and Ritual: The Crowd at Clodius' Funeral." *Historia* 46:82–102.

———. 2002a. "Impersonating the Dead: Mimes at Roman Funerals." *AJP* 123: 559–85.

———. 2002b. "Spectacles and Sulla's Public Image." *Historia* 51:414–32.

Sumner, G. V. 1967. "Germanicus and Drusus Caesar." *Latomus* 26:413–35.

Swartz, Mark, Victor Turner, and Arthur Tuden. 1966. "Introduction." In *Political Anthropology*, ed. Mark Swartz, Victor Turner, and Arthur Tuden, 1–41. Chicago: Aldine.

Syme, Ronald. 1938. "Caesar, the Senate and Italy." *PBSR* 14:1–31. Repr. 1979. *Roman Papers* 1:88–119.

———. 1939. *Roman Revolution*. Oxford: Clarendon Press.

———. 1962. "Missing Persons III." *Historia* 11:146–55.

———. 1964. *Sallust*. Berkeley: University of California Press.

———. 1974. "The Crisis of 2 B.C." *SBAW* 7:3–34. Repr. 1984. *Roman Papers* 3:912–36.

———. 1979. "Problems about Janus." *AJP* 100:188–212. Repr. 1984. *Roman Papers* 3:1179–97.

———. 1982. "Clues to Testamentary Adoption." *Tituli* 4: 1.397–410. Repr. 1988. *Roman Papers* 4: 159–70.

———. 1986. *The Augustan Aristocracy*. Oxford: Clarendon Press.

Szemler, G. J. 1972. *The Priests of the Roman Republic*. Brussels: Latomus.

Talbert, Richard J. A. 1984. *The Senate of Imperial Rome*. Princeton, NJ: Princeton University Press.

Tatum, W. Jeffrey. 1999. *The Patrician Tribune: Publius Clodius Pulcher*. Chapel Hill: University of North Carolina Press.

Taylor, L. R. 1931. *The Divinity of the Roman Emperor*. Middletown, CT: American Philological Association.

———. 1942. "The Election of the Pontifex Maximus in the Late Republic." *CP* 37:421–24.

———. 1966. *Roman Voting Assemblies from the Hannibalic War to the Dictatorship of Caesar*. Ann Arbor: University of Michigan Press.

———. 1971. *Party Politics in the Age of Caesar*. Berkeley: University of California Press.

Taylor, L. R., and T. R. S. Broughton. 1949. "The Order of the Two Consuls' Names in the Yearly Lists." *MAAR* 19:3–14.

Thomas, Richard. 1988. *Virgil: Georgics*. 2 vols. Cambridge: Cambridge University Press.

Thommen, Lukas. 1989 *Das Volkstribunat der späten römischen Republik*. Stuttgart: Steiner.

Tibiletti, Gianfranco. 1953. *Principe e magistrati repubblicani*. Rome: Signorelli.

———. 1959. "The 'Comitia' during the Decline of the Roman Republic." *Studia et Documenta Historiae et Iuris* 25:94–127.

Toynbee, J. M. C. 1971. *Death and Burial in the Roman World*. Ithaca, NY: Cornell University Press.

———. 1973. *Animals in Roman Life and Art*. Ithaca, NY: Cornell University Press.

Treggiari, Susan. 1999. "The Upper-Class House as a Symbol and Focus of Emotion in Cicero." *JRA* 12:33–56.

Turner, Victor. 1974. *Dramas, Fields, and Metaphors: Symbolic Action in Human Society*. Ithaca, NY: Cornell University Press.

———. 1986. *The Anthropology of Performance*. New York: PAJ Publications.

Ulrich, Roger B. 1993. "Julius Caesar and the Creation of the Forum Iulium." *AJA* 97:49–80.

———. 1994. *The Roman Orator and the Sacred Stage: The Roman Templum Rostratum*. Brussels: Latomus.

Vanderbroeck, P. J. J. 1987. *Popular Leadership and Collective Behavior in the Late Roman Republic (ca. 80–50 B.C.)*. Amsterdam: J. C. Gieben.

Vasaly, Ann. 1993. *Representations: Images of the World in Ciceronian Oratory*. Berkeley: University of California Press.

Versnel, H. S. 1970. *Triumphus*. Leiden: Brill.

Veyne, Paul. 1976. *Le pain et le cirque: sociologie historique d'un pluralisme politique*. Paris: Seuil.

Virlouvet, Catherine. 1985. *Famines et émeutes à Rome des origines de la République à la mort de Néron*. Rome: École française de Rome.

———. 2001. "Fulvia the Woman of Passion." In *Roman Women*, ed. A. Fraschetti, trans. L. Lappin, 66–81. Chicago: University of Chicago Press.

Vogt, Joseph. 1953. "Zum Herrscherdult bei Julius Caesar." In *Studies presented to D. M. Robinson*, ed. George E. Mylonas, vol. 2, 1138–46. St. Louis: Washington University Press.

Volkmann, Hans. 1958. *Cleopatra: A Study in Politics and Propaganda*. Trans. T. J. Cadoux. London: Elek Books.

Vollmer, F. 1891. "Laudationum funebrium Romanorum historia et reliquiarum editio." *Jahrbücher für classische Philologie*. Suppl. 18:445–528.

———. 1892. "De Funere Publico Romanorum." *Jahrbücher für classische Philologie*. Suppl. 19:319–64.

Walbank, F. W. 1957–79. *A Historical Commentary on Polybius*. 3 vols. Oxford: Clarendon Press.

Wallace-Hadrill, Andrew. 1982. "*Civilis Princeps:* Between Citizen and King." *JRS* 72:32–48.

———. 1986. "Image and Authority in the Coinage of Augustus." *JRS* 76:66–87.

———. 1989. "Patronage in Roman Society: From Republic to Empire." In *Patronage in Ancient Society*, ed. Andrew Wallace-Hadrill, 63–87. London: Routledge Press.

———. 1994. *Houses and Society in Pompeii and Herculaneum*. Princeton, NJ: Princeton University Press.

Wallmann, Peter. 1989. Triumviri Rei Publicae Constituendae. *Untersuchungen zur politischen Propaganda im Zweiten Triumvirat* (43–30 v. Chr.). Frankfurt: P. Lang.

Walser, Gerold. 1957. *Der Briefwechsel des L. Munatius Plancus mit Cicero*. Basel: Helbing and Lichtenhahn.

Walsh, P. G. 1961. *Livy: His Historical Aims and Methods*. Cambridge: Cambridge University Press.

Ward, Allen M. 1977. *Marcus Crassus and the Late Roman Republic*. Columbia: University of Missouri Press.

———. 2004. "How Democratic Was the Roman Republic?" *NECJ* 31:101–19.

Watt, W. S. 1982. M. *Tulli Ciceronis Epistulae Tomus 1*. Oxford Classical Texts. Oxford: Clarendon Press.

Weigel, R. D. 1992. *Lepidus: The Tarnished Triumvir*. London: Routledge.

Weinrib, E. 1967. "The Family Connections of M. Livius Drusus Libo." *HSCP* 72:247–78.

Weinstock, Stefan. 1971. *Divus Julius*. Oxford: Oxford University Press.

Wesch-Klein, Gabriele. 1993. *Funus Publicum*. Stuttgart: Steiner.

Westall, Richard. 1996. "The Forum Iulium as Representation of Imperator Caesar." *MDAI(R)* 103:83–118.

Wiedemann, Thomas. 1986. "The *fetiales:* A Reconsideration." *CQ* 36:478–90.

———. 1992. *Emperors and Gladiators*. London: Routledge.

Will, Wolfgang. 1991. *Der römische Mob*. Darmstadt: Wissenschaftliche Buchgesellschaft.

Wilson, Lillian May. 1938. *The Clothing of the Ancient Romans*. Baltimore: Johns Hopkins University Press.

Winkler, Lorenz. 1995. *Salus vom Staatskult zur politischen Idee*. Heidelberg: Verlag Archäologie und Geschichte.

Wirszubski, Chaim. 1960. *Libertas as a Political Idea at Rome during the Late Republic and Early Principate*. Cambridge: Cambridge University Press.

Wiseman, T. P. 1964. "Some Republican Senators and Their Tribes." *CQ* 14:122–33.

———. 1971. *New Men in the Roman Senate, 139 B.C.–14 A.D.* London: Oxford University Press.

———. 1979. "Topography and Rhetoric: The Trial of Manlius." *Historia* 28:32–50.

———. 1986. "Monuments and the Roman Annalists." In *Past Perspectives: Studies in*

Greek and Roman Historical Writing, ed. I. Moxon, J. D. Smart, and A. J. Woodman, 87–100. Cambridge: Cambridge University Press.

———. 1987. "*Conspicui postes tectaque digna deo:* The Public Image of Aristocratic and Imperial Houses in the Late Republic and Early Empire." In *L'Urbs: Espace urbain et histoire*, 393–413. Rome: École française de Rome.

———. 1989. "Afterword: The Theatre of Civic Life." In *Roman Public Buildings*, ed. I. M. Barton, 151–55. Exeter: University of Exeter Press.

———. 1992. "Julius Caesar and the Mappa Mundi." In *Talking to Virgil: A Miscellany*, 22–42. Exeter: University of Exeter Press.

———. 1995. *Remus: A Roman Myth*. Cambridge: Cambridge University Press.

Wissowa, Georg. 1912. *Religion und Kultus der Römer*. Munich: Beck.

Wistrand, Erik. 1981. *The Policy of Brutus the Tyrannicide*. Gothenburg: Kungl. Vetenskaps-och Vitterhets-Samhället.

Woodman, A. J., ed. 1983. *Velleius Paterculus: The Caesarian and Augustan Narrative (2.41–93)*. Cambridge: Cambridge University Press.

Yakobson, Alexander. 1995. "Secret Ballot and Its Effects in the Late Roman Republic." *Hermes* 123:426–42.

———. 1999. *Elections and Electioneering in the Late Roman Republic*. Stuttgart: Steiner.

Yavetz, Zvi. 1969. *Plebs and Princeps*. London: Oxford University Press.

———. 1983. *Julius Caesar and His Public Image*. Ithaca, NY: Cornell University Press.

Zanker, Paul. 1968. *Forum Augustum: Das Bildprogramm*. Tubingen: E. Wasmuth.

———. 1972. *Forum Romanum: Die Neugestaltung durch Augustus*. Tubingen: E. Wasmuth.

———. 1988. *The Power of Images in the Age of Augustus*. Trans. A. Shapiro. Ann Arbor: University of Michigan Press.

Zecchini, G. 1982. "Asinio Pollione: dall' attività politica alla riflessione storiografica." *ANRW* 2.20.3:1265–96.

———. 2001. *Cesare e il mos maiorum*. Stuttgart: Steiner.

Zorzetti, Naevius. 1980. *La pretesta e il teatro latino arcaico*. Naples: Liguori.

Index

Entries for persons are alphabetized by *gens* name. References to the notes direct the reader only to substantive discussions. All dates are BC unless indicated otherwise.

Plates

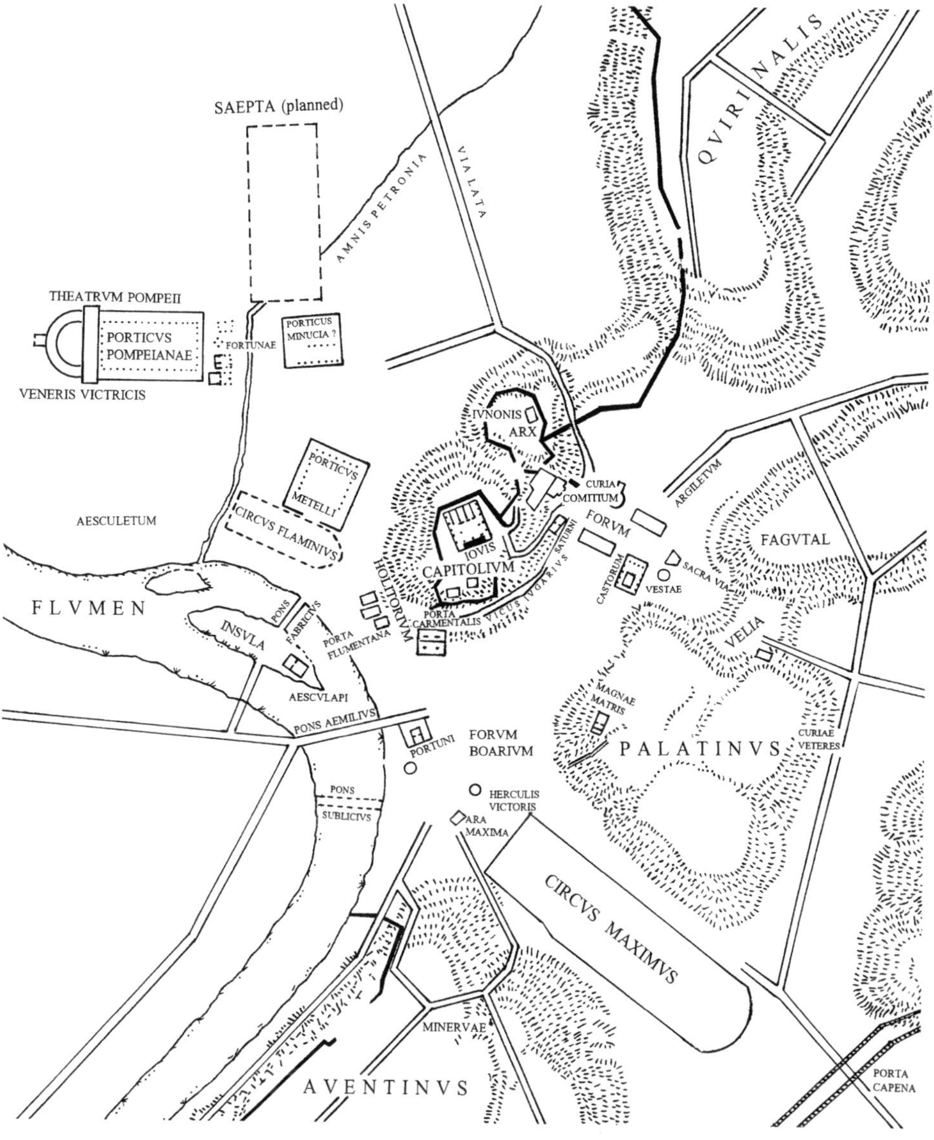

Fig. 1. The Center of Rome in 53 BC. Reprinted from F. Millar, *The Crowd in Rome in the Late Republic* (Ann Arbor: The University of Michigan Press, 1998, Frontispiece), by permission of the publisher. Drawn by Jenny Graham.

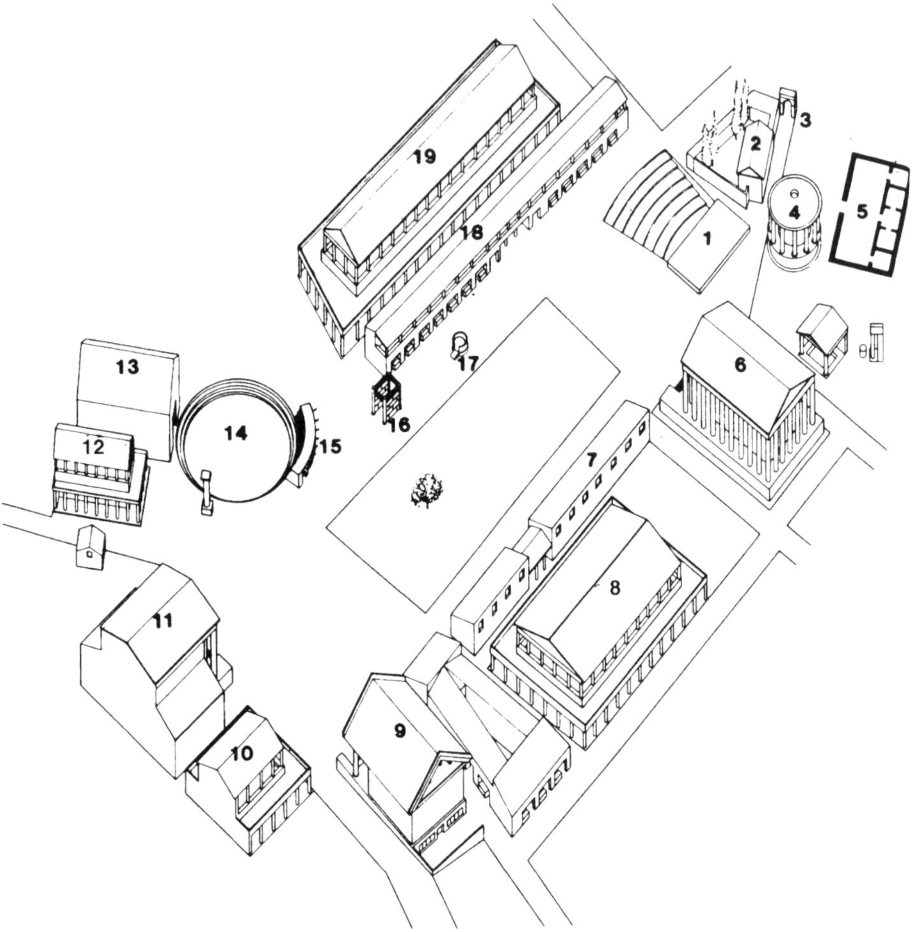

Fig. 2. Drawing of the Forum Romanum, ca. second century BC. E. H. Riorden from J. Stambaugh, *Ancient Roman City*, courtesy Johns Hopkins University Press. 1. Gradus Aurelii; 2. Regia; 3. Fornix Fabiorum; 4. Temple of Vesta; 5. Atrium Vestae; 6. Temple of Castor; 7. Tabernae Veteres; 8. Basilica Sempronia; 9. Temple of Saturn; 10. Basilica Opimia; 11. Temple of Concordia; 12. Basilica Porcia; 13. Curia; 14. Comitium; 15. Rostra; 16. Shrine of Janus; 17. Shrine of Venus Cloacina; 18. Tabernae Novae; 19. Basilica Aemilia.

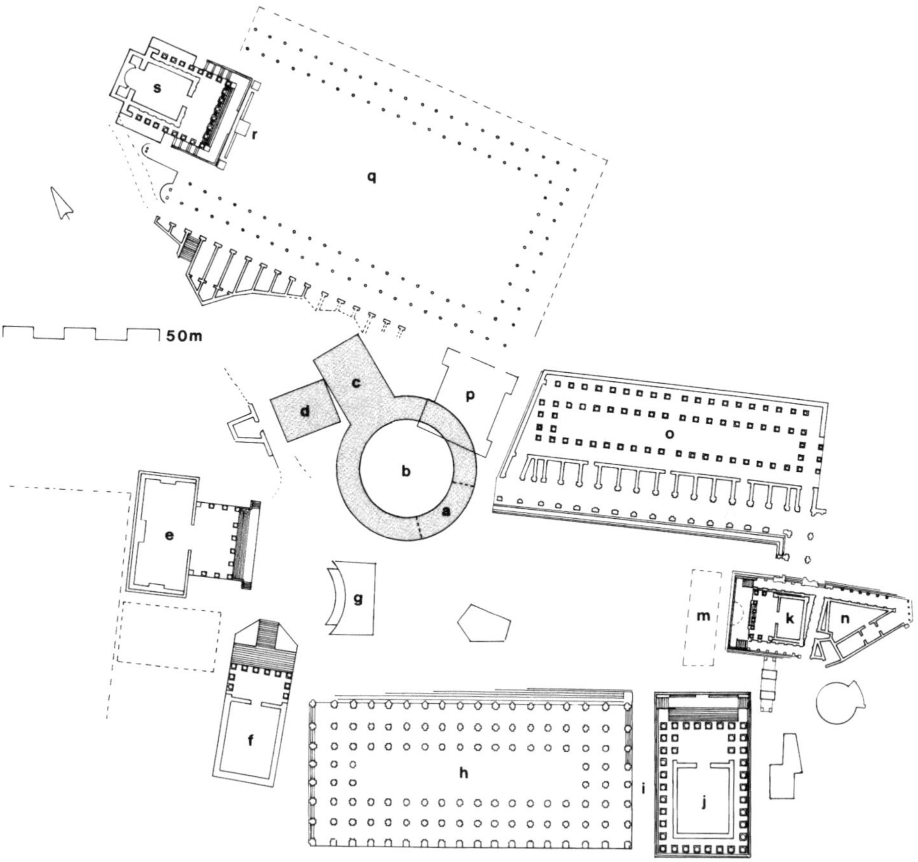

Fig. 3. Plan of the Forum Romanum and Forum Julium (after R. B. Ulrich): (a) Republican Rostra; (b) Republican Comitium; (c) Curia Hostilia; (d) Basilica Porcia;)e) Temple of Concord; (f) Temple of Saturn; (g) Imperial Rostra; (h) Basilica Julia; (i) Vicus Tuscus; (j) Temple of Castor (Imperial phase); (k) Temple of Divus Julius; (m) location of later speakers' platform; (n) Regia; (o) Basilica Aemilia; (p) Curia Julia; (q) Forum Julium; (r) Appiades fountain; and (s) Temple of Venus Genetrix (final form).

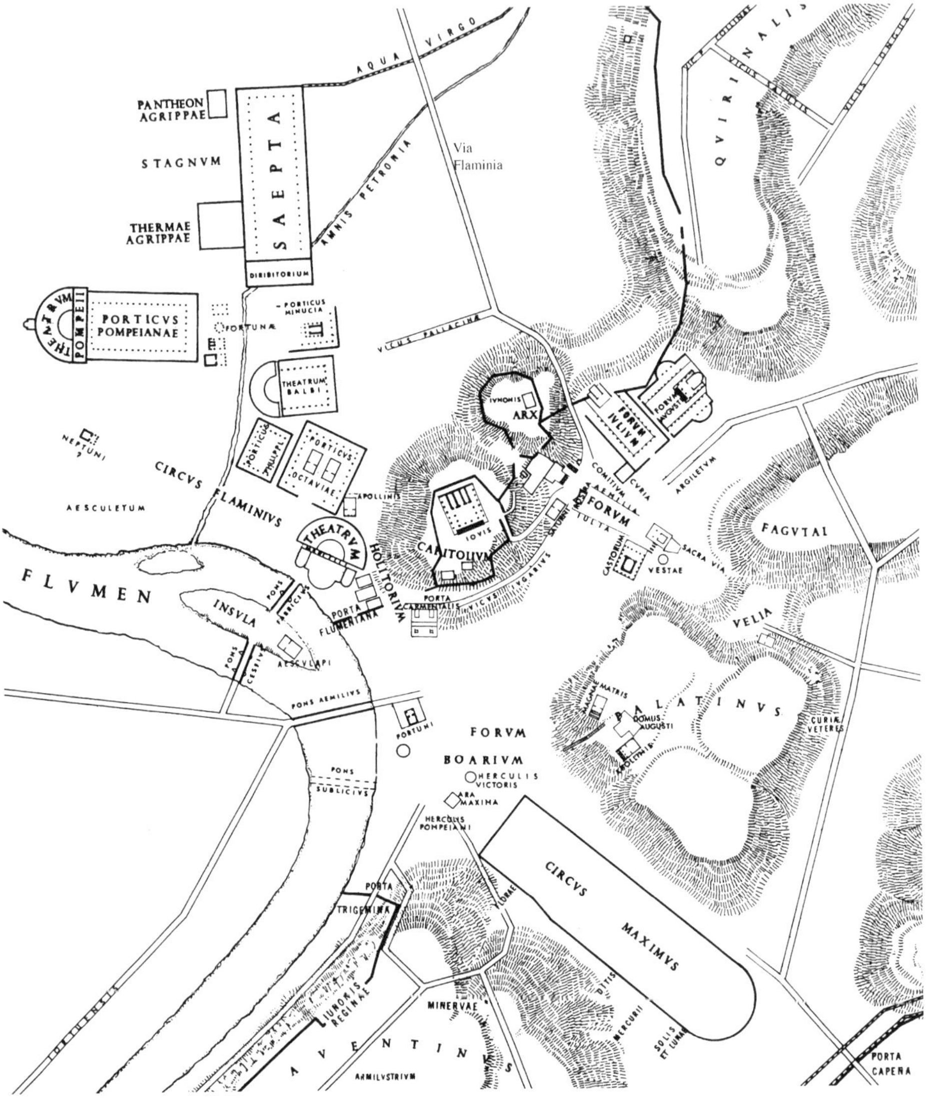

Fig. 4. The Center of Rome in the Augustan Age. Slightly adapted from L. R. Taylor, *Roman Voting Assemblies* (Ann Arbor: The University of Michigan Press, 1966, Frontispiece), by permission of the publisher. Drawn by L. Cozza.